I Didn't Know That!

TORAH NEWS U CAN USE

I Didn't Know That!

JOE BOBKER

gefen
publishing house בית הוצאה לאור
JERUSALEM ◆ NEW YORK

Typesetting: Jerusalem Typesetting, Jerusalem
Cover Design: S. Kim Glassman, Jerusalem

ISBN 978-965-229-398-5

1 3 5 7 9 8 6 4 2

Gefen Publishing House, Ltd.   Gefen Books
6 Hatzvi Street, Jerusalem 94386, Israel   600 Broadway, Lynbrook, NY 11563, USA
972-2-538-0247 • orders@gefenpublishing.com   1-800-477-5257 • orders@gefenpublishing.com

www.israelbooks.com

Printed in Israel   *Send for our free catalogue*

"If you lack knowledge, what do you have?
If you have knowledge, what do you lack?"

– Proverbs

Acknowledgments

I would like to thank my wife Miriam who gives new meaning to the words patience and understanding, without which this book would still be on my shelf instead of yours.

Joe Bobker
Chanukah, 2006

Caution

This book is only intended as an introduction to Jewish law and lore, and should not be used as a halachic guide, nor as halachic rulings, no matter how definitively they are worded, nor as a replacement for studying Judaism and Torah in the conventional way (by *chavrusa*). Its sole purpose is to give the reader a peek into the world of *yiddishkeit* in order to inspire more study. If you have specific questions, consult a qualified rabbi.

The information contained in the endnotes may not always be entirely accurate but will lead you in the general direction for further study.

Introduction

Reb Shneur Zalman of Liadi had a great library that included a rare manuscript of chassidic philosophy. On its cover was the following inscription: "The ban of Rabbeinu Gershom respecting the secrecy of documents is hereby invoked – in This World and the Next!"

One year, there was a fire in the Rebbe's home and his entire collection was destroyed. The Rebbe, distraught and crying, asked his son, Reb Dov Ber of Lubavitch, "Did you ever open this book?"

"No, Father, not once."

"You were never curious? Perhaps you took a glimpse at a chapter, a page? Maybe you recall some of its writings? Even a single paragraph would cheer my spirits!"

"But Father, the ban of Rabbeinu Gershom clearly states that one who opens this manuscript will be cursed in This World and the Next!"

"And you didn't think that the discovery of some new wisdom was worth the sacrifice?!"

Jewish life is a search for knowledge. And knowledge, writes the twelfth-century Spanish poet and Hebrew grammarian Yosef Kimhi (author, *Shekel Hakodesh*), is "the twin to action!"

And so the rabbis of the Talmud urged each Jew, "Let your tongue acquire the habit of saying, 'I do not know!'" Judah haNasi brushed aside any hesitation of shame on this score: "He is great who is not ashamed to admit he does not know!"[1]

This book is not intended to be read in one sitting, but as an envelope to be opened from time to time in order to learn something new.

As the Gerer Rebbe put it, "Each time I learn something, I am born anew!"

---

1.   Berachot 4a; Hagiga 1:8.

A

Abortion

Q **Is abortion an absolute prohibition?**

No. Jewish law neither bans termination of a pregnancy totally, nor does it allow indiscriminate ("on demand") abortion. The general rule? If the well-being of an unborn fetus substantially clashes with the life of an already born person, the autonomous life takes precedence. Thus, abortion is permitted if there is a direct threat to the mother's life through the event of childbirth. In that circumstance, the fetus is compared to a *rodef*, a "pursuer" after the mother with the (unintentional) intent to kill her. Otherwise, "It is a capital crime to destroy an embryo in its womb!" Jewish law recognizes that the threat is not just physical, but can be emotional as well (e.g., in cases of rape or incest).[1]

Abracadabra

Q **I heard this was a Jewishly inspired word. Is it?**

An old folktale claims it is a merger of *bracha* and *davar*, "blessing" and "word." Christian linguists see it as a combination of the initials of *Av, Bar, Ruach*, as in "Father, Son, Holy Ghost." Whatever its origin, it's certainly *not*

---

1. Mishna Oholos 7:6; Sanhedrin 57b.

Jewish! Second-century doctors during the reign of Roman Emperor Caracalla believed that this "magic formula" had the power to cure patients of toothaches, fever and inflammation. The sick wrote it on parchment and wore it as an amulet necklace. I betcha that the Rambam, a Doctor of Reason and a Sage of Rationalism, never used it!

Abraham's mom

Q Who was Abraham's mother?

The Torah does not say, but the Talmud (which also gives us the names of the mothers of Haman, David and Samson) does. According to Rav, a third-century Babylonian Sage, her name was Amatlai bat Karnevo. Rashi says that *kar* refers to a lamb, a clean species of animal, which explains why Abraham became a pious, upright ("clean") person.

Absentee

Q Am I imagining it, or is Philo totally absent from the Talmud?

You're right! He's missing in action! There's not a single reference in the Talmud or in the Midrash to Philo, a gentle, pious, wealthy and prominent first-century Torah Jew in Alexandria, Egypt, at the beginning of Roman rule. Why? I don't know, but here are two guesses. The moment Philo's philosophical writings and Torah commentaries were incorporated by early Christians, they were too "blemished" for inclusion in the Talmud. Or perhaps his unprecedented search for a "Jewish philosophy" turned the pure Torah scholars off, Greek philosophy being seen as a useless, *goyishe* occupation.

Acquittal

Q What did it take to be acquitted in a Jewish court?

The burden of Jewish justice was tough. "A judge should always visualize a sword suspended over him," writes the Talmud's Jonathan ben Eleazar, "and Gehenna [Hell] gaping under him!" If only one of the twenty-three judges constituting a Sanhedrin in a capital case voted in favor of acquittal, the accused was acquitted. What was needed for a conviction? A majority of two. What if all twenty-three judges voted for conviction? The accused was *not* convicted! Why? Because Judaism believes there must *always* exist a possible defense, no matter the gravity of the crime nor the power of the evidence. If not even a single judge sees a hint of "innocence," the law suspects the presence of bias. As the Yiddishists would say: "Better to suffer an injustice than commit one!"[2]

Adam's apple or Adam's apricot?

Q Why is the little projection in our necks ascribed to Adam?

The Adam's apple "bump," formed by the thyroid cartilage in the throat, is derived from an old legend wherein the first man of creation, swallowing a fruit at Eve's invitation, began to resist with his first bite. The result? A piece of fruit stuck in his throat, refusing to go down, unable to be retrieved. Future man was thus born with a throat lump, an "Adam's apple," as a reminder to descendants to resist further temptations. Was it really an apple? No. The Torah even advises that apples are *good* for one's health! And so the Midrash searches for other "fruits" of Eden, suggesting a fig, grape, wheat, quince, pomegranate, nut or the seductive-sounding "apple of paradise." The Ramban identifies it as the citron, influenced by the fact that its Hebrew term (*esrog*) is derived from the Aramaic for "passion, desire" (this is the genesis of the popular slang expression "the fruit of one's deeds"). In short: no one knows what the forbidden fruit was. It could have been an apricot, in which case you'd have an Adam's apricot!

Admiration

Q Can I look at a pretty woman?

Far better to talk to a woman and think of God, goes the Yiddish adage, than to talk to God and think of a woman! When flattering the beauty and body of a woman, the Torah wants us to appreciate not just the created, but

---

2. Yevamos 109b; Rambam, Laws of Sanhedrin, 9:1.

also the Creator; not just the product, but also the Manufacturer. That is why Jews say a special Shehechiyanu prayer of admiration (*Birkos nehenin*, "Blessings of enjoyment") when seeing rainbows, flowers or anything reflective of God's artistic presence in the world.

Adoption

Q Is it a mitzva to adopt a child?

No. There is no halachic obligation "to adopt," which is why there is no adoption mechanism in Jewish law. However, to do so is a great and noble act of *chesed*, praised and inspired by the Torah's Asher; "Serach was Asher's stepdaughter, but because he raised her, people called her 'Asher's own daughter'"! Must the adoptee be Jewish? No. The child undergoes conversion at adoption. Must the child be informed of his status? Yes. When? At "the earliest time" (i.e., maturity). This introduces the possibility to reverse the conversion if the adopted child chooses to do so. How is an adopted child called to the Torah? It's unclear. Some poskim say by his biological name, others prefer that he be called up as the son of the adoptive father.[3]

Aggada

Q Is aggada just legend or should I take it more seriously?

Dismiss it at your own risk; for aggada, "narration," derived from the Aramaic root *ngd*, "to flow," is indispensable to Judaism. Its imaginative narrative, homiletic material, free-floating metaphors and heavily annotated parables flow with such spirit and dazzle that it is a Judaic teaching tool *par excellence*. It brings Jewish history and heritage, law and lore, alive as a powerful (non-halachic) vehicle of aspiration through which each individual Jew can "understand," rather than be forced to accept halacha. Those who were its masters (Yonathan, Abba bar Kahana, Tanchuma) were known as *Rabba Deaggadasa*, "Rabbis of the Aggada." And yet, it is true! Aggada

---

3. Y.Y. Kanievsky, Devar Halacha; Numbers 46:17; Ramban, Numbers 26:46; Iggeros Moshe, Even HaEzer 1:99, 464–2; Kisvei Harav Henkin 2:86, 99; S.Z. Auerbach, Nishmas Avraham, vol. 5.

contains exaggerations and contradictions, which led to early arguments whether it should be preserved in writing. "Anyone recording it has no share in the World to Come," declared Yehoshua ben Levi, third-century CE *amora*. In case no one got the message, the Sage added, "Anyone using a written copy for teaching is liable to excommunication!" But the other scholars (Yochanan, Resh Lakish) won the argument, convinced that the benefits outweighed the potential risks, and ensured that aggada constitutes about thirty percent of the Talmud. The final word goes to the Rambam: "Aggada cannot always be taken literally; rather, it must be interpreted with the understanding that a higher truth is being alluded to!"[4]

Aggressive?

Q Israel is always being accused of being too "aggressive" in its response to terror provocations. What's the halacha?

The *haTorah am'ra*, the general "stated rule of Torah," is *haba l'hor'gecha, hashkem l'hor'go*, "If someone comes to slay you, slay him first!" This is an authoritative order for a pre-emptive strike, derived from the Torah's order to "attack the Midianites and smite them, for they harass you with their wiles."[5]

Ahava

Q What's the Jewish concept of love (*ahava*)?

Frank Sinatra could sing that "love and marriage go together like a horse and carriage," but our Sages were not so naïve. "Love," despite the slogan, does *not* "conquer all," they warn, knowing that love fades and cannot alone sustain a marriage – or as the Yiddish marriage counselor would put it, "Love tastes sweet, but only with bread!" To some, time flies when one is in love, to others, it stands still ("Those who love deeply cannot age!"). The Torah's ideal marital component was not romance and passion *à la* Romeo and Juliet, but "loyalty, togetherness, companionship." The Greeks call this

---

4. Psalms 119:86; Gittin 60a; Shabbat 16:1; Maaserot 111:4; Chagiga 14a.
5. Sanhedrin 72a; Numbers 25:17.

philos (intimacy growing out of friendship), Judaism calls it *reim ahuvim*, "loving friends!" The *Zohar* says love contains the secret of Divine unity. Simeon ben Eleazar says it upsets the natural order. Moshe Ibn Ezra says love is as "blind to faults" as hatred is "blind to virtues!"[6]

Aliya, dead or alive

Q Is burial in Israel a mitzva?

To be buried in the Holy Land is a theme that ripples throughout the Torah. It can be traced to Jacob's last dying wish (expressed to his regal son, Joseph), who asked *twice* that he be buried in Hevron and not in Egypt; Joseph's bones were also reburied in a field in Nablus. But the practice was never codified in Jewish law, even though the Rambam favored it, himself wishing to be buried in Tiberias. Jewish mystics were upset that Jews waited until they died before making aliya, and note the reward given to Joseph for fulfilling the last will and testament of his father, who had lived long enough (to age 110) to see great-grandchildren. The "mitzva" of burial itself is derived from Abraham's reaction to his wife Sarah's death. The first Jew immediately turns to his neighbors, the sons of Heth, with a determined request for a burial site, "that I may bury my dead from before me." Not to be buried at all was considered a punishment from God. To delay burial was disrespect for the deceased, although, if the circumstances of delay lead to "honoring" the body, then Jewish law permits postponing a burial ("to bring mourners, or so that relatives may come, or to make it known to communities").[7]

All about Eve

Q I'm confused. Was Eve a wife, mate, assistant, companion?

Welcome to the club! Several Torah linguists also struggle for an exact translation of the Torah's creation of woman. The first man was originally

---

6. Sanhedrin 105b; Pirkei Avos 5:16.
7. Deuteronomy 28:26, 21:22–23; 1 Kings 14:11; Jeremiah 22:19; Genesis 25:8,17, 47:30; 1 Kings 11:23; Yore Deah 357; Joshua 24:32; Mo'ed Katan 25a; Acharei Mos 72b.

formed alone, until the realization that, as a social animal, it was not good for him to be lonely. Then Eve was created out of a male rib (the word *woman* perpetuates this link to *man*). The Torah speaks of an "opposite…at his side," suggestive of similar yet supplementary. In other words, opposites attract! Is the "rib" to be taken literally? The Torah uses the term *hasela* for "rib," leading several Midrashim to translate *sela* as "side" rather than "rib." Rabbi Samuel ben Nahman interprets it as the "second [side]," because the word reappears with that meaning during the description of the building of the Mishkan. Rav interprets *sela* as "face." The original English word for Eve was *helpe meet*, which meant a *companion* who would *assist* man and *share* in his life and work. The confusion began in 1611, when King James I's scholars chose *suitable* as a synonym for *meet*, which produced, "I [God] will make him [Adam] an helpe meet [suitable] for him." (Luckily, they rejected Wycliffe's incomprehensible version which has God saying, "Make we to hym help like hym!") Sixty years later, Dryden added a hyphen, creating the word *help-meet*. This didn't catch on either, until, a few generations later, it re-emerged as *helpmate*.[8]

Alphabet

Q How many letters in the Hebrew alphabet?

Twenty-two, however they are not literally "letters," but consonants. Which letter appears most often in the Torah? The *vav*. It occurs about 76,922 times. Do all alphabets have twenty-two letters? No. The English one has twenty-six, Russian thirty-six, Spanish twenty-seven, etc. Why do they differ, if they all descend from the one original alphabet? Because the rule of alphabets is based on "one sound, one letter," and thus it fluctuates depending on the various sounds different people can pronounce. Germans are not as guttural as Arabs. The Romans couldn't pronounce the Hebrew "J." The Greeks, similar to today's westerners, have trouble with the Hebrew "C" or "ch." Just watch the Chabad Telethon and you'll see non-Jews struggling with words like *Chabad* or *Chanukah* because they start with the consonant *het* or *chet*, guttural sounds that have no equivalent in English.

---

8. Exodus 26:20; Genesis Rabba 8:1; Midrash on Psalms 139:5.

══ Am I a *shlemazel* or *schlemiel*? ══

Q Sometimes I'm called a *shlemazel*, other times a *schlemiel*! Are they the same? Should I be insulted?

They are not the same, and neither is complimentary! Originally, Schlemiel was a person, son of Zurishaddai, prince of the Tribe of Simon. When the zealous Pinchas ben Eliezer tried to kill Zimri (for having an affair with Kozbi, a pretty Midianite princess), he accidentally stabbed an innocent passerby. The name of this unfortunate bystander was…Shelumiel! Thus, *schlemiel* became a catchword for the unlucky! Meanwhile, *shlemazel* describes "one who has no *mazal*," the unfortunate person on whom the stars do not smile. Mazal, of Akkadian origin, appears in *Tanach*, and is derived from *mazar*, a reference to planets and zodiac signs. Shlemazel is its flipside. Despite its (forbidden) astrological genesis, the term is widely popular. Remember: *mazal tov* does not mean "congratulations" at all. It means "May you have a good constellation [star] for this event." Jewish mystics justify saying *mazal tov* by claiming it merely represents the initial letters of *Makom, Z'man, La'asos*, which means, "Being in the right place [*makom*] at the right time [*z'man*] in order to do the right thing [*la'asos*]!"[9]

══ Am segulla ══

Q What does this mean?

It must be good because all Catholic theologians find this expression scandalous. It reveals that God has bestowed special favor *only* on the Jews, despite their imperfections ("a stiff-necked people," "you are the least of the nations," etc.). This Chosen People theme (*am segulla*), that God's Jews are the "jewel from among the nations," ripples throughout the Torah and all rabbinic writings. In Aramaic, *segulla* means "that which is preferred." Rashi links it to royalty, as in *Segulas melachim*, "Treasures of Kings." Abraham Ibn Ezra, who influenced both the Rambam and Ramban, interprets *segulla* as a "desired and honored" *a priori* object that can never be duplicated. The King James English Bible translates it as the "peculiar people,"

---

9. Kings 11, 23:5; Job 38:32.

but not to worry: in those days "peculiar" stemmed from the Latin *peculiaris*, "special." And yet the Rambam instinctively didn't like the term Chosen People, convinced that "chosen" reflected a prejudicial religious chauvinism that hinted at inherited biological differences between Jews and *goyim* – divisions which didn't exist.[10]

Amen

Q What does this mean?

In loose translation it means "So be it!" The word, derived from the root for *emes* ("truth"), confirms that all that has just been said was "true and reliable." This expression, which appears fourteen times in the Torah, is the most widely used religious word in Judaism. Our Sages link its letters (*alef, mem, nun*) to the first letters of *El Melech Ne'eman*, "God is a faithful King!"[11]

America's Talmud

Q When was the Talmud (*Shas*) printed in America for the first time?

In 1947, a sixteen-volume "Survivor's Talmud" was printed by Carl Winter in Heidelberg, during a time when the town was under United States Army jurisdiction. This made it an "American" Shas. It came out at a time when the future of Jewry looked dim, when a third of world Jewry had disappeared through Adolf's dark hole, when only a handful of *seforim* had survived the inferno of the Hitlerite hordes, when thousands of Jewish DP's (including my parents, my sister and myself) were pouring into Allied camps. Credit goes to Rabbis Philip S. Bernstein, Abraham Kalmanowitz (president of the Mir Yeshiva), as well as Rabbis Samuel Abba Snied and Samuel Jacob Rose (survivors from Dachau). The front page of each volume shows the reality (barbed wire, concentration camps) mixed with hope (sketches of palm trees from the Holy Land).

---

10. Deuteronomy 7:7, 8–16–18; Ecclesiastes 2:8.
11. Sukka 51b; Sanhedrin 111a.

Amplifiers

Q Can I hear the *Megilla* or listen to *havdala* over the telephone?

Sound waves do not negate the performance of a mitzva, say some, who do not distinguish between the original voice and that filtered electronically through an amplifier. Others are undecided and allow it only under extenuating circumstances such as for a patient in the hospital. The general consensus the is that the halachic obligation is to hear the "authentic" speaker's voice.[12]

Anger management for Moses?

Q Why did Moses smash the Tablets?

Simeon ben Lakish gives us a clue: "Anger deprives the sage of his wisdom and the prophet of his vision." The Midrash defines anger and temper as "Death's executioners," and the Talmud compares its destructive presence to "a worm in a plant." Other scholars are reluctant to paint Moses with the brush of rage. Rashbam claims that, at the unholy sight of a calf of gold, Moses' strength simply failed him, causing him to drop the tablets since he was unable to bear their heavy burden when struck with such disappointment. One Midrash suggests that he purposefully caused the *sh'vurei luchos*, "broken tablets," for sheer educational "shock value," in order to emphasize his attitude towards apostasy. Ibn Ezra takes a more mystical approach. By smashing the tablets, symbolic of annulling ("breaking") a contract (*shoveret ketubata*), Moses was actually defending his (adulterous) folk by destroying the "marriage contract between the Groom (God) and His bride (Israel)," thus declaring the calf sin null-and-void.[13]

---

12. Chazon Ish, Minchas Shelomo 9; Minchas Yitzchak 2:113; Even HaEzer 1:33, 4:84; Iggeros Moshe, Orach Chayim 2:108, 4:85, 4:91–4; Tzitz Eliezer 8:11.
13. Pesachim 66b; Sifra, Shemini 2:12; Psalms 6:7; Sota 3b.

—Anti-Semitism

Q Do we know what causes anti-Semitism?

The first mention of the "destruction of the seed of Israel," long *before* Babylon and Rome, and supposed to be the final word on the Jews, was carved into an Egyptian column in 1207 BCE by Pharaoh Merneptah. It was premature. Our Jewish mystics, in surely one of the most startling summations connected to any Jewish festival, trace the history of anti-Semitism directly to the similarity between *Sinai* and *sinah*, the Hebrew expression for hate, as it appears in *mishama yarda sinah la'olam*, "from there originated the world's hatred [*sinah*] of the Jew." English transla-tors of Isaiah's phrase *Eretz sinim* mistranslate it as "the land of Sinim," not realizing that the word refers to a people, not a place. This link is a bizarre paradox. The Torah is riddled with anti-hate laws, so it has to be something else. The clue lies in a verse in Exodus, "Now, if you will truly keep My covenant, then you shall be unto Me a choice from all the nations." This summarizes the handbook of every paranoid and irratio-nal Jew-baiter ever since Balaam first called the *Yiddishe folk* "a people that shall dwell alone." This is the "difference" factor – that Jews eat *dif-ferently*, dress *differently*, behave *differently*. Haman is Exhibit A for the defense. What prompted him to turn to mass murder? The "laws and customs" of the Jews. Which ones? Rava, fourth-century Sage, identi-fies them as *kashrus* ("they do not eat of our food"), non-assimilation ("they do not marry our women nor give us theirs") and Jewish holidays ("they evade taxes by claiming 'Today is the Sabbath,' 'Today is Passover,' etc."). Haman's "dislike of the unlike," centuries before T.S. Eliot devel-oped his own "insane nausea about the Jews," wasn't even original. He simply echoed such other vile men as Cicero and Tacitus ("the Jews sit apart at meals, and sleep apart from foreign women"). Haman takes his defamatory delusions to his boss, whining, "There exists one nation [*Ye-shno am echad*] whose laws do not adhere to the King's customs!" Re-member: he who starts with the complaint that *some* Jews are anti-social irritants inevitably ends with a much more serious charge: that *all* Jews are disloyal *Hofjude*-type citizens. Jewish history is littered with such terminally corrupt Esau-sterotypes as Balaam ("They dwell alone, not to be reckoned among the nations"); Joseph Stalin ("They are passportless wanderers"); Bernard Shaw ("They are enormously arrogant"); Charles de Gaulle ("They are an elite people, dominating"); Voltaire ("What was the Jews' crime? None, other than being born!") – and, of course, Adolf Hitler, *yemach shemo v'zichro*, the inventor of state-sponsored genocide ("They are of a different race with a different smell"). What accounts for this type of Jew-hatred? Menashe ben Israel, seventeenth-century Dutch rabbi, saw *Antisemitismus* (a replacement of *Judenfeindschaft*, "Jew-hatred"), as pure psychological inversion: people who hate something about themselves project it onto the Jews. "People hate Jews because of envy," sighs Ibn Verga, and "for envy there is no cure!"

April Fool's Day

Q Can Jews participate in this day?

Yes. April 1 has no religious underpinnings and thus you can participate in making fools of others to get a laugh – as long as no one is hurt or humiliated. One legend dates the day back to Noah's first attempt, supposedly on April 1, to send a dove to find dry land. Its failure was called a "fool's errand [on] All Fool's Day," the word "all" being derived from *auld* ("old"). The annual custom then arose for pranksters and jokers to celebrate the memory of the Flood with creative ineffectual errands to make another "dull" day fun.

Arise, not!

Q Why are Jews called to the Torah on Simchas Torah in a different manner?

Instead of the traditional way of "calling" someone to the Torah with a *Ya'amod*, "Arise!" followed by his Hebrew name, a highly elaborate formula ("*Mer'shus...*") is used, consisting of sentences that end in the same syllable (*ra*), similar to the formula used by Ashkenazi Jews when calling a bridegroom to the Torah. Penned by the eleventh-century Menachem ben Machir, *Mer'shus* asks God and man to approve the choice of the *chasanim* (*Chasan Torah* and *Chasan Bereishis*) to stress that none be singled out for honor without the approval of the masses.

Aristotelian philosophy

Q Why can't I study Aristotelianism? The Rambam did!

I guess you can, if you do it the *way* he did. The Rambam first finished the entire Torah (witness the *Mishne Torah*) before he looked at the labyrinth of Aristotelian philosophy for one reason only: to help him respond to the "prove-that-I-exist-or-do-not-exist" philosophies of the local heretics (*apikorsim*). When Yishmael ben Dama asked his uncle if he could study Greek philosophy, the Talmud Sage replied "yes," but only *after* completing the entire Torah!

As young as you feel

Q What's the rabbinic concept of aging?

It is a mitzva to "rise and honor the face of an old man." Why? Because with "length of days" (i.e., experience) comes "wisdom and understanding." Shlomo Nissim Algazi, the seventeenth-century Turkish talmudist, was blunt: "Old friends and old wine never lose their flavor!" There is nothing more enviable, notes nineteenth-century Rabbi Daniel Sanders, than to have an old head and a young heart; to which Oscar Blumenthal, the German playwright, adds, "A man is as old as his wife looks!" The Torah frowns on the aged uselessly swaying in rocking chairs in a state of gentility. The significant accomplishments of Abraham and Sarah (the only Jewess in the Torah whose age was revealed) took place not in their youth but during the last quarter of their lives, fulfilling an old rabbinic adage, "At forty, one is fit for discernment; at fifty, for counsel; at eighty, for special strength!"[14]

Atonement

Q Does "Yom Kippur" literally translate as "Day of Atonement"?

No. The English verb "atone" was originally two words, "*at*" and "*one*," implying reconciliation. "Kippur" is derived from a root which means "to

---

14. Job 12:12; Apocrypha, Ben Sira 8:6; Leviticus 19:32.

cover, hide," with a secondary meaning, to obliterate (sin) in order to expiate. Is there any link to *kappores*, the "Ark cover"? Yes. The blood of Yom Kippur sacrifices was sprinkled in the direction of the ark, which required a "cover" protection. This led to the Holy of Holies being called *Beis hakappores*, "the place of propitiation."[15]

Author please?

Q Who wrote the *siddur*?

No one person; it's a collective work. The first prayer book was compiled by Rabbi Amram Gaon in the ninth century CE, in response to a plea from a Spanish *shul*.

Autopsies

Q What's the problem with autopsies?

The Torah prohibition of assault and battery (*havala*) applies to oneself as well as to others; and since the body is "on loan" from God, our Sages saw mankind not as owners but as custodians. Anything that would mar or mutilate the human body was an affront to human dignity and a compromise of God's property – even *after* death. Thus routine, indiscriminate autopsies are prohibited. Is this ban absolute? No. The eighteenth-century Rabbi Yechezkel Landau (*Noda Biy'hudah*) authorized autopsies if they were immediately beneficial to others (*shelefanenu*) who suffered from the same disease. In 1964 this consent was extended by Rabbi Yitzchak Arieli to cover hereditary diseases.

Avram to Avraham

Q Was this name-change mystical in any way?

Yes. Going from Avram to Avraham required adding the letter *heh*, the same letter which created the world, and whose numerical value (five) not

---

15. Leviticus 16.

only symbolizes the five basic Torah elements in the path to repentance, but increases the *gematria* of the word *Abraham* to 248. This is a significant number in kabbalistic circles. Why? Because it matches *ramach*, the number of limbs (248) in the human body, suggesting that the first Patriarch will be *shaleim*, "whole and complete, without any deficiency or blemish." The Torah's new custom of changing names (Canaan to Israel, Sarai to Sarah) had a mystic undertone: to change one's destiny (*mazal*)!

Ayin hora

Q What is this?

One can be forgiven for associating Abraham, the great pioneer of faith, with opthalmology, and yet that is exactly what our Sages, in the tradition of pure symbolism, do. They praise the first Patriarch as a man with a "good eye," a reference not to eyesight but to his *middos* (character traits). The contrast is made between the "good eye, humble mind, lowly spirit" of his disciples to those of Balaam's who possessed "an evil eye (*ayin hora*), haughty mind, proud spirit." The concept is found nowhere in the *Tanach* and first appears in the post-Biblical period, "He cast his eye on him and he died!" After Rav visits a cemetery, he concludes that, "Ninety-nine die through an evil eye for each one who dies from natural causes!" This is the source of the Yiddish expression *keinahora*, in that no evil eye should affect the health or wealth of the Jew, first expounded by Rabbi Joshua in the Mishna, "The evil eye, the evil inclination and hatred of mankind put a person out of the world!" The rabbis of the Talmud related to man's "stumbling" as "only with the eyes!" This led to the Rambam's reminder in his famous *Letter to Marseilles*, "A man's eyes are in front, not behind!" Tradition sees the "evil eye" as a metaphor for greed and envy, and recalls Alexander the Great's visit to the Garden of Eden where he was given an eyeball. He weighed it against all his gold and silver, but the eye was heavier. "Put some dust on it," he was told. The scales tipped in favor of the eye. The lesson? The human eye is never satisfied; the more it sees the more it wants, until finally the dust covers it in the grave. And so our Sages promoted its opposite, *ayin tova*, a "good eye," as an antidote to envy, in that Jews should always see the best, not the worst, in other Jews.[16]

---

16. Shabbat 34a; Bava Metzia 107b; Avos 2:2; Tamid 32b.

B

Baal tashchis

Q What does this mean?

It started as a prohibition against cutting down fruit trees in times of war and was later extended to cover "wastage" of any sort. What qualifies as a "fruit" tree? One over whose fruit a blessing (*borei pri ha'etz*) must be made. Can you cut the branches? Yes. What if the tree is old and no longer able to produce fruit? Then it's OK, especially if it becomes difficult to maintain. Does it matter whether the owner is Jewish, or if there is no owner? No. Some say it's permitted if there is a benefit to it (e.g., if the tree is weakening nearby trees or the wood is more valuable than the fruit). This "do-not-destroy" principle later covered "anything of value" (food, clothing, utensils, etc.). The *Sefer Hachinuch*, a compilation of mitzvos by the medieval Jewish pietists, defined a lover of God as one who could not bear to waste a grain of mustard! Rabbi Chayyim David Halevi saw a *baal tashchis* concern in the custom of throwing ("wasting") sweets, edible items or peeled nuts in *shul* on bar mitzva boys and bridegrooms. He even criticized caterers who decorated their tables with painted vegetables, which made them unfit for consumption.[1]

---

1. Shulchan Aruch Harav, Shemiras Guf V'nefesh 14; Deuteronomy 20:19; Baba Metzia 32b; Sefer Hachinuch 529; Rambam, Sefer Hamitzvos 57; Baba Kamma 91b; Baba Basra 26a; Chasam Sofer Yore Deah 102.

═ Baby naming ═══════════════════════════

Q I'm having a baby. What's the right way to give my child a name?

The Ashkenaz custom is to give a baby the name of deceased relatives. Sephardim name their children after their father's and mother's parents, even if alive. The first child is named after the paternal grandparents, the second after the wife's parents. This is based on the verse, *Ateres zekanim b'nei banim*, "the crown of grandparents is their grandchildren"; thus, when grandparents see the perpetuation of their own names via their grandchildren they feel greatly honored (*kovod*). And so Shimon ben Gamliel named his son Rabban Gamliel after his father, even though his father was still alive, and Chur named his son Kalev after his father, Kalev ben Yefune.

═ Bad advice ═══════════════════════════

Q My friend told me to buy a certain item and it turned out defective. Is he responsible?

It depends. If your friend received payment for his advice, there's liability. If not, there isn't! And was the advice offered as an "expert" opinion, or not? If "yes," and it turns out the "expert" was anything but, there may be some liability for misrepresentation. Unpaid non-expert advisers are still liable if they know their opinion will be relied upon exclusively. In general, to cause indirect losses to another is forbidden, falling within the halachic category of *garmi*, but, as Rabbi Akiva warns, "Beware of unsolicited advice!" because most *batei din* will not award damages in these cases.[2]

---

2. Nesivos Mishpat 306:14; Bava Kamma 99b; Choshen Mishpat 306:6–7; Sanhedrin 76a; Tosafos, Baba Basra 22b; Shulchan Aruch, Choshen Mishpat 386.

Bankruptcy

Q I'm going to file bankruptcy. Am I also relieved "Jewishly" of my debts?

No. It's a Torah obligation to repay one's debts,[3] and filing for bankruptcy protection doesn't exempt you from future repayments. Secular bankruptcy laws, despite the concept that the "law of the kingdom is law (*dina d'malchusa dina*)," may cancel your debts, but they clash with the Torah's attitude to do the right thing ("You shall open your hand to him, according to his needs"), and continue to adjudicate the issues within the *beis din* system. Remember: the Torah prohibits taking collateral forcibly or harassing for repayment ("If you lend money to the poor among you, you shall not be demanding to him!"), whilst not excusing the evasive debtor ("Do not say to your friend, 'Go and come back'"). You can (and should) have the borrower sign a note, and you can (and should) secure yourself, but Jewish law prohibits taking anything that is "essential" for day-to-day living (furniture, clothes, etc.). Remember: loans to widows must be both interest- and collateral-free![4]

Baruch Hashem for Jethro

Q Where does this expression come from?

So overcome is Yisro, Moses' father-in-law, by the charm and elegance of Sinai, witnessing a peoplehood (*ga'alta*) being infused with a religious purpose (*kanita*), that he immediately offers a sacrifice and publicly confirms that "God is greater than all gods!" In fact, neither Moses nor Aaron had thought to offer such a blessing until the arrival of this pagan ex-high priest from Midian and ally of the ruthless Amalek. Yisro (Jethro) is thus *the* epitome of a righteous proselyte (a *ger tzedek*), entering Jewish history as the first person to mutter the now popular expression, *Baruch Hashem* ("Blessed be God"), a potent gentile display of spiritual recognition and

---

3. Kesubos 86a; Ramban, Baba Basra 174a; Responsa Radvaz vol. 2:610, 3, #259.
4. Exodus 22:24, 1:1–2, 22:25; Proverbs 3:28; Deuteronomy 15:2–3,7–8; 24:10–11; 1:3; 2:1–2; 11:4; 18:1–2, 24:6.

incredible allegiance that eventually earns him his self-named Torah portion, the only gentile so honored. Hayyim Ben Alter, the eighteenth-century mystic, believes that Yisro was chosen to demonstrate the need for including the wisdom of other peoples into Jewish life.

Bas kol

Q What is this?

The term, common in rabbinic literature, literally means "the daughter of a voice." Why "daughter"? Because the voice itself is not heard, but an echo of God's message. Since the end of prophecy in Israel, this was God's means of communicating with mankind. It was a *bas kol* that declared the innocence of Tamar and Samuel. It was a *bas kol* that supported King Solomon's cut-the-baby-in-half decision. It was a *bas kol* that intervened on Hillel's side during a three-year argument with Shammai. Does this mean hearing God's Voice can decide Jewish law? No. The general principle, as articulated by Rabbi Joshua, is that "The Torah is not in heaven" but lies in the hands of earthly Sages.[5]

Bas mitzva

Q Can I give my daughter a *bas mitzva*?

A Jewish girl becomes responsible for observing mitzvos at age twelve, yet there are no Torah or Talmud references to any *bas mitzva* ritual. In fact, it was discouraged. Why? For two reasons: modesty, and a frowning on any formal Jewish education for girls (although the Talmud recalls how *both* men *and* women came to hear and learn Torah when the King of Israel convened a national assembly for this purpose). Today, many rabbis endorse *bas mitzva* celebrations whilst admitting they are an "innovation," on the basis that in times when Jewish observance is weak, anything that (respectfully) strengthens *yiddishkeit* is (practically) obligatory.

---

5. Deuteronomy 13:1, 12; Pirkei Avos 6:2; Makkos 23b; Eruvin 13b; Isaiah 30:21; Megilla 32a; Deuteronomy 13:1.

═ Bashert ═══════════════════

Q What does this mean?

The Talmud's concept of *bashert* is that forty days before a male child is conceived, an announcement is made in Heaven as to whom that boy will eventually marry. The theological headaches are obvious. King David had multiple wives; were they *all* his bashert? Perhaps. Remember, polygamy was allowed in those days. In fact, the exact wording (the "daughter of so-and-so is destined for so-and-so") does not say *he* is destined, nor that *a couple* are destined for *each other*. Several wives can thus be destined for one man, thus several basherts. But the reverse is not true. Since women cannot have multiple simultaneous husbands, they are a bashert, singularly. The bottom line: under the *chuppa*, each bride and groom are, by definition, each other's bashert![6]

═ Bathroom blessings? ═══════════════

Q I'm told one has to make a silent blessing after going to the bathroom?

It's called *Asher yatsar*, attributed to the late fourth-century Abbaye, *rosh yeshiva* of Pumbeditha, a scholar who thought Jews should be more aware of the complexity of the human body ("Blessed art thou who has created in man a system of veins and arteries!") He included it in the morning prayers as a daily wish for *gezundt*, physical health.

═ BC (before creation) ═══════════════

Q Was there a "*before*" before Creation?

At first the rabbis of the Mishna, curious and incisive by nature, discuss (negatively) those students amongst them "who contemplate what was *before*" Creation, concerned that reminding God of previous attempts at Creation, which would have been a *quasi* failure, was an embarrassment, akin

---

6. Sotah 2.

to blasphemy. But then they compromised, and limited Creation's esoteric study to a daring few Torah scholar-students, one at a time ("One *may* inquire, but two *may not!*"). And what did these select few see? A Midrash sees the Torah opening with the letter *beis* as a sign; its design is closed in all directions except one – pointing forward, indicating that one can only know what came *after*, not before. Others embraced the simple rabbinic adage, *ein mukdam o m'uchar baTorah*, "There is no such thing as 'early' or 'later' in the Torah." It is easy to see why: they wished to avoid chronological confusion, sequence distraction, historic disputes, contradictions of time and space, and such ambiguities as having two accounts of the Creation of man (the first account describes how male and female were created "in the *image* of God" but says nothing about their bodies; the second describes how only Adam was fashioned from earth dust and had the breath of life instilled into his nostrils through a Godly kiss). Meanwhile the Ramban saw time-Torah uncertainties as a purposeful desire by God to withhold information, and the twelfth-century Rashbam (Shemuel ben Meir, grandson of Rashi), adopted the policy of *peshatot hamihaddeshim bechol yom*, which required re-reading the old "in new ways!"[7]

═ Be aware! ═

Q How do we know if our leader is a phony?

The road to holiness requires sincere leadership. It is the ultimate challenge for the layman to recognize the seductive ambiguity of the rascal rabbi, the phony prophet, the mischievous miscreant messenger of God. Commenting on the verse "You shall seek out [*tidreshu*] His Presence and come there [*u'baasa*]," our Sages note that "to seek out" is written in the plural, whilst "to come" is singular in tense, implying that the responsibility to root out any corruptive leadership masquerading under a cloak of righteousness rests not with any individual but with the *Klal* ("community").

---

7. Chagiga 11b, 16a; Genesis 1:26–28, 2:7–22; Ramban, Genesis 46:15, Exodus 10:2, Leviticus 9:3, Numbers 16:5.

═ Beards and *peyos* ═══════════════════════════

Q Is shaving forbidden?

The Torah prohibits cutting "the five corners of a man's beard" by means of an instrument with *one* cutting edge (e.g., a razor). Electric shavers are acceptable because of their multiple cutters. What constitutes "corners"? And how far does one have to cut for the action to become "cutting"? Ah, that's the big question! The sideburns that link the head to the beard definitely constitute "a corner," but how much to chop off is based on custom. Why are they called "*peyos*"? The Torah's term for "corners" is *peoth*. Is there a consensus as to what exactly this means? No. That is why the *Shulchan Aruch*, to be on the safe side, includes the mustache. Why are they called "earlocks"? Because their length must at least reach the lobes of the ears. Why is the Torah even concerned with such "hair-splitting"? In order to differentiate the people of Israel from others, especially primitive pagan cults that made shaving, tattooing and body disfiguration obligatory. In those days, the cutting of flesh and skin was equated with the cutting of hair. This is why Sephardim call side locks *simmanim*, "signs [of Jewishness]." The rabbis of the Talmud considered a beard, especially one that was white, symbolic of dignity and wisdom. Does it follow that every Jew with a long beard and *peyos* is pious? No. As the seventeenth-century Italian Dr. Joseph Solomon Delmedigo put it, "If men be judged by their beard, then goats are the wisest of creatures on earth!"[8]

═ Belief ═══════════════════════════════════

Q Somebody at work asked me what the main beliefs of Judaism are. I said I'd get back to him/her. What should I say?

There are two answers. The approach of the Rambam and that of the *Sh'ma* (the central prayer of Judaism); both can be found in *the* best book of Jewish belief, the daily *siddur*! Maimonides' Thirteen Principles appears (in revised form) in the *Ani Ma'amin* ("I affirm, the coming of the Messiah")

---

8. Kitzur Shulchan Aruch 170:1; Leviticus 19:27–28; Deuteronomy 14:1; Jeremiah 16:6, 48:37; 1 Kings 18:28.

and represents the more philosophical, clinical approach that was inspired by the "doubting" moods of his time. The *Sh'ma* is a straightforward, no-nonsense belief ("Hear, O Israel! The Lord is God, the Lord is One!").

Belts and shoes

Q We bless God for belts and shoes?

Yes. Witty Yiddishists preferred to link praise to "real life," and so when the cock crowed its wake-up call, God was praised for giving it enough intelligence to know the difference between day and night. Upon opening one's eyes? God was blessed for "opening the eyes of the blind." Shoes and belts? God is praised for "supplying all my needs [and] for girding Israel with might!"

Best Man

Q I was asked to be my friend's "best man" at his wedding. Is this OK?

Technically, there's nothing wrong with it, but it's not a Jewish tradition. The closest thing we have is a *shomer* ("guard") who is usually a friend (or relative) of the *chasan* charged with keeping the groom company (and thus safer) during the wedding week. The concept of "best man" started in antiquity, when soldiers "grabbed" brides, sometimes literally from the arms of their fiancés. Men were hired to provide armed "muscle" to defend the groom. Later, the fathers of brides wanted their daughters to have their own protection, so they hired what we now call *bridesmaids*!

Better than patriarchs and prophets!

Q Why so much emphasis on the kids?

"Who exactly is going?" Pharaoh asks Moses, in response to the request to let the Jews take a three-day leave from their serfdom to pray to God. "*Our young* and our old," replies Moses, the inspiration for the daily Psalmist's "lads and maidens, old men *and youths*." Moses mentions Jewish children first, an order of priorities. In contrast to pagan Egyptian religions wherein the young were of no significance, Jews place their children on a spiritual pedestal, considering it incomprehensible not to have the young (symbolizing the future) stand together with the old (a holy link with the past). Even Pharaoh knew this! By trying to keep the youth, he hoped to slash the chain of tradition in which fathers teach sons ("Remember the days of old, ask your father and he will tell you"). And so Pharaoh offers to openly let the "adult men" leave. The offer is rejected, and the ninth plague, a palpable, three-day deathlike eclipse of "total darkness" (*choshech*), is on its way. The pre-birth of Judaism thus revolves around children. And so King David sang how "happy the man that has his quiver full of them"; the Midrash's Rabbi Meir declared that they were "the best surety, better than patriarchs and prophets!" – and the Yiddishists concluded that insanity was hereditary, gotten from one's kids!

Billboards

Q Billboards? In the Torah? Where?

The first billboards in Jewish history, dedicated to the public ratification of Torah, are found in the Torah portion of *Re'eh*, when the Jews, having crossed the Jordan River into Israel, find themselves upon the slopes of two opposing mountainsides (Mounts Gerizim and Ebal). The nation stands literally at a crossroads, between wandering and settlement, past and future, blessings and curses. God challenges them to Judaic graffiti, an encouragement to "cement the Covenant" by carving it on "great stones, coated with plaster" in seventy different languages, one for each nation. What exactly did God want written? The entire Torah? The Ten Commandments? A list of mitzvos? No one knows. But the order to write embodies a famous rabbinic axiom, *Lo hamidrash ikar ela hama'aseh*, "It is not the talking that is important, but the doing!" After forty years of wandering and whining, it was time for the People of Israel to become the world's first Jewish historians; and so the people sit, reminisce and record the momentous events that brought them to this day, the miraculous entry into the Promised Land and onto the stage of Jewish history. Don Isaac Abravanel, statesman of Spanish Jewry, saw these spiritual billboards as the *mezuzos* to the nation's "gateway" into the Holy Land, its text reaffirming acceptance of Sinai.

— Biological battles

Q Are there any instances of biological war in the Torah?

The fifth and sixth plagues that God hurled against Pharaoh involved a fatal attack on the skin and lungs of "all the cattle of Egypt" and affected their "horses, asses, camels, oxen, sheep." The Hebrew word *dever*, which is not used anywhere else in the Torah, translates as "a very grievous murrain." Murrain, the merger of two Latin words, *mor* and *ine*, means "a death plague." Anthrax was a known deadly disease among animals in the ancient Mediterranean terrain. In modern Hebrew, afflictions are named as follows: rabies is *kaleves* from *kelev* ("dog") whooping cough is *sha'eles* from *she'ul* ("cough"), jaundice is *tsaheves* from *tsahov* ("yellow"), etc. When Philologos, the formidable lexicographic giant of the newspaper *Forward*, applied this method to *paheles*, Hebrew for "anthrax," from the Greek *anthrax*, "coal" (from the Latin *carbunculus*, which described an inflamed boil on the skin), he noted that God's next order to Moses was to take "handfuls of furnace ashes" (i.e., disintegrated coal) and release it in the air. This plague produced a lethal skin disease, "a *shehin ava'bu'ot* [boil] upon man and beast." Ash in the Torah is *pi'a*. Coal is *peham*. Add the two, and voilà – we get *pahemes*, Hebrew for anthrax!

— Birth control

Q Is contraception totally forbidden?

The Torah's traditional attitude is based on the positive duty of procreation ("Be fruitful and multiply"). However, in certain situations, if a pregnancy or childbirth might cause harm to the mother, Judaism demands that the wife practice artificial birth control. To the parent who argues that more children are an economic inconvenience or a social hardship, our Sages caution that preventing a birth deprives not only a Jewish family of blessings but also the world of a possible genius – maybe even the Messiah![9]

---

9. Genesis 1:28.

Birthright

Q Is being the "firstborn" a big deal in Judaism?

And how! Jewish families were considered "incomplete" without at least *one* male offspring. It was *he* who carried the family name into the future, provided protection, and, unlike daughters who were given away in marriage, remained at home. The male firstborn received rights and privileges (e.g., a double portion of the inheritance) and, being the oldest, was expected to carry on the family business whilst acting in the role of the "elder" spiritual model.

Bis 120

Q Is this a literal number? To live to be "a hundred 'n' twenty"?!

Past and future; future and past. The story ends as it began! When we first meet Moses, he is "going out" to witness the oppression of his people. When we last see Moses, a hundred twenty years later, he is still "going out" (*vayelech*), giving a farewell speech confessing how hard it is to "stand still" (*netzavim*). It is from here that the popular Yiddish birthday expression, "May you live to be a hundred and twenty years!" stems. Of course, in reality, this age is rarely reached, which is why the great Sforno, a sixteenth-century Italian Torah commentator, taught that it is simply suggestive of having lived to a good ol' ripe age!

Blessing George Bush

Q If I see the President of the United States, who is not a "king," must I still bless him?

Yes. Respect for government stems from Jeremiah ("Seek the well-being of the city, for in its peace shall you have peace") and the rabbis of *Pirkei Avos* ("One should pray for the welfare of the government, since, were it not for the fear of it, people would swallow each other alive"). What are the words of this blessing? No one knows. We do know it was said "after the reading of the Torah" and after *Kol Nidrei*, when Jews asked God to ensure that their ruler show them compassion. Any elected or official leader with the power or authority to affect the Jewish community is considered a "king." The Chasam Sofer and Rabbi Ovadia Yosef define "power" as being able to pardon a convicted killer. What about leaders such as Adolf Hitler or Stalin? Should we have to bless Saddam Hussein with "much nachas"? No. Why not? Tyrants lose their moral authority when they disregard the laws of God and become immediately ineligible for any such Godly blessings. Nevertheless, Russian Jews, even during pogroms, prayed for the health of the Czar (who was followed by Stalin!), and in Germany Jews prayed for the health of the Kaiser (who was followed by Adolf Hitler!).[10]

═ Blue for girls? ═

Q We're expecting our first baby. Should I color the bedroom blue if it's a boy and pink for a girl?

The color blue for ribbons, clothing or bedroom decoration has no basis in Judaism. The color is pure superstition, from an ancient time when infant mortality was high and someone decided that the evil spirits which preyed upon babies were allergic to certain colors. Why blue? It was considered the most potent distinctive pigment to keep them at bay. Is that why all the Arab windows and doors frames are painted blue? No. Their fear was to keep out the "blue-eyed" demonic European Crusaders. Why not blue for girls? Since girls were considered inferior to boys, it was assumed they were of no value to the spirits. Baby girls had no color for centuries, until someone decided the neglect was unfair, and chose pink. Because roses were pink!

═ Blue Moons? ═

Q Do moons get "blue"? How does that affect Rosh Chodesh?

It is only a moon's *shape*, whether waxing or waning, and *not* its color, that interests Jewish law. Besides, the moon is never "blue" (even though it has inspired love-struck poets, songwriters and such crooners as Ella Fitzger-

---

10. Radbaz, Sefer haEshkol; Proverbs 24:21; Jeremiah 29:7; Pirkei Avos 3:2.

ald, Bill Monroe and Elvis Presley). The "Once in a Blue Moon" expression refers to a one-time occurrence, in 1883, when a major explosion on an Indonesian island threw up clouds of enormous volcanic dust and water vapor that circled the world for a few weeks, making the earth's light rays to the moon appear bluish. When astronomers see two full moons in one calendar month, a very rare event – although it occurred on July 31, 2004 – they still call the second one "the Blue Moon."

Body piercing

Q Does Judaism allow tattooing and body piercing?

Tattooing and body piercing fall under the prohibited category of self-mutilation, known as *k'toves ka'ka*, "imprinting a mark." Tattos are also taboo because they are either idolatrous in origin, or humiliating marks of servitude.[11]

Botox

Q My face looks awful. Can I use Botox?

Rabbi Eliezer Waldenberg describes the shallowness of cosmetic surgery as "cosmetic perjury," and adds that, "There is no artisan as our God, who formed every one of His creatures in His image that suits Him, not to be added to or subtracted from." After a person in the Talmud was called "ugly," his immediate retort was "go tell the craftsman [God], who made me, how ugly this item He crafted is." Does this mean no effort should be made to look pretty? Of course not! The Torah frequently mentions precious spices and oils as a means of enhancing female beauty, and describes how brides spent a long time beautifying themselves. In other words, our rabbis encourage beauty and desirability but simply don't equate those goals with Jewish girls turning into walking, talking, surgically perfected Barbie Doll mannequins, engaged in esthetic pop-culture superficial frenzies over pixelation, faultless facelifts, flat torsos and narrow waists. This is why Isaiah, urging moderation in beauty aids, disapproved of "anklets,

---

11. Leviticus 19:28; Rambam, Hilchos Avoda Zara 12:11; Exodus 21:6.

fillets, crescents, pendants, bracelets, veils, head-tires, armlets, sashes, rings, nose-jewels, and aprons." It's obvious what the prophet would say today to society's frenetic search for the Holy Grail of reed-thin cybermodel beauty via liposuction, laser-blasting, exfoliation – and Botox![12]

Bowing down

Q Is bowing down to another person an *absolute* prohibition?

No. According to thirteenth-century Egyptian chief rabbi Avraham ben HaRambam, son and successor to his own illustrious father, it depends on intent. If it is an act of honor or homage, and there is no innuendo about gods or godly symbols present, then there is no deification involved.

Boxing Day

Q Does December 26 have any religious undertones?

Boxing Day, a British custom, has nothing to do with boxing, pugilists or prize fighting – and everything to do with giving a gift *in a box* on a day honoring Christianity's first martyr (St. Stephen). Its connection to religion is vague because it's purely secular today; however, its timing, the first weekday after Christmas, is uncomfortable, and thus Jews should treat it as any ordinary day.

Breakfast cereal

Q There are so many ingredients in breakfast cereal; what *bracha* do I make?

Here's all you need to know. Any cereal that contains one of the five species of grain (wheat, barley, spelt, rye, oats), or its basic ingredient is baked or cooked rice, requires a mezonos. A cereal made only of whole "milled" corn is a *ha'adama*. If you mix milk with cereal there is no need for a *shehakol*

---

12. Isaiah 3:18–23.

because the milk[13] is only there to help you eat your cereal (this applies to such other "extras" as raisins, sliced bananas, etc.). What if you mix cereals? If either one requires a mezonos, then a mezonos it is on all. In the real world, it's practically impossible to keep up with the manufacturer's ingredients, so most scholars suggest that, when "in doubt," eat your cereal as part of a meal, whose blessing is not subject to debate.

Bribes

Q I'm a builder and I know an inspector from the city who can be bribed. Should I?

No. Bribery can be found, together with lying and irresponsibility, in the "non-kosher" category of business ethics, based on a Torah observation that it "blinds the eyes of the intelligent and perverts the words of the righteous." Bought prophets are phony prophets, warns the text, railing against the *Och'lei shulchan Izevel*, those who "ate at the table of Jezebel."[14]

Brother, can you spare a dime?

Q Is *tzedaka* the same as "charity"?

No. The word comes from *tzedek*, which means "righteousness" or "justice" in how you conduct yourself at all times. Charity comes from Latin (or, in Greek, "philanthropy") and simply refers to a vehicle of benevolence to the poor and needy, an indication of compassion and respect to mankind. Jewish law urges the Jew to give anonymously, so that donor and beneficiary are unaware of each other's identity. This is based on the Temple's *Lishkas chasha'im*, a "chamber for secret charity," whereby contributions were deposited and disbursed in secrecy. The Torah does not state "*do* kindness" but "love [*to do*] kindness," which is why Jews are ordered to "give with a good heart" and the proper attitude. "If one gives his fellow all the good things in the world but with a sullen face, it is as if he has given nothing;

---

13. Iggeros Moshe Even HaEzer 1:114; Rama Orach Chayim 208:8; Mishne Berura 168:46, 208:37; Orach Chayim 208:7, 212:1; Shaar Hatzion 31; Iggeros Moshe Orach Chayim 4:43; Biur Halacha 212:1.
14. Deuteronomy 16:19; 1 Kings 18:19.

but he who receives his fellow man with a pleasant countenance, even if he gives him nothing, it is as if he has given him all the good things in the world!" A beggar once asked a man for money. The man replied, "I'm sorry, brother, but I have nothing myself and cannot help you." "I am very content," said the beggar, "because you called me 'brother!'"[15]

Buying shares

Q Can I buy shares based on zodiac signs?

No. Astrology is irrelevant since *ein mazal l'Yisrael*, "the people of Israel transcend astrological influences." The Talmud, which has not a single reference to zodiacs, criticizes *Ov'dei kochavim umazzalos*, the "worshippers of the stars and planets." However, this didn't stop the Children of Israel from acting as though the stars didn't influence their lives, despite the rabbinic adage, *Hakkol biy'dei Shamayim,* "everything is in the hands of Heaven."[16]

---

15. Deuteronmy 15:10.
16. Yore Deah 179:1; Shabbas 156a; Jeremiah 3, 10:2; Brachos 33b.

C

Cain's wife

Q **How did Adam and Eve have grandchildren if there were no girls for their sons to marry?**

The First Couple definitely had daughters-in-law ("Cain knew his wife and she conceived and bore Chanoch"), but the Torah is mute on who they are – yet the Midrash is not. Cain's wife was his sister. Who else could it be? The Midrash goes one step further, blaming Cain's fratricide on being jealous of his brother Abel's (more) beautiful wife (another sister).[1]

Calories

Q **Is Pesach fattening?**

Are you kidding! Is the Pope Catholic?! Despite the matza's entree into the Jewish kitchen as a bread of "affliction," Jewish women have managed to create exquisite Pesach cuisines by using matza as a flour replacement in matza pies, matza balls (*kneydlach*), matza *brei* (*gefrishte matza*). It has never ceased to amaze me: each year there are more inventive foods, more wines and more recipes for Pesach than all other Jewish festivals combined! Pharmacies in Israel report a fifty percent increase in sales of digestive stomach

---

1. Genesis 4:17.

medication after Pesach. How many calories in a typical seder meal? Three thousand! How many in a single matza? A hundred forty, the equivalent of two pieces of bread. And drinking? One standard glass of sweet red wine and grape juice has a hundred seventy calories.

Cannibalism

Q Is cannibalism kosher?

Of course not; the notion is morally repugnant. In his five-volume Holocaust *responsa* (*MiMa'amakim*, "Out of the Depths"), penned on torn cement sack paper and hidden during the war in tin cans, Lithuanian Holocaust survivor Rabbi Ephraim Oshry, a graduate of the Slobodka Yeshiva who helped sustain the religious morale in Nazi concentration camps and ghettoes, says that he was *not once* asked this question despite the hunger, privation and unbearable suffering.

Cantillation

Q What is this?

Cantillation comes from a Latin word (*cantare*), which describes a method of singing that "heightens, stylizes, or freezes" vocal sounds in order to get a "uniform ritual practice." After the destruction of Jerusalem, our rabbis, as a mark of mourning, discouraged the use of music and choral singing and began to chant instead (in Eastern Europe, there was even a rabbinic injunction against reading the Torah without a melody!). The magnetism of music is indicative of the Jews' longing for the past, in that its melody and harmonious consonance always returns to its fundamental root note, to its "hook" as they say in the trade, to the *do* as in *do, re, mi,* etc. The eighth-century rabbis of Tiberias, wishing to preserve this singsong scriptural style during exile, codified a syntax system (*ta'amei hamikra*) that punctuated the emotional-dramatic impact of Torah's song, whilst retaining the serene beauty of its original monophonic melodic line. As "proof" of their brilliance, it is still in use today!

Captives 'n' hostages

Q How important is the issue of captives?

Ransoming a hostage is placed on a higher halachic pedestal than feeding the needy and clothing the poor. Rabbi Joshua ben Hananya held a vigil outside a Roman prison ("I will not budge from here until I ransom [this young boy with curly locks], whatever the price!"). The boy was released and grew up to become Rabbi Ishmael ben Elisha, a great scholar of Israel. However, to "pay any price" was frowned upon by the rabbis of the Mishna, who feared that kidnapping Jews would turn into a booming business. "Captives should not be ransomed for more than their value, as a precaution for the general good!" The thirteenth-century Emperor Rudolph imprisoned the famous Rabbi Meir of Rothenburg (*Maharam*), but the rabbi refused all efforts to be ransomed, concerned that the sums offered for him would simply set a terrible precedent. And so Rabbi Meir spent the last seven years of his life behind bars. When he died, the emperor kept the body for fourteen years, denying it burial, until the Jews paid for its release. Many Jewish communities in medieval Europe had full-time societies (*Chevrath pidyon shevuyim*) with *parnasim*, "communal wardens," whose sole purpose was to raise funds to liberate Jews incarcerated by pirates and gangs, or who had been sold into slavery, or were being held for outstanding debts. Those in charge of Jewish law even laid down priorities: one must ransom a teacher before a father, a scholar before a king and a mother above everybody else![2]

Car *mezuzos*

Q Can I put a *mezuza* in my car?

If you insist! But remember, a *mezuza* is not a "good-luck" amulet and should be limited to places where you live, eat or sleep. There is nothing *technically* wrong with it but, according to Rav Ovadia Yosef, you must be respectful, which means you can't dangle it from the mirror (just like you can't hang *tefillin* off a wall!). Both Rav Ovadia and Rav Moshe Feinstein

---

2. Gittin 58a, 4:6.

allow wearing a *mezuza* on a neck chain (if the parchment is enclosed) because the King of Israel once walked among the folk with a *Sefer Torah* on his arm.

Celibacy

Q Should I get married if I don't want to have children?

In the Richter scale of mitzvos, marriage is right up there, and the "be-fruitful-and-multiply" clause is, within the context of creating a family, literally, the Number One order from God. When celibacy for Christian clergy became an issue in the Middle Ages, our rabbis produced reams of polemics against it. One thirteenth-century *sefer* (*Nitzachon Yashan*) bluntly states that clerical celibacy is a fiction, and would tempt priests to "wallow in licentiousness in secret." The Jew who deliberately renounced marriage lacked joy, blessing, happiness, peace and more: the celibate also deprived society. How? Who knows what blessing one's child might bring to the world? After all, *someone's* child has to be the Messiah! There is only one recorded instance of a Talmudic rabbi (Ben Azzai) who chose not to marry, and he was roundly criticized for his excuse: "What shall I do, my soul embraces Torah. Let others perpetuate the world!"[3]

Chai luck

Q How is the word *chai* associated with the lucky number "eighteen"?

By reversing the two Hebrew letters *yud* (the numerical value of which is ten) and *ches* (eight), we get the combined *yud-ches* (eighteen) – which yields the word *chai* (meaning "alive"). The "luck" associated with this number, or any multiples of it (180, 1,800, etc.) is the reason it is widely used in giving *tzedaka,* as in, say, "two times *chai*" (thirty-six), "three times *chai*" (fifty-four), and so on.

---

3. Yevamos 63b.

═ *Chalav Yisrael* ═══════════════════════════

Q Is *chalav yisrael* more "kosher" than kosher milk?

In order to protect the unsuspecting kosher consumer from any inadvertent consumption of non-kosher milk (a remote possibility today), a more stringent process was initiated that required that the milking of kosher animals be supervised by a Jew. That milk is known as *chalav yisrael*. Drinking unsupervised milk (*chalav akum*), a rabbinical prohibition, is disallowed even if there is no other milk available, or when supervised milk is very expensive. Does this also apply to powdered milk? Yes, but in Israel unsupervised powdered milk is still considered *chalav yisrael*. However there were times when unsupervised milk was as kosher as kosher could be. When there were there no "non-kosher animals" around, the *Pri Chadash* allowed it because the odds of a non-Jew mixing the two were practically nil. His opinion was not universally accepted. The *Chasam Sofer* defined the decree as a "permanent ordinance," never to be abrogated. Yet leniency was a common occurrence. Reb Yaakov Kamenetsky allowed plain milk when *chalav yisrael* was unavailable (e.g., in hospitals, on business trips), and Rav Moshe Feinstein allowed "plain company milk" (*chalav stam*), which is neither *chalav akum* nor *chalav yisrael* (although he himself refrained from drinking it).[4]

═ Charity ═══════════════════════════════════

Q I don't want to overdose on charity. Since I can't please everyone, whom should I help first?

Basically, charity begins – but does not end – at home. Rashi explains the Torah's order of priorities. If a close relative ("one of your brethren") is a "needy person," he or she has greater priority than a stranger. Local Jews ("within your gates") must be helped before the Jew in "the land which God gives you" (i.e., Israel).[5]

---

4. Chasam Sofer, Yore Deah 107; Iggeros Moshe, Yore Deah 1:46, 1:49, 2:35, 2:47; Aruch Hashulchan 115:8; Chazon Ish, Yore Deah 41:4; Teshuvos Radvaz 4:74; Emes L'Yaakov, Yore Deah 115:1.
5. Deuteronomy 15:4–8.

Chazanuth

Q Our *shul* is looking for a *chazan* for *yom tov*. I don't see the point. Do you?

Yes. In the "old days," when an atonement-seeking Jew arrived at the Temple with a sacrifice, the "mind-reader" priest in residence would try to read his thoughts. If he sensed that the Jew was "faking it," he asked the Levite choir to sing a *niggun* to help *nudge* the sinner to full *teshuva* (repentance). Today, this role is fulfilled by cantorial skill. However, the *chazan* need not give us a "delightful little concert," nor a great musical *weltanschauung*, but a truly uplifting religious experience. Remember: his audience is not only God, but a community that he must inspire, stir, arouse.

Cheating the government

Q Should religious Jews be held to a higher standard when it comes to crimes against the government?

Cheating the authorities is wrong, whether you are religious or not! However, being "religious" means you are (or *should* be) much more halachically aware of *chillul Hashem*, the "profanation of the Divine Name," and sensitive to guilt via association. Not only are *all* Jews bruised publicly from such disclosures in the media, but Judaism itself suffers disrepute.[6]

Check it out!

Q How often should I check my *mezuza*?

It depends. Is it public or private? If public, it only has to be checked every twenty-five years. If private, then you should inspect it twice in seven years, however if it is a private (i.e., residential) *mezuza* exposed to the elements (sunshine, rain), then you should do it more often. I have friends who make it an annual duty, and check their *mezuzos* every Elul, and not just for *kashrus*. To make sure they're still there! Do you need a professional

---

6. Gittin 10b; Chullin 94a; Tosefta Baba Kamma 10.

sofer? It's preferable, but not necessary, if you are competent in Hebrew and know the laws. If a *mezuza* has to be replaced, must a temporary one be put up? Yes, if it will take several days to replace it. Or, you can renounce your ownership of the house, making it *hefker*, temporarily – but don't tell your lender![7] Should one examine *mezuzos* if a tragedy strikes the family? Some do, but every Jew reacts to misfortune differently, and since no Jew has a direct hotline to God, no Jew knows whether the *kashrus* of a *mezuza* is the direct cause-and-effect of calamity.[8]

Cherem d'Rabbeinu Gershom

Q What is this?

It describes a *takkana* ("prohibition") from Gershom ben Judah (known as the "light of the exile") against marrying more than one wife; the *cherem* ("excommunication") adjective was tacked on to warn violators of its gravity. Were "spouses" (plural) considered immoral? No. Rabbeinu Gershom was concerned with gentile resentment, and social preservation. Remember: the Jews of Europe lived under the Christian thumb, and Rome was totally against polygamy. Was the ban intended to be permanent? No. Rav Moshe Isserles (*Rama*) says it was temporary, only until the year 5000 (which has since come and gone, and yet the ban stays in place). Was it universally accepted? No. Only Ashkenaz Jews (Germany, France, Poland, Russia) were OK with it; Sephardic Jews (southern France, Spain, Italy, Greece, Turkey, Israel, Africa, Asia) were opposed. What if a Polish-Ashkenaz Jew moved to a Sephardic communuity in Salonika, or Constantinople? Then, according to Rashba, Maharil and Yosef Caro, he can marry as many women as will have him. Rav Emden goes one step further: since the *takkana* was based on fear of Christians, it did not apply to Jews in any non-Christian country. Were there general exceptions? Yes. For example: if a wife had no children, or had ceased to have children, or had gone insane (which required the husband to get permission from a hundred rabbis in three countries).[9]

---

7. C. Kanievsky, Mezuzos Beisecha 289:6; Kuntres Hamezuza 289:6.
8. Yore Deah 291:1; Iggeros Moshe, Yore Deah 1:183; Aruch Hashulchan 291:1; Kitzur Shulchan Aruch 128:3; Rashi, Yuma 11a; Teshuvos Chasam Sofer 283; C. Kanievsky, Mezuzos Beisecha 289:6; Teshuvos Maharil 94.
9. Sh'eilos Ut'shuvos HaRashba, vol. 3, 446; Maharil, Sh'eilos Ut'shuvos HaMaharil He-

Chevra Kadisha

Q When did this concept begin?

The earliest mention of a "community burial society" dates back to when a Talmudic Sage (Hamnuna) arrived in a town and noticed an unattended dead body. Appalled, he decided to place the entire Jewish community into *cherem* (excommunication) for violating Jewish law (burying the dead takes precedence over everything else). But the Rav desisted when he discovered that the town had a burial society, and he made it their responsibility. Since then, the *Chevra Kadisha* has become every community's primary cause, its establishment even *more* important than that of a *shul, cheder* or *mikva*.

Chewed cuds and split hooves

Q How, within the myriad of food products, am I supposed to know what's kosher and what is not?

By way of a *hechsher*, a rabbinic seal of approval, and *hashgacha*, rabbinic supervision. The basic rules are these. A kosher animal? One that chews its cud (ruminant) and has split hooves. A kosher fish? One that has both fins and scales. A kosher bird? Since the Torah only lists non-kosher birds, one deduces that all the other birds are kosher.[10]

Chicken

Q How do we know that a chicken is kosher?

There is no such thing as a "kosher bird," but we deduce through default. If it is not listed among the Torah's twenty-four non-kosher species, then it's OK.

---

hadashos, Machon Yerushalayim, 202; Otzar Haposkim, Even Haezer 1:10; Tashbetz Sh'eilah 94; Beis Yosef, Sh'eilos Ut'shuvos HaRan 48.

10. Yore Deah 117:1; Rambam, Guide for the Perplexed, 1:35.

═ Child custody ═══════════════════════════

Q Do parents automatically have child custody "rights"?

The conflict is between "parental rights" and what's in the best interest of the child. The *Rosh*, a leading fourteenth-century Talmudic authority, awards the children to the parent "fittest" to support and them. Rav Shlomo ben Adret (Rashba) of Spain agrees on support, but doesn't grant the parents automatic custodial rights. In the olden days, Jewish children became the responsibility of the Jewish courts (*beis din avehern shel yesomin*, "guardians of all children!") who tried to apply formulas: maternal custody of sons and daughters under six; paternal custody after six (unless either parent was unfit, which changed the rules). These were guidelines, not law.

═ Christmas trees ═══════════════════════════

Q My Jewish neighbors claim their Christmas tree is harmless, secular and just decorative. Are they right?

No. It is as pagan as pagan can get. It began in Norse mythology, associated with the death of nature during the winter solstice; its leaves represent immortality, its branches and roots supposedly connect heaven to hell. The Romans used it to display decorated images of their gods, in an attempt to ward off Saturnalia, the husbandry-vegetative god of Saturn. When the Church adopted it, it tried to link it to Isaiah, who spoke poetically of the "righteous branch" (but the Hebrew prophet was referring to the trees that beautified the Jewish Sanctuary). My suggestion? Buy your neighbors the biggest menorah you can find and ask them to try it on for size!

═ Chronological order ═══════════════════════

Q Is the Torah sequential?

The Ramban says "yes" (*Yeish mukdam u'm'uchar*), the Torah flows in chronological order; but most scholars disagree, including Rashi, the "prince" of Torah commentators, who claims that certain themes and Torah topics are organized thematically, with no chronological relationship to how they were given by God to Moses. For example: the mitzva to build the Tabernacle was given *after* the Golden Calf sin because of the thematic similarities to *that* specific event.[11]

Chametz and shares

Q Do I have to sell my shares every Pesach in a public food company that deals in *Chametz*?

Yes: to a non-Jew, together with the rest of your *Chametz*, and you cannot buy or sell them during *chol hamo'ed*.[12]

Chumros – light!

Q *Chumros*? What does this mean?

It depends on whom you ask! Basically it means self-imposed religious stringencies, over-and-above what Jewish law requires, for the purpose of showing greater devotion to God. Examples would include *glatt kashrus*, a married woman wearing a *sheitel* plus a hat, etc. The Torah actually contemplated that some Jews would feel the need to go above-and-beyond the cause, and thus instituted an "excessive" category, with its own specific laws. Welcome to the *Nazir* Jew who seeks abstinence and lives a life with "fewer" pleasures, eschewing wine and haircuts. Yet, the Talmud still warns the Nazir to give up his "anti-extras" after thirty days, warning that long periods of such conduct become "counter-productive." And more! He then has to bring a sin offering to "apologize" for his self-stringencies and is ordered to celebrate his return to "normality" by drinking wine. Thus, whilst it's good to give a mitzva some "extra" attention, the Jew is advised to be modest in his behavioral patterns (*chumros* – light!), and avoid extremism. In fact, if the purposeful and public pursuit of *chumros* is seen by others as arrogance, then it's better to lie low.[13]

---

11. Exodus 25:1; Exodus 32:1.
12. Mishne Berura 448:12.
13. Numbers 6; Nazir 1.3; Baba Kamma 59b; 80b.

Chuppa, in or out?

Q Where should it be? Indoors or outdoors?

No difference. Originally, *chuppa*, derived from the Hebrew root "to cover," didn't even refer to a public wedding canopy, but to the privacy of a "marriage tent" (or room), a legal precondition of marriage (Psalms sings about a wedding couple *emerging* from their "*chuppa*" to a morning sunrise). When the ceremony was later moved outdoors, under a textile covering on four poles, a "new" custom known as *yichud* ("privacy") was instituted to allow the couple "a few minutes alone" elsewhere. How long is this brief intimacy? The time it takes to start throwing dishes at each other? No! According to Rama, it's long enough "to eat [something that breaks the fast].")[14]

Church

Q My friend is getting married in a church? Can I go?

No. Jews are prohibited from going into a place of worship whose symbols, theology or liturgy are incompatible with Judaism or monotheism; despite the Torah's ethic of harmonious relationships (*darchei shalom*, "the ways of peace") with others. What about a funeral in a church? No, unless it's an absolute necessity. For example: if you're a chief rabbi, and one of the mourners is a head of state, and your absence might jeopardize the safety of the Jewish community, then *maybe* it's OK.[15]

Cloning

Q Is this permissible?

The question for Jewish law is not whether cloning is permissible *per se*, but on the clone *itself*. Is it fully human? Does it have human rights? Who is the "real" mother? If either "mother" is not Jewish, Rabbi Shlomo Zalman Auerbach requires the child to have a conversion. Where the ovum

---

14. Psalms 19:6; Joel 2:16; Rema, Even HaEzer 55, 61:1; Rema, Yore Deah 391.
15. Gittin 61a; Shulchan Aruch, Yore Deah, 150; Iggeros Moshe, Yore Deah 3.

was provided by a donor, Rabbis Yosef Shalom Elyashiv and Shlomo Zal-man Auerbach *pasken* that the child belongs to the donor-mother. So, is cloning a monster unleashed? The Torah's attitude to cloning is the same as its approach to such medical breakthroughs as artificial insemination and surrogate motherhood. If it can save or protect life, by treating infer-tility, diabetes, Parkinson's or Alzheimer's, it's OK (Judaism considers the doctor as doing "God's work"). However, any exercise in "playing" God is forbidden. The Talmud claims three areas whose domain the Heavens have retained for themselves, and one is childbirth. Thus cookie-cutter humans ("an athlete, please"), baby farming ("one boy, no girls, please"), or baked to order ("I'll have a blue-eyed child instead of brown-eyed to go, thank you") are banned by Jewish law because of their immoral intent. But wait! Didn't Hanina and Hoshaya "fashion" a calf? Didn't Rava manufacture human life that only lacked the ability to speak? Didn't medieval Jewish mystics fiddle with creating "golems"? Yes, but since none of these activi-ties used pre-existent human genetic ("God-given") material, they are not defined as cloning.

Codex Theologicus Graecus Number 31

Q **What is this?**

It is the catalog ("shelf") number designated by the Austrian National Li-brary for the most beautiful illuminated sixth-century Book of Genesis ever found, known as the *Vienna Genesis*. It is made out of purple parch-ment (the color that symbolized imperial rule in the early Middle Ages), is written in silver ink letters, and has about five hundred exquisitely stun-ning miniature scenes.

Cohen in love

Q **I'm a *cohen* in love with a convert. Can I marry her?**

Sorry, no. Is this a reflection on the convert? No. *Cohanim* have serious ritual responsibilities that come with certain restrictions (e.g., they cannot come into contact with a dead body; they cannot marry a divorcee, nor a convert).

═ Coincidence? ═

Q How many enslaved Egyptian Jews actually left for Israel?

Exclusive of Levites, women and children, 603,550 males. Is this a guess? No. The Book of Numbers owes its very name to a God-ordered "counting," via the submission of *shekalim* ("coins"), as the basis of the future division of Israel. A coincidence? Six hundred thousand (approximately) is also the number of Holocaust survivors who left Europe for the same Holy Land, and who initially left the Soviet Union (*Operation Exodus I*), the proportional equivalent of moving the entire population of France to the United States! A coincidence? This is also the (approximate) number of Hebrew letters in the Torah, the word *Yisrael* being an acrostic for *yesh shishim riboah l'Torah* ("There are six hundred thousand letters in the Torah"), or *yesh shishim riboah anashim l'Yisrael* ("There are six hundred thousand Jews").[16]

═ Communion ═

Q Is this related to anything Jewish?

Yes. The Church hijacked the symbols of bread and wine from the Jews, the two critical ingredients that started the holy Shabbas day of the week. So how did they get the "thin wafer" from our *challa*? Because they borrowed the imagery of the "Last Supper," ostensibly a pre-Pesach meal, wherein unleavened bread (matza) was used instead of ordinary loaves.

═ Compassion ═

Q If I'm not, by nature, a compassionate person, am I still Jewish?

This question is not as stupid as it sounds. Although the traditional answer to *Who is a Jew?* is "one born to a Jewish mother, or converted by Jewish law," the Torah adds a unique, mystical "kindness" factor when deciding *What makes a Jew*. This led the rabbis to a stunning conclusion: that

---

16. Exodus 1–4, 26; 30:11–16; 38:26; Numbers 1:46, 26:53.

hardheartedness (of the Pharaohnic kind) is a Judaic anomaly ("Whoever does not have compassion and mercy [is] not of the seed of Abraham.") In other words, a *sine qua non* for being a "spiritual disciple" of Abraham requires an inbred ability to be sensitive, to care for others, to sense their hurt, to respond unselfishly to their needs. A Jew in deed *as well* as in birth, notes *Pirkei Avos*, must have three characteristics: a "good eye" (benevolence), a "humble temperament" (contentment), and a "lowly spirit" (non-materialistic). In short: manners and *middos* are mandatory for the Jewish soul!

Competition

Q Can I open a pizza place next to another pizza place?

Yes. Our rabbis don't consider this a *hasagas gvul*, which literally means, "removing a neighbor's landmark" (i.e., "unfair competition," as in depriving another of his livelihood). Rashi, a proponent of free choice, agrees, on condition that there is no unfair advantage, or bad faith. An example? If you are subject to lower taxes and, as a result, can offer similar pizza at lower prices. Or you indulge in cutthroat business. An example? Offering a pizza at a price that your competitor cannot match, in order to drive him out of business. What about "stealing" customers? This is a "gray" area (known as *s'michus da'as*, "assumptions and expectations") that recognizes the "exclusivity" relationship between a vendor and a steady customer (although some scholars tolerate "customer-baiting," if that's the norm in a particular type of business, such as insurance).[17]

Compulsory pledges

Q What's my obligation towards *shul* pledges? Can I change my mind?

If you make a vow or pledge to donate money to a *shul*, or a *shul* cause, the commitment has to be honored ("Observe and perform the utterance of your lips"). And, if all, or even the majority of, a *shul*'s members vote in

---

17. Baba Basra 21b; Shulchan Aruch, Choshen Mishpat 156:5; Chasam Sofer, Choshen Mishpat 61; Minchas Yitzchak 2:94; 3:127; Beiur haGra, Choshen Mishpat 156:5.

favor of a particular cause, then *every* individual must contribute because the decision is collectively binding. Why? Because *everyone* benefits from this approach, one that systematizes welfare instead of leaving it up to the whim of individuals.[18]

Computers and God

Q Can I "delete" God's Name on the computer?

Jewish law demands that God's manifestations in print be treated with respect (i.e., stored or ritually buried when no longer needed); however Rabbi Moshe Shaul Klein ruled that the word "God" can be "erased" from a computer screen, or disk. Why? Because pixels are not considered letters.

Concubines 'n' wives

Q What's the difference between a wife and a concubine?

An Arab oil magnate once entered London's *Marks & Spencer* department store and asked for a hundred nightgowns from different counters. "But, sir," said the surprised salesgirl, "these are of various shapes and sizes." "So are my wives," he replied. The Torah uses both terms (wives and concubines) synonymously, although the expression "concubine" only applied to "plural," second-class wives, a status that was critical for inheritance (concubine children received gifts before death but no inheritance afterwards). The Torah frequently alternates between the two (e.g., Keturah is called both a "wife" and a "concubine"), as are David's wives. Meanwhile, Rehoboam had sixteen concubines and King Solomon broke all records with three hundred concubines. Who was the first to deviate from the one-woman-as-exclusive-soulmate? Lemech, a degenerate great-grandson of Adam, who had two wives (Adah, Zillah). The Laws of Moses once tolerated more than one spouse; however our Sages never idealized the situation and instead filled their rabbinic texts with teachings that stressed monogamy as the most satisfying spiritual and physical nourishment.

---

18. Deuteronomy 23:24.

═ Confidentiality ═══════════════════════════

Q I have a defective gene. Do I have to disclose this to a *shadchan* or a potential spouse?

Yes. In fact, failure to disclose physical defects or illnesses, according to Rabbi Judah, is grounds for marriage annulment. Can a relative disclose the information? Yes. The Chofetz Chayim declares that this (non-obligatory!) disclosure is *not* a form of "tale bearing" (*loshen hora*) if it could be a determining factor in one's decision. Is there anything that one *absolutely* must divulge? Yes. Heretical beliefs![19]

═ Congregation B'nai Bingo ═══════════════════

Q Can I donate my gambling winnings to the local Jewish day school?

The first question is whether you should be gambling at all. Most scholars permit "social" gambling, although some consider it a form of theft, and Rashi explains that because gamblers play with expectations of being winners, their consent is not entirely voluntary. Jewish teaching distinguishes between professional, compulsive gambling, and occasional gambling. In a famous Mishna, a professional dice player (*M'sachek b'kuvya*) is stigmatized and excluded from giving testimony, or becoming a judge. In contrast, the occasional social gambler was tolerated. Why? Because he had a "constructive occupation," although he was aware that the moment he "stepped overboard" he faced potential denial of any communal office. What was the fear? Obsessive gambling was addictive, led to financial strain, and made one a useless member of the community (both winner and loser, according to eleventh-century Rabbi Joseph Tov-Elem, "forsake life eternal [for] temporary existence and nonsense!"). Therefore, organized casinos in *shuls*, such as the relatively innocuous form of Bingo, or gaming fundraisers for *yeshivos*, schools and Jewish charities, are to be handled-with-halachic-care.[20]

---

19. Sefer Chassidim #507; Chofetz Chayim, Laws of Talebearing, 9, 3:4.
20. Sanhedrin 3:3, 24b; Rama, Choshen Mishpat 370:63.

Connoisseur

Q I love fine things. Is it OK to surround myself with beautiful objects?

Sure, go right ahead! Our rabbis, convinced that "a beautiful wife, a beautiful dwelling place and beautiful furnishings broaden the mind of man," demanded that anything "unseemly" be removed from civic sight, so as not to spoil the splendor, and urged Jews to appreciate such natural beauty as birds, mountains and lakes. Why? Because all creativity awakens a sense of wonder, and acts as a reminder not to take surroundings for granted. Rav Samson Raphael Hirsch, when asked why he was going to Switzerland, replied: "As an old man, I'm afraid that when I appear in front of God, He will ask me, 'Did you see My mountains in Switzerland?' and I will not know what to answer." Judaism also recognizes that such man-made beauty as music and art, done tastefully and in moderation, can elevate the soul as well. An example? Shaul, first King of Israel, recovered from his melancholy after the music of David's harp forced a "bad spirit" to leave him – an incident that inspired several Psalms to jubilate how "spiritual victory is achieved through the art of music (*Lamnatzeach bin'ginoth*).[21]

Contradict

Q Can one rabbi disagree with another rabbi?

It is disrespectful, says Rashi, for a *rav* to question another's ruling; in fact, the ruling in itself gives the matter at hand a special *ipso facto* special status (known as *na'aseh chaticha de'issura*). Others agree, but for a different reason – so as not to imply that there are two Torahs.[22]

---

21. Brachos 57b; Baba Basra 2:9; Shmuel II, 16:25; Psalms 4:1.
22. Niddah 20b; Ran, Ra'avad, Ritva; Avoda Zara 7b.

Convert caveats

Q Does Judaism accept converts?

Yes, but with a caveat. They must be sincere, with no ulterior motive. That is why our rabbis are first obligated to deter potential converts by emphasizing all the negatives of being a Jew. Neither "persuaded nor dissuaded," notes ancient sage Eleazar ben Pedat in an entire Talmud tractate that reads like a guidebook-for-potential-proselytes! Judaism is not an aggressively outgoing missionary religion (Jews, unlike Christians, do not have a theological imperative to convert people "to the faith"), but, once accepted, the convert is highly praised, "dearer to God than Jewish saints!"[23]

Convert's *kaddish*

Q Can a convert say *kaddish* for his non-Jewish parent?

It's optional, but not forbidden.[24]

Copycat

Q If I copy my friend's tape, am I breaking copyright laws?

It's complicated. On the one hand, if your friend has fully paid for it, he can do whatever he wants with it, even giving you permission to copy it. However, Jewish law not only prohibits you from depriving another of his income (*parnosa*), especially if that cash flow comes *only* from creative labor, but also has a provision of *Shiur b'mechira* which describes sales "subject to" some restrictions, which could, legally, disallow copying. Rav Moshe Feinstein forbids copying even a Torah cassette tape without the producer's explicit consent. What about copying book pages? That depends. If it's for educational purposes it's probably OK (because the publisher would likely not object to this form of promotion), however you cannot profit from

---

23. Gerim 1:3; Yore Deah 268:12; Yevamos 47; Simeon bar Yohai, Mishnat R. Eliezer; Numbers Rabba 8:2.
24. Aharon Walkin, Z'kan Aharon, vol. 2, no. 87.

the "copied" material. What takes precedence? Jewish law or government copyright law? The latter. Why? Because halacha is subordinate to any law of government enacted to (financially) protect its citizens.

Cosmetic surgery or cosmetic perjury?

Q My daughter wants a face-lift. Should I let her go through with it?

Ancient Greeks bound female breasts for shrinkage, African tribal women extend their necks with graded rings, and other cultures still use nose and genital piercing to "improve" their beauty. In contrast, Judaism prefers to leave the manufactured goods the way the Manufacturer made them. Since the body is "on loan" from God, our rabbis see mankind not as owners but as custodians, and includes our bodies in the Torah's prohibition of assault-and-battery (*havala*). Jewish law thus frowns on the shallowness of cosmetic surgery ("cosmetic perjury") as an exercise of sheer vanity, but permits it for medicinal reasons (e.g., after an accident). What about tattoos? This self-mutation, known as *k'toves*, "imprinting a mark," is forbidden for additional reasons: it was once a mark of slavery and popular amongst those worshipping idolatrous gods.

Costs too much!

Q Why are *tefillin* so expensive?

Like a *mezuza* or *Sefer Torah*, they must be handwritten by a pious scribe with a quill pen; this takes time, care, patience, practice and expertise – which are reflected in the price. But spare no expense! They're the best investment you'll ever make!

Count down, or up?

Q Isn't the *sefiras ha'omer* expression, to "count down," incorrect, and confusing? Shouldn't it be a "count-up"?

The count is a very carefully worded one: instead of saying this is the eighth day, we say, "Today is one week *and* one day of the omer," a methodology that the Rambam calls a *mitzva atsei,* one that creates a greater anticipation and motivates us not just to count the omer – but to make the omer count. Why do Jews start counting the *sefira* from one *up* to forty-nine, and not from forty-nine *down* to zero? I'm not sure. Perhaps by ticking off the days that have passed, we accustom ourselves to appreciate each passing day, in the vein of the Psalmist's reminder, "Teach us to count our days rightly, that we may obtain a wise heart."[25]

Coveting and craving

Q Aren't these the same things?

No. So, how to tell the difference? By the level of behavioral intensity; in other words, if you crave, you will (ultimately) covet and, once coveted, an item will (ultimately) be stolen, and so on. British Chief Rabbi Joseph H. Hertz defines them both the same way: "Anything that we cannot get in an honest and legal manner!" The nineteenth-century *Malbim* agrees with the sixteenth-century Ovadiah Sforno that coveting is "tangible, specific" (e.g., seeing, then wanting the neighbor's car), whilst craving is "intangible" (e.g., seeing the neighbor's wealthy lifestyle and wanting to be rich). Coveting even includes trying to *buy* something that's not for sale, for *full value*! An example? If you talk your neighbor, who's not in the business of selling cars, into selling you his great car because you just gotta have it at any price, you are actually transgressing not one, but *two,* Torah prohibitions: *lo sachmode,* "You shall not covet," and *lo sisaveh,* "You shall not desire your friend's property."[26]

Cremation

Q If someone is already cremated, can his or her ashes be buried in a Jewish cemetery?

No. There is no ambiguity: cremation is prohibited, even though it is not specifically mentioned in the Torah. Why? It is forbidden to destroy or

---

25. Rambam, Hilchos Temidin U'musafin, Ch 7; Menachos 66a.
26. Mechilta; Rambam, Hilchos Gezeilah 3; Exodus 20:14; Deuteronomy 5:18.

mutilate a human body, even *after* death; it was a pagan practice and a blatant denial of resurrection. Therefore "ashes," indicative of a renunciation of fundamental Jewish beliefs, have no place in the mitzva of burial (*k'vuras hames*), which *only* applies to a human body revered. What if a will demands cremation? A reputable *Chevra Kadisha* will ignore such wishes. And if cremation does occur? Judaism holds the next of kin responsible for the severe transgression.[27]

Crescent moons

Q Is the Islamic symbol of a crescent moon Jewish in origin?

Yes. Our rabbis waxed poetic, and halachic, about the waning and re-emergence of the moon (Rosh Chodesh). Mohammedans "borrowed" the philosophy of a moon in a state of increase, worshipping the day when it (as a symbol of Islam) would conquer the world "all around."

Criminals

Q I have just been sentenced to prison. Can I be counted in a *minyan* behind bars?

Yes. You may be guilty of desecrating God's Name (*chillul Hashem*), a major transgression in Judaism, but you haven't permanently forfeited your "spiritual" rights. There is a law (one offense doesn't excuse another), and a principle involved (do not "close the door before penitents").

Culinary Judaism

Q Am I right? Do all Jewish holidays rotate around food?

Yep, you're right. All Jewish holidays involve a specific delicacy and a cornucopia of symbolic foods that borders on a halachically mandated Culinary Gastronomic Judaism (in fact, three out of the first five commandments that Israel received as a nation have to do directly, or indirectly, with eating!).

---

27. Joshua 7:15; Isaiah 30:33; Leviticus 20:14; 21:9.

Try to imagine a Rosh Hashana without apples and honey cake; a Purim void of *hamantaschen*; a Shavuos absent blintzes and cheesecakes; a Succos without stuffed cabbage and *kreplach*; a Chanukah minus doughnuts and potato *latkes* – and what is a Shabbas without *challa*, *gefilte* fish, *cholent* and *kugel*? What about bagels and lox! No, they are unrelated to the Jewish calendar! God's sole positive and negative commands to the First Couple in Eden related to permissible foods ("from all the trees"), and forbidden ones ("from the Tree of Knowledge"). Thus food, discipline and survival are synonymous from the get-go, which is why our rabbis structure the art of eating as a powerful act of sanctification. From washing of hands, blessings, "breaking" *challa* and sprinkling salt, each meal is a mini-reenactment of the priest's Temple procedures. The logic was simple. The Torah was likened to sustenance, in that if the body needed food to sustain itself, then the soul also required spiritual nourishment.[28]

---

28. Exodus 21:1.

D

Democracy

Q Who pioneered democracy?

Your first thought might be the Greeks, but the democracy of Athens relied
on subjugating and depriving the populace of their human rights. In contrast,
the Torah declares, "This is the book of the generations of man," which our
Sages interpret to mean *all* men, *all* created equal in God's image, *all* (even
the "stranger within the gates") entitled to dignity and freedom "as of right"
(*even* slaves were assured freedom after seven years!). Israel was the pioneer
of the "no one is a nobody!" democratic theory, even as it struggled with the
concept *lo tih'yeh acharei rabbim l'hattot*, to "follow the majority." Majorities
can go wrong. When Elijah disagrees with the four hundred prophets of the
god Baal, despite the four-hundred-to-one odds, he sides with the minority.
Rabbi Joseph Hertz reads the verse as "a warning not to follow a majority
blindly for evil purposes." The adage "tyranny of the majority" is no empty
slogan. Consider: Germany in the 1930s, when Hitler, having received the
popular vote, used it to construct Auschwitz. This is why the Torah tacks
on *Asher tasim lifneyhem*, "You [Moses] should put before them," an order
to place reasoning, logic and common sense (*seichel*) in preference to blind
obedience.[1]

---

1. Genesis 5:1.

Dowry

Q Who usually pays the wedding dowry?

Since the wife was chosen by "the boy's side" (usually the father), it is "they" (usually the father) who paid the dowry. How much? It differed, determined by social status and wealth. In 1618 the rabbis of Rome, concerned that dowry pressures were getting out of hand, limited *shadchanus gelt* for the father to two hundred scudi. Ben Sira agreed, and described the Have-Money-Will-Marry ritual as "hard labor and a disgrace!" Is this fee compulsory? Yes. There are repeated Torah references to "marriage gifts" and "bride prices" during Isaac's courtship of Rebecca, Shechem's pursuit of Dina, David's marriage to Saul's daughter. What about poor boys? They ended up like Jacob, working for their father-in-law as an *Eidem auf kest*, "resident son-in-law." Today the custom is reversed. The girl's father is expected to pay, and pay, and pay even more if the chosen *chasan*-to-be is a proven Torah scholar, or *claims* to be one, or even just *promises* to become one![2]

Drafting *yeshiva bochurim*

Q Should all Jewish men, including full-time Torah students, serve in the Israeli army?

Unfortunately, this is a major wedge lodged in the throat of national Jewish unity. The idea of an "obligatory war" is carved into Jewish law, as is the creation of a standing army. Self-defense is such a fundamental commonsense Judaic concept, that, in the face of an implacable enemy whose hobby it is to blow up Jewish children in school buses and pizza parlors, it is *forbidden* to be a pacifist. Let's see what the Torah says. At the end of the Book of Numbers, Moses is faced with a disturbing request from certain tribes (Reuben, Gad and the half-tribe of Menashe) who refuse to cross the Jordan with their kin and settle in western Canaan. To a leader the issue is obvious: in a situation where the nation goes to fight a war of survival, it is irresponsible and intolerable in the context of national unity and collective fairness for some members to (unilaterally) decide to "sit it out." Moses'

---

2. Genesis 24:53, 34:12; 1 Samuel 18:25.

response is basic and timeless: "Are your brothers to go to war while you stay here?" Moses compares their request to the report of the failed spies (*meraglim*) whose fear and slander led to national disaster, an entire generation dying in the desert. The Torah describes them as *tarbus anashim,* a "breed of sinful men," who selfishly struck at the safety and security of the people of Israel, their lack of shared values accelerating the nation's demise. So how could anyone justify, in the face of suicide bombers, missiles and public Arab intent for a genocidal sequel to Hitler, not to "cross the Jordan" with his brothers-in-arms? Even the ancient Levites were actively engaged soldiers charged with protecting the Sanctuary, because dead Jews, *religious or secular,* are of no use to Torah or God!

═ Do's 'n' don't's ═

Q It seems the majority of Torah laws are on the "negative" side. Am I right?

Yes. The "do not's" account for seventy percent of the Ten Commandments, and about sixty percent (365) of the 613 mitzvos. Isn't this intimidating? No. A long list of "to do's" would be far more consuming and exhausting; in contrast, "*not* doing" instills a healthy discipline of restraint.

═ Dress reversal ═

Q Was fashion more important than food?

What a dumb question! Or is it? "If need be, spare from your stomach, spend on your back," goes an old Talmudic proverb, to which the cynical Yiddishists of central Europe respond, "Beautiful clothes do not hide the hump!" Judaism has considered one's clothing a weapon in the fight against assimilation ever since the enslaved Jews used their distinct attire to prevent wholesale integration into Egyptian society. The Rambam takes the Torah's focus on priestly clothing and extends it to the rabbinate. The clothes of a *rav*? They must be "suitable, clean, with no stains or grease-marks, and not drag along the ground [in order not to] bring disrespect to the wearer." A *tallis katan*? Don't wear it "conspicuously long." Why not? "It appears like haughtiness!" How about patched shoes? *No, no, no!* Unless it's winter, and you're "a poor man!" How about perfume? No. Scented garments? A definite no! Why not? "To avoid suspicion." A noble appearance gives rise to awe and respect. The Torah even implies death for those who conduct the Temple service in the absence of a regal appearance; note how close the Hebrew word for clothing (*b'gadim*) is to betrayal (*b'gida*)! The Hebraic term for wearing a costume, *lehit'hapes,* comes from the root *lehapes,* which means "to look for," because costumes hide the truth. The ancient Greeks called the masquerade of slaves pretending to be free "pretend play at the theater." On Purim the masks make it a *yom tov* not of dress rehearsal but dress reversal!

Does my guest have to wear a *sheitel*?

Q Well, does she?

In the pursuit of bringing Jews "back" to keeping Torah laws, does anything go? No. The popular adage "the end justifies the means" is a foreign, non-Jewish philosophy. Jewish law rejects anything done in its name which compromises Torah standards, even for such a noble goal as being *mekarev* other Jews. In the "real [halachic] world," this means you cannot invite a Jew for a Shabbas meal if he will drive there. Can you invite a married Jewish woman if you know she's not going to wear a *sheitel* or otherwise cover her hair? I don't know; it's unclear.[3]

Don't try this at home!

Q Has anybody counted the letters in the Torah to see which one is in the "middle"?

After the age of prophecy ended, a generation of rabbis called *sofrim*, which literally means "counters," became the first Jews to "count" Torah letters, words, verses. In their desire to "break" the Torah text in half (by "halving," they sought to *double*), these rabbis identified God's middle pair of words as being in *parshas Tzav* (*Leviticus*), with the middle letter a *vav,* a symbol

---

3. Minchas Shelomo 2:4–10; Iggeros Moshe, Orach Chayim 1:98–99; 4:71, 1:39, 42, 43; Orach Chayim 3:23, 24.

of progression, a letter that always acts as a "hook" between two words; or in this case, a staple that held the two halves of Torah together. This coveted *vav*, written larger than the other letters, was found in the word *gachon*, "belly"; and, lying at the center of this conjunction, they met the mysterious *Urim VeTumim*, a breastplate that Aaron wore, which acted as a conduit that connected the Jew and God through Time and Space. Don't try this "search-for-the-center" at home. Why not? It no longer works. Most Jews today use the popular Jerusalem-published *Torah, Nevi'im, u'Ketuvim* edition of 1962 which is different; not only does it have forty-five letters *less* than the oldest complete manuscript of the entire Bible, but it places the Torah's middle letter and middle words some 4,830 letters and some 933 words *away* from the previous location. At least those who compiled this edition were intellectually honest enough to warn, "We do not claim that we have established our edition on the basis of the tablets that Moses brought down from Mount Sinai"; and the humble Talmud admits, "We are not expert on full and defective spelling," conceding the impossibility of determining whether any middle letter truly belongs in the first or second half of the Torah.[4]

Deathbed confessions

Q My mom's in the hospital with a terminal disease. Is the family obligated to get her "to confess" before she dies, or is this a Christian thing to do?

It's a Christian thing. The "Jewish" thing is epitomized by the death of Rabbi Akiva (at the hands of the Romans), who used his last ounce of strength to say the *Sh'ma*, the last mitzva available to him. This "dying prayer" then took on a religious significance. Meir ben Yehiel, thirteenth-century poet, recalls Akiva's martyrdom, "his soul departed with *echad*," solidifying the trend that saying the first words of *Sh'ma* ("Hear, O Israel...") is a pre-death obligation to sanctify God's Name.[5]

---

4. Kiddushin 30a; 11:42; Tzav 8:8; Leviticus 8:28, 8:15,19; 10:16; 11:42.
5. Kiddushin 40b; Ezekiel 33:12; Sha'arei Teshuva 1:9.

═ Death penalty ═

Q Did the death penalty exist in ancient Israel?

Yes. There was stoning, burning, beheading and strangling. Male idolater-blasphemers were executed and hung in public until nightfall. Other corporal punishments included a beating of thirty-nine lashes; however, no punishment was meted out without explicit witness testimony, a rule that totally negated confessions and circumstantial evidence. Judges were commanded to judge justly, show no mercy to those deserving of punishment ("Your eye shall not be merciful!"), and be careful not to discriminate between the poor, rich, wicked and pious.[6]

═ Devil's in the details ═

Q Is the concept of a "devil" Jewish or Christian?

Jewish mystics ascribe the powers of the "evil inclination" (*yetzer hora*) to Satan and see his negative influence right from the start as the serpent in Creation. *Sitra achra*, "the other side," is an Aramaic term for the devil that comes straight from the *Zohar*. Whenever the term "Satan" appears in the Torah, it does so not as a name but as a noun, as a hostile "adversary" to God. In the Book of Job, he's the "Devil's Advocate" in the court of Heaven, a (non-demonic) prosecutor with no dogmatic or authoritative significance. His role in history was enlarged later by Christians who made their opponents (Jews, then Romans) out to be Satan's evil instruments, determined to lead the world to damnation.[7]

═ Defining Judaism ═

Q Is Judaism a race, religion or nationality?

Judaism is a religion. "We are a people," declared Saadia Gaon a thou-

---

6. Numbers 15:30; Leviticus 19:15; Deuteronomy 19:13, 21; 25:2–3, 26:12; Exodus 23:1–3, 6; 23:7.
7. Psalms 109:6; Zechariah 3.

sand years ago, "by virtue of the Torah," with unique practices (mitzvos) designed to propel a mission (*tikkun olam*), whilst forging a nationalistic identity. Those who call Jews a race (popular since the nineteenth century) by classifying them as "Semites," are driven by anti-Semitic motives, in an attempt to genetically isolate and categorize Jews as "inferior." In the race to the finish line, there's no such thing as a "Jewish race"!

Do, obey? Obey, do?

Q Well, which one is it?

Torah linguists point to the Jews' response at Sinai, *Na'aseh v'nishma*, "We will do and obey," as being in the wrong order, since "doing" usually comes *after* "obeying." A more correct translation of *nishma* is "understanding," since religious acceptance flows from actions. Yet, there *is* a vagueness. When God "spoke all of these words," the Torah doesn't tell us to whom. Ibn Ezra argues that everybody heard everything. The Rambam disagrees and claims that only Moses understood the content, the Jewish people *hearing*, but not *comprehending*. What does Rashi say? Like the Ramban, he suggests a compromise: all Ten Commandments were given by God; however, only the first two ("I am the Lord, You shall have no other gods") were understood by the children of an Egyptian polytheistic culture; the other eight required further explanation by Moses, implied by the Torah's switch from first-person-singular to third-person.[8]

Do I need a Phase I?

Q Was the Torah concerned about the environment?

The Torah abhors widespread environmental devastation. Since Mother Nature, notes the Baal Shem Tov, is "the very essence of God," our ancient Sages grappled with such "contemporary" issues as hazardous waste, dump sites, air pollution. The heads of the *beis din* would personally inspect the water in the wells. The Talmud forbade Jews to live in any city that had no

---

8. Ibn Ezra, 20:1; Rambam, Hilchos Yesodei HaTorah 8:1, Guide for the Perplexed 32, 33; Exodus 20:1.

gardens, foliage, vegetables. Yoseph Caro, author of the *Shulchan Aruch*, ordered Jewish communities to plant trees. Acha bar Rabbi Chanina warned, "What appears as superfluous [*meyutarin*], like flies, fleas, mosquitoes, are not!" Such supreme halachists as Yitzhak ben Sheshet and Jacob Ettlinger dealt with urban and noise pollution, and the Rambam, a doctor by day, noticed the ill effects that nature degradation had on asthma, and so, as a Talmudist by night, focused on environmental issues.[9]

= Darkness to dawn =

Q Why does every Jewish festival begin at night?

Rav Samson Raphael Hirsch compared "the waxing and waning of the moon to Israel's renewal, for even in its darkest wanderings, Israel, like the moon itself, is never lost." The nineteenth-century Chassidic Sage Yehuda Leib Alter (*Sfas Emes*), commenting on a Mishna that collates the transformation from Egyptian suffering to joyful freedom as going "from darkness to great light," concluded that "Israel orders its calendar by the moon, for it is used to living in the night of history." Jewish festivals begin at night in order for the Jew to emerge in the dawn, the morning light, with an affirmation of survival. This belief, that those who cling to Torah, heritage, lore and law have the power not only to persevere through darkness but also to turn that darkness into light, was in sharp contrast to the Egyptians who regarded darkness as superior to light (which is why they deified blind field mice). When Isaiah calls out to the Heavens, "Watchman, what of the night?" Rashi describes "nighttime" as the "domain of the destroying agencies." The *Zohar* agrees: nighttime is a "barren dust that rules over Israel, who are prostrate to it." And so our rabbis composed *Hashkiveinu*, a prayer that God protect Jews from the terrors of nightfall, a plea based on precedent. All thirteen events, as compiled by the *Beis Halevi* and listed in the lyrics of *Vayehi bachatzi halayla*, take place on Pesach eve, *at night*! This convinced Jewish mystics that the final redemption, an event which will be "as clear as day" (*u'keor boker yizrach shemesh*) would appear during the darkness, when all hope seems lost; at a time of heightened fear,

---

9. Exodus Rabba 10:1; Ribash, Responsa 196; Ettlinger, Responsa Binyan Zion, 137; Genesis 2:15; Brachos 40a; Baba Basra 25a; Likutei Moharan 2:12; Zohar 3:225a; Job 12:7–9.

insecurity, deep anxiety. Why? So that the Jew could awake to the light and confidence of a new world order, and know no more of the dark, inauspicious, "it-came-to-pass-at-midnight" dread.[10]

— Divorce

Q As a wife who wants a Jewish divorce, can *I* institute proceedings?

Technically, no. It is the man who takes the initiative, based on the Torah's wording on both marriage ("When a *man* marries a woman") and divorce ("*He* shall write *for her* a bill of divorce"). Yet you *can* begin divorce proceedings under certain conditions. Examples? If your husband has a loathsome disease, or refuses to give you support, or is cruel, licentious, impotent or deprives you of your conjugal rights. The *beis din* then has the power to force the husband to give a *get* by fining him a set amount for each day he refuses to do so. Early Mishnaic texts (including the remarkable documents preserved from the fifth-century BCE Elephantine Jewish community) discuss the extent of a husband's fines, and what exactly constituted husband-breaches. The question is obvious: why do we have the major problem of *agunos,* "chained wives" who cannot remarry because their husbands refuse to grant them a divorce? This heartbreaking status has nothing to do with any "harsh, man-made" laws of Moses and everything to do with the total collapse of the *beis din*'s authority in modern westernized society.[11]

— Drinking, or sleeping?

Q I don't want to drink on Purim. Can I sleep away the hours instead?

Yes. In fact, not everybody was happy with Rava's Purim dictum to drink so much that one's intoxicated senses "can't differentiate between cursing Haman and blessing Mordechai," and decided, perhaps influenced by the

---

10. Rashi, Exodus 12:22; Baba Kamma 60b; Psalms 90:14; Exodus 21: 11.
11. Deuteronomy 24:1; Exodus 21:10.

Rambam's ruling that one may drink just enough to fall asleep, that sleeping accomplished the same result as wine-soaked blurriness.[12]

Do not enter!

Q **Is it forbidden to enter the Temple Mount?**

Yes, until we know where it actually stood. Until then, the uncertainty makes much of the grounds "hallowed," under the concept of *tuma*, the Laws of Defilement. When Sir Moses Montefiore walked on the site in 1867, with permission from the Sultan of Istanbul, he was immediately placed into *cherem* (excommunication) by Rabbi Yosef Moshe of Lissa. Montefiore, a religious Jew, quickly apologized and said he had misinterpreted a halachic ruling by the *Raavad*. Can you touch the stones of the Wailing Wall? If you're looking for a "yes" answer, go to Maharil and the Sochatchover Rebbe. A "no" response would be given you by the *Aderes*!

Debate or deny?

Q **Is to quarrel with God an act denying God?**

No. Rabbi Akiva's death accelerated the search for some order to the universe, something that would explain the acceptable coexistence of a good God and a bad evil. This exercise, known as theodicy, is as old as time itself and can be traced back to Deuteronomy's doctrine of *mipnei chatoseinu*, "on account of our sins." Our rabbis plead, "Do not give up because of sufferings," even as they painfully acknowledge that "if you want to endure this world, equip yourself with a heart that can withstand pain!" Meanwhile, the saintly *Chofetz Chaim* cries, "When the going gets tough, look at the jewels [Torah] you are carrying," in a desperate attempt to review the glorious past in the light of the grisly present. Rav Ami, a student of Rabbi Yohanan, tried to explain the ultimate *Mysterium tremendum*, why bad things happen to good people, by declaring *Tiyuvta d'rav ami tiyuvta*, that every death and suffering is caused by sin. It didn't work. He was rebuked by the Heavenly angels themselves. This led the Yiddishists of East-

---

12. Sukka 51a.

ern Europe to proclaim as an article of faith: "In life, be careful. Ask God questions and He may insist you come up to hear the answers!" The Holocaust may jolt us into asking "Where was God?" but it is also a reckoning of "Where was Man?"

Day the music died

Q Were does the idea that song *equals* Torah come from?

From a Biblical injunction of Moses, "And now write for yourselves this song," a position supported by King David ("Thy statutes have been my songs!"). Convinced that Moses was equating "song" with the entire Torah, the Rambam made it a positive command for every Jew to write a *Sefer Torah* for himself, one "which contains *shira*, an element of song." Song was, and still is, a favorite form of religious self-expression, especially for Chassidim. The Baal Shem Tov introduced joy via singing as a way of serving God, and made it a point to learn as many *niggunim* ("melodies") as possible. Chassidim would "borrow" tunes, rhythms and dance steps from the local White Russian *prisiudki* or gentile Romanian shepherds, and then add Hebrew words and allegorical Judaic content (nothing beats Ger's Shabbas marching tunes, with Modzhitz coming a close second!). In fact some of our favorite melodies (*Ma'oz Tzur, Adir Hu*) are derived from non-Jewish folk songs and European operatic arias (even Napoleon's march somehow found itself into the Kol Nidrei liturgy!). Many of the songs we hear these days at Jewish weddings and other simchas are no more "Jewish" than Mick Jagger wearing *tefillin*, or Led Zeppelin blowing the shofar. Original Jewish music was more chant than rant. The Judaic music tradition goes back to the first-century Jews of Jerusalem, whose hereditary caste of musicians (the Levites) played intricate instrumental and choral music with silver trumpets, drums and reed pipes during the three-times-a-year agricultural pilgrimages. The day the music died was the day the Romans entered as professional pyromaniacs and burnt the House of God to the ground.

Dancing with the Torah

Q Can I dance on Simchas Torah if I'm not holding a Torah?

"Jewish life is a symphony whose score is the Torah, whose composer is God, whose orchestra is the Jewish people," writes Rabbi Jonathan Sacks, "and whose most moving performance is on Simchas Torah." The charismatic Chassidic leader Israel ben Eliezer (*Baal Shem Tov*) once danced with the Torah, stopped, put it aside – and continued dancing and clutching it in its invisible form. This ability to perceive something that is not there, and continue as though it is, is the single most remarkable strength of the *Yiddishe folk*. It is confidence personified, *emuna* on a stand, "evidence," according to Menachem Mendel of Kotsk, that "faith is clearer than sight!"

Dates

Q I'm very confused with what happened, and when, in early Jewish history.

Here's a clue: everything rotates around the Exodus! And here's an (inexact) summary. Two hundred fifteen years pass between Abraham's journey from Mesopotamia to Canaan and Jacob's migration to Egypt (c. 1700 BCE), four hundred to 430 years are spent in Egyptian slavery, therefore around 645 years is the time span between Abraham's entrée into Jewish history and the epochal Exodus. If we use the Bible's timing of Solomon's construction of the Temple ("in the fourth year of his reign"), which is about 480 years after the Exodus (c. 960 BCE), we can backdate the exit from Egypt to around 1436 BCE (i.e., 960 minus four plus 480), with the invasion of Canaan forty years later (c. 1400 BCE). This calendar formula identifies the oppressive Pharaoh as Thutmose III; unfortunately, non-Jewish historians don't agree. Why? They claim the Pharaoh (Rameses II) who built the cities in the Torah (Pithom and Raamses) lived between 1290 and 1224 BCE. So, join the club! I'm not so sure of the dates either![13]

---

13. Exodus 12:40; 1 Kings 6:1; Exodus 1:11.

Dehiyyah molad zakein

Q What does this mean?

The lunar month is totally indivisible within a solar year, causing a "deficiency" of about half a day in each month. So, why not just "fractionalize" the day? Because Jewish law didn't want Rosh Chodesh to arrive *during*, instead of *at the beginning*, of the day. In order to always get a "full day," the rabbis alternated the months between twenty-nine and thirty days, created up to a two-day postponement (so that Yom Kippur not fall on a Friday or Sunday, nor Hoshana Rabba on Shabbas), and delayed Rosh Hashana a day until the *molad* was more defined. The time of the *molad shel tohu*, on the first day of Tishrei in the Hebrew year 1, is known by an acronym: *baharad*, wherein *beis* stands for "Monday," *hey* for "five hours," *resh-daled* for "204 parts." This exercise is known as *dehiyyah molad zakein*, the "Old [or Obsolete] Moon Rule," and is derived from a Rav Zera dictum which supposedly guarantees the New Moon's visibility on Rosh Hashana (but has never been proven!). Was Zera's decision universally accepted? No. In fact, it created major *machlokes* between a Torah genius in Palestine (Aaron ben Meir) and his formidable competitor in Babylon (Saadia Gaon). The result was mass confusion. Jews who followed ben Meir (who thought the maximum *molad* was thirty-five minutes, forty seconds), celebrated Pesach, Shavuos, Rosh Hashana, Yom Kippur and Succas two days *earlier* than the followers of Saadia Gaon! In the end, Saadia won the argument and calendar unity was restored.[14]

Doctor in the house

Q I heard that seeing a doctor showed a lack of faith. Does it?

No, but it *is* a time for prayer! *Doctor* means "one who instructs," *patient* means "suffers," *nurse* means "nourishment," *hospital* stands for "guest house." The first surgery in the Torah was performed by Dr. God Himself, with the excision of a rib from Adam. And it was done under a God-induced anesthetic (He caused "a deep sleep to fall upon the man"). Preventive

---

14. Rosh Hashana 20b.

health is a must in Jewish law, and even the laws of the holy Shabbas can be suspended in order to protect life. The Chinese had it right: they put their doctors on their payroll and stopped the checks the moment they got sick. Is there anything Jewish about the symbol of medicine, the staff-and-serpent emblem? Yes. Jews who were bitten by poisonous snakes during their years in the dangerous wilderness had to make a snake out of copper and hold it high over their heads on poles. Why? I don't know. The Torah is mute on reasons, but obviously saw some power of healing in sticks 'n' snakes. Even the pagans acknowledged the Torah source. The Greeks, who considered their god of healing (Aesculapius) the father of all physicians, drew him holding a staff on which a snake is coiled. So does seeing a doctor signify lack of faith? Of course not, despite the Torah's declaration, "For I, God, am your healer!" A doctor is God's agent "granted the privilege of healing," no less than the priests once supervised medical treatments and disbursed various remedies. The debates in the Talmud are full of medical references, anatomical-physiological information, basic psychiatry – and who would dare accuse the medicine-practicing Rambam of usurping any Divine prerogative? In fact, a sick person who does *not* call a competent doctor immediately is breaking Jewish law. How? By relying on a miracle to cure him![15]

═ Drugs? No thanks! ═

Q Does recreational drug-taking infringe on Jewish law?

Yes. The Torah prohibition of assault and battery, known as *havala*, applies to oneself ("You shall diligently guard *your* life") as well as to others. Since the body is "on loan" from God, our rabbis saw mankind not as owners but as custodians. Judaism's method of getting "high" is through the ecstasy of spirituality, and an encouragement to "take a trip" through the exhilaration of Torah study and the joyful art of doing mitzvos. Apart from its harmful effects on the individual, family and community, drug abuse infringes on several basic halachic principles. If the body is not "ours" but "His," our Sages saw these regulations as being "more stringent than ritual prohibi-

---

15. Exodus 15:26, 21:19; Baba Kamma 85a; Chazon Ish, Kovets Iggerot, vol. 1, #138; Peirush Hamishnayos, Pesachim 4:6; Kiddushin 39b.

tions" since man is made in the Divine image. Therefore any activity that threatens the body (including smoking, excessive drinking, etc.) falls into the forbidden category of self-mutilation.[16]

Disabilities

Q Does Judaism discriminate against Jews with disabilities?

Yes, and no. There are laws that diminish the sanctity of Jews with certain disabilities. An example? Priests with "blemishes" (*mum*) were prohibited from performing sacrifices in the Temple. But scholars were extremely sensitive to these issues in real life. Jewish history is chock-full of giants of Torah who were handicapped. Moses had a stutter; Sarah couldn't bear children for a long time; Isaac and the Torah Sages Yosef and Sheshet were blind; Mefiboshet, Saul's grandson and an outstanding scholar, could scarcely walk; and Rabbi Zeira was described as "the one with short legs." And more! Not only did our Patriarch Jacob limp, but his new name, *Israel*, is a direct reference to his disability.[17]

Dove

Q Why are the children of Israel compared to a dove?

When all other birds grow tired, they find rest upon a rock or the branch of a tree. But when the dove tires, she does not cease flying; instead she rests one wing and flies with the other, under a watchful Divine Eye.

Death

Q What is Judaism's attitude to death?

"The Angel of Death always finds an excuse," goes the Yiddish proverb. There is no immunity from the great certainty of death; it is inevitable, part

---

16. Deuteronomy 4:15; Rambam, Hilchos Chovel U'Mazzik 5:1; Eruvin 54b; Chullin 10a; Genesis 1:26.
17. Leviticus 21:16–23; Brachos 7:7; Megilla 24b; Mishne Torah 9:13–15; Yoma 85b; Biur Halacha, Shulchan Aruch, Hilchos Shabbas, section 329; Genesis 32:23–33.

of life, none is exempt ("Moses died, who shall not die?"). Death, says the Midrash, is part of God's pattern for history, allowing one generation to make way for another. And yet, it still remains a great theological mystery: is death an end, or a transition? Judaism believes (although there is no empirical evidence) in a life (*Olam Haba*) after this one (*Olam Hazeh*) but scrupulously discourages speculation about its nature. "There's only one [death] per customer, so it must be a real bargain," cracked that famous Jewish philosopher, Milton Berle. Judaism has a unique view of death and dying, one often based on humor and wit – despite the Torah view that death is (sometimes) a punishment for sin. There is no reality like mortality, death's popularity coming only by abstraction since, by its very definition, it is what happens to somebody else. It is the one great adventure in life of which there are never any survivors' accounts, eyewitness testimonies, reliable reports or experiences. "This world is only a hotel, the World-to-Come is our home," was a favorite theme of the Baal Shem Tov. That is why the Hebrew word for a funeral is *levaya,* or *halvayas hames,* which means, "*accompanying* the dead." It's a universal truism: since everyone is uncomfortable dealing with an angel called Death, our rabbis optimistically call a cemetery a *beis chayim*, a "house of *life!*" Death, notes thirteenth-century Joseph Zabara, is "the terror of the rich, the desire of the poor." Its cause? Life! [18]

18. Genesis 3:22–24; Zabara, Sefer Shaashuim.

E

Evolution

Q I'm going to college next year and want to study the natural sciences. Is that OK?

The Rambam claims the study of natural science fulfills a primary twin-mitzva, to "love" and "fear" God. So is it OK to study evolutionary biology? No. Rav Moshe Feinstein condemns as sheer heresy any evolutionary text-book or Darwinian analysis that supplants the Torah's account of Creation – yet he does allow the generics of biology, *absent* its apostatical nature, to be studied. Can non-Jews study evolution? It's unclear. Some rabbis interpret the Noahide provision "that they [non-Jews] honor the Torah" as a *sine qua non* directive *not* to delve into such a heretical doctrine as humans evolving from monkeys.[1]

Eclipses

Q Does Judaism view an eclipse as a bad event?

No. Jeremiah's warning, "Be not dismayed at the signs of Heaven," refers to

---

1. Exodus 21:19; Leviticus 18:5, 19:16, 18; 25:36; Deuteronomy 22:2; Shulchan Aruch, Orach Chayim 6:1; Sanhedrin 99a; Rif 19a; Rosh 11:3; Iggeros Moshe, Yore Deah 3:73; Mishne Halachos 2:35; Chullin 92b.

eclipses. However, whereas other nations (the Chinese see it as a "sky dog" eating up the sun) regard eclipses as evil omens, Judaism accepts them as a part of the Divine system. In fact, the sun "stood still," twice in the *Tanach*, with such eyewitnesses as Joshua and Hezekiah.[2]

═ Eulogy ══════════════════════

Q I've been asked to give a eulogy. Any suggestions?

Yes. Keep it short ("I decree," the Chassidic Aaron of Karlin requested, "that no praises be spoken of me"), honest ("orators and Amen-sayers will be punished for false eulogies") and extravagance-free ("To ascribe to one merits which are not his is really to approach him!"). When the Heavens lionize Moses, the most illustrious rabbi of all time, they do it in two short, direct words: he's an *eved Hashem*, "servant of God." There is no great oratory, no flowering poetry, no tomes of accolades for his unstinting devotion, remarkable humility, calm leadership, pristine prophecy. The Torah focuses only on his *raison d'être*, his fidelity to God. Abraham, at Sarah's funeral, the first recorded in the Torah, first eulogizes and only *afterwards* does he cry. And so the Torah uses a miniaturized letter for *kaf* in *livkot* ("to cry"), a sign, explains the *Baal Haturim*, a fourteenth-century halachist, that weeping be restrained and grief subdued.[3]

═ Eggs, onion, garlic ═══════════════

Q I was at my grandmother's and she wouldn't let me eat a peeled egg. Why?

Included in the litany of "life-threatening acts" to be avoided (not counting the obvious, such as walking too close to a cliff edge, contracting a disease, etc.) are non-physical elements that the Torah considers spiritually "bad for the soul." These include eating peeled eggs, onions, garlic (and maybe radishes) left overnight. Why? We don't know; just like we don't know the resultant danger, if any, from eating meat and fish together. The rabbis

---

2. Jeremiah 10:2; Sukka 29a; Joshua 10:12; II Kings 20:8.
3. Brachos 62a; Zohar Genesis 232b.

claim that these foods attract the same *ruach ra'ah* ("spirit of impurity") that rests on one's hands during nighttime sleep, and requires washing (*netilas yadayim*) immediately upon wakening. Whatever the reason, the Torah takes it seriously, even to the extent of accusing the Jew of committing a form of suicide for its neglect.[4]

Ethical will

Q Is there such a thing as a will with no "hard" assets?

Yes. Judaism believes that simple good advice from a parent or role model is an incredibly valuable asset, worthy of being "passed down." Jacob's deathbed scene, of final blessings and lavish advice, is the foundation for this custom. Jacob was the first Jew to establish an ethical will, and was also the first Jew in the Torah to suffer from an illness before dying. His example sets the tone for the last wills of future Torah personalities. They leave not riches nor material goods, but the philosophy of morality. So on their deathbeds King David advised his son Solomon to "keep faith, walk in God's ways"; Eleazer ben Hyrkanos instructed "Let your children sit at the knees of wise scholars"; Moses Sofer taught, "If you can do only a little, then do that little with utmost devotion"; the Ramban exhorted, "Speak in gentleness to all men, at all times"; and when Yehudah ibn Tibbon died, he passed on to his children his view on *seforim*: "Make bookshelves your pleasure gardens; gather their fruit, pluck their roses and take their spices and myrrh!"

Enhancers

Q How do I know which *bracha* to say if my meal comes with "enhancers"?

It's complicated, but the general rule is this: a primary blessing (*bracha rishona*) over a main dish (*ikar*) also covers the dish's "enhancer" (*tafel*).

---

4. Brachos 32b; Rambam Hilchos Rotzeiach 11:4; Chosen Mishpat 427:5; Pesachim 76b; Orach Chayim 173; Yore Deah 116:2; Chazon Ish, Archos Rabbeinu 1:210; Minchas Yitzchak 2:68, 9:28.

An example? If you sprinkle matza crumbs over your schnitzel, no blessing is said on the matza because it's considered "secondary, insignificant." If your "enhancer" isn't enhancing, there's obviously no issue! If an "enhancer" consists of one of the five traditional species of grain, then it is a separate, stand-alone *mezonos*. An example? Your blessing over vegetable salad wouldn't cover any side croutons; nor would a blessing over chicken soup extend to the noodles. Are there exceptions? Yes. A *shehakol* on an ice-cream cone covers both the ice cream and the cone, despite the fact that the latter is a *mezonos* item.[5]

Euthanasia

Q I have a patient in pain who wants to end his life? Shall I assist?

No. The moral right to Life, *the* supreme sanctity, is absolute, not relative. In contrast to the ancient Greeks and Romans, who dismissed the old and seriously ill as useless, Judaism views each human, regardless of the patient's age, background, profession, social status and condition, in the image of God, and thus to write off a life is to diminish God. Jewish law ("a dying person is alive in every respect") even forbids writing a eulogy or making funeral arrangements before death. Since only God has the prerogative of ending life (because the body is considered His property), the deliberate shortening of life, even by a moment, is considered a form of murder ("Whoever closes the eyes [of a dying person, a *gosses*] is deemed to have taken his life"). However, in a display of compassion for the dying, the Torah allows the removal of "artificial" obstacles that do not cause, but delay, death. An example? "If there is something which inhibits the soul's departure, such as a nearby noise of knocking like wood-chopping, or if there is salt on the patient's tongue and these [irritants] hinder the soul's departure, then it is permitted to remove them."

---

5. Mishne Berura 205:11, 208:23, 212:5; Orach Chayim 208:2; Magen Avraham 205:6, 208:7.

═ Etiquette ═════════════════════════

Q Is Judaism a religion of etiquette?

Yes, despite the fact that etiquette is a French term, meaning *label* or *card*, which came into use when guests at French royal functions were handed little cards instructing them on how to behave. These cards were called "*etiquettes*." Jews have the same cards. They're called mitzvos!

═ Eschatology ═════════════════════

Q What does this mean?

Eschatology is theologic discussion on the "end of days," the fulfillment of messianic hopes. Isaiah's expression (*aharis hayomim*) is not original. It first appears in the Torah when Jacob, having gathered the future twelve Tribes of Israel, tries (unsuccessfully) to tell them what will "befall you *in after days*." So, do we know when the exile will end? No. And we're not supposed to guess, but many try. Jacob knew, and, as he was about to tell his sons, he was struck with amnesia ("It was hidden from him!"). The second scholar, Jose ben Halafta, warned that those who try to calculate "the end will have no share in it!" Jonathan ben Eleazar, a third-century Palestinian *amora*, minced no words: "Blasted be the bones of those who calculate the end, for when the calculated time comes and Messiah does not appear, people despair of his ever coming!" Our Sages explicitly warn not to calculate any salvational arithmetic about the end of this planet, but this did not stop the Ramban, who toyed with messianic maths, from declaring that the Jewish year 5118 (1358) was a likely Messianic candidate. In case you haven't noticed, he was incorrect.[6]

---

6. Genesis 49:1; Genesis Rabba 96:1, 98:2; Tosefta Derech Eretz 6:13; Sanhedrin 97b, 98a; Shabbas 118b; Shir Hashirim Rabba 2:24.

Earner-learner

Q What should I look for in a spouse?

An earner-learner is a modern-day term to describe potential husbands who will manage to earn (a living) whilst learning (Torah). Learning, on its own merits, somehow seems inadequate; and pure earning (a job, profession, etc.) seems spiritually lame. A combination is the ideal.

Equinoxes and solstices

Q Should Jews care about equinoxes and solstices?

Yes. Why? By acting as calendar anchor points, they fix certain start dates in the diaspora. An example? Sixty days after the autumnal equinox (around December 5th–6th), Jews begin to say the prayer for rain in the daily *amida* (*Vesen tal umatar livrachah*) until Pesach. Who arrived at this formula? The Talmudic Sage Shmuel codified the four quarter-year "periods" (*tekufos*) for the Jewish calendar (*Nisan* – Spring, *Tammuz* – Summer, *Tishrei* – Fall, *Teves* – Winter), known as *Mahzor Hagedola* (or *Hamma*, the "Great Cycle"). This is the *only* secular date in halacha. How reliable is it? Very. Every twenty-eight years, like clockwork, the *tekufa* of Nisan reverts back to where it started. And the time between Pesach and Shemini Atzeres equals the days (185) between the vernal and autumnal equinox. A coincidence? I don't know, but unlikely.

Epitaph

Q Is it tacky to compose one's own epitaph?

Maybe, but Moses did it! "There has not risen since in Israel a prophet like Moses," he wrote, *before* dying, with tears in his eyes (although some scholars, uncomfortable with this example of haughtiness, claim these words of praise were penned by Joshua after Moses' death).[7]

---

7. Baba Basra 14b–15a; Deuteronomy 34:10.

Ephraim and Menashe

Q Why do parents bless their children that they be like Ephraim and Menashe?

Before blessing his own sons, the bedridden Jacob singles out and blesses two of his grandchildren (sons of Joseph), an honor that catches the attention of all Torah scholars, especially since so little is known about them. And more: by placing a hand on each child's head, the *zeida's* interaction has trickled down the centuries to become *the* traditional *erev* Shabbas parental model for *birkas habanim*, the poignant blessing that all Jewish sons "be like (the modest) Ephraim and (the strong) Menashe." But why? Why not strive for a son to be like Moses or Abraham? Contentiousness among Jews seemed to be a pattern, a Judaic Greek-style family tragedy, until Ephraim and Menashe, two brothers who never fought, broke the trend. They are thus the Torah's epitome of sibling compatibility, an inspiration for the Davidic lyrics, "How good and pleasant is it for brothers to sit peacefully together." Neither Abraham nor Isaac had such *nachas*, and the next generation (Joseph and his siblings) was even worse! Ephraim and Menashe's entry into the Torah's Hall of Fame is also existential. They symbolize survival, continuity, and eternal conservators of Jewish traditions and values. Why? Because they were born not in Israel but in *chutz la'aretz* ("in the land of Egypt"), and yet maintained their identity.

El Al: Every Landing Always Late!

Q Is *being late* a Jewish addiction?

Sadly, it seems so. *El Al* once stood for "Every Landing Always Late!" No Jewish function begins when it should, since Jews keep "Jewish time," which has no relation to "real time," despite a Torah that insists on promptness and punctuality. And yet *even* God is accused of lateness! "How long, O Lord?" asks the Psalmist, surely aware that God is "outside time," yet nevertheless perturbed that the Heavens have not intervened in Jewish history sooner. One episode is a sad reminder of the consequences of delay. The impatient folk of Israel make a calf of gold only when "Moses is slowed [*boshesh*]" on the Mount. How late is he? Six hours. How do we know? The Midrash breaks the word *boshesh* into *ba shesh*, "He arrived (at) six!"

= Es past nisht

Q What does this mean? I hear it all the time in my grandparent's home.

It is a powerful Yiddish expression, "That's not how a Jew is supposed to behave!" a nod to the mission of the Jewish people, to be always seen as holy couriers of the Jewish God. The Yiddishists of pre-war Europe used this phrase as a constant reminder of who they were ("Remember the days of old, consider the generations long past"), where they were heading and how to get there (via *middos un mitzvos*). *Es past nisht* was a timeless Judaic motto of pride and purpose that once helped Benjamin Disraeli, the Earl of Beaconsfield, reply to an anti-Semitic remark, "Yes, I am a Jew, but when your ancestors were brutal savages on an unknown island, mine were priests in the Temple of Solomon!"[8]

= Errors

Q Does anyone check a Torah scroll before it is sold?

Yes, and the results are scary. Nearly thirty percent have one or more unintentional mistakes. There are over three hundred thousand Torah letters, so even the most scrupulously careful, steady scribal hand can make an error (e.g., spelling Noach with a *chaf* instead of a *chet*, or writing a word twice). However, technology has come to the rescue! No more personal painstaking efforts to detect a mistake; computer scans now compare every column for spelling errors, fading, and cracked writing, against a perfect text.

---

8.   Deuteronomy 32:7.

E-mail ethics

Q Do I have to watch what I say over the internet if my identity is secret?

Yes. The ethics of e-mail are not different from the ethics of speech ("Wise people, be careful with your words, for if speech is worth a *sela*, silence is worth two!"). Despite the subtle advice to "regard the speech, not the speaker!" Rabbenu Gershom, famous for his polygamy edict, had another *takkana* as well: he forbade opening other people's mail (including family members), which he defined as a form of theft, a precursor to today's "insider trading."[9]

Embalming

Q Are Jews allowed to embalm the dead?

No. Embalming is quintessentially an Egyptian, not a Jewish, burial rite, one of a panoply of practices designed to obscure the reality of death. This very idea is anti-Genesis, which considers human life an extension of the earth ("For dust you are, and to dust you shall return"). This is why Jews in Israel are buried without a coffin. And yet, for some inexplicable reason, both Jacob and Joseph, senior patriarchs, requested that their bodies be embalmed, the only two to do so in the entire Torah. At first, Joseph is reluctant to comply with his father's dying wish, an act of great theologic schizophrenia, but ultimately does so. He is rewarded with long life (110 years, long enough to see his own great-grandchildren), but the Midrash blames his death before his brothers as punishment for ordering Egyptian physicians to embalm his and his father's bodies.

---

9. Pirkei Avos 1:11; Megilla 18a.

Employee obligations

Q I work in a factory. What obligations do I have to my employer, and vice versa?

The Mishna defines an employee as a *shomer sochor*, a "paid watchman," and makes him responsible if his negligence on the job causes losses, or theft of his employer's property. Whilst employed, all of his actions must be solely for the benefit of his employer, and thus, within the category of *hashavas aveida*, the "return of a lost article," he is required to "prevent" a potential, involuntary, loss. But employer-employee relationships are not a one-way street in Jewish ethics; for "whoever acquires a servant acquires a master over himself," which literally means, in the colorful rabbinic phrase, that an employer is at his or her workers' mercy. Yes, workers must not take advantage of their employer, and must work efficiently, energetically, and not waste their employer's time or money; but neither can the employer behave like a tyrant. The boss is forbidden to exploit, cheat, undermine his staff, delay their wages ("On that day shall you pay his hire; the sun shall not set upon him") or make them feel like slaves ("Whoever shames his fellow human being in public, it is as if he has shed his blood"). The ideal is for the two to work, together, as a *de facto* partnership; a boss needs workers in much the same way as an army general needs privates; sports captains need players; orchestra conductors need instrumentalists. The Torah's role model for respectful labor management relations is Boaz in the Book of Ruth. When Boaz came into the field, he said, "The Lord be with you," and his reaper workers replied in respectful kind, "The Lord bless you!"[10]

Excommunication

Q Where did this concept come from?

Originally the term *cherem* (excommunication) was only applicable to "stuff" (not people), objects that God described as "abominations." The

---

10. Choshen Mishpat 306:1; Teshuvos Chasam Sofer, Choshen Mishpat, Siman 140; Shulchan Aruch, Choshen Mishpat 259:9; Kiddushin 20a; Psalms 115:6; Deuteronomy 24:15; Baba Metzia 58b.

expression (also known as *niduy*, a less severe status) was later extended to those folks who offended not just God, but other Jews. It covers about twenty-four offenses, ranging from *chillul Hashem* (desecrating God's Name), to insulting Torah scholars and purposely tripping a blind person. When the power was vested in the rabbinate, excommunication was a dramatic social-death verdict, a punitive punishment that few Jews could endure. It meant being shunned by the entire community, dead or alive (some being denied burial), having *mezuzos* removed from one's home, and an order not to teach nor marry nor do business with the family (in some cases, even a *bris* was denied!). The announcement of a *cherem* was made publicly in packed *shuls*, accompanied by the sounds of a shofar in front of the Ark opened especially for this embarrassing moment. The audience would hold black candles and somberly snuff them out at the end of the hearing.

Extradition

Q Are Jews allowed to extradite Jews from the Land of Israel?

Yes. Although the Torah defines "all the people of Israel" as "partners," and grants every Jew an inalienable halachic right to live in the Holy Land, it exempts "idolaters" and "apostates." Rambam, responding to a question of extradition for criminal prosecution, rules that a Jew cannot be turned over to a non-Jew for execution unless he has committed a capital crime. The Taz goes one step further: he allows extradition of anyone whose activities endanger the wider Jewish community.[11]

Elders of Zion

Q Who are the recognized Sages of Israel?

The *Tannaim* of the Mishna (70 CE–200 CE); *Amoraim* of the Talmud (200 CE–500 CE); *Savoraim*, the classical Persian rabbis (500 CE–600 CE); *Geonim*, of Sura and Pumbeditha, Babylonia (650 CE–1250 CE); *Rishonim*,

---

11. Yesodei HaTorah 5:5; Yore Deah 157:8.

of the early medieval period (1250 CE–1550 CE); and the *Acharonim*, the rabbis of 1550 to the present.

Equidistant letter sequences

Q What is this?

The assumption that the Torah contains hidden patterns and word sequences of sanctified Hebrew letters that are equidistant from each other is known as ELS's, "equidistant letter sequences." They form the basis of the "Bible Code" which supposedly alludes, cryptographically, to future (or past) historical events such as the Holocaust, the 1991 Gulf War, the assassination of Yitzhak Rabin, etc. A typical example? To "prove" that there was a predestined link between Moses Maimonides and his writing of the *Mishne Torah*, bibliomancy starts with the letter "m" in Moshe (Exodus 11:9–12:13) and counts every fiftieth letter to spell out the word "Mishna." Then, starting with the second "t" letter (in Exodus 12:11) again, counting every fiftieth letter, they spell out the word "Torah." The number of letters between the first "m" and the first "t" is 613, as in the 613 mitzvos that the *Mishne Torah* discussses. Don't try this at home. It's an exercise in futility, the epitome of "fuzzy maths." When Brendan McKay, a computer science-mathematician, applied the same formula to Melville's *Moby Dick* he "proved" that the fictional novel predicted the assassination of Leon Trotsky, John F. Kennedy and Martin Luther King, Jr.

Eye for an eye

Q Was this punishment ever carried out literally?

No. The famous "eye for an eye, tooth for a tooth" passage is probably one of the most misquoted of all Torah verses. Anti-Semites, in their desire to denigrate the Old Testament, often point to this dictate as "proof" that the Jews, and their vigilante God, were barbarous, stern, primitive seekers of blind vengeance. Nothing could be further from the truth. Yes, the phrase is dramatic; no, it does not require the gouging of an eye for an eye, but the financial compensation of the value of a "lost" eye. This establishes a principle of justness and fairness: that the punishment must fit the crime; not too harsh, nor too lenient.

Eden's Torah

Q Was there a different Torah before Sinai?

Jewish mystics made their debut during the first centuries of the Common Era as couriers of a celestial spiritualism that spoke of ecstatic time "travels" to God's Throne on Ezekiel-type chariots (*merkava*) that crisscrossed seven spheres of Heaven. By the Medieval Ages, especially in Spain, they were less interested in spiritual travel through time, and more interested in "communing with Judaism itself," an exercise of exploring the unknowable Oneness (*Ein Sof*, "Infinite") within a "hidden" world of Creation itself divided into ten *sefiros* ("realms," or "planes") – and, in a stunning declaration, regulated by a different Torah altogether. This version of Torah was called *Gan Eden Torah* and is described by the mystical *Sefer Yetzirah* as one long unbroken sequence of letters that could be "split" into words and sentences in innumerable ways (*Tikunim HaZohar*, "Perfections of Splendor," translates just the first six letters of the Torah in no less than seventy different ways).

Ein mazal l'Yisrael

Q What does this mean?

When the Jews of Pumbeditha asked Rabbi Joseph to become their *rosh yeshiva*, he declined. Why? He was afraid: a stargazing Chaldean had predicted that if he took the post he would die in two years. Instead Raba got the job and lasted twenty-two years. When Raba died (330 CE), Rabbi Joseph was again pressured. This time, he took the job…and died two and a half years later. No wonder that the future Yiddishists in Eastern Europe turned the old rabbinic adage, *ein mazal l'Yisrael*, "Israel is not subject to the signs of the Zodiac," into the popular cynical folk saying "The Jews have no luck!" Even Jewish vocabulary is infused with superstition. Consider: when our rabbis advise one not to be led by fortune they are using the name of a Roman goddess (*Fortuna*), which itself meant "chance"; and when advised that to rely on the stars was to court disaster, Torah scholars were again in a linguistic cul-de-sac. Why? Because the word "disaster" means "an unlucky star."

Exercitus Judaicus

Q **What is this?**

The overconfident bar Kochba marked the great Jewish divide of history, from Jerusalem to Auschwitz, from being a stubborn "stiff-necked" fighting force for independence to a passive diaspora-entrenched serf folk. After his revolt failed, the Romans were more determined than ever to uproot all things Jewish. And they succeeded beyond their wildest dreams! The messianic dream had collapsed, and the dismemberment of the children of Israel began with a long, bitter, humiliating and genocidal exile of eighteen hundred years. In his report, Dio Cassius, the enemy general, takes credit for wiping out fifty-two Jewish strongholds, 985 Jewish villages, selling hundreds of Jewish women and children through the Hevron-Azza slave markets for less than the cost of a horse, killing 580,000 Jews by Roman swords, and allowing an unknown number to die of hunger, fire, disease. The death statistics? A third of the Jewish community. This annihilation was celebrated with a new currency: minted coins marked *Exercitus Judaicus*, "Good riddance, Judaism!" Prematurely, it turned out. The Roman Empire is gone, the Jewish people remains.

Ex-Cohen?

Q **I am a cohen who left Judaism, but have returned and done *teshuva*. May I still *duchan*?**

Yes. The Talmud has an analogy: a *cohen* with a physical blemish is not allowed to minister at the altar but is allowed to bless the people (unless the blemish is on his raised hands). The lesson? You, as an apostate *cohen*, once had "a blemish" on your record, but your return in sincerity now allows you to return to priestly blessings. Rashi, faced with multiple such cases of "returning *cohanim*" during the bloody Crusades, responded with leniency which he thought was mandatory in the absence of the Temple. Rabbenu Gershom agrees and warns Jews not to embarrass any *cohen* with reminders ("Remember your previous situation"), which he calls "verbal oppression."[12]

Exodus: coming or going?

Q Does "Exodus" mean "to go"?

The dramatic Torah portion that chronicles the departure of Jews from Egypt is called *Bo*; however, it does not mean "Go [*bo*] to" but "come to Pharaoh," as in, "Come to Pharaoh, I will be with you," a literary hint that the confrontation is about to become up-close and intensely personal. Joseph ben Isaac (*Bechor Shor*), twelfth-century French scholar, reads the "I" as a royal "We," a sign of God's effort to lift Moses' spirits after the failure of several plagues, reassuring him to carry on ("*Come*, let's join forces and *go together!*"). What's the term for "go"? This was already established by God's *lech* ("go") directive to Abraham; thus, "exodus" is an expression of a continuing process, one of coming *and* going.

Exogamy

Q What is this?

It means "outmarriage," a serious problem dating back to Biblical times that even plagued the wisest of the wise. King Solomon, in an act of calculated political expediency, married hundreds of "foreign" wives whose "imported" pagan baggage led directly to his fall from grace. When Jehoram, king of Judah, married Athalia, daughter of King Ahab, the gentile Queen's idea of royal *shalom bayis* was to murder all her potential successors!

---

12. Ta'anis 27a; Megilla 24b.

Ezras Hashem

Q I hear the expression *b'ezras Hashem* all the time. What does it mean?

It means "with God's help." We see it in the Torah verse, "For they did not come *l'ezras Hashem* [to the place where God can be of aid]," a reference to the fact that the Jews of Reuben, Gad and Asher didn't respond to Devora's call for help against nine hundred of King Jabin's chariots. The purpose of saying *l'ezras Hashem* in daily life is a reminder, and a hope, that God will continue to lead Jews to "places" where they can have their faith renewed and reinvigorated. This was the case for Barak and the Hebrew tribes that did show up for Devora, and witnessed "the strong hand of God's deeds" (wherein the enemy, Sisera, has a tent peg attached to his head!). Devora, a prophetess, thus criticizes the absent Jews out of pity, not malice.[13]

---

13. Judges 5:16–19; Exodus 14:31.

F

Father

Q If the mother determines her child's Jewishness, what does the father contribute?

The father determines a child's Judaic identity, whether a *Cohen*, Levite, or Israelite. What if dad's a gentile and the mom's a *Cohen* or Levite? The child stays an Israelite. What if a *Cohen* marries a divorced woman? He automatically compromises his regal status (*Halal*), and his children are no longer considered *Cohanim*.

Freemasons

Q Is freemasonry considered heretical?

No. Freemasonry does not claim to be a rival religion, has no theological underpinnings, and its members believe in monotheism. If you flip through a Freemason booklet, you'll find numerous quotes from King Solomon, ethical Jewish-based allegories, (mostly misspelled) Hebrew words, and Midrashic narratives.

Frequent flier

Q When do I have to say the "Prayer for Travelers"?

The timing is flexible. Try this. If your travel exceeds three miles outside the metropolitan area, say *Tefillas haderech* just *before* you cross that line. But you can also say it at home before you leave, or just before you arrive at your destination. If you travel several times a day, you need only say it once. What if it's a long trip, over several days? Frequent mileage doesn't mean frequent prayers. Say it once, on the first day, then repeat daily but without saying God's name, until destination.

From *sizkeit* to *mizkeit*?

Q Are Jewish women allowed to "show off" their beauty?

"Looking good" is not a modern invention. When archeologists opened *Babatha's Archive*, a cave near Ein Gedi, they found expensive antique cosmetics from the era of the second Jewish revolt. The British Museum displays a five-thousand-year-old mummified Egyptian woman who was found with her finger and toenails still painted red! Women of antiquity shaved off unwanted hair, applied makeup to their eyes and colored their lips. Queen Jezebel of Israel even applied makeup before she threw herself out of a window, wanting to die attractively. The Midrash relates how the "beauty" of Jewish women once saved the Jewish people from extinction during Pharaoh's genocidal decree to murder all male infants. The Talmud describes how these Jewish women (guided by the motto *Passions are Fashions!*), would polish pieces of copper into mirrors so they could see their reflections. So proud was God of their bravery that He instructed Moses to fashion their copper "mirrors" into the washing vessels that the priests used during construction of the Tabernacle. "Vanity of vanities, all is vanity!" screams out Koheles; however, although beauty for its own sake may be the ultimate vanity, there is no automatic contradiction between a girl's desire to look good and Sinai's traditional concept of modesty. It's all in *intent*, the Torah differentiating between being *attractive* and being *attracting*![1]

---

1. Ecclesiastes 1:2.

Free will

Q Do we truly have free will?

The two most baffling questions in Jewish thought are the suffering-of-the-righteous inconsistency, and freedom-of-will-vs.-determinism. No scholar has even come close to a satisfactory answer; thus when Jews declare, *Hakol min haShamayim chutz mi'yiras Shamayim*, "everything is from Heaven (determinism) except the fear of Heaven (freedom of will)," they accept this belief as a matter of pure Jewish faith. If you search the Torah for some clues, you'll only be confronted with more, not fewer, theological dilemmas. An example? Abraham's promise ("Your descendants will be aliens in a land, slaves for four hundred years") *required* God, in order to fulfill His *own* words, to *force* Joseph into Egyptian exile, create all the sibling hatred, prearrange Joseph's sale and ultimate elevation to regality, cause a famine, and then, finally, propel Jacob and his sons to Egypt – and still have the spiritual *chutzpa* to blame them for *their* troubles? And yet freedom of will somehow functions. How? We don't know. All you can do is file it under "Great Paradox of Human Existence."[2]

Fast for falling?

Q Do I have to fast when a pair of *tefillin* falls on the ground?

It depends. Are you a Torah scholar, teacher, communal activist? If yes, then your profession exempts you from fasting (but you must give charity instead). Were they your own *tefillin*? If yes, you must fast; however, if you didn't personally witness the fall, or if you did but it was somebody else's *tefillin*, then no fast is required. What if it's an accident, not negligence? Charity is sufficient. What if the *tefillin* were still "covered" (i.e., in the box)? Then you don't have to fast, but need to give *tzedaka*. When should you fast? It's unclear, but either on the same day, or the next day.[3]

---

2. Genesis 15:13.
3. Ben Ish Chai, Chayei Sarah 18; Orach Chayim 571:1; Mishne Berura 40:3; Shaarei Teshuva 40:1; Iggeros Moshe, Orach Chayim 3:3; Mishne Berura 40:3; Y.S. Elyashiv, Avnei Yashfe 2:1.

Flower halos

Q I want to wear a halo of flowers at my *chuppa*. My father says it's not for Jewish girls. Is he right?

Yes. The halo is purely pagan in origin. Centuries *before* the Church turned it into a symbol for angels and saints, idolaters would ornament their heads with a circle of feathers to show their devotion to their Sun-god. If you look at old Indian, Greek and Roman paintings, all their deities come equipped with halos; and Roman Emperors, imagining themselves as megalomaniac divine gods, never went anywhere in public without putting on their "celestial" (halo) crowns first.

Flags

Q Is flying a flag too "nationalistic" for Jews?

No. Some of the first "flags" in history were carried by Jews. Upon leaving Egypt, the nation identified each of its tribes via an ensign. Menashe's was jet-black with a figure of a Capricorn, Zevulun's was white with a ship, etc. So that they could be seen from afar, they were mounted on banners and tied down with streamers that flew in the wind. But, as usual, it was left to the enterprising Chinese to perfect the concept. In the twelfth century BCE, the founder of the Chou dynasty never left home without his (white) flag. Today's flag of Israel, designed by David Wolffsohn for the first World Zionist Congress in 1897, is adorned with a blue-and-white *mogen Dovid*, a nod to the original colors of the *tallis*.

First words

Q I just had a baby boy. What are the first words of Torah I should teach my son?

Go to the Torah portion *Zos Habracha*, "This is the blessing," a reference to Moses' final blessing for health, happiness and prosperity. The reappearance of this *bracha* at the climax of the Torah, first used by Jacob when blessing his children, is a reaffirmation (as Jacob's new name, "Israel," implies) that he remains *the* progenitor patriarch and founding father of the Jewish nation. Our rabbis thus chose from here the first words a Jewish child should hear, *Torah tziva lanu Moshe, morasha kehillas Yaakov,* "Moses commanded us to keep the Torah, it is an inheritance [*morasha*] of the community of Jacob." This obligatory sentence helps give the children of Israel a sense of status, permanency and purpose.

From BE to AE

Q Did Judaism have anything to do with these abbreviations?

Yes. Pesach, being such a significant event, changed the basis of the Jewish calendar. It went from BE, "before Egypt" (when the Jewish year began in autumn – Tishrei) to AE, "after Egypt" (with a Torah dictate to "observe spring – Pesach"). This forced the rabbis to count their months from spring (*Aviv*), the end of the rainy season, when fig trees bud, grains ripen, fruit trees blossom, wheat stalks harden and silos begin to fill up with harvested grain.

Full shekel or half-shekel?

Q What was the point of the half-a-shekel collection?

Jewish law didn't allow counting people, so surrogates, such as a half-shekel coin, were used. Their original purpose was a "poll tax" for the Temple's upkeep. Remember: the shekel was a weight before it became a coin, and metaphorically meant that every Jew was required to "weigh in" as an equal contributor. The Hebrew term for "counting their number" and "lifting their heads" is the same (*ki sisa*), since giving was considered an act of spiritual elevation. Torah linguists note that *sapar* (to count) is similar to *sipayr* (to tell a story), in that the tale itself affirms that each Jew is incomplete until he joins his brother's other "half" donation, thus rendering them both complete, and thus united – the whole being not only the sum of its parts, but *greater* than its parts.

Funeral processions

Q Do I have to attend?

Yes. As that great philosopher once quipped, "If you don't go to other people's funerals, they won't come to yours!" Attending a Jew's funeral is a primary mitzva of loving-kindness, because the dead return no favors. You must accompany the procession for at least six feet, and those who don't are compared to the cruel who mock the poor and needy.

Friends like these

Q Why are Christian evangelists so friendly to Israel?

The affection comes in sugar coating, but the shell is deadly. Evangelical friendship is not unconditional. The theological precondition for complete Christian redemption is the annihilation of the entire Jewish people in the Holy Land, a goal shared by Israel's implacable Arab enemies. This is why the fundamentalists encourage *aliya* and donate tons of money to the Jewish state, to get as many Jews there as possible. This "final solution" is perversely called "the redemption of Israel" by the Church, a prerequisite for the return of their Savior. Why the messenger of world peace and compassion can only return over the bloodied and mutilated Armageddon bodies of millions of Jews is still a mystery to me. However, in a world where Jews have so few friends, we'll accept a friend in deed (today), and let the future worry about itself!

Father comes first

Q Is Jewish schooling the preferred method of Jewish education?

No. Originally, based on the order within the *Sh'ma*, the obligation to teach children fell on parents, not teachers: "Ask thy father [first and then] thine elders!"). Originally, Jewish elementary schools were established to cater to orphans, and to children whose parents were unable to teach them (that is why it is a great mitzva to teach other people's children) and not for the general public. By the first century BCE, non-parental teaching was so commonplace (because of the rise and popularity of Greek-Roman schools, and the growing complexity of Jewish knowledge), that Shimon ben Shetach had no choice but to rule that all Jewish children must attend school, "for otherwise the Torah would be forgotten." How important was Jewish schooling? Rabbi Hamnuna linked the destruction of Jerusalem itself to its neglect of the school system; and Shimon bar Yohai even ordered certain towns in Israel to be abandoned simply because they didn't maintain salaried teachers!

Flowers, no fruit

Q What was the main difference in outlook between the Greek and the Jew?

The Greek adored the philosopher, the Jew the "wise man, Sage" (*chacham*), despite the interesting fact that "school" is not once mentioned in the Torah. The word comes from the Greek *skhole* (or *schola*), which does not mean "education" but "leisure." Why? Only the non-working class who had time to study were educated. The ordinary guy-in-the-street was too busy earning a living to indulge in the luxurious leisure of learning. Not so with the Jews. The Greeks, notes Judah Halevi, produced flowers, but no fruit. Their accomplishments were intellectual, not moral. Meanwhile, the Sanhedrin, guided by High Priest Joshua ben Gamala and Rabbi Shimon ben Shetah, was pioneering Jewish education, creating the world's first (compulsory) public school system. Consider the contrast: the typical carefree Greek and Roman spent his leisure hours at the arena, but the Jew, fixated on education and appalled by illiteracy, was found in his academy of learning. *Quid Athenis cum Hierosolymis*, said the early Christian Tertullian, "What does Athens have to do with Jerusalem?" In regard to the value of education, obviously not much!

Forgive them not, Father...

Q How did the Holocaust happen?

When, in January 1933, "the reign of the beast began," all the highly Christianized European countries stood by silently or actively cooperated with a satanic Austrian psychopath as he slit the throat of world Jewry. This was not just a one-night fleeting participation in mass-murders. Practicing Catholic communities, together with their Catholic heads of state and leaders, were there – day-by-day, night-by-night – undisturbed by a freakish sideshow that left six million (an average of twenty thousand Jews per week, nonstop for over three hundred weeks) of their neighbors bleeding to death on their doorsteps. Is it a coincidence that history's worst conflict devoured, decimated, destroyed and devastated the Chosen People right in the heart of Christian society? No. Thousands of "ordinary men," raised on the theory of Deicide, saw no contradiction between their New Testament's compassionate "love-thy-neighbor" dogma and their Church's dance to the evil tune of Adolf, the Choreographer of Death – a vegetarian who lavished nonstop affection on his shepherd dog Blondi and yet ordered all Jewish children to be snuffed out like shadows in the wind, and all adults who were once present at a mountain in Sinai to be gassed into mountains of human misery. This irrational brother hate began a long time ago when the Christian child (Christianity) left its Jewish womb (Judaism). Since then it has suffered from such complex and convoluted mother-hatred pangs that no psychiatrist could untangle its gratis streaks of parental cruelty. In its infancy, as it waltzed across the gentile playgrounds of the world, this daughter gave her Jewish mother an unusually ferocious and brutish nickname: Killer of Christ, eaters of matza dipped in blood. Millions of young, impressionable, innocent Christian children were raised on such hatred that it was natural for them, as adults, to savagely redefine the Jew in their midst not as a person but as some evolutionary freak of history, one to be hounded, humiliated, converted, expelled, gassed.

Flogging

Q Is this still a custom?

Some Yom Kippur customs have survived the ages (kneeling, *kappora*, *vidui*), but *malkus* ("flogging"), a classical Hebrew term for Biblical punishment, has not. In the *shtetlach* of Eastern Europe, the job of lashing went to the poor, who would then get "tips" from their "victims." During Rashi's time, flogging was an activity of symbolic atonement, being executed (pun intended) just before entering *shul* for Kol Nidrei (this is not to be confused with the Rosh Hashana tradition, *hataras nedarim,* whereby three Jews act as a *beis din* whilst a fourth asks for exoneration of unfulfilled vows). The ritual involves one Jew (Jewish women were excluded for reasons of modesty) lying on the ground and being struck three times by another. Wait! Why three? Isn't *malkus* thirty-nine blows? Yes, but the point was not to actually hurt anybody, especially a Jew voluntarily seeking repentance, so the rabbis devised a substitute formula. Those administering the three blows had to recite a certain Psalm instead (78:38). Why? Because it contained thirteen words. So? Well, thirteen times three equals thirty-nine! Once again, Jewish numerology to the rescue!

═ Fringe benefits ═

Q What is a *tallis katan?*

The mitzva of the four-cornered garment, and its requisite fringes (aka *tzitzis*), is the only article of clothing that all male Jews are ordered to wear (other than the *kippa,* "head covering," which was only mandatory for the priests). This command is an unusual one. Why? It is one of the few that the Torah explains with a rationale: to teach Jews to be constantly aware, "Look at it and be reminded of all the commandments." *Tzitzis* thus joins the list of such "remember and observe" signs as a rainbow, *bris,* Shabbas and *tefillin.* This reminder "to see" rather than "to hear," is why our rabbis stress that "seeing leads to remembering, remembering brings to action!" Is there a blessing required? Only if you do not yet wear a *tallis* (i.e., you're Ashkenazi and unmarried), in which case you say "*al mitzvas tzitzis.*" The mystic Ramban takes the numerical value (*gematria*) of the *tzitzis* strings (eight), adds it to their knots (five), arrives at *echad* (thirteen), and notes that this is the last word in the *Sh'ma,* which means "One." The implication? *Tzitzis* fringes are akin to the unity of God. But today's garments are not "four-cornered!" That explains why Jewish men wear a specially made *tallis katan* under their regular clothes. Should it be worn at night? No. Why? Because it's impossible "to see" (this is why Chassidic Jews wear theirs over their clothes).[4]

---

4. Numbers 15:38, 39; 1:3, 6, 9; 3:7,10–12; Deuteronomy 22:12; 3:1–2, 4–6; Mishne Berura

═ Forbidden return ═══════════════════

Q Why did Jews go back to Egypt when the Torah prohibited it?

The Jews were told not once, but *thrice*, not to go back to Egypt, land of heretical beliefs, causing the Rambam to make a startling codification: "A Jew may settle anywhere except in Egypt!" The implication of returning to the "crime scene" of bondage motivated our rabbis to link Israel's survival to its avoidance of Egypt. They even blame the disappearance of the large, faithful Jewish community of Alexandria on its continued stay in this "evil and sinful" place. But wait! Didn't the Rambam *himself* live in forbidden Egypt? Yes. This "history" led the sixteenth-century Radbaz to conclude that the ban only applied to "permanent" residency (the Rambam stayed there only to earn a living as a doctor), and the seventeenth-century Maharshal to argue that it was only operative when Jews lived in their own land as a free people, a physicality of holiness intended to make the diaspora less inviting.[5]

═ Final chance? ═══════════════════

Q I'm confused. Until what date in Tishrei does God listen to our prayers for forgiveness?

If you're not forgiven on Rosh Hashana, you get a second chance up to Yom Kippur; and if you're not forgiven on Yom Kippur, you might squeeze in by Hoshana Rabba (in other words, Three Strikes 'n You're Out!). Our rabbis deduce this from Isaiah's observation, "They seek Me day by day," and identify the two days on which people seek God: Rosh Hashana and Hoshana Rabba. And so the seventh day of Succos has a redemptive dimension, a time when messianic footsteps can be heard.[6]

8:24, 30; Aruch Hashulchan 8:2, 16; Y.Y. Kanievsky, Orchos Rabbeinu 1:4; Iggeros Moshe, Orach Chayim 4:4; 5:20–25

5. Deuteronomy 17:16; Hilchos M'lachim 1:1, 5:7; Sukka 51b; Sefer Hachinuch, Mitzva #500.

6. Rosh Hashana 4:8; Isaiah 58:2.

Faith and reason

Q Why should I follow the mitzvos that I don't understand?

Rabbi Yitzhak has a straightforward answer. Reasons are not always given because some may assume they are therefore not applicable. King Solomon made this mistake when he expanded his harem in contradiction to Torah order. He was so self-confident that, when he read the reason why ("Lest his heart be swayed from following My ways"), he simply decided his heart would never sway (and was proved wrong). Rashi advised his students, "Don't investigate laws, simply say it's a decree from Above!" Not all scholars agreed. Saadia Gaon and Ibn Ezra saw reason as "God's emissary," whilst Shneur Zalman of Lyady argued for it ("Virtue arising from reason is higher than virtue which is not founded on it"). Levi Yitzhak of Berdichev hedged his bets. Yes, there are reasons but they are only known to the spiritual soul, not the physical intellect. The Gerer Rebbe (*Sfas Emes*) was convinced that understanding of mitzvos would come in due course, but only *after* their repeated performance. The Rambam ("Reason is more to be trusted than the eye") disagreed. The lack of reasoning, he warns, would drive many Jews into assuming that "God's actions are purposeless." All mitzvos are ultimately "unfathomable decrees" designed to test the obedience of the Jews. "The reward for a mitzva is a mitzva," was the tradition, despite an extensive literature known as *ta'amei hamitzvos* (literally, "the tastes of the mitzvos") which attempts to "explain" the orders of Sinai. So, does Judaism disapprove of rational understanding? No. The Torah frowns on a belief system that requires leaving one's mind behind before entering. Yehudah Halevi, as well as other great rabbinic philosophers, believed that if reason contradicts Torah, then the textual interpretation is incorrect!

Fashion mavens?

Q Jews as fashion trailblazers? Is that possible?

Jewish law, at a time of mourning, dictates the tearing of one's garment. In the case of parents, the rip was never sewed back, thus slits in coats and jackets served as a permanent reminder of the children's personal tragedy. Over time, the "cut" became so widespread that even Christians began to wear slits, unaware of their "mournful" origin as a gesture of sorrow. Today, the slit in the lapel of a man's jacket is a decorative must. Tailoring (which became a Jewish art) started in Paradise, with Adam and Eve being motivated by shame to cover themselves. What did they use? Probably fig leaves from Eden's garden, wrapped like an apron, supplanted later, according to the Torah, by animal skins. Were Jews responsible for trousers? No, the horse was. Riders quickly discovered how uncomfortable, and restrictive, it was going on horseback wrapped only in a (short or long) flowing sheet or animal skin. *Voilà!* Trousers were born – but prohibited to Jewish girls! Why? Because originally only barbarians and warriors on horses wore them, but mainly for modesty reasons and the Torah's wish to keep the sexes looking and being apart, since close mingling led to promiscuity. Is that why men and women wear their buttons on opposite sides? No. The button, introduced in the thirteenth century during the reign of King Charles I, was first worn by royalty. Men buttoned their own clothes, from left to right; women of nobility had maids do it for them. Thus the buttonholes were reversed to make it easier for them, facing their boss, to button from right to left. So? Is it true? Clothes make the man? Yes. The Torah portion for Purim (*Tetzaveh*) discusses the special clothing (*bigdei Kehuna*) that the priests would wear upon entering the Tabernacle or Temple to perform their services (*avoda*), including a special hat, pants, belt, shirt; all entirely white, notes the *Sefer Hachinuch* (a classic medieval work on the meanings underlying the mitzvos), in order to symbolize purity. This priestly wardrobe, designed to express "honor and splendor" as shown by royalty (Ramban), was serious business. The Torah even implies death for those who conduct the service in the absence of a regal appearance. Jewish mystics paired each garment, as atonement, to a different sin (e.g., trousers for adultery; tunic for murder; belt for improper thoughts; breastplate for miscarriage of justice, etc.) and warned that these sins were a result of lack of *middos* (commendable character traits), which in Hebrew also means "measure"; in other words, a priest's appearance had also to be a perfect (spiritual) fit, *mido vad*, made to measure![7]

---

7. Yoma 23b.

First-person singular

Q Is Judaism a singular, or communal, religion?

Judaism is essentially a religion not of the mind nor the heart, but the hand. It is a religion of individual action, presented by God *not* collectively by the use of the plural "you," but in the second-person singular (i.e., *thou* shalt not, and *thou* shalt). Why? The intent was that each Jew's obedient behavior needed to contribute to the sanctity of the people as a whole, a body in common, always referred to in the plural (e.g., "I am *your* [plural] God who…brought *you* [plural] out of Egypt"). The nineteenth-century Tzadok Hacohen of Lublin, one of the great leaders of the Chassidic world, explains that the Ten Commandments, the most famous injunctions in Western civilization, are phrased in the second-person singular (i.e., "I am the Lord *your* God"), because God spoke, and continues to speak, to every Jew individually ("according to what he is"). This "single-hearer" communication is unique: it allows each man, women and child to hear the voice of Heaven within his, or her, own inner world (or as the Psalmist put it bluntly, "One thing God has spoken; two things have I heard!").[8]

First "second-generation" Jew

Q Who is the world's first "second-generation" Jew?

The Torah gives us a dramatic tale of family and kinship, of intrigue and jealousy; a unique snapshot of the fractious, complex world of the House of Isaac as it erupts onto the opening stages of Jewish national history. The illustrious Isaac may have lived in an *ohel* (tent), but it was Jacob, father of sons, whose twelve tribes ultimately merge into the House of Jacob, a *bayis* that Abraham initiated and Isaac guarded. Yet despite all the attention, we never really get to know Isaac, the world's first second-generation Jew and most passive of the three patriarchs. The rabbis of *Pirkei Avos* crown this purely spiritual Jew as *the* personification of might (*gevura*), his strength being defined in Torah terms, as a possessor of self-control, discipline, "one who conquers his passions." Incredibly, his entire biography is condensed

---

8. Exodus 20:2; Rabbi Hacohen, Resisei Lailah, 15; Psalms 62:12.

into only one Torah portion, and even there Isaac seems to be playing a cameo "walk-on" role, cast as an unlikely hero whose needs are always being subordinated to those of others. The Rambam calls him a loner, uninterested in maintaining a circle of disciples, satisfied with a single student: his son, Jacob. It is understandable. Jewish history finds Isaac sandwiched between an intense father figure (Abraham) and his revolutionary new spiritual vision, and a determined son (Jacob-Israel) who is busy reconstructing a family into nationhood. Isaac's primary claim to Judaic fame is thus generational. He is *the* biological progenitor of the entire Jewish nation, and the only patriarch who never leaves Israel. That is why, in their search for a worthy Biblical figure, in the context of Isaiah's famous messianic prophecy of peace ("they shall beat their swords into plowshares"), our rabbis skip over such heroes as Abraham, Moses, and David – and choose *only* Isaac ("You are our father!")

Funny, you don't look Jewish!

Q I just had my chromosomes tested. Can they tell me if I'm really Jewish?

Your DNA test is more reliable than the old-fashioned way, looking to see if you have a Jewish nose or a *Yiddishe kop* (head)! Recent cutting-edge genetic technology (which requires taking a long swab from inside the cheek to obtain a sample), has defined the vast majority (seventy percent) of today's Jewish priestly class as descendants of a single ancestor. This is a rare example of science confirming a three-thousand-year-old Jewish (gene) tradition. Genetic profiling has another serious purpose. It can determine whether a person is the carrier of a genetic disease (including the devastating Tay Sachs). If found positive, the person will be advised not to marry someone who is also a carrier, in order to prevent transmission of the disease.

Fill of grapes

Q I work in a grocery store. Can I take some grapes when the boss ain't watching?

Here's the relevant verse: "When you come into your neighbor's vineyard, you may eat your fill of grapes, but you shall not put any in your vessel." Does that answer your question? I didn't think so! Going "into your neighbor's vineyard" cannot mean trespassing, otherwise the "grape eating" would be theft (which it's not); therefore the Torah must be referring to a laborer (or, like you, a shop assistant), and *permits* tasting the goods – but *not* during work hours (a form of theft, by infringing on the boss's time). So yes, you *can* eat the store's grapes but *only* during your break. How much can you eat? By using the words "*your* fill," the Torah only allows what will satisfy *your* needs (which means you can't stuff your pockets and underwear with grapes and take them home).[9]

Finder's fee

Q I mentioned a house for sale to my friend who eventually bought it. Can I ask for a commission?

It depends. If you told your friend it was "a favor," you get nothing. Intent is the key. If you were expecting a fee, even if you didn't specifically say so, you are entitled to one, just like *shadchanus gelt* ("Any person who does a favor, the recipient is not able to say, you did this for free because I didn't ask you, rather he must pay him"). How much? You're entitled to the same sales or referral rate that local licensed real estate agents get.[10]

---

9. Deuteronomy 23:25.
10. Baba Kamma 101a; Rema, Choshen Mishpat 264:4.

══ Family Feud ══════════════════════════════

Q Does the Arab-Israeli conflict have anything to do with the old hostility between Isaac and Ishmael?

Today's antagonists are *both* the descendants of Abraham, Ishmael being Abraham's son by Hagar, and Isaac being his son by Sarah. The current conflict does seem to have a continuing fraternal metaphysical aspect, with the two half-brothers still fighting over their "father's" inheritance. God had sealed His main covenant with the Jews through Isaac, but, in response to a plea from Abraham, promised that He would "bless" Ishmael. How? By making him "fertile and exceedingly numerous." Although we take their animosity for granted, in the two or three places where Isaac and Ishmael are together in the Torah (one being at their father's burial), there is no direct suggestion of tension or conflict. (The first time they appear together is after the death of Sarah.) But there is no doubt about their characters. Ishmael, whilst in the womb, is already called a "wild ass of a man," a guy who would end up fighting with everyone and everyone with him. All the major medieval Torah commentators (Rashi, Ibn Ezra, Ramban), Psalms, and several Midrashim link the "aggressive troublesome" nature of his descendants to this descriptive prophecy. Resh Lakish, third-century Sage, commented that, whilst others were merely thieves, the Ishmaelites were murderers. *Pirkei de Rabbi Eliezer* actually lists fifteen crimes of the future that Ishmael would commit against the Jews in *Eretz Yisrael*, including perhaps the mother of all evil crimes, the purposeful delaying of the Messiah. So is there hope for an end to the tragic clash, a reconciliation of family? Yes. In the end, God promises Hagar, her son will "turn from his evil ways [and] shall dwell alongside of all his kinsmen." We're still waiting, and praying.[11]

══ Fighting priests ══════════════════════════

Q Were the priests also called into battle?

Torah students were encouraged to lead the way for Jewish soldiers, on the

---

11. Genesis 16:12; Genesis Rabba 30:4; 38:12; Brachos 16b.

theory that the possessors of faith would inspire. No, in those days, sword-bearing warrior *yeshiva bochurim* were *not* excluded from military duty! In fact, ancient Israel even had a special title, *Cohen mashu'ach lamilchama,* "the priest anointed for battle." His sole role was morale, to address the common folk and urge them not to be afraid, because God was with them. The "war Cohen" is the precursor of today's military chaplain, a position that George Washington brought into law in 1775 with a short *dvar Torah,* "The blessing and protection of Heaven are at all times necessary, especially so in times of public danger" (the first Jewish Marine chaplain in America was Rabbi Roland Gittelsohn, who fought at the battle of Iwo Jima). The term "chaplain," however, is un-Jewish. It is derived from the French *chapelains,* from *cappellanus,* the men who go into battle carrying the *cappa* (Latin for "cloak"), symbolic of the tunic of Martin of Tours, a fourth-century Roman soldier convert to Christianity, who was later canonized.

Foreign language

Q How do you say "God" in Chinese?

In 1875 Samuel Schereschewsky, a Jew who converted out, becoming known as "the missionaries' bishop" in Shanghai, was the first to translate the Bible into demotic Chinese, wherein God became *T'ien Chu,* a merger of *t'ien,* "Heaven," and *chu,* "ruler."

G

Gematria

Q **Is it OK to use this method of numerology?**

Sure, but don't let this fascinating and enjoyable arithmetic exercise become a substitute for traditional methods of study or help you decide halacha. Hew does it work? Here's an example. The Torah tells us that Abraham had 318 skilled staff members, which also happens to be the sum of the letters in the name Eliezer; thus the "318" servants must mean Eliezer! Want something more complicated? The *mispar kidmi* of each letter is the sum of all letters from *alef* (one) to itself, the "triangle" of a number (or letter) is the sum of all numbers from one to itself. Thus, 820 (*etz*, in *mispar kidmi*) is the triangle of forty (the sum of all numbers from one to forty). The letter *mem* (which stands for "water," considered the fountain of life), adds to *etz* to spell *etzem*, "bone" or "skeleton," a derivative of *etz* in Hebrew, as in, the skeleton of the human body being its innermost "tree of life." The mystic numerologists then matched 820 to the letters of both "the wellspring whose might ever increases" (*ma'ayan hamitgaber*); and "and you shall love your fellow as yourself" (*v'ahavta l'reiacha kamocha*).[1]

---

1. Genesis 14:14, 15:2; Nedarim 32a.

═ Guarantors? ═

Q In the Covenant between God and Jews, is there a "guarantor" on our side?

Yes. When God called for a guarantor, Abraham stepped forward, warranting that the "study of Torah will never be abandoned." God refused his offer, saying his guarantee was insufficient. Each patriarch, plus Moses and Aaron, then stepped forward, willing to act as guarantors. All were rejected. Then the Jewish children offered themselves and God quickly agreed because *Yiddishe kinderlach* ensure the future of the Jewish nation.

═ Going once, going twice.... ═

Q I think the "For Sale" signs on *hakkafos* is too commercialistic for a holy day. Am I right?

There is neither right nor wrong concerning this custom, although I must confess that I am also a bit "turned off" by the "auctioning" of Torah parts to money "bidders." This practice, traced back to the *Tanach*, only got "serious" in Eastern Europe when somebody decided to pay off *shul* deficits by selling *aliya* "honors." What sections have the most "value?" The first and last *Simchas Torah* portions (*Chasan Torah, Chasan Bereishis*), and although the highest bidder would traditionally pass the honor to either the rabbi or a worthy congregant, my experience has been that the *truly* "worthy" (and usually poorer) members always seem to be unfairly ignored, even publicly dishonored.

═ *Gola* or *galus*? ═

Q What's the difference between *gola* and *galut* (or *golus*)?

These two terms, derived from the verb *gala*, "to be exiled," are used interchangeably, and can mean exile *in general*, or a *specific place* of exile, or a *community* of exiles. The Torah uses the expression *gola* far more often than *galut* (forty-one to twenty-six), in the context of a specific physical place in *chutz la'aretz* (outside of Israel); whilst *galut*, especially in kabbalistic circles after the 1492 Spanish exile, referred to either a theoretical state of dispersion (as in "as bitter and long as the *golus*"), or the duration of exile, or a spiritual state. Joseph B. Soloveitchik (*Rav*), notes that *geula* is only used twice in the *Tanach*, at the Egyptian redemption and with reference to the messianic age. Seventeenth-century Lurianism then popularized the mystic concept of *golus haShechina*, the exile of God literally, from Himself. The Yiddishists then had a field day with this dogma (*Zayn bay emitsen in golus*, "to be in *golus*," or *Oprikhtn golus*, literally, "to undertake *golus*") to describe their state of misery, wretchedness, anguish.

God, dating?

Q Is this true? God dates?!

God Himself is described in the Old Testament as being married to Israel and Judah (a "youthful bride"), not in the form of an interesting metaphor but, as Hosea and the later Hebrew prophets repeatedly stress, as a legal reality, traced with the bold themes of unfaithfulness, forgiveness, reconciliation. God's promises to Jerusalem include a pledge to "clothe" her priests and feed "her poor." It is from here that the rabbis of the Mishna conclude that a husband's obligation is to provide his wife with money for food and clothing.

God's scorekeepers

Q Are we allowed to speculate on what caused any particular tragedy?

No. Jews are not God's scorekeepers! The sheer scope of Jewish suffering throughout Jewish history has led to three common, yet dangerous, myths. Myth Number One: "To suffer is a mitzva." This is religious nonsense; only the Church and Islam embrace a permanent suffering-as-good-for-the-Jews dogma, because it neatly coincides with their own anti-Jewish doctrines. To suffer was *never* a Jewish choice, *never* a positive command. The Laws of Moses elevated joy, not pain, to a spiritual level. Myth Number Two: "All *yissurim* are a form of punishment." Not true; whereas all punishment contains *yissurim*, not all *yissurim* are punishment. Some are challenges (Job, Abraham's ten tests) and some are normal results from one's self-selected labor (e.g., it would be absurd to claim that a trench digger's pain from his labors is Divine "punishment"). Myth Number Three: Some Jews are able to correlate the cause and effect behind Jewish suffering. No such Jew exists. When Rabbi Levi Yitzhak of Berdichev cried, "I do not want to know why, only if I suffer for Your sake," the *Chassid* knew that pain has a purpose in the higher scheme of things. So if your rabbi tells you that he knows what causes someone's suffering, get another rabbi, one with no such spiritual arrogance.

Guests and fish

Q Why do we always have to be hospitable?

Welcoming the stranger with receptive enthusiasm is an important mitzva, known as *hachnasas orchim*. The Biblical equivalent of a welcome mat is the sight of Abraham sitting at his tent door under a glaring sun, generously inviting passing strangers to enter, and determined not to miss any opportunity of cordiality. As the *Yiddishe mama* says, "A dish tastes best when shared with a guest!" Abraham's attitude was more than just good manners. In the harsh desert climate, this bed-and-breakfast refuge saved nomadic lives. This behavior served as the motivating factor for the rabbinic Sage Huna to start each meal by shouting, *Kol dichfin yaytay v'yachol*, "Let all who are hungry, come and eat!" the phrase that opens the Pesach Haggada (expressed in Aramaic so that the Aramaic-speaking masses would understand, and respond). Abraham, now an active ambassador for the Jewish God, would gently explain to his satisfied guests that their scrumptious meal and unleavened "cakes" (*ugos matzos*), were a gift that deserved a hearty "thank you" (*Yasher koach*) not to man, but to God. When he asks God to wait as he welcomes three visiting angels, Abraham sets forth a revolutionary Torah maxim: the mitzva of hospitality is greater than maintaining the presence of the Divine (*kabbalas P'nei Shechina*). "Nowhere," notes Russian Rabbi Leib Kagan, "does the Torah say, 'invite your guest to pray,' but it does tell us to offer him food, drink, and a bed." This echoes Joshua ben Hanania's observation: the poor does for the host more than the host for the poor! The Yiddishists were, as usual, cynical: "House guests and fish," they declared, "spoil on the third day!"[2]

---

2. Shabbas 127a; Ta'anis 20b; Leviticus Rabba 34:8.

God against the gods

Q When did monotheism become the accepted practice among non-Jews?

The cessation of the steady slide from monotheism to polytheism can be traced to the zealotry of King Josiah, seventh-century BCE ruler of Judah, who burnt the bones of idol-worshiping priests on the destroyed altars of their gods. Josiah held the traditional "fort" for monotheism until Emperor Constantine the Great made Christian monotheism the official religion of Rome in the fourth century CE. When his nephew, Julian the Apostate, came to power he brought back polytheism into the pantheon, but he was to become the Roman pagan emperor. Today, more than fifty percent of the world's population identify with a monotheistic faith. About thirty percent adhere either to non-theism or polytheism, and twenty percent profess the disbelief of atheism, a religion that worships Nietzsche's *théologie du jour* ("God is dead!"). Shmuel, a notorious atheist and hard-core Communist, once strolled into a *shul* on Rosh Hashana and, when asked why, replied that he had come to talk to his friend Yossi whilst Yossi talked to God. "In order not to offend anybody" is how the world-famous violinist Yehudi Menuhin responded when asked why he, a non-believer, still went to *shul* on Rosh Hashana. Or as a Chassidic Rebbe once assured an apostate, "Have no doubt – the God *you* don't believe in, I don't believe in either." In other words, even fervent atheists believe in something!

Gemilus hasadim

Q What is this?

You gotta be kidding! This is the most important all-encompassing concept in Judaism, called a *shekula*, qualitatively equal to all other Sinai commandments. The entire Torah is based on *chesed*. It starts with God providing clothes for Adam and Eve and ends with God burying Moses, a moral set of bookends for Jews to try to pursue *imitato Dei*. "If it's good enough for God…!" The first time this expression appears is when the second-century Shimon Hazaddik concludes that "the world rests on three things: Torah, worship, *gemilus hasadim.*" Since *gemilus hasadim* requires compassion, concern, caring, understanding and sensitivity, qualities that cannot be legislated, it has no special place in the *Shulchan Aruch*, in contrast to the laws of *tzedaka* which require community codification in Jewish law. The final word goes to Moshe Leib of Sasov: "If someone asks your help, you shall act as if there is no God, as if there were only one person in all the world who could help him – only yourself!"[3]

= Globe

Q Is there any connection between cosmic shapes and the Torah?

When asked why the world was constructed round, the formidable *rosh yeshiva* Chaim Volozhiner replied that a circular world was necessary to create different time zones. Why? In order that a spot of daylight existed at all times, to ensure that Torah learning not stop for a moment. Rashi elaborates on this Creation-Torah linkage in that the original term for Creation completion (*vayechal*) only reappears at Sinai when Moses completes (*cichalato*) the receipt of Torah. Jewish mystics then link *vayichulu* to *kalla* ("bride"), hinting at the marriage between God and the Jews.

= Good neighbors

Q Was there any specific layout to the camps of Israel?

Yes. As soon as the Twelve Tribes coalesced into a community, they encamped in a four-direction Star-of-David layout, whose twelve focal points were linked to guard the "thirteenth" spot, the "heart of the nation," the holy inner Sanctuary (*Ohel Moed*, "Tent of Assembly.") The Ramban, the first to merge kabbala into Torah, places this vigilance around God's "Home" on a halachic parallel with all the other laws of Sinai. However, this positioning and marching formation puzzled Don Isaac Abravanel, the classic fourteenth-century exegete of Torah. Why? Because, for the first time, the traditional order had changed; usually, everything revolved around the wives of Jacob, whereby Leah's five boys went first, followed by Rachel's three sons,

---

3. Sota 14a; Pirkei Avos 1:2; Sukka 49b; Seder Eliyahu Rabba 34; Ramban, Leviticus 19:2.

and then four sons from the handmaidens. A Midrash explains why: the layout is a cleverly orchestrated effort to forge multifaceted partnerships, each group installed, not by rank, but in a spot best befitting *it*. Thus the large *avant garde* tribe of Judah, being destined for the monarchy, led the others; the leadership of Yissachar-Zevulun, camped to the east of the rising sun, provided "light"; Dan accompanied Naftali-Asher in order to benefit from their special blessings, and so on. "Cling to a good neighbor, shun an evil one," warn the Mishna rabbis, who, if they were here today, would put it this way: Hey, watch out who you hang around with!

Gilgul

Q What is this?

It's a mystic term, popularized first in the thirteenth century after the *Zohar* was published, then again in the sixteenth-century era of a revitalized (Lurianic) kabbala, and amongst the eighteenth-century Polish Chassidim. *Gilgul* refers to the physical re-embodiment of a soul who had lived in a previous time. What purpose is there for souls to "re-juvenate?" Jewish mystics believe that God allows souls to emerge for a second chance, to complete something (usually a mitzva) they started but never finished. Chayyim Vital was convinced that only "males" fit this "halachic opportunity" category, because Jewish men were obligated to keep more Torah commands; however, his teacher, the wonder-working Ari, felt that *gilgul* was also a form of generational punishment, and was convinced that Yosef Della Reina, a fake Messiah, was "reborn" as a black dog! The Baal Shem Tov (*Besht*), founder of Chassidism, saw "holy sparks" in everything, and legend has it that he "elevated the soul" of a frog whose *gilgul* had been a previous Torah scholar found guilty of not washing his hands before a meal![4]

Grandchildren! Should 'a' had 'em first!

Q Are there any grandparently obligations?

It was easy for the first generations of Jews (Abraham to Jacob) to raise

---

4. Sefer Hagilgulim, Katzenelenbogen, 1885.

children primarily in the Holy Land, where being "Jewish" was a natural; not so the next generation in *chutz la'aretz* (Egypt), a hostile gentile environment, exposed to the climate and curse of assimilation. If it was hard to raise "Jewish" children, imagine the challenge of "Jewish" grandchildren! The ability of Menashe and Ephraim, Jacob's only Egyptian-born grandchildren (from Osnat, his daughter-in-law), to grow up in the lap of Egyptian royalty yet withstand the temptations of exile, notes Rav Yaakov Kamenetzky, makes them *the* primary role models for all future "second generations." Jacob touched on a sensitive subject that few Jews ever consider: mortality! Or, bluntly, how do I want to be remembered after I am dead? The powerful Joseph, second only to Pharaoh, may have had affluence and prestige, but Jacob was more concerned with future Jewishness, hence the prayer, "Bless the lads: may they grow into a great people!" This is why Jewish history calls him *Yisrael sava*, "Israel the old one," the grandfather-educator *par excellence*, fulfilling the Mishna's ideal of *mispar hadoros lefanav*, "connecting the generations" in the covenant of fraternity. Or, as the Yiddishists say, "If I knew having grandchildren was so much fun, I would have had 'em first!"[5]

Green belts

Q Do Jews believe in landscaping?

And how! When the Torah details the borders of the Promised Land, it throws in an ethical gem with amazing modern relevance. Create a green belt, a mandatory "open land round the cities." Why? "To beautify" the environment. Explains Rashi: to provide air, space, greenery, foliage, flowers, playgrounds.

Graves

Q Why do Jews go to graves to pray?

"It is pleasant," sighs the Talmud, "to find rest among one's ancestors!" To visit, say *tehillim*, *kaddish* and pray for mercy at the graves of the pious

---

5. Genesis 48:15–16; Genesis Rabba 70:1.

(*tzadikim*) on certain days (fast days, *erev* Rosh Hashana) is an ancient custom. Joseph cried at his mother's grave, and the Jews, as a people, cried at the grave of Rachel. Yet, despite additional encouragement from the *Zohar*, many scholars frown on this practice, fearful of the prohibition against "consulting the dead."[6]

Great Synagogue, or Great Assembly?

Q Which one's right?

They're one and the same. When *Pirkei Avos* was first translated into English, the term "synagogue" was used at a time when it referred not to a house of worship but, as per its Greek connotation, to a religious assembly. Jewish history's first "Great Assembly," a body of a hundred twenty members, was formed by Nehemiah and Ezra, two underrated Jewish heroes responsible for the continuity of Judaism. "When the Torah was forgotten from Israel, Ezra came up from Babylon and established it!" What exactly did the Great Assembly do? A lot! It spread knowledge of Torah, established regular prayer and Torah readings, started schools, appointed judges, and arranged the *Tanach*, guided by its own principle: "Be deliberate in judgment, raise up many disciples, make a fence around the Torah."[7]

Ger

Q Is there more than one kind of *ger*, and is this term masculine or feminine?

Originally, the term *ger* was generic and simply referred to those (even Jews) who were living amongst "others" (e.g., the Jews were themselves considered *gerim* "in the land of Egypt"). A male convert is a *ger*, a female a *gera* (or *giyores*), both derived from the verb *gur*, "to reside" or "to dwell." And yes, there are several categories of proselytes (in Latin *proselytus*, in Greek *proselutos*). There is the *ger tzedek*, the "righteous" (or "full" convert)

---

6. Birkei Yosef, Yore Deah 344:17; Ta'anis 16a, 23b; Sotah 34b; Rama, Orach Chayim 581:4, 605:1; Divrei Yoel 99:4; Minchas Yitzchak 8:53; Kitzur Shulchan Aruch 581:27.
7. Pirkei Avos 1:1; Sukka 20a.

who was showered with praise ("dearer to God than all the Jews who stood before Sinai") because he chose to join the people out of belief, conviction, without ulterior motives. There's the *ger toshav*, the "resident alien" (or "partial" convert) who simply lived amongst Jews and followed certain selected mitzvos (such as Pesach, Yom Kippur, mikva). There's also the *Yerei Elokim*, "God-fearing *ger*" (in Latin, *metuens*, in Greek *phoboumenos*), who identified with the Jewish God of monotheism but was lax in observing mitzvos. And the *ger sheker*, the "mendacious *ger*," who converted for ulterior motives, such as materialistic reasons (similar to the vast majority of today's converts who do so for marriage), despite the fact that halacha is supposed to disqualify applicants with vested non-Jewish interests. There was even a class of *ger arayos*, the "lions' ger," who converted in the hope that their newly found "holy" status would protect them against the lions roaming the hills of Samaria![8]

Gold, or gold-plated?

Q If the Ark is so important in Judaism, why was it only gold-plated and not pure gold?

You're right! Raiders of the lost Ark (in Hebrew, *aron*) would be disappointed to find their discovery to be made of gold-plated acacia wood instead of the real thing. However, this is what God ordered. Why? Because the Ark, the first of the sacred objects, was designed to house something even *more* sacred, the holy stone tablets engraved with the Ten Commandments, God's message to Israel at Sinai. Wood was chosen because, unlike the "stationary" gold, it came from a tree (*etz*), an object that the Torah associates with growth, development, continuity, and life (*chai*) itself.

Giraffe

Q Can I eat giraffe meat?

For all you anxious giraffe eaters out there, the answer is… yes! Although

---

8. Numbers Rabba 8:2; Tanchuma, Lech Lecha; Isaiah 56:6; Exodus 12:48: Leviticus 16:29; Numbers 19:10; Yore Deah 268:12.

some question not whether a giraffe has split hooves (it has; and it also chews its cud), but whether they are split enough (which would make it unkosher, like a camel whose toes are only partly split). This argument was settled by Saadia Gaon, *rosh yeshiva* of Sura and translator of the Torah into Arabic (the *Tafsir*). Saadia translated the Torah word *zemer* as a kosher *Camel Leoparadous* (Rome considered a giraffe a hybrid between a camel and leopard). So why don't you see kosher giraffe meat on your butcher shelves? It simply doesn't pay. The size, shape and thick skin of a giraffe makes it difficult to *shecht* (kill) and expensive (which is why you don't see *treif* giraffe meat either!)

Golem

Q Where does this word come from?

It appears in Psalms. As a *Maharal*-type "creature of clay"? No, but as a fetus: "Thou [God] hast covered me in my mother's womb. Thine eyes did see my unformed substance [*golmi*]."[9] In his proto-kabbalistic *Sefer Hayetzirah*, "Book of Creation," the twelfth-century Rhineland rabbi Eliezer of Worms uses the expression in its humanoid sense. When the term is used in *Pirkei Avos*, it simply means a "thoughtless, idiotic person." It reappears in several Talmudic tales, ranging from God breathing life into Adam ("made into a golem)" to Rava creating a man out of clay for his friend Rabbi Zeira (who wasn't amused and ordered him to return it to dust!).

God's Name(s)

Q What is God's true name?

No one knows for sure because there are so many different metaphors and names, each attributed to a Godly attribute (e.g., *Hashem* symbolizes "compassion"), or image (e.g., "the Shield of Abraham," "the Mighty One of Jacob"), all merely reflections of many-faceted similes within human experience. That is why there are no nouns to be found in the *siddur* in reference to God (other than "King," or "Father") but merely "descriptions" cast in

---

9. Psalms 139.

the language of multiple action verbs (e.g., Jews praise God "Who Blesses the years," "Who Redeems the people," and so on). Remember: there is only one name in English for God and that's "God," a noun, not a verb. The terms "Lord," "Almighty," etc., are concepts wherein God is different in each. The Torah allocates no fewer than seventy different "aspects" to God (excluding *Hashem*), whilst Jewish mystics are far more aggressive: they have somewhere between forty-two and 231 names, not counting a plethora of synonyms. In the early years, up to the third century CE, God was simply referred to generically, as *HaMakom*, "The Place" (i.e., He Whose place is everywhere). Later, God appears only in quotations, prayers and synonyms, the most common being *HaKadosh Baruch Hu* ("The Holy One, Blessed be He"), a description that appears no less than thirty-nine times just in Isaiah's writings. This popular expression fell out of favor when Christianity began conferring "holy" cultic status on mere humans (popes, saints, etc.). So what's God's true name? In all humility, I would like to venture a guess. Only one Divine name appears just *once* in the entire Torah, and it is the mysterious and ambiguous response of God to a direct ("Who are you?") question from Moses: *Ehyeh asher ehyeh*, "I am/shall be/become what I am/shall be/become," from the verb "be" (in short, "I Am Who I Am"). This is not a name as we know names to be, but an "essence of being." When Rav Hayyim, famed *rosh yeshiva* of Volozhin and renowned student of the Vilna Gaon, declared that "a person's name is the very essence of his soul," his choice of the word "essence" was not accidental. Derived from the Greek word for "being," it is directly traced to the consonants of the four letters in God's Name, traditionally voweled as *ah-oh-oi* (in Hebrew, *Yud, Heh, Vav, Heh*), making it grammatically close to the verb be/become. How was the "Name" pronounced in its original form? No one knows. Why? Because it has been forbidden for so long.

P.S.: After having asked and gotten an answer, Moses never repeated the question![10]

---

10. Exodus 3:14–15.

Goats 'n' sheep

Q What's wrong with mixing goats and sheep?

This is related to the Torah demand for separation (*kappora*) and has to do with the Judaic law of *sha'atnez*, which declares it forbidden to mix wool and linen. Very few Jews comprehend its serious significance; it is in fact a Torah ordinance carrying the same weight as such other Biblical ordinances as "Thou shalt not kill."

Golden Rule

Q What's so "golden" about the rule to "love your neighbor"?

The Torah's most quoted passage and most famous of all ethical mitzvos is *V'ahavta l'reiacha kamocha*, "Love your neighbor as yourself," a five-word directive that Rabbi Akiva, the second-century Talmudic giant, crowns as the "fundamental principle of the Torah (*zeh klal gadol baTorah*)." At first glance, this Golden Jewish Rule sounds selfish – "as yourself" surely seems egotistic. Chassidus takes the words *l'cha pesel* from "Do not make for yourself a graven image," and notes the similarity to *p'sol l'cha*, from "Hew for yourself two tablets of stone," and concludes that if the Jew puts *l'cha* ("himself") first (i.e., on a pedestal) that it approaches idolatry (an I-doll!). The Ramban, noting the concern, points out that the text does not say *V'ahavta es reiacha*, but *l'reiacha*; not *es*, which implies that "I" and "my neighbor" are on a par, but "I," which denotes "for" (i.e., my duty is not necessarily to love my neighbor as *myself*, but to love "for" him *that which I love for myself*; in pragmatic terms, as I wish to be done to me, so must I do to others!). Hillel's position, "What is hateful to you, do *not* do to your fellow," was in reverse to Akiva's. Why? In order, writes the Ramban, to reinforce that an assault (physical or verbal) on a fellow man is an assault and mutilation of God's image (*demus deyukano*). Linguists point out that *kamocha* ("as yourself") is not used adverbially but as an adjective on the basis of *b'tzelem Elokim* (all are created in the image of God), and that the Hebrew verb for love (*ahava*) does not only describe an emotion but an action, because it requires the preposition *l'*, which means "to," or "for." The Midrashic Sifrei's explanation, "In your love for your neighbor you shall find God," makes the Golden Rule concerned with love in its qualitative, *not* quantitative sense!

Goyim

Q When did a gentile become a "*goy*"? Isn't this term demeaning?

No. The word *goy* began its lexicon journey as "nation" or "people," and, in Biblical times the term applied to both gentiles and Jews. "The nations of the earth" were *goyei ha'aretz* or *hagoyim asher*, even as the Jews were to be a *goy kadosh*, "a holy nation," and Israel a *goy echad*, a "unique nation." The term also described rites, not folks, as *chukkos hagoy* simply referred to "(pagan) customs." Demeaning? No. Even when the expression came to denote "them" (as in, "not us"), the Rambam insisted that Jews respect Christian-Muslim "*goyim*" for their monotheism, and Jewish law ordered Jews to behave morally towards non-Jews, despite the bitter experience the Jewish nation has long suffered at the hands of a hostile gentile world.[11]

Gomel bensching

Q What does this mean?

Gomel means "bestows [goodness]." *Birchas hagomel* is the act of blessing and thanking God after emerging safely from a dangerous situation. This prayer replaced the (optional) "thanks offerings" at the altar (*korban toda*). Do we need a *minyan* to say it? Yes. Can it be said in private? Yes, but without God's name. When do we say it? Within three days of coming out of harm. Do we have to wait until full recovery? No. Do we say it by day or night? No difference. Can one express gratitude on behalf of another? No. In some communities, it was customary to make a donation to charity equal to the value of the animal sacrifice (this is what Chayei Adam did when he survived an explosion in 1804). Are women obligated? In the olden days, yes, even women brought the *korban toda*, but not today (in the Ashkenaz world). Why not? For modesty reasons, since it required saying it in front

---

11. Leviticus 20:23, 25:44; Genesis 18:18; Exodus 19:6; I Chronicles 17:1; II Kings 17:8; Gittin 61a.

of a *minyan* of ten men; however, women should say this blessing and major halachists (Rav Moshe Feinstein, Rav S.Z. Auerbach) provide opportunities to do so (some common customs include saying it in the home, or from behind the *mechitza*). After childbirth, the mother can simply answer "amen" to her husband's *aliya* if he does so with a specific intent to fulfill his wife's *hagomel* obligation. Do minors have to recite this blessing? No. Can a father do so for his child? No. What defines a "dangerous situation?" There are four categories. A serious illness or operation (including childbirth); a risky journey (e.g., air flight, especially in a world of terrorism); surviving an accident; release from prison. What's the source of these categories? The Psalmist defines four types of people who are God's "redeemed": travelers, captives, invalids, and sea voyagers.[12]

Gezeira

Q What is this?

A *gezeira* is a binding rabbinic decree, a precautionary measure intended to lessen the probabilities of accidentally transgressing the Torah. For example: in order to maintain the spirit and aura of Shabbas, the forbidden work categories (*melachos*) had "fences" (*takkanos*) added as a form of "protective legislation." Thus, climbing a tree was forbidden *only* because it might lead to breaking a branch, or tearing a leaf. Certain items, such as a pen, money, and a hammer, were defined as *muktze* for one reason only: to prevent accidental writing, lending, hammering. Even reading *Megillas Esther* was prohibited because it could perhaps lead to disappointment, since the "eyes of the poor are lifted [in expectation of getting Purim *gelt*]." Is a *gezeira* the same as a mitzva? No, but since they're both equally binding, the end result is the same, except in the degree of punishment, and the fact that the *gezeira* is temporary in theory, and can be modified, even abrogated, by the rabbis.[13]

---

12. Shulchan Aruch, Orach Chayim 219; Psalms 107; Brachos 10:8, 54b; Orach Chayim 219:3, 6; Mishne Berura 20, 8:13, 213:12, 219:3; Chasam Sofer, Orach Chayim 51; Akiva Eiger, Orach Chayim 219:5; S.Z. Auerbach, Hilchos Shelomo 1:23–24; Iggeros Moshe, Orach Chayim 5:14.
13. Yad, Shabbas 21:1; Rashi, Shabbas 14b, 49b; Ramban, Leviticus 23:24; Pirkei Avos 1:1; Chayei Adam 9:1; Megilla 4b.

= Gambling

Q I'm a gambler. Am I doing anything wrong?

The odds are on "yes"! The root cause of gambling is man's innate urge to take a chance, not merely to acquire money but as a means of escapism, as a stimulus, or to relieve tensions – and the *nachas* of maybe getting something for nothing! Dice-throwing goes back five thousand years. Knucklebones and pebbles were the first dice, marked not with numbers but signs of "good luck" and "bad luck." African tribes believed that dice revealed the will of gods, and threw them on the eve of battle. The way they fell predicted success or failure. Playing-cards consisted of a slew of idol emblems, allowing itinerant gypsies to create a whole industry of fortune-telling (*Hearts* were symbols of ecclesiastic powers, the three-leaf *Clover* represented the Trinity, etc.). Judaism considers gambling an artificial adventure and allows it as amusement, but only in moderation. If you are a professional or compulsive gambler, the Torah considers you as contributing nothing to the betterment of society. The rabbis taint you as *ein lo ummanut ella hu*, "lacking an occupation," and disqualify you (*m'sachek b'kuvya*) from being a witness in a Jewish court of law.[14]

= *Gezundheit*

Q How did the custom of saying *gezundheit* after a sneeze begin?

Once upon a time, a sneeze was more than just a sneeze. It was associated with fear. Thus the popular slang expression, "not to be sneezed at!" Early Jews believed the sneeze was a prelude to death. The Romans saw it as an evil omen. The Greeks considered it a sign of pending danger (during the catastrophic Athenian plague, sneezing was endemic). Having determined that man's soul (*neshoma*) was the essence of his life, Jewish mysticism, noting that the dead cease breathing, associated breath with soul. The source? God Himself. At creation, man was fashioned from dust, but in order to become a living soul, God "breathed into his nostrils the breath of life." Since the sneeze let out air ("breath"), the superstitious reacted in apprehension

---

14. Sanhedrin 3:3.

and alarm, convinced that the *neshoma* had just been deprived of some of its essence. One old legend claims that Jacob died at his first sneeze. Thus, the custom of wishing the sneezer long life and good health (*gezundheit*). It was this same concern (and *not* good manners) that led to the custom of covering one's mouth when yawning.

Genetics

Q Can I use gene therapy to ensure that my baby is the best in sports, intellect, looks?

Jewish law approaches genetic engineering the same way it does science and technology – with indifference! Why? Because Judaism is only concerned with aim and purpose. Thus, if the scientist's desire is to exploit genetic engineering for immoral goals (e.g., to create another Adolf-style evil master race), or genetic determinism (e.g., manipulating genes to create the Perfect Child), then it is *verboten*. If the motivation to modify genes is to correct serious hereditary defects, then this search would constitute a great mitzva, similar to *pikuach nefesh*, the saving of life. If gene therapy can cure diseases, it is not different from the discovery of antibiotics, and a genetic review of family before marriage is already a recognized custom! The real question is this. How can the Torah demand a code of ethical behavior, if programmed into people are genes that give them a predisposition to murder, theft, aggression? In the *Genes vs. Free Will* battle, the Judaic winner is a mother's nurture over Mother Nature. Natural predilections never excuse one's evil nature (*yetzer hora*), which remains a perpetual internal battle over moral responsibility. Even the great Moses, notes *Tiferes Yisrael*, the nineteenth-century commentary on the Mishna, was born with a natural predisposition to be bad, but by overcoming it, he turned out exceptionally excellent.

Get

Q Is a Jewish divorce similar to that of other religions?

No. Divorce in some societies was informal, footloose and so fancy-free that, in Tonga, a man simply told his wife to go away and he was legally divorced. An Eskimo legally leaves his wife just by moving into another igloo. Early Roman husbands got a "quickie" divorce by having a servant deliver a letter to the spouse saying they no longer had any feelings for her. Arabs repeat one word (*Ittalak*) three times, just as in *Beetlejuice*, and the wife is automatically dismissed (the word literally means, "Go to the Devil!"). In contrast, our Sages made divorce difficult, in an attempt to preserve the family. Jewish law had precise detailed language (identifying clearly the parties, the location, etc.) that had to be written by special expert scribes in a legible "writ" (*get*). Three judges and two witnesses had to be present. It was read out aloud. Then the husband had to physically hand it to his wife and say the right words. The wife then passed the document to the *av beis din* who tore it partially (to prevent its use for fraudulent purposes), and stored it in a safe place for future reference.

Glatt

Q What does "*glatt kosher*" mean?

This expression, which has become a code word for "strictly kosher," literally means "smooth." It refers to the examination, externally, for a blemish or adhesion to the lungs of an animal. Does *glatt kosher* apply to chickens, or fish? No, chicken's lungs can't be inspected, and fish don't have lungs. The expression is misused greatly. For example: to have *glatt kosher* toothpaste, cake or bread is meaningless, since the term *glatt* only applies to meat.

Growing pains

Q We're expecting our first child. What obligations do we, as parents, have?

You have a three-pronged responsibility. To raise them in the ways of God (to show them right from wrong falls on the mother's shoulders). Teach them how to make an honest living. Inspire them to become productive members of the Jewish community. The Torah understood that these were difficult tasks, requiring discipline and "tough love," and thus dangled a carrot in front of the children as well. The very first commandment that comes attached to a promise (long life!) is to "honor parents." And yes, you *can* hit a child (but only with the force of a shoelace!), for "who spares the rod hates the son."[15]

Good luck charm?

Q I'm putting up my *mezuzos* this week. Are they supposed to bring me good luck?

No. The sole purpose of a *mezuza* is to publicly identify which house on the block is Jewishly dedicated to God. However, over the years, as misfortune continually struck Jews and Jewish communities were surrounded by hostile gentile neighbors, it became associated with warding off evil, akin to the Angel of Death that "passed over" the Jews of Egypt. Jewish mystics see the term *mezuzos* as a merger of *zaz mavea* ("death departs"). The thirteenth-century Meir of Rothenburg spread twenty-four *mezuzos* throughout his home, convinced that "no demon has power over a house where the *mezuza* is properly affixed" (the rabbi credited his study door *mezuza* for his successful afternoon naps, uninterrupted by tormenting evil spirits). Today it is common (especially in Chabad circles) to inspect *mezuzos* for flaws after a tragedy. Israeli soldiers carry *mezuzos* hoping to deflect enemy bullets; some wear a *mezuza* necklace as a protective charm. The final word goes to the Rambam who criticizes Jews "who convert a command intended primarily to imbue a belief in God, into a mere talisman which they in their foolishness think has some magical power!"

15. Exodus Rabba 28.2; Exodus 20:12; Deuteronomy 5:16; Proverbs 13:24.

H

Hakoras hatov

Q What does this mean?

The popular slang, "Don't bite the hand that feeds you," is a direct hand-me-down of the Talmud's "Do not throw stones into the well that you drank from!" The purpose of this expression of appreciation (*hakoras hatov*) is, according to Rav Eliyahu E. Dessler, not just for the benefactor, but for the recipient. In fact, to "give thanks" is the very genesis of the term "Jew," whose Hebrew counterpart (*Yehuda*) is derived from *hoda'a* (thankfulness), the name chosen by Leah for her fourth child [Yehudah] from Jacob. Why was the matriarch so grateful? Because this was the child that tipped the balance in her favor, contributing the largest number of children to the twelve tribes of Israel.

Hot hell!

Q Are there any "Jewish" sins that lead to a Christian-type "hot hell"?

The Torah describes three levels of sin. Intentional, committed in deliberate defiance (*pesha*); done knowingly (e.g., lust, or uncontrollable emotion), but not done to defy God (*ovon*); and the innocent, unintentional sin (*cheit*). God, recognizing that no one is perfect, and that Jews, being fallible, are prone to sin (*aveira*), always tempers justice with mercy – and thus no one is ever condemned to eternal damnation!

Half or whole?

Q What does "half" Hallel mean?

Hallel is a song of praise sung by Jews *and* angels in its entirety (*Hallel Shalem*, "Whole Hallel") on twenty-one days a year; generally on days when weekday work is prohibited (Succos, Chanukah, Shavuos). The concept of singing praise to God is derived from Isaiah, "You shall sing a song [*shir*] as on the night when the festival [Pesach] is sanctified." Thus, if the time is similar to the night of Pesach, then "whole" *Hallel* is said (with a blessing). So when is the time not applicable? "Singing and rejoicing" are inappropriate emotions on life-and-death judgment days (Rosh Hashana, Yom Kippur), on occasions when "your enemy has fallen" (the last days of Pesach and its "intermediate days," *chol hamo'ed*), and on days that do not commemorate a national *nes* (miracle) or are not full Jewish festivals (Rosh Chodesh). Is it literally "half"? No. Only two paragraphs are omitted: *Ahavti* and *Lo lanu*. Should one say a blessing on a "half" *Hallel*? It's in dispute: the Rambam says "No." Rabbenu Tam (Rashi's grandson and famed *tosefos*) says "Yes." What's the issue? Whether one can say *v'tzivanu*, "God has commanded us," over a custom (*minhag*).[1]

Hypnosis

Q Is hypnosis considered witchcraft, or an acceptable practice?

Rabbi Jacob Ettlinger, the formidable nineteenth-century halachic authority, allowed Jews to undergo hypnotism (then called "magnetism," or "mesmerism") after doctors assured him the procedure had nothing to do with necromancy and had potential mental health benefits.

---

1. Isaiah 30:28.

Health

Q Does Judaism have any health tips?

Sure, many. Here's one: "Too much sitting aggravates hemorrhoids; too much standing injures the heart; too much walking hurts the eyes." The conclusion? "Divide your time between the three!" Want more? See a doctor.

Hear or heed?

Q Is "Hear" O Israel, the correct translation of the *Sh'ma*?

No. Although the conventional translation of the *Sh'ma*'s first sentence is, "Hear, O Israel! The Lord our God, the Lord is One [*echad*]," a more literal, and accurate, translation is, "Take heed, O Israel! The Lord, our God, alone is God." This emphasizes monotheism's contrast to polytheism, in that the God of Israel is *not* "one," as opposed to *two or more* gods, but rather is the *only* One and unique God. But if the *Sh'ma* is a personal, *internal* declaration of faith, why does it begin with an order to a third party, "Hear, O Israel?" Again, a mistranslation: *Sh'ma* does not mean "to hear," but "to listen," a prerequisite of first grasping Moses' words, and only *then* accepting God's existence. Thus, "O Israel" is a declaration of group identity, communal cohesiveness, a United-We-Stand dogma – and an acknowledgment that the individual Jew can only flourish in personal faith if, and when, the entire community of Jews does so as well. Does this make the *Sh'ma* an exclusive Jewish possessiveness of God? No, not at all: it simply places a responsibility, called *kiddush Hashem*, solely on the Jews to behave appropriately, in order to spread, via association, the sanctity of God's Name.

Human rights, why bother?

Q Why should we, as Jews, worry about the human rights situation in other countries?

Affinity for human rights, and not just Jewish rights, is rooted in thought and practice of Judaism, despite there being no Hebrew or rabbinic word for "rights." Today's term, *zechus*, denotes purity and innocence. In fact, the "as of right" concept is generally absent in Jewish law. The command to give charity does not *entitle* the poor to receive *tzedaka* "as of right." The command to love your neighbor does not *entitle* him to your affection "as of right." The key Torah concept is *duties*, not entitlements, and these duties were governed not by man's definition of right and wrong but by God's. The Torah frowns upon Jews, even kings and rulers, doing "that which was right in his *own* eyes." And what did God promote? Justice, justice, *above* all, to *all*, by virtue of their common humanity and ancestry – binding, incidentally, not just on mankind but also on God Himself.[2]

Heaven, or Hell?

Q **What happens after we die?**

Ah, the timeless question. Obviously, no one knows. The consensus is of an *Olam Haba* ("The World to Come"), a state of non-physical being where the still-active soul (*neshoma*) basks in the *joie de vivre* of God's glory, and Torah scholars study Torah perpetually ("When you awake [a reference to a 'future world'], it [the Torah] shall talk with you"). What is Hell? I guess it's the absence of Heaven!

Heidenheim and Roedelheim

Q **I found these names in my grandmother's *siddur*. Who are they?**

The first is a name, the second is a suburb. Wolf Benjamin, born in 1757, was known as *Ish Heidenheim*, the "man from Heidenheim" (a Bavarian village) and had a printing shop in Roedelheim, Frankfurt-am-Main. Driven by passion and scrupulous perfection, the obsessive Benjamin published *machzorim* and *siddurim* of the highest quality. In an (unsuccessful) attempt to prevent plagiarism, he stamped *Heidenheim/Roedelheim* on his title pages, and then signed his name underneath in Hebrew. How can you

---

2. Judges 17:6; Deuteronomy 16:20, 17:14–20; Sanhedrin 37a; Genesis 18:24–25; Leviticus 19:15.

spot a fake? Look at the title page, and if you see the words "as correct as any edition ever printed," it's a fake.

Hair, O Israel

Q How important is hair in Jewish folklore?

"May God pluck your beard!" is one of the most feared curses among Bedouin. Why? Because hair was associated with faith, strength, some sanctity; in fact the Torah rails against the cutting of "the corners of the beard." A long beard was a sign of wisdom (Jewish texts describe an elder as "the bearded one"), male power (kings in the second century BCE who couldn't grow beards used to wear fake ones in public, made of metal and held in place by special chinstraps), strength and vigor (when Samson's locks were cut he lost his power), piety (the *nazir* ascetic swore to let his hair grow as a service to God), opportunity (Alexander the Great's soldiers had to go into battle clean-shaven to deprive their enemies of the opportunity to grab them by their beards), income revenues (Queen Elizabeth I taxed, based on their social standing, those whose beards had more than two weeks' growth), vanity (French King Francis I grew a beard to hide an ugly chin scar), and sympathy (eighteenth-century Spaniards went around beardless because their king was unable to grow one).

Hapax Legomena

Q What is this?

There is a great Yiddish saying: *Ven Got vil bashtrofn an am'orets, leygt er em a loshn-koydesh vort in moyl arayn,* "If God wants to punish an ignoramus, he puts a Hebrew-Aramaic word into his mouth!" There are certain Hebrew words whose meaning is still a mystery (*Hapax legomena* in Greek). Why? Because they appear only once, and thus we are deprived of context. Even Sifrei, an ancient midrashic anthology nearly as old as the Talmud itself, shows frustration with rabbis who can't get their Hebraic act together (specifically, they vent their wrath at scholars who mix "*ayin* and *alef*," and confuse "*tsadik* with *gimmel*"). A perfect example? No one knows what *azazel* means. Some say it refers to "the goat that is sent away" (scapegoat), others see it as a combination of *ez* ("goat") and *azal* ("went"), or perhaps, since *az* means "strong, rugged," the term describes "the harsh mountain" over which the animal of atonement was thrown. In summary? After three thousand years, it's still a mystery word!

Harry Potter

Q I wasn't allowed to see this movie because of its "witchcraft" content. Does Judaism have an opinion on superstition, zodiacs, demons, etc.?

To ignore the zodiac influence in Judaism is to rewrite history. All the Latin names for zodiac signs were Hebraicized (*t'leh* for Aries, *shor* for Taurus, *sivan* for Gemini, *sartan* for Cancer, *aryeh* for Leo, etc.). Signs, motifs and diagrams appear in early Jewish architecture. Zodiac wheels with astrological signs for the Hebrew months were discovered built into the mosaic floor of Israel's oldest find, a sixth-century Bet Alpha Synagogue. Halachic documents (ancient *kesubos*) and prayer books (thirteenth-century German *machzorim*) display drawings of goats sipping water, a combination of the zodiac signs for Capricorn (goat) and Aquarius (water carrier). Rabbinic texts (the tenth-century *Sefer Yetzirah*, "Book of Creation," and the *Pesikta Rabbati*) dare to connect each zodiac sign to a major event in Jewish history. And then there are the entire delightful (*Aggada*) and mystical (*Zohar*) writings that have no qualms about explaining "troubling" Biblical passages via the use of cosmic astrology, coupled with a catalogue of mythopoeic supernaturalism that contains enough ghosts, poltergeists, dybbuks, devils and *di gute* or *rekhteleit* ("right-handed") demons in *Yenne's Velt* to fill dozens of J.K. Rowlings's *Harry Potter* books and surely every episode of the *Twilight Zone*. When Tevye, in *Fiddler on the Roof,* concocts the ghost of Tzeitel to fool Goldie, the ghost might have been fictitious on stage, but not to Goldie, nor to the masses of Yiddish audiences throughout Eastern Europe.

High days and holydays

Q Is "High Holydays" the correct term?

No. The expression comes from an old popular English phrase, "high days and holydays," wherein the terms *holydays* and *holidays* were used interchangeably – "holiday" being a contraction of "holyday," and "holy" being derived from the Middle English *hool*, which means not "sacred" but "whole," or "excellent" (and no, High Cholesterol is not a religious holiday!). The problem is obvious: neither word is a literal translation of the Hebrew *yom kadosh*, a "sacred day." Even Yom Kippur is frequently mistranslated as the "Day of Atonement," a result of the English verb "atone," a combination of *at* and *one*, denoting atonement to reconciliation. In Hebrew, however, the word *kippur* is derived from the root "to cover, hide," or "to obliterate" (as in sin), and thus "to expiate." What's the correct term? *Aseres yemei teshuva*, "Ten Days of Repentence," or the *yamim nora'im*, "Days of Awe," not to be confused with *yamim narronim*, which means "the days of idiots"!

How high?

Q How tall does a *mechitza* have to be?

High enough to prevent communication, sight, or interaction. Rav Moshe Feinstein defines this as at least eighteen *tefachim*, which is around sixty to sixty-six inches (however, more stringent scholars claim a *mechitza* must completely block out the entire women's section). Is a full glass partition OK? No, it defeats the purpose. Remember: a "physical barrier" is technically needed wherever men and women pray, or are publicly invited (weddings, etc.). How about at a *shiur* (a public learning session)? This is a gray area, although separate seating should be maintained, Rav Moshe concluded that if its presence might cause people not to come, then it is better to do without, in the spirit of bringing Jews back to Judaism.[3]

How long a wait?

Q I just had a hamburger; how long do I wait before I can have a chocolate milkshake?

The only reference in the Torah to meat and dairy (*basar b'chalav*) is the

---

3. Sukka 52; Iggeros Moshe, Orach Chayim 1:43; 3:23, 3:24; 4:31; M'haram Shik 77; Shevet Halevi 1:29; Shabbas 92a.

prohibition against cooking them together ("Do not cook a kid in its mother's milk"); which is where the Oral Law comes in. The custom varies: Dutch Jews wait one hour; German Jews wait three hours; but our family (Polish) waits six "full" hours (a "quarter of the day and night"), which is the custom practiced by most Jews today. When do the six hours start? From the end of *bensching*. Is this universal? No, some start the clock from when they finish eating meat. The question is obvious: why not just switch to the Dutch custom? It's not allowed, under a rabbinic concept known as "fence breaking" (*poretz geder*), which considers you guilty of *al titosh Toras imecha*, "Do not forsake the teachings of your mother." Why is there (considerably) less wait after *milchigs*? Because the taste of meat lingers on, its "fatty" residue remains in the throat and stuck between the teeth.[4]

Holocaust and the halacha

Q **Did complex and unprecedented issues of Jewish law arise during the Holocaust?**

Yes. Rabbi Ephraim Oshry, who was born in 1914 in Kupishok, near Ponevezh, north-central Lithuania, relied on memory to compile his responsa, adding to a long Jewish tradition that has so far recorded over 250,000 *sheylas un tshuvas* ("Questions and Answers"). Rav Oshry hid his covert work in a milk can and published it after liberation (telling a *New York Times* reporter, "Some resist with a gun, others with their souls!"). The questions that Jews asked were heartbreaking: Can one perform a Caesarean on a dead Jewess? Yes. Could a poverty-stricken wife remove her dead husband's gold teeth? No. Could a Jew buy a Christian baptism certificate to try to escape? No. [After the war] could one have his concentration camp tattoo removed surgically? No (in order not to erase the memory of the greatest crime ever perpetrated against the Jewish people).

---

4. Darkei Teshuva 89:6; Shiyurei Bracha 89:4; Chayei Adam 127:10; Aruch Hashulchan 89:4, 7; Ecclesiastes 10:8; Rashi, Proverbs 1:8; Chulin 105a; Rambam, Maacholas Assuros 9:28.

Hundred a day

Q I just heard we should say a hundred blessings a day! Isn't that a lot?

Commenting on the Torah verse, "What [*mah*] does God ask of you?" our rabbis interpret *mah* as *me'ah*, "hundred." It sounds like a lot, but it's not if you add up the obligatory daily blessings. Try this: start with the fifteen early morning blessings, add nineteen *amida* blessings thrice daily, then throw in all the eating *brachos*, plus your regular day-to-day experiences, and you get…close to a hundred! Is this Jewish law? No, it's Jewish lore. The number is symbolic of "a lot," and the exercise is a voluntary one, encouraging the Jew to spend each day in recognition of God ("Know Him in all your ways").[5]

Hunting, shooting, fishing

Q I would like to go away for a weekend to hunt and fish. Is that OK?

How many hunters in the Torah? Three. Nimrod, Esau, Ishmael – and not one is a role model! Hunting as a hobby or sport is considered ethically unthinkable, "downright cruelty," according to Rav Landau, eighteenth-century halachist. Is the ban absolute? No. It's allowed in the context of food, protection, or prevention. Just look at Solomon's daily diet: wild game – deer, gazelles, roebucks, fowl; and fish was a delicacy for the Jews during Egyptian bondage.[6]

Hygiene

Q Is *mikva* simply a ritual of hygiene?

No. The Torah required that ritual impurity, whether from contact with a corpse, childbirth, menstruation, skin infections, disease, mildewed clothing, etc., be symbolically "washed away," through immersion. Cleanliness

---

5.   Deuteronomy 10:12; Meir, Menachos 43b; Psalms 3:6; 16:8.
6.   Genesis 10:9, 21:20, 27:5; Leviticus 17:13; Numbers 11:5; Isaiah 19:8.

may have been a side benefit, but hygiene was never the primary purpose of the mitzva of *mikva* (hijacked by the Church, and transformed into baptism). Jews and water were thus linked from day one at sacred moments. Priests washed whenever entering the Tabernacle; Jews wash their hands first thing in the morning, again before *davening*, and before and after meals. And then they rinsed for special occasions: Abraham offered to "wash the feet" of three visiting angels; Ruth bathed before meeting Boaz; David did the same to mark the end of his mourning, and for his sinful Bathsheba saga ("cleanse me, wash me, and I shall be whiter than snow"). Which brings us to soap. No, there wasn't any, but vegetal-mineral substances and after-bathing deodorants were popular. Jeremiah's favorite? Potassium niter and vegetable alkali (*borit*). Perfumed oils were a best seller, even used "religiously" to anoint the kings of Israel.[7]

═ Honoree ═

Q Why do we give public awards at dinners? It seems so "distasteful."

It's complicated. Yes, the Mishna frowns upon those who "chase honor," warning them that this "removes a person from the world." However there is a fine line between active "pursuit" and simply accepting an honor. If the awardee acts humbly, he can actually set a good example and inspire others to emulate him in good deeds. In this case, the honor becomes not an end in itself, but a means to an end. And more: it's important to give recognition (*hakoras hatov*) to those amongst us who are deserving of it (and while we're on the topic, awards to schoolchildren are very, very desirable, because the pride it generates [in the parents] is the result of a major mitzva, *kibbud av v'eim*, honoring one's parents).[8]

---

7. Deuteronomy 23:12–13; Leviticus 13:47–59, 14:33–57, 17:15–16, 16:24; Exodus 30:18; Shabbas 25b, 109a; Genesis 18:4, 19:2; Ruth 3:3; II Samuels 12:20; Psalms 51:7; II Samuels 12:20; Ruth 3:3; Ezekiel 16:9; Jeremiah 2:22; I Kings 1:39.
8. Pirkei Avos 4:28.

Hamantaschen

Q Where does this word come from?

Who knows? Not I! This triangle-shaped sweet pastry, filled with prunes, poppy-seeds or jelly (*hamantaschen* is plural for a *hamantasch*) originally had no Purim connection at all, and was simply referred to as *mohntasch*, "a pocket of poppy seed." This later became *Haman-taschen* the moment their popularity as a sweet Purim delicacy spread. Jewish mystics broke it down into *tasch* (*kocho shel*) *Haman*, "may Haman's strength become weak," and suggested that its three corners were symbolic of the shape of Haman's hat. Others saw its contour as reflecting our three Biblical Patriarchs, whose merit saved the Jews of Persia from destruction. The Otzar Dinim is convinced that the word "Haman" was mistakenly used for "manna," claiming it should have been called *Mantash*, "a bag of manna," but instead, through human error, became *Haman-tash*. During the days of Abravanel there was even a cake called *oznei Haman*, "Haman's ears," that was baked in the shape of human ears and dipped in honey. Why? Immanuel of Rome recalls a legend wherein Shushan's Jews cut off Haman's ears after he was hanged (in line with local custom, whereby a thief's ears were chopped off as punishment). Kreplach, another three-cornered delicacy, is associated with the meals of Purim, erev Yom Kippur, and Hoshana Rabba. Why? They share a commonality: striking or beating – our heart (on Yom Kippur), willow branches (on Hoshana Raba), Haman's name (on Purim). Perhaps the term *kreplach* is an acronym of Kippur (k), Hoshana Raba (r), and Purim (p)?[9]

Humility

Q How important is this?

It's considered the greatest of Judaic traits; even King Solomon advised those seeking wisdom to "Go to the ant, sluggard; look at her ways, and become wise. She, who has no prince, officer, or ruler, provides in the summer her provision, gathers in harvest-time her food" – to which the rabbis

---

9. Midrash Megilla 12.

add that, if the Talmud had not been given, we would have learned "decency from the cat, not to rob from the ant, fidelity from the pigeon, and modesty from the rooster."[10]

═ Holocaust ═

Q Where does this word come from?

During the era of the Judges, God ordered Gideon to construct an altar and to offer a "holocaust" (a "burnt offering'); the term then appears again when an angel invites Manoah, Samson's father, to offer "a holocaust." Prior to the generation of Holocaust survivors the Heavens allowed only three men to see both destruction and reconstruction in their lifetime: Noah, Daniel and Job.[11]

═ How to blot! ═

Q Is there any "right" way to show disapproval of Haman?

No. The sky's the limit! Reb Heschel the Scribe would test his ink quills during the year by writing the word Haman, and then literally blotting it out. On Purim, in addition to hissing, booing, stamping one's feet and rattling *graggers*, some communities bang together two smooth stones or wooden blocks inscribed with the name "Haman." Others write his name on the soles of their shoes and then stamp, jump, and rub their shoes on the ground. In Iraq they burnt entire life-size effigies of the "wicked one." Yemenite Jews made large human-shaped Haman effigies from intertwined pieces of wood smeared with paint and clay, and then, having hung the villain on a high tree in the synagogue yard, hurled arrows and stones at it until it fell down in pieces. Why the noise? It's a mitzva to obliterate the memory of Amalek (*mocho timcheh es zecher Amalek*); it helps keep children's attention late at night (similar to how the *afikoman* works on Pesach); and, according to a mystic Midrash, each generation's "bang and stamp" is still personally felt by Haman!

---

10. Eiruvin 100b; Hullin 60a; Proverbs 6:6–8.
11. Judges 6:25–26.

═ Hands off! ═══════════════════

Q What is the meaning of the expression "fences around the Torah"?

To lessen the possibility of Shabbas desecration, our rabbis added dozens of additional "thou-shalt-nots" (*takkanos*) that act as "fences" (*seyag la Torah*). An example? Certain objects (cash, radios, pens, etc.) were made *muktze*, "excluded" (i.e., forbidden to touch), on the grounds that to touch was potentially to use. What's the legal basis of this extraordinary power? "You shall take measures to safeguard that which I give you." But there were caveats. No "double-dipping" (*gezeira l'gezeira*) was allowed (i.e., one protective measure could not safeguard "another protective measure"). "Do not make the fence more important than what it fences in!" reminds the *Yalkut Shim'oni*, a thirteenth-century compilation of earlier rabbinical literature, for "if there be no vineyard, why a fence?"[12]

═ Head over heels ═══════════════

Q Is there any significance in Jacob's grabbing his sibling's heel in the womb?

Yes. Judaism lends great significance to names, in that they reflect a person's essence. Esau's name is derived from *seir*, a Semitic root meaning "thick-haired"; however, the Midrash links it to the Hebrew *asui*, "fully formed, complete [at birth]" – a reference to his emergence from the womb as a "mature" infant, with a full head and body of hair, whereas "Jacob" relates to the Hebrew word *eikev* (Yaakov), which means "heel." Esau saw himself as a finished product with no need, nor interest, in growth, static as far as his Judaism was concerned. In contrast, Jacob perceived himself to be at "the heel" of his spiritual growth, sensing that he still had much to learn. Ovadiah Sforno, sixteenth-century Italian Torah commentator, relates to "heel," being at the end of the body, as a positive attribute for Jacob, a nuance for "he will remain at the end," suggestive of persistence and adaptation. Mystics see his "heel grabbing" in the womb as the start of Jacob's

---

12. Pirkei Avos 3:13; Exodus 23:13; Leviticus 18:30; Deuteronomy 17:10–11; Baba Metzia 5b; Beitza 3a.

tenacious and prolonged struggle to win his brother's birthright. By insert-ing the ominous word *yipparedu* ("they shall be separated"), the Torah im-mediately disrupts the rhythm of its own poetic hemistich-couplet, "Two nations are in thy womb." Rashi, the father of all Torah exegetes, derives "struggle" from the Hebrew root of "run" ("and her sons ran [*vayitrotztzu*] around in her womb"), and traces the genesis of disorder to each fetus's natural tendencies; Jacob "struggles" to emerge when his mother passes synagogues or schools, in contrast to Esau's longing which stirs towards idolatrous temples.

Honor

Q Why is the Fifth Commandment (to honor parents) flanked among the man-God duties?

By honoring parents, we honor God, for only through our parents, act-ing as Divine agents, has God given us life. This mitzva is one of the few, and the *only* one of the Ten Commandments, that comes attached with a reward: old age ("Your days may be long upon the land"). The *Zohar* has a different outlook: "your father" is God, and "your mother" is the Com-munity of Israel, implying that Jews who "take the fifth" actually honor *two* commands – a spiritual and interpersonal human one.

Have an "easy fast"

Q What can I do to make my fast "easier"?

Erev Yom Kippur we wish each other a *tzom kal,* "an easy fast," which is easier said than done – but here are some tips for the day before the fast: drink a lot, eat in moderation, take plenty of carbohydrates (pasta, rice, potatoes, etc.), avoid salt, sweet foods, coffee, and coke.

Hiddur mitzva

Q What is this?

The halachic source of *hiddur mitzva*, the performance of a mitzva in the most beautiful way possible, lies in the melodic highlight of the *Shabbas Shira*, a magnificent eighteen-verse *Shirat Hayam* ("Song at the Sea"), the greatest ode in the entire Torah. As a source of collective memory, it is a central part of our daily prayer (*Mi Chamochah*, and "Blessing of Redemption (*geula*)," an elated Psalm of praise and crooning *niggun* of redemption, spontaneously sung by a relieved and rescued people who had just witnessed the dramatic drowning of the Egyptian cavalry ("They sank like a stone and lead, consumed like stubble!"). It is here, among rich language, vivid metaphors, and lyrics of passion and appreciation, that Miriam, co-orchestrator of the chorus, is first identified by name, as a prophetess. That an exhilarated nation responds not in prose nor study, but in poetry and tune, the most liberating and soul-uplifting of all activities, with such lyrics as *Zeh kayli v'anveihu* ("This is my God and I will praise, beautify and exalt Him"), becomes the epitome of *hiddur mitzva*.

Hatikva

Q Where did Israel's national anthem come from?

The nine-stanza poem, *Hatikva*, "The Hope," was penned by a Polish-born, Austrian-raised perpetually wandering Jew (Naftali Herz Imber) who dedicated it (seventy years before the Third Jewish Commonwealth arose), together with a bunch of other poems he wrote, to his close Christian-Zionist Scottish friend Laurence Oliphant, who eventually became a member of the British House of Commons. The word *tikva* appears often in rabbinic writings, ranging from Proverbs to Jeremiah to Ruth. The *Hatikva* is a song of optimism, a hope and a prayer that prophecy would soon come true and the Jews be returned to their ancestral homeland. How did Naftali choose his title? In 1878, on a trip to Palestine, he was impressed by the idealism of some Jewish settlers who founded their colony in a malaria-ridden swamp, and named it "the Gate of Hope" (a quote from Hosea). Is the tune original? No. Naftali "borrowed" (OK, stole!) it from an old Spanish-Slav folk song (you can hear it in Smetana's composition *Die Moldau*). What happened to Naftali? Did he die a wealthy man from royalties? No. He died broke, destitute, an alcoholic. On the streets of Zion? No, on the Lower East Side of Manhattan![13]

---

13. Proverbs 11:7; Jeremiah 31:17; Ruth 1:12.

⸺ Haircut ⸺

Q I'm uncomfortable going to work unshaven during the Three Weeks. Any suggestions?

You need a lenient opinion. Both Rav Moshe Feinstein and the Chasam Sofer permit you to shave (but not during the Nine Days), not because of potential embarrassment, but *only* if the alternative is losing money. There is another exemption: a *bris* ceremony, which allows a father, *sandek* and *mohel,* to the delight of the local barber, all to have haircuts. Can you arrange that?[14]

⸺ How sweet it is! ⸺

Q Can God smell?

Metaphorically, yes. When Noah, grateful for his survival from the Flood, gave thanks via animal sacrifices, the Torah describes how "God smelled the sweet odor," perhaps the first recorded instance of *perfume,* a Latin term which literally means "through the smoke." Ancient Greeks called perfume "the scent of Divinity," and when archeologists opened the Egyptian Tomb of Tutankhamen in 1922, they uncovered several vases of still fragrant perfume dating back to 1350 BCE! In the olden days, our rabbis used the sense of smell for a semi-religious experience, with incense in the Temple, *havdala* spices, etc. Doctors used to diagnose diseases through smell, and food was judged not by taste – but by smell!

⸺ Help! ⸺

Q I'm on the rabbi committee. How do I choose a rabbi?

The rabbis of yore were known for their intellect, piety and personal qualities. But the times they were a'changing. In 1951, *Time* magazine quoted the advice one rabbi gives another: "Unless you can play baseball, you'll

---

14. Chasam Sofer, Orach Chayim 158; Iggeros Moshe, Orach Chayim 4:102; Mishne Berura 493:13; Kitzur Shulchan Aruch 122:15.

never get to be a rabbi in America!" The final word goes to Yehoshua ben Gamla. After being appointed Rosh Sanhedrin, he confessed that, "Before I accepted this office, if anyone had suggested it to me, I would have tied him up in front of a lion." Is this an admission of humility? Yes, and no, for he goes on to say, "But now that I have this office, if anyone were to ask me to step down, I would pour a pitcher of boiling water on him!" In other words, I can't help you!

He's mine – no, mine!

Q **How could Leah and Rachel, sisters, marry the same man? Isn't that prohibited? How did they get along?**

The familial tension in the Torah is *not* Oedipal; in other words, Jews don't agree with the Greek myth that siblings are *always* the cause of family stress. Yet, it's true. In the case of Leah and the "blue-eyed and golden-haired" Rachel, relations are strained. They not only enter a marriage forbidden in the Torah ("Do not marry a woman as a rival to her sister and uncover her nakedness in the other's lifetime"), but, as co-wives, find themselves in an untenable position, suffused with envy ("When Rachel saw that she had borne Jacob no children, she became envious of her sister; while Leah complained: 'You have taken away my husband!'"). So how did this union happen? The rabbis give several explanations. One is timing. Our forefathers only kept the mitzvos in the land of Israel, and not in *chutz la'aretz* (in this case, in Haran), which is why Abraham could serve his guests mixed meat-milk meals. The next is meta-spiritual. This marriage law was suspended by Divine sanction in order to allow the future progeny, the twelve tribes of Israel, to emerge. Jewish mystics argue that the necessary characteristics of the twelve boys came about *only* via a cosmic merger of Rachel's physical self (*alma d'itgalya*), combined with Leah's spirituality (*alma d'itkasya*). The Ramban then adds a reason of fear: both sisters knew that whoever didn't marry Jacob would end up with Esau; so God, the Ultimate *Shadchan*, saved them by letting them both marry "the better man." Jewish history has the final say! After ten of the Tribes are lost, *only two* sons remain, one *each* from Rachel (Benjamin) and Leah (Judah).[15]

15. Leviticus 18:18; Genesis 18:8; 39:1, 30:15; Gur Arye, Tikune Zohar 40.

Hair covering

Q Must a married woman always have her hair covered?

No, only outside her home. However, even though a Jewish woman who fails to do so forfeits her *kesuba* (marriage contract) and should technically be divorced, the halachic standards today accept the reality that many sincere wives erroneously believe they are not required to cover their hair; therefore the husband cannot initiate a *get* because his wife is acting in ignorance, and not by willful disregard for Jewish law. Are divorced or widowed women required to cover their hair? Yes, although some authorities differ, on the basis that it is a rabbinic and not a Biblical obligation.[16]

Halachic hour

Q How long is a "halachic hour"?

"One twelfth" of the day. Well, how long is "a day" for Jewish law purposes? From seventy-two minutes before sunrise until fifty minutes after sunset. The length of a halachic hour therefore varies according to the season – longer in the summer, when days have more sunlight, and shorter in the winter.

Halloween

Q Is collecting candy on Halloween a harmless pastime?

No. Unlike Thanksgiving, the "holiday" of Halloween has its origins in the pagan Celtic autumnal festival of Samhain, a sinister day on which the devil invoked divinations of resurrection, calling on a weird litany of "dead souls, ghosts, witches, hobgoblins, and demons." In the Middle Ages, even the Vicar of Rome tried (unsuccessfully) to counteract Halloween's heretical cult by initiating *All Saints Day* on October 30–November 1. Yes, I know. The majority of those who collect candy and go trick-or-treating do so with

---

16. Mishne Berura 75:14; Biur Halacha; Iggeros Moshe, Orach Chayim 4:112, 75:2, Even HaEzer 1:114, 1:57; Machazeh Eliyahu 118–120.

no religious motives; however, the Rama forbids Jewish participation. Well, what if your non-Jewish neighbor's child comes a' knocking? In the spirit of *eva* (good neighborliness), smile, and give the kid a candy![17]

Hester panim

Q What does this mean?

During his final farewell speech, given in song (perhaps the world's first Soul Symphony), Moses is given a glimpse of the future. In a few, brief sentences, an acrimonious God, reacting to a befuddled generation of Jews (*dor ikesh u'ftaltol*) who had flirted with "unfamiliar" demon-gods (*hadashim mikarov ba'u*) "whom your fathers did not know" (*lo se'arum avoseichem*), opens a startling Pandora's box of the sorrow and anguish, woe and distress, depression and vexation that await His people ("I will heap evils upon them, I will consume them"). In fact, *the* most ambiguous of all teasers takes only six words (*Eino yachol liros es Panai*, "No one can see My Face"), a warning that there will come times during the history of Israel (such as the incomprehensible Holocaust), when God will be *Deus absconditus*, an absent ("hidden") *El Mistater* who purposefully conceals (*hester panim*) His ways from us mere mortals. The Midrash extrapolates from this Torah portion the traditional words of hope ("His work is perfect, His ways are just") used during painful episodes (at gravesides, in eulogies, etc.), timed to coincide with Hosea's urgent call ("Return, O Israel, to God!") on *Shabbas Shuva*, the "Sabbath of Repentance," a special Shabbas that falls between Rosh Hashana and Yom Kippur.[18]

---

17. Yore Deah 147:4–7; 178:1.
18. Rabbi Elimelech bar Shaul, Maarechei Lev, 2; Deuteronomy 31:17, 32:4.

I

Insurance fraud

Q I run a car repair shop. My customers always want me to include claims for damages that are covered by their policy. Can I?

No. This is a classic example of "thievery," and any proceeds you receive must be returned.[1]

Intoxication

Q If smoking and drinking are so bad, why do I see so many orthodox Jews smoking and drinking?

Judaism, based on the principle of *shmiras haguf*, the prevention of bodily harm, differentiates between smoking (full abstinence) and drinking, with which it has no problem, unless it is excessive. Unfortunately, many Jews smoke, but so far alcoholism is not rampant in orthodox Jewish communities (and each year more rabbis speak out against boys going overboard on Purim and Simchas Torah). In fact, the Torah identifies wine as the source of Shabbas and *yom tov* joy, and associates its use with happy life-cycle events ("Wine gladdens the heart of man"), even as the Prophets raged against the sin of wine (Isaiah blamed "strong drink" for causing certain Prophets and

---

1. Shulchan Aruch, Choshen Mishpat 348:1, 359:1.

priests to misbehave). Our rabbis trace Jewish sobriety to the lessons of Noah and his vineyard, causing the witty Yiddishists to conclude, *shikker iz a goy*, "only gentiles get drunk!"[2]

Is there a doctor in the house?

Q Are professional doctors mentioned in the Torah?

No, not explicitly; however, if you're looking for diseases and sicknesses, there's no shortage. The Torah talks about apoplectic fits and fevers (intermittent, bilious, inflammatory), paralysis, leprosy, blindness, inflammation, dysentery, sunstroke, epilepsy, diarrhea, and a slew of skin rashes – not to mention attacks of madness and melancholy.

Images

Q Why can't Jews have images?

The Torah rejects all forms of physical worship, graven images, holy relics or man-made symbols, preferring actions and beliefs. One of the first acts of the first Jew (Abraham) was to smash idols that were "religious," and the greatest collective sin of the Jewish people was building a calf of gold.

It's mine, all mine!

Q Am I right? There's no word in Hebrew for "possession"?

Not quite, but you're close. Hebrew has no expression for the English equivalent of "to have." That's why, if an Israeli wants to say "I have," he or she says it in a roundabout way: *yesh li*, "it is to me." The difference is deliberate! The Torah only related to "possessions" in their use for specific holy purposes, not with the "object" itself *per se*; in other words, money, for example, was only as good as its ability to be spread around amongst the poor and needy.

---

2. Psalms 104:15; Judges 9:13, Ecclesiastes 10:19.

= Isaac and blindness =

Q Is the fact that Isaac was blind significant?

Yes. It is a deprivation of an important sense, a tragic personal event that coincides with his family's disintegration. How did he go blind, and when? No one knows. One Midrash traces it to the smoke of the neighborhood's idolatrous practices; another Midrash refuses to accept his blindness as a "medical" (physical) fact, claiming that the patriarch, helpless in old age and facing a confrontational, dysfunctional family, retreated into a self-inflicted "spiritual" (emotional) blindness. The rabbis of the Talmud described his status as *sagei nahor*, "full of light," akin to the temporary loss of sight a Jew experiences when covering his eyes during *Sh'ma*, trying to better focus on God's presence.

= In the beginning... =

Q Is there any special significance to *Bereishis*, the very first word of the Torah?

Since Judaism accords deep significance to every letter, word and phrase in the Torah, even if seemingly superfluous, many a Torah scholar has had a field day with the symbolic exegesis (*remez*) of the first Torah portion. The word *Bereishis* seems simple to explicate. It comes from *b'kadmin*, which means "genesis" or "beginning," but as *the* sole originator, the Mother of all Words, serving as a prelude to the entire Torah, it has naturally attracted intense scrutiny from an army of Torah scholars. The Hebrew root of *Bereishis*, writes Rav Samson Raphael Hirsch, is *bara*, a Chaldean word which means "health" or "outside" (taken from the traditional expression "*Bereishis bara*"), indicating that "bringing something out into the open" was a healthy spiritual exercise, in the spirit of ben Sira's advice: if one has health, he has everything! The mystic *Zohar* expanded the center root *rosh* ("head") to *reishis*, and then linked it to *b'chochma* ("with wisdom"), a derivative of *b'kadmin*, in order to infuse the first Torah portion with a specific egocentric function: that the Jewish people's relevance hinges on wisdom obtained by their continuous commitment to Torah. To Rav Tzvi Hirsch Meisels (*Veitzener Rav*), *Bereishis* is an acronym for *bris eish*, a Covenant of

Fire, implying that each Judaic heart, mind and psyche carries within it a Jewish spark (the *pintele Yid*) just waiting to connect, to help "shed a light," and ignite the People of Israel into an aspiring "light unto the nations."

Interior decorating

Q Was furniture important to the Jews of the Bible?

Sure! Interior decorating was a give-away for class. Since most Jews slept on floor mats or on animal-skin covered benches, beds were considered a sign of great wealth. Well-made beds, considered the epitome of luxury ("I have covered my bed with colored linens from Egypt. I have perfumed my bed with myrrh, aloes and cinnamon"). When he wanted to criticize the rich for being "idle," the eighth-century prophet Amos couched his complaints in terms of beds and linen: "You lie on beds inlaid with ivory and lounge on your couches!" Pillow customs varied. Jews preferred goatskin pillows stuffed with wool or feathers. Egyptians preferred raised pillows, used as head supports. The Assyrians liked low, soft pillows. The other sign of wealth was a dining table. Saul had one, and the Queen of Sheba was impressed with King Solomon's extravagant table. The "ordinary" Jews would simply sit or recline on the floor on animal skins or straw mats, or on wooden boards, passing a common tray around. Whenever the Torah refers to a "table," it's not necessarily a table as we understand a table to be. Instead, it is often used in a metaphoric sense to indicate the owner's hospitality.[3]

Infallibility

Q Are our rabbis or rebbes infallible?

No, you are mixing us up with that other religion. The concept of human infallibility doesn't exist in a Torah that goes out of its way to reveal *tzadikim* as ordinary, frail, human beings, warts and all, men who can succumb to sin at any time (and often do). The Torah contemplates errors by

---

3. I Samuel 19:15–16, 20:29, 28:23; II Samuels 4:7, 9:7; Proverbs 7:16–17; Amos 3:12; 6:4; I Kings 10:5; Psalms 23.

its rabbinic couriers (even Moses erred), which is why there were specific communal sacrifices (*par he'elem davar shel tzibur*) for leadership mistakes. Look in Tractate Horiyot: it is dedicated to what must be done when the rabbinate rules in error. To infuse confidence in their pronouncements, God gracefully promises, *Elokim nitsav beadas kel,* that He will try to help the Sages in all their deliberations.[4]

Inheritance

Q Can I bequeath everything I own to the poor?

Sure, I'll send you my address! Actually, it depends. If you are giving to charity in order to deny your own children, then you cannot. If you die without naming any beneficiaries, Jewish law automatically gives your assets to your children, because it's forbidden to ignore natural heirs. Parents who exclude sons are called "outright sinners"! You can't even show favoritism between sons, good and bad. Why not? Because you don't know God's plan. Perhaps your "bad" son's grandchildren are destined to be more worthy than the grandchildren from your favorite son![5]

I just don't get it!

Q I read the *Zohar* but haven't got a clue what I'm reading. Am I missing something?

To understand the esoteric doctrines of the *Zohar* one must be able to study the Torah using one of three hermeneutic methods. *Temura,* which means "change," in which each letter of the Hebrew alphabet is interchanged with another (e.g., *aleph,* the first letter, becomes *lamed* by interchange with the twelfth, or the last letter replaces the first, and so on); *gematria,* which calculates the numerical values of words via their letters and matches them with the numerical values of other words or letters; and *Notarikon* (Latin

---

4. Leviticus 4:13–21; Teshuvos Hage'onim, Harkaby, 394; Guide for the Perplexed 3:14.
5. Iggeros Moshe, Choshen Mishpat 2:50; Maharam, Shibolei Haleket, II, 132; Shulchan Aruch, Choshen Mishpat 252:2.

for *notarius*) which involves reconstructing a word by using the initials or all the letters to form a sentence.

Internet, not?

Q Some rabbis have banned the Internet. What should I do?

If they are "your" rabbis, you must follow their rulings. However, there are dozens of reputable rabbinic teachers who are effectively using the Internet and e-mail to spread Torah knowledge (complying with an Isaiah vision, *Yagdil Torah v'ya'adir*, "He magnifies the Torah and makes it glorious"). And yet, like other forms of entertainment, the net must be used in moderation and responsibility, and not become an undiscriminating and obsessive pastime.[6]

Ich lern

Q What does this mean?

Only amongst Jews in the Torah world can someone answer the question, "What are you doing?" with *Ich lern*, which simply means, "I'm learning." Yes, it *is* an incomplete answer, but complete enough not to have to ask *what* is being studied. The answer is obvious: Torah, a term derived from the root *yud, reish, heh,* which means "to teach" or "to direct," thus making it, in Rabbi Berel Wein's words, the "Manufacturer's Instruction Manual of Life."

Is it edible?

Q Is all vegetarian food kosher? Can I eat in a vegetarian restaurant?

The term "vegetarian" is a misnomer even for vegetarians, and more so for the kosher consumer. Kosher-vegetarian still requires the absence of *fleishig* dishes, etc.; and even if a non-kosher vegetarian restaurant were truly vegetarian, it would still be unacceptable. Why? Because of other halachic is-

---

6. Isaiah 42:5.

sues, ranging from Shabbas, the proper checking of fruit and vegetables for insects, *bishul akum* ("non-Jewish cooking"), the appearance of eating in a non-kosher establishment, etc.

Incense

Q Why is there no incense in *shuls*, considering that it was used in the Temple?

Incense was so popular in those days that the family of Avtinas, responsible for its preparation, was severely criticized by the rabbis for keeping its "sweet savior recipe" to themselves. The *siddur* still contains a rabbinic attempt (*pittum haketores*) to reconstruct the incense ritual. The custom was abandoned after the destruction of the Temple; and yet the words of the Psalmist ("Let my prayer be set before You as incense") continued to ring in certain Jewish circles. In Eastern Europe, some Chassidim smoked pipes, or perfumed cigarettes, before *davening* (rumor has it that the Baal Shem Tov even said a *bracha* before smoking his *lulke*), convinced that sparks of tobacco helped one's spiritual elevation, akin to the mystical elevation provided by the aroma and aura of the incense in the Temple. The closest thing to incense in Judaism today is the smelling of spices at the end of Shabbas (*havdala*). Its purpose is mystical: that the fragrant odors help revive the joy in the Jew after his "extra" Shabbas soul has departed and comforting that same soul which is headed for the fires of hell. The havdala box became known as *hadas livsamim*, because the myrtle *hadas* became the most popular "sniffing" spice in the Middle Ages.[7]

Inscriptions

Q Can I put an inscription on a tombstone?

Yes, but it's best to restrict it to three facts, ironically, over which a person has *no control*! The Hebrew name of the deceased, and the Hebrew birth and death dates. Before the name put a *peh, nun* (Hebrew initials for "Here lies buried"). After the name put the letters *tav, nun, tzadi, bet, heh* (Hebrew

---

7. K'ritot 6a; Psalms 141:2; Pesachim 112b.

for "May his/her soul be bound up in the bond of life." Remember: keep it modest, and if you want to use a symbol, stick to either a *mogen dovid* or *menorah*. No statuettes, no photos allowed. When should a headstone be erected? Customs differ, but it's best to do so as soon as possible, either after *shiva*, or near the first anniversary.

IRS

Q Do I have to pay income taxes?

Yes. The Torah has a series of different taxes ("tithing") for different reasons. Some taxes were directed towards the Sanctuary; some toward helping others. The purpose was not just to raise funds for worthy causes, but to instruct both intellectually (*L'maan tilmad*, "so that you may learn") and emotionally (*L'yirah es Hashem*, "to revere the Lord"). Why? So that even during the time of earning money, the Jew was already thinking of how to disburse it, Jewishly. The payment of income taxes rests on both halachic (*dina d'malchusa dina*, "The law of the government is law") and moral principles (the prohibition of *chillul Hashem*, "desecration of God's name"). It is also against the Torah to obtain benefits to which one is not entitled, including the benefits that come from falsifying government forms. Although Jewish law considers non-payment of taxes a form of government theft, it allows legal loopholes. Why? Because, as Tevye would confide to his horse, "It's no mitzva to overpay!"[8]

Is seeing believing?

Q Do you have to believe *before* you observe, or can you observe without yet believing?

Yes, to the latter. Moses' initial encounter with God at a burning thorn bush in Midian, one unconsumed by its own flames, helps him rediscover the legacy of Abraham. Why is this site of desolation chosen for such a revelatory experience? To teach, says the Midrash, that seeing-*is*-believing;

---

8. Choshen Mishpat 369:6; Deuteronomy 14:22–23; Gittin 10b; Deuteronomy Rabba 3:5.

that God can be both found and felt in the unexpected, that no place on earth is too humble or too low to receive the spirit of Godliness. "To see" became the title of a Torah portion (*Re'eh*), one that laid out "blessings and curses" in such a way that it became clear: the Jews' future well-being was not predicated on an ability to feel, smell, hear (*sh'ma*) or listen, but to "see," as in "to grasp" and "comprehend" that behavioral choices have consequences. The Sifrei, an important early Midrashic work, was blunt: "If you observe a little, you will end up hearing much!" These two verbs ("observe and hear") sum up a Judaism that grows on you – that through beginning to observe, you come to believe.

Ink

Q **Can we use ink to write a *Sefer Torah*?**

Yes. Ink (Greek for "a branding iron") is even mentioned in the *Tanach*. Baruch, Jeremiah's secretary, when asked how he recorded the Prophet's words, replied, "He pronounced them to me, and I wrote them with ink in the book." Originally, carbon ink was used, but the early scribes didn't like it: it washed off easily, and clogged the quill. In the sixth century, iron-gall liquid ink mixed with minerals was a big hit with Jewish scribes. Why? Because it penetrated the parchment better.

It's about Time!

Q **How many years from Creation to the Exodus?**

A grand total of 2,448 years. When was the Temple built in relation to Creation? The year 832 BCE. How do we know? Add 480 years to 2,448 to arrive at 2,928, then deduct 2,928 from 3,760, the year the Common Era began.

Illustrated 'n' illuminated

Q **What motivated illustrators to illustrate Torah texts and manuscripts?**

Illiteracy. The illustrations (*scriptoria*) were supposed to literally "shed light" on their related texts (which is why they used exquisite bright colors and precious metals that "glittered," such as gold) for those who couldn't read. Sometimes sophisticated miniature pictures were drawn into the text's letters themselves. In the Middle Ages, drawings of the author were added; so, in the thirteenth century we see decorative likenesses of King David, Solomon, Joshua, and, in the introduction of *Sefer Isaiah*, a sketch of the prophet being sawed in half. Did they think Isaiah was a magician? No. It was a nod to the fact that he had died, yet lived!

Intuition, to spare

Q Are Jewish women more "spiritual" than men?

Yes. Jewish tradition traces this greater spiritual enthusiasm to Eve, and claims that if *she* had heard God's "do-not-eat" command directly, instead of through Adam, her innate spiritual instinct would have prevented them both from straying. Our rabbis endow women with a greater degree of *bina* (intuition, understanding, and intelligence), in that woman was "built," not "formed." The Hebrew roots of *build* and *bina* have the same consonants. The Talmud has no problem with wise women (the halachic opinions of Berurya, wife of Rabbi Meir, sometimes overruled those of her male contemporaries), and Rabbi Akiva's son's *kesuba* (marriage contract) obligates his wife to teach her husband Torah. A Talmudic adage: when a pious man marries a wicked woman, the man becomes wicked, but when a wicked man marries a pious woman, the man becomes pious![9]

Is it theft?

Q Can I copy and distribute pages from *seforim*?

The spirit of copyright protection is commercial, not educational (i.e., to prevent resale for a profit); thus Rav Eliezer Waldenberg (*Tzitz Eliezer*) allows it for purposes of *chinuch*, as long as credit is given to the author and source. Others (*Shach*) claim that there is no concept of "stealing" when it

---

9. Exodus Rabba 28:2; Genesis 2:22; 2:7.

comes to *divrei Torah*. Thus, if you see a *Sefer Torah* and want to use it for *leyning* or learning, the owner is powerless to stop you![10]

Israelis or Hebrews?

Q Which is more correct?

I don't know, but perhaps Moses gives us an inkling. When he addresses Pharaoh (a foreigner), he refers to his people as "Hebrews," but when he speaks to them directly, he fondly calls them "Israel." The term "Hebrew" (*Ivri*) appears for the first time during Abraham's battle with several kings. What does the word mean? It is related to the root meaning of "to go over," or "to go across," thus, a "Hebrew" was someone who "went from place to place," like Abraham, a nomad, a wanderer.

---

10. Baba Basra 21b; Deuteronomy 19:14; Chasam Sofer, Choshen Mishpat 2, 79; Beis Yitzchak, Yore Deah 2:75; Baba Metzia 34a; Baba Basra 63a; Iggeros Moshe, Orach Chayim 4:40–19; Beis Yitzchak, Yore Deah 2:75; Shach, Yore Deah 165:8.

J

Jews 'n' trees

Q That all Jews are responsible for each other is a famous rabbinic adage; but are trees also accountable to one another?

Apparently, yes. In a startling discovery, scientists have found evidence that when a tree is physically injured or is being infested with worms and bugs, it responds by changing its chemical balance by secreting a chemical substance called *phenol* which acts as a protective covering. This poisonous protective kills the worms, and keeps others away. When this happens, all adjacent healthy trees respond to the warning in the same way, vaccinating themselves against similar danger. This vegetative protection against a "common enemy" contributes to the long-term survival of the species as a whole – just like Jews who are repeatedly commanded to be concerned with the health of the larger Jewish community in which they live.

Jabbok vs. Jacob

Q Why can't Jews eat thigh bone meat from kosher animals?

We are probably the only people named after a disability; and Jewish law even extends the handicap of a limp by making it forbidden (for the descendants of Noah, as well) to eat not just an animal's thigh muscle "on the socket of the hip," but anything (nerve-sinew-tendon) through which the sciatic nerve runs. Jacob's wound, the result of an all-night struggle ("wrestle") with a messenger of God on the banks of the River Jabbok, caused his name to be changed to *Israel*, and motivated Rabbi Eleazar to warn that it's not safe for Jews to go out at night, alone, in the dark, when there's no moon. The *Zohar* claims the weather conditions were perfect for Lilith, the evil night-temptress, to seduce – i.e., "wrestle with" – Jacob. The Rambam is convinced that Jacob was wrestling with himself, the darker side of his own being. Did the wound heal? Yes. By the time Jacob and Esau meet, the "sun rose upon him, limping on his hip, and healed him"; however, by keeping the episode alive through a name (Israel) and religious practices (*kashrus*), the emblem (*gid hanefesh*) of a patriarch's struggle remains timeless.[1]

Jews as "letters"

Q Is it true that every Jew is supposed to represent a letter in the Torah?

The Baal Shem Tov revolutionized Jewish history with a simple all-consuming passionate philosophy: "To pull a friend from the mud, don't hesitate to get down and dirty." On his thirty-sixth birthday (18 Elul, 1734), the founder of Chassidism announced a new movement (*Chassidus*) based on an old but neglected Torah principle of Rabbi Akiva: *ahavas Yisrael, ahavta l'reiacha*, "love of our fellow," which included a belief that every Jew resembled a Torah letter, and the Jew who "failed" to be a Jew harmed his people in a way similar to the missing letter that disqualified and made a *Sefer Torah* unfit for use (*pasul*). This is based on the tradition that the number of Jews who left Egypt equals the number of Hebrew letters in the Torah; and so our Jewish mystics expanded the letters of "*Yisrael*" into several acrostics, such as *Yesh shishim riboah l'Torah*, "there are six hundred thousand letters in the Torah," and *Yesh shishim riboah anashim l'Yisrael*, "there are six hundred thousand Jews."

---

1. Genesis 32:23–31, 33; Zohar 1, 169b; Rambam, Guide for the Perplexed 2:42.

= Just another Yiddishe mama? ==========

Q How come we never hear about Jesus' mother? Surely she's not to blame for the religion that turned her son into a phony messiah many years after her death?

You're right. She was just another first-century Jewish mother, a hard-working daughter of Israel trying to raise a family in Nazareth, an eyewitness to the brave Galilean hero Hezekiah who led an uprising (53 BCE) against Rome's puppet-ruler, Herod. What do we know about her? From Jewish history, nothing (although we can assume, because her son adhered to Jewish law, that she ran a "Jewish" home). From non-Jewish sources we're told that: she was born to very elderly parents (like Isaac), her mother died in childbirth, she had a cousin (Elizabeth), she was a vegetarian, raised in the Temple (like Samuel), married within the faith (Joseph), and after her son's brutal murder by crucification at the hands of Pontius Pilate, moved into a Jewish convent in Jerusalem with other Jewish women. The problem is not with her *per se*, but the incongruous mother of all paradoxes, the adjective "immaculately conceived" (*pre partum, in partu,* and *post partum*) that the Roman Catholic Church attached to her name in 1864, the "Virgin" Mary (the *goyishe* version of her true name, Miriam, or *Maryam*, in Aramaic, after Moses' sister), and her idolatrous place in Church theology, as an *Isis*-type Magna Mater, "Mother of God." Where did this non-Jewish distortion of scriptural virginity come from? An Isaiah term, *almah*, is its genesis, with Christians adopting this verse ("Behold an *almah* shall conceive, and bear a son, and shall cause his name Immanuel [which means, God is with us]") as a supposedly prophetic innuendo to the "Virgin Mary" (Jerome's fourth-century Latin version of the Torah translates it as *virgo*). Rashi translates *almah* as "virgin" (as do the third-century rabbis of the Greek-Torah version, *Septuagint,* using the term *parthenos*); but the Radak and other scholars claim it simply means a "young, unmarried girl," and that the correct Hebrew word is *betulah* (the feminine version of *elem*).[2]

---

2. Isaiah 7:14.

Jewish partridge

Q Is there such a food?

Yes. Dating back to the eleventh century, it has, naturally, a heavy North African-Arab influence. Jewish partridge included eggplants stirred with couscous and semolina flour, served with almond paste. You want the recipe? Its cavity was stuffed with almonds, pine nuts, oil, eggs, and garum sauce (courtesy of fermented fish), coriander, cinnamon, pepper and nard, an aromatic herb. Got that? You then place it all over red-hot embers in a heavy clay pot and stew with a sauce of oil, vinegar, mint, citron leaves, salt and murri, a pungent paste. And *voilà*! You have Jewish partridge! But wait! You have to serve it correctly, with a garnish of hard-boiled egg yolks, sprinkled with pepper, cinnamon and sugar.

Judaism's Number One enemy

Q Who is Judaism's major enemy?

In the abstract, it's the nation of Amalek, the eponymous ancestor of all evil, wickedness, racism, and anti-Semitism, seared into Jewish history's consciousness as the first enemy encountered after the crossing of the Red Sea. And they were not just the first, but also the *successful* first, wreaking continuous disaster and losses, attacking the Jews from the rear, which allowed them to direct their hostility against the Judaic weak and tired. In a paradox, the Torah demands that Jews "erase the memory of Amalek from under heaven, thou shall not forget" – ordering the Jew to simultaneously erase and yet never forget. Do we know Amalek's identity? Yes. He was born to the concubine Timna, sister of Lotan, son of Seir the Horite (where Esau lived). Who was the father? Eliphaz, the son of Esau's son. In a startling statement, the rabbis of the Talmud, in an extraordinarily courageous accusation, blame our patriarchs for the birth of Amalek. After asking why Timna would marry Eliphaz, they give us an astonishing reason: "Timna desired to become a proselyte, so she went to Abraham, Isaac and Jacob, but they did not accept her. So she went and became a concubine to Eliphaz, the son of Esau, saying: 'I would rather be a servant to this people than a mistress of another nation.'" From her, Amalek was descended, who afflicted Israel. Why so? Because "they should not have repulsed her!"[3]

Just the facts, ma'am!

Q What was the cause of death that killed the students of Akiva?

We're not exactly sure, nor do we know the death toll (possibly 300, 12,000, 24,000 or 48,000), nor the reasons why. The Talmud says they died because they did not treat each other with respect; but the Midrash blames the envy they had for each other (either way, they surely don't qualify as *groyse tzadikim*). Isn't this disrespectful? No, even Rabbi Akiva is highly critical of his disciples, warning a future generation, "be not like them!" Our rabbis try to link the punishmental manner of their death to their sin, claiming that the cause of death (*eskera*, a throat ailment that resembles croup) was that they (mis)used their throats to revile, slander, and envy one another. The question is obvious: why recall *their* deaths by refraining from marriages, when, reminds Asher, this "honor was not conceded to any Patriarch or Prophet?" I don't know; but this is why many Torah historians trace this custom of "no weddings" not to Akiva but to the tragedies of the Crusades in the Middle Ages, when some of the most horrific slaughters of Jews occurred during the *omer* period.[4]

Justice, justice

Q Why does the text repeat "justice" twice?

The Torah's psychologically profound sensitivity to justice is emphasized by its famous phrase, *Tzedek, tzedek tirdof*, "Justice, justice shall you pursue," a doubling of "justice" that has given rise to many midrashim. Why "justice" twice? Bachya ben Asher saw the doubling of "justice" to mean, "Justice, whether to your profit or loss, whether in word or action, whether to Jew or non-Jew!" In other words, Jews are to pursue justice by just means, by giving equal justice to all, by ensuring that the appointed judges and

---

3. Deuteronomy 25:19; Genesis 36:2, 12; Sanhedrin 99b.
4. Yevamos 62b; Kesubos 63a; Nedarim 50a.

officers are beyond reproach (i.e., *Shoftim v'shotrim titen l'cha*, "Judges and enforcers you shall give yourself," fit to judge justly). The Torah views justice by itself as insufficient, and demands *mishpat tzedek*, "righteous justice," using two linguistic mechanisms: a powerful verb, "shall *pursue*" instead of simply commanding us to "*do* justice," or "*be* just"; and the use of *loshen yeserah*, "redundant language," by repeating "justice" twice in order to emphasize that real righteousness is a result of expanded righteousness. The next question is obvious: what's the difference between "justice" and "righteous justice"? The latter, say our rabbis, is a "love-tempered" judgment, fueled by compassion and mercy (based on the two major names for God: *Elokim*, symbolizing justice, and *Hashem*, representing love and mercy) – an acknowledgment that everybody, even criminals, has a spark of Godliness in him!

Jeremiads

Q Is this grim expression of Jewish origin?

Yes. Of the many Hebrew prophets, it was Jeremiah's reputation as a gloomy doomsayer that gave birth, in seventeenth-century Christian Europe, to the unflattering term "jeremiads." This word comes from the French *jérémiade*, to describe chronic *kvetchers*. Even the rabbis of the Talmud describe him (hyperbolically) as being "all destruction," in contrast to the "all consolation" approach of Isaiah, whose inspiring words became the *haftoras* for many *Shabbasos*.

Juries

Q Is trial by jury a Jewish concept?

No, but the number of jurors ("twelve good men and true") is based on the twelve officers appointed by King Solomon (this act being itself inspired by the "twelve" tribes of Israel). The term *jury* stems from the French, to "take an oath." Why do Jews always seem to gravitate towards social justice issues? It's no accident that the Five Books of Moses are known simply as "the Law." If Judaism has a passion for anything as a religion, it is for justice, that right prevail over wrong, that the perpetrators of evil must be punished, and that those administering justice be wise, just, honest, skillful, and (most important of all) compassionate! The concept that "justice is blind" implies impartiality, no prejudice nor favoritism between rich and poor, mighty and downtrodden (the Egyptians took this concept literally, and their courts met in a darkened chamber, so judges could only hear and not see the parties; that is why the famous Old Bailey statue of justice in London's Central Criminal Court is literally blindfolded).

Judah Who?

Q Did Judah use the name Maccabee?

Probably not; it's more likely that he simply called himself by his real name, Yehudah ben Matisyahu, Judah the son of Mattathias the *Cohen*. The *Maccabee* name came later; any additional adopted name would have been a reference to Chashmon, which was the name of his great-great-grandfather, and of the village of Cheshmon, from where we get Hasmonean, the rabbinic reference. Does Maccabee appear in the Jewish texts? No. It's found in the non-Jewish *Books of Maccabees*. Why is Judah's name absent from rabbinic writings? I don't know, perhaps for the same reason that Moses is omitted from the Haggada: to prevent a Judah-cult from arising.[5]

Jacob or Israel?

Q Why does the Torah switch back and forth between these two names?

Israel or Jacob? The former is symbolic of the "struggle" between man and angel, its essence is thus *ongoing*; in contrast, Jacob's name remains *fixed*, on the threshold of life, its essence a reminder of the potential to improve oneself. The Hebrew root of *Yaakov* (Jacob) also forms "skill," a necessary quality of life, in contrast to the root of *Yisrael* (Israel), which connotes "honor, nobility, virtuousness," the spiritual results of overcoming adversity by a Torah way of life. Unlike Abraham and Sarah, whose name changes were instituted via only one letter (*heh*), Jacob's is a totally new name al-

---

5. Joshua 15:27; Middos 1:6; Shabbas 21b.

together. The contrast is dramatic – from one word, "Jacob," derived from *akev*, a "heel" (suggesting a "supplanter") to "Israel," derived from *sar*, a "prince" (suggesting superiority). The old Jacob attempted to succeed by deceitfully seizing blessings; the new Israel intends to earn his kudos and glory through his own efforts. The question is obvious: Jews *never* refer to Abraham by his previous name (Avram), so why is it OK to use either Jacob or Israel? The Vilna Goan (*Gra*) had the answer: Abraham's was an instantaneous, irreversible transformation, "with immediate effect (*ve'hoyo*)," whereas Jacob's came only "later" (*yihye*); thus either name is permissible, depending on its context.

J.C., the unmentionable

Q Does Jesus appear in Jewish texts?

Yes. The Talmud, written several hundred years later, refers to him as *Yeshu* (probably short for Yeshua, but we're not sure). One source even tries to trace his heresy on an insensitive Jewish *tanna* ("teacher") identified as Yehoshua ben Pirhiya, who turned him off Judaism ("Always let the left hand reject and the right hand draw close, not like Rabbi Yehoshua Ben Pirhiya, who pushed Jesus [away] with two hands!"). How credible is this theory? Not at all. The timeline is wrong, set during the era of Alexander Yannai, who ruled in the early first century BCE, whereas Jesus was not even born until the start of the Common Era. Yet its import lies in the fact that our rabbis were willing to learn from their educational errors. Why, historically, is this name barely mentioned in Jewish circles, either in speech or in texts? Jews detest Jesus because of the horrific, horrendous and horrifying anti-Semitism committed in his name. Jews for Jesus? Is this possible? No. It's the mother of all oxymorons. Ignore them!

Job security

Q Can I approach a worker at another company and offer him a job?

No. Employers are not allowed to lure employees from their jobs, unless other potential employers are *already* actively recruiting the person; and the reverse: you cannot accept an unsolicited offer for a job if it means another Jew will lose his job (unless it's well known that you're dissatisfied, or you were only hired on a "short-term" basis to begin with).[6]

Joshua's wife

Q Did Joshua ever marry?

I don't know. There's not a single reference in the entire Book of Joshua of a marriage, or even a family life. Yet the notion of a bachelor status for a leader of Jews seems bizarre, thus the Midrash goes searching for a "Mrs. Joshua" – and suggests Rahab, a harlot who housed the twelve spies, of which Joshua was one (perhaps that is why, during the battle of Jericho, the first Jewish war, her family is the only one saved from the wrath of the Jews). But a harlot?! Maybe not: Rashi translates her description (*isha zona*) as an "innkeeper," one who feeds people. Even so, the question then becomes: since she belonged to a forbidden Canaanite nation, how could a Jewish leader marry her? According to the Radak, she and her family had converted before the Torah's prohibition of not intermarrying with "the seven nations" took effect. Now that we've located a wife, how about children? They must have had some, since Joshua's progeny includes such famous descendants as the prophets Jeremiah and Hulda.[7]

Just judges?

Q I'm confused. Were Jewish judges just judges?

No. Several judges were chosen not for their judicial or religious qualities, but for other charismatic traits, such as leading their people into battle (e.g., Ehud and Gideon, who repelled the Moabite, Ammonite, Amalekite and Midianite foreigners). Eventually this military function was assumed by the kings of Israel, and the role of overseeing justice was left to the judiciary branch.

---

6. Choshen Mishpat 237:2, Shulchan Aruch Harav, Hasogas Gevul 12; Teshuvos Alshich 67.
7. Joshua 1, 6:25; Megilla 14b.

K

Kvetching Jews

Q **Are Jews chronic complainers?**

You mean perpetual *kvetchers*? It would seem so! Kvetch comes from *quetschen*, German for "to squeeze," as in the reflexive Yiddish phrase, *Kvetshn zakh*, or *Gebn a kvetsh*, as in, "exert yourself!" Just imagine this! Despite their awe-inspiring brush with God at Mount Sinai, and their stunning leap from abject servitude in Egypt to miraculous freedom, the Jews, cantankerous and querulous, are simply unable to seize their history and destiny. *Vayehi ha'am kemitonenim*, "The people took to complaining bitterly." It's embarrassing, *especially* when the French notice ("The Jews have always been malcontents!" roars the nineteenth-century Bernard Lazare). After His unruly folk loudly accuse Him of "bringing us out into this wilderness to starve to death," God responds with a shower of manna. When they whine about thirst, God responds with water gushing from a rock. When they complain that the water is bitter and undrinkable, God makes it sweet and potable. So, what are the Jews *kvetching* about? They're bored. They're unhappy about their limited culinary pickings. They have suddenly developed a "gluttonous craving" for such Egyptian delicacies as "cucumbers, melons, leeks, onions, garlic, meat, fish." They conveniently forgot what they had for desserts! Hundreds of years of lashes and oppression served up on trays of humiliation!

= *Klotz kashes* =

Q What does this mean?

"Tis better thrice to ask your way," Guiterman's poetry advises, "than even once to go astray!" The art of questioning is at the heart of the Jewish religion, even *Klotz kashes*, Yiddish for the most ridiculous queries of them all! "Who is ashamed to ask," notes Moshe Ibn Ezra, "diminishes in wisdom"; or in the wit of our Yiddishists: "Each wherefore has a therefore!" But even if you fail to find the rationale you seek for a mitzva (*ta'amei hamitzvos*), you're still not exempt from it. "The components of Torah remain the law," writes Rav Samson Raphael Hirsch, "even if we have not discovered the cause and connection of a single one!"

= Kneeling =

Q Isn't kneeling on Yom Kippur a "Christian" activity?

No. The practice of kneeling was common in Biblical times, a defiant "No-one-will-prevent-us-from-acclaiming-the-true-God!" spiritual battle cry. Prostrating one's body to the ground was more than just symbolic; it was a humbling gesture of ultimate submission, a human vassal in front of the King of Kings, an act of self-abasement not just of the mind but the whole body. The Hebrew word for praise is rooted in the term "knee" (the Muslims "borrowed" this expression, and the word "Mosque" refers to a "place of kneeling"). King Solomon knelt during his dedication of the Temple; Daniel knelt thrice daily in prayer, and kneeling played a dramatic role in the Yom Kippur service. Today we prostrate ourselves during the *musaf Aleinu* on Rosh Hashana and Yom Kippur to re-enact the Temple ritual. Why do some Jews place newspapers and tissues (it used to be sand) on the floor before kneeling? To stop their suit pants from getting dirty? No. In order to avert any suspicion that they are bowing down to stone![1]

---

1. Leviticus 26:1.

Keep it short!

Q Are there times when prayer is the wrong response?

Yes. Imagine this scene. The Jews are trapped in tumultuous terror at a place called Pi-Ha'hirot. Behind them are the thundering horse sounds of six hundred well-armed, vengeful Egyptian chariots. Ahead lie the pounding, drowning waves of a Red Sea. Their immediate reaction? Hysterical desperation! They first "cry out to God [*vayitzaku*]" in "panic and prayer," followed by a sarcastic assault against Moses, blaming him for their predicament: "We would rather serve the Egyptians than die in the desert!" A stunned Moses turns to God and pleads for Divine intervention. God's response is unexpected! Stop wasting My time in "lengthy" prayers (*Ma titzak elai?* "Why do you cry out to Me?"). "Go forward," He advises, in the Torah's foremost lesson of survival – take matters in your own hand! The lesson is clear: action always takes precedence over contemplation! But trust in God is insufficient if one lacks the courage to trust in oneself. One Jew (Nachshon ben Aminadav) gets the message. Nachshon's spirit suddenly shifts from passive to active as he bravely steps into "the midst of the sea," causing the waters to split into "a fortress wall" (*homa*) of protection. This single act of faith and ennoblement marches an entire nation forward through a dry seabed, an act that symbolizes the final and full transition of a people from slavery to freedom.

Kalla my world

Q Is God in favor of marriage?

What a dumb question! Marriage was so critical to Jewish continuity that the Torah even carved out a special joyful time of marital (no, *not* martial!) pursuit in the Jewish calendar. The merry Tu b'Av, 15th of Av, is Jewish history's first Torah-sanctioned annual marriage marketplace day, nothing less than *Hitna'ari me'afar kumi*, the "secret" of Jewish regeneration. It is a desire-driven entrepreneurial day of *shadchanus*, "when the maidens come out to the vineyards of Shilo to dance" in the hope of catching the eye of their *bashert* ("destined one"). God's motto became "*Kalla* My World," in line with the tradition that, after Creation, He has kept Himself busy making marriages.

Khazars

Q Is Judah Halevi's famous *Sefer Hakuzari* a work of fact or fiction?

Fiction, yet it accurately described a formerly nomadic Turkish folk (the Khazars) whose belligerent ruling class mass-converted to Judaism around 740 CE, and then established an impressively powerful empire that stretched from the Crimea to the Aral Sea. What caused the conversion? Legend has it that King Bulan was impressed by the convincing arguments made by the Jews in a three-way debate between representatives of Judaism, Christianity and Islam. What happened to Khazar Judaism? After 965 CE, the state began its decline, finally disappearing in 1237 as an ethnic group, courtesy of a wave of savage Mongol invasions.

Kosher

Q Why should God care what we eat? Does it have to do with health?

It is a myth that *kashrus* has to do with health considerations, or that some animals have a level of "uncleanliness," or that we should avoid predatory creatures lest we prey on others, or that we must avoid those creatures that were once worshipped as gods. None of this matters, except in a spiritual manner – i.e., a healthy mind needs a healthy body, and a healthy body comes from approaching everything basic in life, including – no *especially* – eating, in a moral, sanctified fashion. Non-kosher animals are to be avoided, advises Rashi, the classic medieval Torah commentator of commentators, simply because God said so ("You are a people consecrated!"). Why *kashrus*? "To train us to master our appetites!" replies the Rambam (so what's a balanced diet?...a cookie in each hand!). Since what-and-how-we-eat affects character and soul, attention to food was present from Day One, when both God's positive and negative commandments to the First Couple of Eden involved eating ("Eat from all the trees of the garden; do not eat from the Tree of Knowledge"). Does anybody doubt that *kashrus*, by drawing lines of demarcation between Jews and gentiles, has significantly preserved Jewish identity, commitment and history? The discipline of *kashrus* helps the Jew attain a certain spirituality, an armor, so to speak, of self-control against the daily temptations of a "non-kosher" lifestyle.

Kesita

Q What is this?

When Jacob buys a gravesite in Shechem from Hamor's children, he gives them a hundred *kesita*s. How much is a *kesita*? No one knows. In the history of numismatics, "coins" only became a method of payment during the seventh century BCE in Asia Minor. Commercial Biblical transactions were conducted either via units of metal (brass, silver, gold bars), weight (goods and services), or, as in Jacob's case, barter (one *kesita* equaling one sheep).

Kingly priesthood, or priestly kingdom?

Q Are we supposed to take the Torah term "a kingdom of priests" literally?

No. Obviously, not every Jew in the world is a "king" or "priest." And even priests are not kings, nor were kings automatically priests. These are categories originally defined by different tribes. Only the Jews from the tribe of Levi, freed from life's day-to-day concerns, were the predestined "Priests of God," whilst candidates for the post of king only need apply based on genealogy. This changed dramatically with the Hasmonean revolt. At first, the Maccabean Jews kept the tradition of priestly families, until Jonathan, brother of Judah, crossed the halachic red line. By unilaterally crowning himself king *and* priest, he illegally consolidated political and priestly leaderships into one single entity, throwing ambiguity into the Torah's original meaning of a "kingdom of priests." The vagueness had begun. From the original Hebrew phrase, *mamlechet cohanim v'goy kadosh*, the Latin translators produced *regnum sacerdotale*, a "priestly kingdom," whilst the Greeks turned it into *basileion hierateuma kai ethnos hagion*, a "kingly priesthood."[2]

---

2. I Maccabees 2:1; 2:54; Isaiah 61:5; II Samuel 7–11–16; Genesis 49:10.

Klezmer

Q Where does this word come from?

The recent wave of nostalgia for the *krekhs* and *kvetsches* (groans 'n' sobs) of the mix of violin, clarinet, cimbalom, and bass of Eastern European music is a reminder that Jews themselves were once considered walking instruments. Klezmer, a Yiddish term, comes from merging *k'li* ("vessel, instrument") and *zemer* ("song"). The musicians used to metonymically describe themselves as *k'li zmorim*, in that, by singing *together*, in unity, they were performing a semi-sacred task. Jeremiah compared the Jews of Judah to a *k'li rek*, an "empty pot" (for failing to resist King Nebuchadnezzar). In his prayers, the fourth-century Rava referred to himself as "a vessel [*k'li*] full of shame." The Torah calls the holy Temple vessels *k'li kodesh*, and holy books *k'li yakar*, "precious vessels." A major Torah scholar even called himself the *K'li Yakar*!

Kov'ea seuda

Q Can I, or my wife, eat before hearing the shofar on Rosh Hashana?

Yes, if you are weak, elderly, or ill. Otherwise no, if it's a full meal (*kov'ea seuda*). Ah, so what's a "full" meal? Anything more than a *k'beitza* (two to 3.5 ounces) of bread or cake. How about a light snack? It's unclear. Some permit light food (fruit, cheese, rice cereals, etc.) before *tekias shofar*, others actually encourage it and serve a special *kiddush*, yet some object to it strongly. But all agree that drinking (tea, coffee, juice) is permitted. What's the concern? Our rabbis were not worried about food *per se*, but about distraction from the mitzva at hand (some allow eating if a *shomer*, a "guard," is there to remind you when to stop eating!). Inexplicably, the *Shulchan Aruch* prohibits eating before *netilas lulav* and *Megillas Esther*, but says nothing about *tekias shofar*. Your wife? She can eat at any time. Why? Because none of these mitzvos are applicable to Jewish women, since they are all exempted by the "time-sensitive" rule.[3]

---

3. Chasam Sofer, Yore Deah 7; Minchas Yitzchak 5:11; Mishne Berura 235:18, 652:7, 639:15, 692:14; Chayei Adam 119:7; Aruch Hashulchan 431:26; Orach Chayim 286:3, 639:2, 652:2,

Kids, kids and more kids

Q Why do some Jewish families have so many children?

The main reason for large families pertains to religion ("Be fruitful and multiply"). Children, symbols of hope, anticipation, and familial happiness, were "proof" that God had bestowed favor on the family. But if children were a blessing ("a heritage of God"), then the reverse was also true: childlessness was an abnormality ("a childless person is like dead"), and barren women a curse from God. So Jewish law created a halachic exit from marriage if, after ten years, there was no child. Eleazar ben Azariah charged those who "refrain from begetting" with the crime of "impairing the Divine image." Eliezer ben Hyrcanus was uncharacteristically blunt: "Who brings no children into the world is like a murderer!" In 1939, on the eve of the Holocaust, there were more Jews alive than ever before in history. Sixty-five years later, the number is down by a third (from eighteen million to twelve million). Thus credit must be given where credit is due, to those with large families. Jews, being an endangered species (Jewish reproduction rates are less than half those of the world in general, not to mention the catastrophic loss through intermarriage), rely *solely* on birthrate increases to prove Arnold Toynbee wrong in his smug observation, "It seems safe to prophesy that in a hundred years there will be no Jews anywhere!"[4]

Kochba, Simon bar

Q Well, was he the Messiah, or not?

Obviously not. Simon bar Kochba, who eventually became the Prince (*Nasi*) of the Jewish state, led tiny Israel through a series of stunning victories between 135 and 132 BCE against Rome, the mightiest superpower of antiquity. But he eventually proved to be no match for the Roman Emperor Hadrian and his top general, Julius Severus. Roman troops poured into the Holy Land from Britain, Switzerland, Austria, Hungary and Bulgaria and

---

692:4; Divrei Yoel 1:29; Sedei Chemed, Rosh Hashana 2:31; Chayei Adam 141:7; Kitzur Shulchan Aruch 129:19.

4. Genesis 1:18; Psalms 127:3, 5; Joshua b. Levi, Nedarim 64b; 1 Samuels 1:1–8; Yevamos 6:6, 63b; Leviticus 20:20–21; Genesis Rabba 34:14.

wore the Jews down through simple attrition. When Severus's troops, after nearly four years of bloody warfare, entered the fortress city of Betar, the Jews' last stand, their horses waded in rivers of Jewish blood up to their bellies. And Bar Kochba? His body was never found.

Kneidlach

Q **What's wrong with eating *kneidlach* (matza balls) on Pesach?**

Nothing. Then why do some Jews avoid it? These Jews have imposed upon themselves a *chumra* (stringency) based on *kneidlach* being made by kneading matza meal with liquid. Does this produce *Chametz*? No. Many Chassidim, wishing to show there's nothing wrong with *kneidlach*, make a point of eating them on the eighth day of Pesach!

Keviyya

Q **What does this mean?**

With no less than fourteen different ways to lay out the Hebrew calendar, the primary arithmetic factors are known as a *keviyya*, a pair of numbers that represent the day of the week on which Rosh Hashana starts, and the length of the year it is about to inaugurate. A *haser* ("deficient") year, denoted by the Hebrew letter *het*, was one whose length is shortened because a day was taken away from Kislev. Meanwhile, a *kesidra* ("regular") year, denoted by the letter *chof*, refers to a year whose months are unchanged, and a *shalem* ("abundant") year, denoted by the letter *shin*, occurs when a day is added to the month of Cheshvan, and so on.

Kosher crab and certified kosher bacon bits

Q **Should Jews be vegetarians?**

When asked if he was a vegetarian for health reasons, Isaac Bashevis Singer replied, "Yes, for the chicken's health!" In the utopian Garden of Eden the original Divine plan was vegetarianism, based on the order that mankind should only eat plants and fruit. Meat eating became permitted after the

Flood as a concession to human weakness, a hint of which is evident in the derogatory tone of the Torah's *ta'avas nafschecha*, that the consumption of meat comes from "the craving of the soul." And so the rabbis, having declared that "only in meat is there joy," make eating meat an obligatory part of the *simchas Yom Tov* (the "joy of Jewish festivals"). To which the great Yiddishist Shalom Aleichem cynically adds, "The best of milk dishes is a slice of beef," a contradiction of sorts which found its true expression (*only in America*) where kosher creativity has produced "kosher crab," processed "fin fish," and certified "kosher bacon bits"!

Knock, knock, knock

Q I notice that some people "knock on wood." Is this a Jewish custom?

No. This is a psycho-pathological superstition that began when talking of good luck or one's prosperity was considered a challenge to fate. Touching, then knocking on, wood, was considered a precautionary measure, designed to block their words from an adversary's hearing. In pagan times, trees were deified (e.g., the god of lightning and thunder supposedly dwelt in oak trees), thus to touch the wood was a "religious" experience. Later, those who sought sanctuary would simply have to touch the wooden doors of a church to be considered by the local authorities to be under the official protection of the Church.

Kill or murder?

Q Is the Sixth Commandment "Thou shalt not kill" or "Thou shalt not murder"?

Pacifism is not a Jewish ideology; capital punishment is. Thus the Hebrew is crystal clear, *Lo tirtsach*, from the root *ratsach*, means "do not murder." Killing *is* justified, says the Torah, even morally mandatory in certain circumstances ("He who comes to kill you, kill him first!"). So, where does the confusion arise? From the King James English version of the Torah, where "Thou shalt not kill" appears in a distorted attempt to promote traditional ("turning-the-other-cheek") Christian, *not* Jewish, values. The British were not the only ones who made mistakes. When Louis 11 brought out the French version, it contained, "*Tu ne tueras point* [you shall not kill]," as did Martin Luther's German edition ("*Du sollst nicht töten* [you shall not kill]"). In an older, fourth-century Bible, St. Jerome, in his Latin Vulgate version, hedged his bets, using an ambiguous phrase, *non occides*, that can be read either way; likewise the third-century Greek edition of the Torah (*Septuagint*) with its *ou phoneuseis*, designed to please both sides (and thus pleasing neither!).

Ketiv system

Q Can I rely on modern-day Bibliomacy?

No. Here's the problem. Bibliomacy relies on the accuracy of the popular 1962 Koren edition of the *Torah, Nevi'im, u'Ketuvim*, which has forty-five letters *less* than the oldest complete manuscript of the entire Bible. And further. When compared to other Torah editions, it has dozens of words that are spelled differently. In fact, the compilers of the Koren edition were intellectually honest enough to *admit* in their own preface, "We do not claim that our edition is based on the tablets that Moses brought down from Mt. Sinai." Bibliomacy is an impossible science because no two texts are alike. The Rambam embraced the Aleppo Codex 32 as the most reliable of all Torah texts, yet a study reveals it has *fewer* Torah letters than *Mikra'ot Gedolot*, a sefer which incorporates the seventeenth-century masoretic *Minhat Shai*. Rabbi David Kimhi (*Radak*), the formidable twelfth-century medieval grammarian, noted that the Masorete *ketiv* (*keri*) system itself was created only because earlier Bible texts were lost during the Babylonian exile, and the best scholars of the land had been killed. Not wanting to "edit" the holy Torah, these Jews accepted the commonality of manuscripts; however, when they couldn't decide on the accuracy of the text, they showed different possibilities in their notes. These ancient humble Jews were closer to the source, yet, after laboring for several centuries before producing the basis of today's *Tanach* (the Masoretic Text), they admitted the impossibility of determining the Torah's exact middle letter ("We are not expert on full and defective spelling").[5]

---

5. Kiddushin 30a.

Koy

Q What is this?

It's a mythical beast that the Mishna refers to and is indicative of the diffi-
culties the early rabbis, who abhorred mixtures (*sha'atnez*), encountered,
when trying to describe biological hybrids (the Torah describes creatures
that cannot be classified as fish, flesh or fowl as "abominations"!). In this
particular case it was taxonomy, the offspring of a gazelle (a wild creature)
and a goat (a domestic animal). The expression (*koy*) thus became a Mishnaic generic word, a metaphor for anything that seemed to disturb the
fragile sense of cosmic order (a mule's sterility was seen as Mother Nature's
punishment for crossing an ass with a horse).[6]

Kill them?

Q Does the Talmud advocate killing idolaters?

It's unclear. The problem lies in centuries of both Jewish and Christian censorship. The Midrash originally took the word "idolaters" from the verse
tov sheba'akum harog, "Kill the best of the idolaters," and said it only referred to *Mitzrim* (Egyptians), *K'na'anim* (Canaanites), or just plain *goyim*
(gentiles) – whether they were idolaters or not! But some Torah linguists,
concerned that this sounded too ethically offensive, translated *harog* not
as "kill" but as a verbal noun, meaning "a killer," which made it read, "The
best of the idolaters is a killer" (a bitter truth considering the Jewish experience with outsiders!). But even then, our rabbis didn't want to be automatically quoted as justifying the harsh killing of Egyptians, Canaanites,
heathens, or anyone else for that matter. So they added qualifications. "Kill
the best of the heathens," said Shimon bar Yochai, adding the reservation,
"but only *in time of war*!"[7]

---

6. Hullin 79b.
7. M'chilta B'shallach 15:9.

= King James ===========================

Q Did the King James English translation of the Torah affect Jews?

Yes. Touted incorrectly as the *authentic* "Word of God," James's Bible was composed by fifty scholars between 1604 and 1611, at the time of Shakespeare, when the English language was at its zenith. Incredibly, the result was not "a camel being a horse designed by a committee," but a cohesive, virtually seamless work that somehow merged the smoothness of a Jacobean English with the rhythms of ancient Hebrew, Aramaic and Greek. Not all translations came out equally "holy"; a misprint in a 1631 issue, known by collectors as the "Wicked Bible," omitted the word "not" from the seventh commandment! Thanks to King James, an Anglican who believed in the Divine right of Kings, Jews and Jewish texts, we have such imaginative English idioms as "to lick the dust," "to fall flat on one's face," "a man after his own heart," "the land of the living," "sour grapes," "from time to time," "the skin of my teeth," "to stand in awe," "to put words in his mouth," "to go from strength to strength" – and the ominous "like lambs to the slaughter"!

L

Leaving the fold

Q **If I leave Judaism, am I still Jewish?**

Yes, always and forever! "Even though one has sinned, he is still a Jew!" – or, more bluntly, "A myrtle, though it stands among reeds, is still a myrtle!" Surely, there must be *some* restrictions placed on such a Jew? Yes. He cannot be called to the Torah and, if a *Cohen*, cannot bless the community (*duchan*).[1]

Land for peace

Q **Are there any Jewish laws that impede giving up parts of Israel?**

Yes. In debating the Torah instruction *lo t'chonnem*, "do not be gracious to them," the rabbis link *t'chonnem* with *chana*, "to encamp," and conclude that once territory falls into Jewish possession it becomes a religious obligation not to transfer it, nor be alienated from it. There is (perhaps) one exception: the duty of saving lives (*pikuach nefesh*), an obligation to cede territory to an enemy, but only in return for a "real" – not a phony land-for-rockets – treaty.[2]

---

1. Sanhedrin 44a.
2. Deuteronomy 7:2; Avoda Zara 20a.

= Language ==========

Q In what language did Adam speak?

Early Christians said the language of the Garden of Eden was Syriac. St. Augustine bet on Hebrew. Jan Van Gorp, a sixteenth-century Dutchman, using etymological gymnastics, "proved" that Adam spoke Flemish. Gott-fried Leibniz was convinced that the *Ursprache* of Adam & Co. was Cum-brian, a German dialect. Andreas Kempe, a seventeenth-century Swedish *meshugene,* taught that the snake spoke in French, Adam in Danish, and God's reprimand was in Swedish. All we know as linguists is, by the time of Babel, "Everyone on earth had the same language and the same words," proof that all languages derive from a common proto-language. Was it He-brew? The Torah doesn't say, but there is a clue. All the people "branched out" from the sons of Noah "according to their clans and languages." If He-brew was one of these Semitic "branching" languages, named after Noah's son Shem, that suggests that there was a "language ancestor." If we knew that, we'd know what language the snake used to seduce Eve![3]

= Lying on the stand ==========

Q I'm supposed to be a witness. Can I lie on the stand?

Sure, you can do anything; however, the Torah defines you as "a wicked witness," and the punishment is creative. It matches what the defendant receives, or would have received, on the basis of your false testimony ("You shall do to him as he plotted to do to his brother!"). But there's also an obligation on the judges to do their job properly, to question witnesses carefully, to "inquire, investigate, ask thoroughly!" in order not to reach a verdict based on people like you![4]

---

3. Genesis 10:32; 11:1.
4. Deuteronomy 13:14, 19:15–19; Numbers 35:30.

═ Lies, lies, lies ═══════════════════

Q Can a Torah scholar lie?

Scholars and Sages are granted three acceptable areas of "white lies." They can lie about their Torah learning (to maintain humility or modesty), marital matters (best kept private), and where they stay when traveling (so as not to burden the host with fans, followers, etc.). Jewish law recognizes that not all lies are equal in gravity. Rabbi Yonah lists nine different categories of lies in their order of severity, starting from "the worst" (cheating in business) to "the least" (changing details when telling a story).[5]

═ Lamentations ═══════════════════

Q This word sounds very "un-Jewish." How did it enter our vocabulary?

You're right! It was King James, and not the Jews, who first called Jeremiah's book "Lamentations," in an attempt to describe the national degradation and destruction of Jerusalem. In Hebrew, it is *Megillas Eicha*, "The Book of How" – as in, "*How* can it be?!"

═ Long life ═══════════════════

Q How did our ancestors live such long lives?

When asked to explain how Biblical people lived to be hundreds of years old (with no help from medical technology), Rabbi Meir Leibush (*Malbim*) traces the phenomenon to the post-Flood time, when the Heavens inform Noah that from now on there will be constant changes in the seasons. Until then, there were no seasons, and the weather was always temperate, which somehow allowed long life. And after the Flood? "The earth's axis tilted in relation to the sun," he writes, "thus, the earth's climate changed drastically,

---

5. Sha'arei Teshuva 3:178–186; Brachos 43b; Pesachim 112a; Sukka 34b; Yevamos 65b; Baba Metzia 23b, 30a.

resulting in a weakening of the human constitution and ability to withstand these constant changes in weather [leading to a shorter life span]."[6]

Lord of the flies

Q Is Beelzebul (or Beelzebub) Jewish or Christian in origin?

Christians consider Beelzebul the *rosh* (head) of all powerful demons; however, the name derives from *Baal z'vuv*, "Lord of the flies." The *Tanach* names Beelzebub as the god of the Philistine enemy, and the god whom King Ahaziah consulted (against God's will, naturally) when he was ill. Why *this* particular "god"? In ancient times, flies were held responsible for plagues. Beelzebub had it made as the anti-fly "god"![7]

Left-handed

Q I am left-handed; does that mean I'm "left out" as far as Judaism is concerned?

Sorry, but the fact is that the Torah *does* consider the right hand more significant, even complimenting God Himself, metaphorically, for being right-handed ("Your right hand, O Lord, is glorious!"). And, I'm sorry to reveal, if you're a left-handed *Cohen,* the Rambam would disqualify you (unless you were ambidextrous) from offering sacrifices in the Temple because of your "physical blemish." Consider: Jacob places not his left but his *right* hand on Ephraim's head. Batsheva sits at Solomon's *right* hand. The singer of Psalms feels secure only because "[God] is at my *right* hand." And don't forget Jerusalem! Otherwise your *right* hand "will wither." This "left-sided" prejudice wasn't restricted to Jews. The Latin word *sinister,* which means "left," became symbolic of hidden evil. Getting up "on the wrong [i.e., left] side of bed" was a superstition that ruined the mood for the rest of the day. Romans never entered a house with their left foot first (the rich ones employed special servants to ensure no one entered that way, hence the word *footman*). Cesare Lombroso, famous Italian criminologist, concluded

---

6. Genesis 8:22.
7. Ecclesiastes 10:1.

that being "a leftie" led to insanity and criminality. The preference is also reflected in Jewish law. Since the right hand was the "stronger," wedding rings went on a bride's right-hand finger, *mezuzos* were nailed to the right-hand doorpost, *tefillin* are wrapped by the "muscular" right hand on the left arm. Jewish mystics concluded that the evil of *Sitra achra* can be found on a person's *Sitra smola*, "left side!"[8]

Leap Year

Q Is this good for the Jews?

Yes. Judaism adopted the Leap Year, a *shana me'uberes*, literally, a "pregnant" year, after it was introduced by Meton, an innovative fifth-century BCE Athenian astronomer-philosopher, who lived at the same time as Ezra. Incredibly, by using naked-eye observations only, Meton found that if, every four years, all the "extra" hours, minutes, and seconds of the solar year were added up, they would equal an extra day, and that 235 lunations (or "synodic months") were equal to nineteen solar years. So? Is this good for the Jews? Yes. Despite being "off" by about two hours per cycle, his became *the* rabbinic calendar correction of convenience. Why? Because it avoided clashes with "religious" days that were seasonal in nature. Remember: our ancient rabbi-mathematicians had to satisfy a certain Jewish law, that some *yomim tovim* must fall within certain seasons (Succos in the fall, Pesach in the spring). This required balancing two conflicting requirements – lunar months according to the Moon, solar years according to the sun. The solar year, which describes the earth's complete orbit around the sun, is critical to Judaism. Why? Because it is subdividable, and can thus accommodate the seasons. This calendar incompatibility, which caused many a sleepless night for the early rabbis, started when the Babylonians, the grand astronomers of the Middle East, decided on a solar year of 365 days, five hours, forty-eight minutes and forty-six seconds – a number that exceeded the Jews' twelve lunar months by ten days and twenty-one hours. This differential produced an excess thirty days over three years. Therefore, if no adjustments were made, such summer months as Av or Elul would shift

---

8. Exodus 15:6; Bechoros 45b; Hilchos Bi'at Hamikdash 6:1, 8:1, 11; Genesis 48:14; 1 Kings 2:19; Psalms 16:8, 137:5; Menachos 34a; Menachos 37a; Shulchan Aruch 27:6.

into winter, causing, for example, Pesach to wander aimlessly. So our (un-named) rabbis formalized Meton's computation and added an extra "leap (intercalary) month," called *Adar Sheni*, the "second Adar," seven times in the course of each nineteen-year calendar compensatory cycle (i.e., twelve years of twelve lunar months, and seven years of thirteen lunar months). This synchronization, known as *machzor*, "cycle," was calculated so well that after every nineteen years the course of the sun and the moon coincided again, almost exactly. The introduction of this supplemental month sometimes had nothing to do with synchronizing time to the festivals. In a remarkable letter to diaspora communities, Rabbi Gamaliel II, first-century Sage, suggests, on behalf of himself "and his [rabbinic] colleagues," to "add thirty days to this [upcoming] year." Why? Because "the lambs are still too weak, the chickens too small, the grain is not ripe." Meton, are you listening?[9]

Lions

Q The lion seems to be more prominent in Judaic art than other animals? Is it?

Yes. The lion (*aryeh*) is *the* most common motif in Jewish ceremonial art, and the only specific creature to be found on Ark curtains, Torah covers and breastplates. God's own voice is compared to the powerful roar of a lion, a "king of beasts" which became the emblem of the city of Jerusalem. The Torah compares the people of Israel to a lion, golden lions stood on either side of King Solomon's throne, and the Mishna describes those who do God's will as having the "bravery" of a lion! In a display of courage, both David and Solomon kill lions. Why such feline fixation? Because the lion symbolized dignity, majesty, strength – the very qualities desired by a nation-in-formation.[10]

---

9. Exodus 12:1, 13:3; Leviticus 23:10–12.
10. Brachos 3a; Hagiga 13b; Numbers 23:24; 1 Kings 7:29, 10:19–20; Pirkei Avos 5:20.

═ Leather ═══════════════════════════

Q Why can't I wear leather shoes on Yom Kippur?

Two reasons. As Moses approaches the Burning Bush, considered holy ground, he is ordered to "remove your shoes"; similarly, as a sanctuary in time in which Jews draw near to God pleading for forgiveness, Yom Kippur is also holy ground. Secondly, leather shoes were solid and comfortable (which is why they were worn by the rich), and thus symbolic of the physical pleasures forbidden on Yom Kippur, the day Jews must "afflict their souls." Consider: when the rabbis urged husbands to buy their wives gifts for *yom tov*, they singled out "new shoes" as the most appreciated present![11]

═ Life ═══════════════════════════════

Q Is there any logic to a person's life span?

I have no idea. A Midrash, attributed to Simeon ben Eleazar, breaks life into the following seven categories, each stage called an *olam* (world): the first year (when a baby is called "king," adored by all); between two and three (called a "pig," wallowing in dirt), at ten (the child "jumps like a young goat"), at twenty (one becomes egocentric, a visceral "horse," motivated by physical appetites, not spiritual nor intellectual), upon marriage (one becomes a "donkey," loaded with responsibilities), upon having children (the person becomes a brazen "dog," aggressively pursuing a livelihood), and then, finally, old age (when the unlearned becomes a "monkey" and the Torah Sage a "king").[12]

═ Living room or bedroom? ═══════════

Q I lost my *kesuba* (marriage certificate). Am I still married?

Good try, but it doesn't work! You're still married, although you should

---

11. Exodus 3:5; Leviticus 23:32; Kesubos 5:8.
12. Ecclesiastes Rabba 1:2; Pirkei Avos 5:21.

get a substitute one ASAP and keep it with you at all times. Under Jewish law, a marriage lacking a proper *kesuba* is not a legal Jewish marriage. The *kesuba* gave women, at a time when they had none, certain security and financial, conjugal, emotional and burial rights. This is such a serious document that its content is purposefully rigid. It has to be read publicly, in front of, and signed by, two valid (unrelated) witnesses, and specifying exact names, date and place of marriage. Where should you display your *kesuba*? In the living room, dining room, family room, bedroom? No matter. The only requirement is that a couple keep their marriage contract close by. When arguing couples approached him for advice, the eighteenth-century Baal Shem Tov, charismatic founder of Chassidus, urged them to reread their *kesuba*, the ancient Aramaic mutual pledge made "according to the tradition of Moses and the Jewish people," in the hope that they would be reminded of the good ol' days of being brides and grooms.

Levirate marriage

Q What is this?

If a man dies childless, his oldest brother, on his father's side, must marry his widow. Why? So that "his name not be blotted out of Israel." And what if he (or she) doesn't want to? There is a halachic exit door. It's called *chalitza*, a symbolic ceremony wherein "she shall go to the elders and pull his shoe off his foot (*chalitza*) and say, 'Thus shall be done to the man who will not build his brother's house.'" If she refuses to go through this process, can she remarry? No. If she does, what's her status? She is her brother-in-law's divorced wife. This is not to be confused with lineage endogamy (aka parallel cousin marriage), a vehicle to ensure continuity when a father only has daughters. How does this work? A daughter inherits property but must marry a son of her father's brother to keep the assets in the family (i.e., their patrilateral parallel cousin).[13]

13. Deuteronomy 2:18, 25:5,7,9; Leviticus 18:6.

Lenders

Q I have cash, and my assets are very liquid. Should I lend money to other Jews?

Yes. Lending money to other Jews is not only a "positive" command (*im kesef talveh es ami*, "You shall lend money to My People), but an even *greater* mitzva than giving *tzedaka* (charity)! Why? Because there is less embarrassment in being a borrower than a beggar. And more! A loan gives a person the business opportunity to improve his lot, and thus to be in a position to lend to others. To whom should I lend first? A relative or a stranger? The former, who takes precedence over a Torah scholar (*talmid chacham*) – unless your *mishpacha* is wealthy, or has other resources to tap. What's better? To lend five thousand to one person, or five hundred to ten people? The Lubavitcher Rebbe said it is better to make smaller loans to more people (unless the larger loan is an emergency, and can avert a financial catastrophe), because that forces more Jews to interact.[14]

Learning, or working?

Q I can't decide whether to work and learn part-time, or devote myself to full-time Torah study. Any suggestions?

There is a classic debate between Yishmael and Shimon bar Yochai. The former interprets the verse "You shall gather your grain" to mean that Torah study must be combined with a worldly occupation. The latter, commenting on the order "Six days shall you work," considered employment "a positive command, in and of itself." Yet the mystic Sage also hedged his bets, concerned by a Godly warning, "This book [Torah] shall not depart from your mouth, you shall meditate therein by day and by night," which left him wondering, "If a man ploughs, sows, reaps, and threshes – what is to become of the Torah?" So, who won this lively debate? According to Abaye, those who "followed Yishmael [balancing study with work], were successful, whilst the followers of Shimon [committed to Torah study exclusively] were not so successful." And so *Pirkei Avos* advises that "Torah is

---

14. Exodus 22:24.

better with *derech eretz*" (i.e., gainful employment), and our Sages warned parents that "if they don't teach their son a trade, they teach him thievery!" Yosef Caro, of *Shulchan Aruch* fame, concludes that "if Torah is not accompanied by work, it will ultimately be nullified." Rabbi Yisrael Meyer HaCohen (*Chofetz Chayim*) disagreed, and supported the full-time yeshiva kollel lifestyle, but with a caveat – that in each generation only a few outstanding individuals merit the right of sole Torah immersion. What do Rashi and Rambam, the ivy league of Torah scholars, say? They both agree! It is a serious halachic duty to teach one's children a profession (*umanus*) – *even* on a Shabbas! Rashi, in an uncommonly ominous warning to parents, says that depriving a son of the means of a livelihood will turn him into a common *ganef* ("thief")! Flip through the Talmud and you'll find dozens of Torah scholar-tradesmen (shoemakers, tailors, carpenters, etc.) who are held in great esteem for *both* qualities. The Rambam is also unusually blunt in his disdain for Jews who ask for handouts in order to learn Torah exclusively, accusing them of "defaming God's name, cheapening the Torah, extinguishing the light of faith, removing himself from the World to Come." Now, if that's not enough reason to get a job, I don't know what is![15]

Law and order

Q When did the twelve tribes of Israel coalesce into a monarchy? Was it successful?

No. The unending tragedy of the Jews has been the House Divided complex. Even when finally settled in the Promised Land, the Jews lacked political cohesion; in fact, there was no king, no capital, no central government, no army, no taxation, no outside trade, and, incredibly, "Every man did what was right in his own eyes!" Only the common threat of foreign invasion motivated unity; the Jews went from forty years of a socially close-knit unit in a desert to being geographically distant from each other's tribes. Did the popular "election" of Saul help? No: he abused his position through favoritism, granting "fields and vineyards" freely to family and followers,

---

15. Deuteronomy 11:14; Joshua 1:8; Brachos 8a, 35b; Kiddushin 29a, 82a,b; Shulchan Aruch, Orach Chayim 151:1; Shabbas 150a; Rambam, Hilchos Shabbas 24:5; Orach Chayim 306:6; Baba Metzia 30b, Nedarim 49b; Rashi, Makkos 8b.

creating an elite class, separated from "the people of the land." What about David? At least he tried. David pushed for spiritual-political solidarity, established Jerusalem as the capital, centralized the priesthood, organized "cabinet officials," a standing army, civil servants, etc. But was he triumphant? No. Success waited for Solomon who acted more like a king than a father. Solomon fortified Israel's borders, established international trade and foreign alliances, improved the nation's lifestyle, and oversaw the grand opening of the First Temple ("God's House"). But the wisdom of Solomon showed serious flaws, from unpopular taxation and conscription to forging a marriage alliance with Egypt that allowed foreign wives to "import" their foreign gods. The result? Solomon's heart "turned from God," and the ominous beginning of the end – division of the kingdom, two rival kings, two capitals, two armies, conflicting Jewish laws – began.[16]

═ Leviathan ═

Q What is this creature?

The Leviathan is a legendary sea-monster, described by Job as the most powerful of them all, unconquerable by man, able to be vanquished only by God who, when He's finished with him, shall serve the beast to "the pious, in banquet." This "final supper" is timed for their resurrection, each portion depending on the *tzadik's* rank when alive. First-class *tzadikim* get tents from the creature's hide, the second rank receives girdles, the third level gets chains, and the final category of piety receives necklaces. What does the Rambam, super-rationalist, say to all this? He sees the banquet of the Leviathan as allegory, in that the pious have a spiritual and intellectual status in the afterlife.[17]

═ Libel ═

Q I assume libel is prohibited?

And how! The risk has been there ever since God gave man the capacity for

---

16. Judges 17:6; Joshua 13:22; I Samuel 22:7; II Kings 21:24.
17. Job 40:30.

speech. The danger of words becoming harmful missiles hurled at others caused the wise Solomon to declare, "Death and life are in the power of the tongue!" And the punishment? Lashes, bans, ostracism, social sanctions, financial damages. And no one was immune! Aaron and Miriam were punished for their slanderous comments about their brother's wife. The fourteenth-century Asher ben Yechiel (*Rosh*) writes about the custom of the courts which fined "those who put others to shame with their [written or oral] words." Does libel apply only to an individual? Is there group libel? Yes. The Chofetz Chayyim argued that it was as wrong to slander the Jewish people as a whole as to defame an individual, based on God's response, "You may speak evil of yourself, but not of My children!"[18]

Letter of the law

Q What's more important, the spirit or the letter of the law?

This is Judaism's great paradox! Jeremiah cautions the Jews that even their most meticulous offering carries less weight with God than their personal conduct – a stunning acknowledgment that the Heavens judge *not* by the letter of the law but by its spirit. "A handful of flour brought by a poor man voluntarily is, according to the midrashic Isaac Nappaha, more precious than two handfuls of incense brought by the High Priest!" On what does Jeremiah base this supremacy-of-ethics lecture? On the fact that God's appearance at Sinai was accompanied not by any specific mention of sacrifices but by the morality of the Ten Commandments.

Long prayers

Q I get bored very quickly in *shul*. Can't the services be shortened?

I don't know; but I do know that when his sister Miriam was sick, Moses' entire prayer consisted of five words: "God, heal her now, please."

---

18. Proverbs 18:21; Kiddushin 28a; Numbers 12:1–13; Isaiah 6:5; Sanhedrin 46a; Deuteronomy 22:13–21.

═ Lord's prayer ═══════════════════

Q Does this Catholic prayer have a Jewish origin?

Yes. Its phraseology is the epitome of religious plagiarism, being a direct derivative from several Jewish sources, especially the *kaddish* and the silent *amida*, having "borrowed" such classic Hebrew phrases as "Our Father in heaven," "Hallowed be Your name," "Your kingdom come, Your will be done on earth as in heaven." Even its final phrase ("Yours is the kingdom, the power and the glory") is a direct quote from Jewish sources![19]

═ *Lo sisgodedu* ═══════════════════

Q What does this mean?

This is a severe Torah warning, derived from the verse, *Lo sa'asu agudos agudos* ("do not mutilate yourselves"), that some say includes the order for Jews not to "mutilate" themselves by breaking up into "splinter groups." This admonition is also directed towards the rabbinate and *batei din*, in that they must avoid issuing conflicting rulings. Why? Because "two Torahs," warn Abaye, Rashi and the Rambam, paves the way to disunity and discord. However, Rava supports different schools of thought, Beis Shamai-Hillel style, as being the very nature of Torah, yet he frowns on "split decisions" from "different Torah factions" which allow Jews to choose one rabbi over another. "Differences of customs," warns the Vilna Gaon, "lead to differences of the hearts!" Rashi ruled that each community can do as it pleases if the custom did not apply to an actual halacha. The Rambam frowned on this approach, which is why he wrote the *Mishne Torah*, to provide Jews with one single halachic source.[20]

---

19. 1 Chronicles 21:11.
20. Deuteronomy 14:1; Rashi, Sukka 44a; Yevamos 13b; Rambam, Avoda Zara, 12:14; Pesachim 4a, 51b; Sha'arei Teshuva 693:1; Iggeros Moshe, Orach Chayim 1:159; Aruch Hashulchan 651:22; Chayei Adam 32:33; Orach Chayim 468:4.

═ Lost and found ═══════════════

Q I found a wallet in a phone booth. Can I keep it?

No. The laws of *hashavas aveida*, "returning lost objects," and "caring for lost property," are derived from *v'hitalamta*, which means one must "not remain indifferent," as in to "pretend" not seeing a lost object. However, apart from not picking it up on Shabbas, the item must seem abandoned, and be worth something (at least a *perutah*, which is about a nickel). However, even if its value seems insignificant, it might be priceless to the owner (e.g., a photo, a single glove, etc.). Rabbi Hanina once found some hens accidentally left on his doorstep, and soon they began to lay eggs. Instead of using them as food for his family, the rabbi set both eggs and hens aside until he ran out of space. Forced to sell them, he used the money to buy goats. One day, the owner of the hens showed up, and Hanina presented him with the goats, a prime example of *kiddush Hashem*, the sanctification of God's Name.[21]

═ Lost in translation ═══════════════

Q How widely spread is the Torah today in other people's languages?

Not very. Out of the 6,800 languages in the world, the Old Testament has been translated into about four hundred, including Attie (spoken by 300,000 people in the Ivory Coast), Nyaboa (spoken by about 43,000 folks), Baoul (the language of over two million people), Obolo (spoken by 100,000 people in Nigeria), and Sabaot (spoken by 150,000 Kenyans). So, how do you say "Let My people go!" in Lama, spoken by nearly 200,000 people in Togo? I haven't a clue.

---

21. Kiddushin 34a; Choshen Mishpat 259:5, 359:1; 262:1, 266:1; Aruch Hashulchan 259:7; Chasam Sofer, Orach Chayim 42; Mishne Berura 308:13; Moshe Feinstein, Hashavas Aveida, Responsa 1, 4.

═ Lottery tickets ═══════════════

Q Am I allowed to buy a lottery ticket? Is this considered a form of gambling?

Yes, you can; and no, it's not. In fact, "casting lots" dates back to Torah times. On Yom Kippur, lots were cast to decide which goat to designate for God and which for *Azazel*; the allocation of territory among the Tribes of Israel was carried out by lot, as was the honor of doing service in the Temple. Some *shuls* even have a custom of casting lots to see who gets an *aliya*, and the right to say *kaddish*. Buying a lottery ticket is not gambling if it's done occasionally, in moderation, as a harmless source of enjoyment; however, compulsive buying with large (unaffordable) sums, is forbidden, an addiction known as *m'sachek b'kuvya*, "one who plays with dice," and would disqualify that person, regarded as having no constructive occupation, from being a credible judge or witness in a Jewish court.

═ Love-at-first-sight ═══════════════

Q Is this a good thing?

It worked for Jacob. The third Patriarch was immediately mesmerized by the girl of his dreams (Rachel), a shepherdess who turned out to be his cousin, daughter of his wily Uncle Lavan. The Jacob-Rachel sparks are the Torah's best example of Love-at-First-Sight, and quantitatively different from his father and grandfather's spousal unions, who deferred revealing their emotions and feelings until *after* they established a relationship. So instantly smitten was Jacob that he agreed to seven years of hard work in return for Rachel's hand in marriage, his love so strong that the years "seem like only a few days." Which direction is right? They both are, says the Midrash, approving the active enthusiastic Jacob-style ("he went forth"), and the passive appreciative Isaac-style ("he watched the caravan approaching"), disapproving only of those who procrastinate, delay, and dilly-dally in pursuing marriage.

Look at Moses' thighs!

Q Do appearances matter?

Yes. The question of appearances is important – even if one is not transgressing any law ("You shall be innocent before God and before Israel!"). This dictate is even more important for leaders of Jews, so "whenever Moses went out of the tent, each person stood at his own tent door, gazing at Moses until he was gone into the tent [and then the Jews would whisper to each other], 'Look at Moses' thighs, how thick they are. Of course! He eats and drinks what he takes from us!'" And this was directed towards the trustworthiest Jew of the time! In order that one's integrity be obvious to his fellow family, neighbors and friends (and not just to God), it was decided that any Jew in charge of Temple moneys couldn't wear "a cloak with folds, or lining, or shoes, or sandals, or *tefillin*, or an amulet." Why? Because they all allowed valuables to be concealed![22]

Leprosy

Q What is today's equivalent of leprosy?

Leprosy was incurable in Bible times. Today the disease is called Hansen's disease and can be cured with modern medicines.

Land laws

Q Whence do we get "land rights"?

The general principle about real estate ownership in *Eretz Yisrael* is simple. God is Landlord ("the land is Mine") and everybody else ("the sons of men") are, at best, "merely resident tenants." The validity of the lease on the Holy Land was contingent upon the morality of the Jews' behavior. The Torah's fixation on land is not lost on Jeremiah, a lonely and sad prophet who, despite sitting in a Jerusalem prison under Babylonian siege, is still focused

---

22. Numbers 32:22; Exodus 33–8; Bikurim 3, Halacha 3; Mishna Shekalim 3:2; Midrash Shemos Rabba 51:1.

on paying his cousin seventeen shekels of silver for his property "in the territory of Benjamin." Jeremiah acts in accordance with the "duty of property redemption," a first right-of-refusal that obligates relatives to retain ancestral holdings within the family or tribe. This is why Naboth refuses to sell his inherited vineyard to King Ahab, even at a substantial profit; why Boaz exercises his right of redemption in the Book of Ruth; and why Jewish women who inherit family property in the absence of male heirs marry men of their own tribe in order to keep the assets "in the family."

Let My people know

Q Is ignorance bliss?

This idea is alien in a religion that believes every "why" invites a "because." Centuries of religious literature show an overwhelming index of challenging questions and humble answers. To help prepare ourselves, we are even encouraged to begin asking questions about the laws of Pesach thirty days before. "If the other does not know how to ask," teases the Haggada, "ask for him!" Why? "Because the finest quality of Man is asking questions, since his wit is judged better by his questions than by his answers!"

Laundry

Q Can I do laundry on *erev* Pesach?

Not after midday (*chatzos*). Nor can you have a haircut (but if you *must*, you have to use a non-Jewish barber), shave, sew new clothing, or cut your nails. Ironing, polishing shoes, cutting nails, sewing buttons, minor mending and lengthening or shortening hems is OK. How about a shower or bath? Probably, but it's not so clear. Why the strictness? These acts are considered "work" (*melacha*), and *erev* Pesach, during the time of the Temple, was a *yom tov*, with an obligation to bring sacrifices (*korban Pesach*). Others disallow it for purely pragmatic reasons: why are you having a haircut when you should be preparing for the seder![23]

---

23. Mishne Berura 468:5,7, 468:1; Chazon Ish, Orchos Rabbeinu 2; Rema, Orach Chayim 468:2; Pnei Yehoshua, Pesachim 50a; Biur Halacha 468:1.

═ Last Supper ═══════════════════════════════════

Q Christians claim the Last Supper was a Jewish meal. Are they right?

No. The Church takes it for granted that Jesus' Last Supper was a traditional Pesach seder; but it was not. How do we know? Because all three of the synoptic gospels (Matthew, Mark, Luke) that describe the connection totally ignore Judaism's plethora of compulsory seder elements (e.g., there is not a single reference to paschal lambs, matza, *maror, charoset, Ma Nishtana,* narration of the Exodus story, etc.). And more! The fourth gospel (John) doesn't even get the date right, placing the final Supper one day *before* Pesach! In any event, even if Jesus & Co. thought they were participating in a *seder tisch*, the whole meal was totally invalidated by Jewish law. Why? By substituting the paschal lamb symbol with Jesus (the "lamb of God"), they made a heretical mockery of the entire custom.

═ Lawyers ═══════════════════════════════════════

Q Is there a place for lawyers in Judaism?

The original Jewish court system had no place, *nor* patience, for "professional" attorneys. Lawyers were simply unnecessary. Why? Because the parties themselves presented their own case, and witnesses were examined directly by the judges. So why do we have so many lawyers today (Israel, with a population of around six million, has twenty-five thousand lawyers; in contrast, Japan, with a population of one hundred twenty-five million, has only eighteen thousand)? The ambivalence towards the "profession" eroded when litigants became (Jewishly) inarticulate, unable to speak for themselves. And so the *beis din* reluctantly began to allow spokesmen, just as God appointed Aaron as Moses' spokesman (not his lawyer!) in addressing Pharaoh. It was then inevitable: the spokesmen, learned in Jewish law in order to be effective, became "lawyer-spokesmen," despite the axiomatic fact that the *dayyanim* (judges) already knew the law. What about Jewish lawyers who represent Jews in the general court system, an act that transgresses God's order that Jews, because of the inherent justice of the Torah, litigate their differences only within the Jewish legal system? This prohibition is directed to the litigant, not the lawyer.

═ Late with the rent? ═

Q Can I be late with my rent?

The same Torah verse (*ein adam l'chaveiro: lo salin*) that commands a laborer be paid "on *that* day" (i.e., on time, on the day the work is done), also applies to rental fees – although there is a dispute as to whether this applies to real estate rentals.[24]

═ Living in Israel ═

Q Is it mandatory to live in the Holy Land?

The Ramban describes it as an active *mitzvas asei,* on the basis of a Torah directive, "You *shall* possess the land and you *shall* settle in it!" And yet the Rambam decided not to include *aliya* in his catalogue of commandments. Why? He believed that it was no longer obligatory after the destruction of the Temple and dispersion of Jews to exile. Hayyim Cohen, a twelfth-century halachist, ruled that *aliya* was obligatory unless there was danger involved, in either traveling or living there. Rav Moshe Feinstein classified *aliya* as a *mitzva kiyyumit* (an observance) instead of a *mitzva hiyyuvit* (obligatory). The Rav (J.B. Soloveitchik) was of the opinion that *both* the Rambam and Ramban *had* codified *aliya* as a mandatory act, applicable even today, and cited the reliable *Avnei Nezer* as his source. Most scholars agree with the Ramban, but were reluctant to be strict. Why? Stringency would automatically put thousands of Jews worldwide (except those involved in Jewish education) in violation of a "positive" halachic command.[25]

---

24. Chofetz Chayim, Ahavas Chesed 9:5; Pischei Teshuva 339:1.
25. Sefer Hamitzvos, #4; Numbers 33:53; Tosafos, Kesubos 110b; Iggeros Moshe, Even Haezer 102; Yore Deah 454:2.

══ Last mitzva ══

Q I know what the first mitzva is, to "be fruitful." What's the last?

The final command of them all, number 613, appears in the shortest Torah portion of them all (*Vayelech*, which means "and then he went," a reference to Moses' appearance amongst the people to announce that, at the age of 120, he is too old to continue as an active leader). The final mitzva is to "write (*kitvu*) down this poem [a Torah scroll]," which is the genesis of the label "People of the Book." Moses jumps at the opportunity to create the first written scroll of God's teachings, which he does in the spirit of *zerizim makdimim l'mitzvos*, "diligent people are quick to observe the commandments." Why? Because he instinctively recognizes the power of preservation as the key to the survival of Torah; and, in order to dispel any future doubts as to its sanctified authority, Moses places it in the Holy Ark, right next to the Tablets.[26]

══ Lord of the Rings ══

Q I'm buying my bride a wedding ring. Is this absolutely essential for a Jewish wedding?

For *shalom bayis* (peace-in-the-home) and for *parnossa* (of the diamond dealer), it is. For technical Jewish law, it isn't. The ring only entered the Jewish world in the eighth century CE, replacing the tradition of handing the bride a small coin (symbolic of "value"), which acted as a "promissory note," securing a husband's promise to support his wife. Worn conspicuously on the finger, the ring was a permanent, visible confirmation of the husband's contractual pledge, and a subtle sign that the bride was "taken" already. Its circular shape always had mystic connotations (being endless, it symbolized harmony and perfection), and was not restricted to fingers (ancient ornaments circle wrists, ankles, and waists). Primitive man even bound a rope around his wife, on the theory that this "magic circle" would bind her to him through supernatural forces! In the Torah, rings (and their signets) represented power, and handing one to another was a transfer of

---

26. Proverbs 10:4, 13:4.

authority. "You shall be over my house," said Pharaoh as he handed his ring to Joseph, "and according to your word shall all my people be ruled!" And let's not forget how Purim started! With the transfer of a king's ring to Haman!

M

Marriage counseling

Q Is there any marriage guidance in the Torah?

Yes. The first marriage counselor was God, His first client was Abraham, and His first advice was, "Whatever Sarah says to you, listen to her!" And *voilà*, the rules of Who-is-the-boss-in-the-Jewish-household were laid down forever.

Mitzva haba'a b'aveira

Q What does this mean?

This describes one who, whilst trying to fulfill one *mitzva*, acts in a way as to transgress another. In other words, a process that starts "religiously" and ends "irreligiously," thus negating its original intent. An example? Let's say you're called up to the Torah and, in your zeal, you knock me, an older man, over, thus reducing the *mitzva* of *aliya* by your recklessness.

Masculine or feminine?

Q Is God masculine or feminine?

Neither. The Torah speaks of God as "Him," but other texts confer on God both masculine and feminine loving attributes. *Tehillim* compares His compassion as "a father" to his children, whilst Isaiah compares His comfort as "a mother" to her child. Kabbala frequently switches genders, although Jewish mystics tilt, allegorically, towards the feminine verbage. The Hebrew expression for "God's Presence," *haShechina*, which does not even appear in the Torah, is derived from *shochen*, "dwells," which is "neuter" in English (as in "it") but feminine in a grammatical sense. Remember: *all* nouns in Hebrew are either masculine or feminine![1]

Mezuza, behind bars

Q I have a friend in prison. Should I send him a *mezuza* for his cell?

It depends on the length of his sentence. If he's only "in" for a matter of days, then it's not needed. A *mezuza* has certain criteria. It goes "on the doorposts of your house and on your gates." What constitutes a "dwelling house (*dira*)?" Two things. Its size (more than eight square feet) and its purpose (eating, sleeping, working). Thus a car, a temporary prison cell, or a market stall don't qualify.[2]

Medicinal *Chametz*

Q I need to take medicine daily. What do I do over Pesach? Is it considered *Chametz*?

The definition of *Chametz* has to do with "edibility," defined as to whether a dog would eat it. Thus cosmetics, ointments, and medication are permitted to be stored over Pesach, because they are *nifseda tzuras haChametz*, have "lost their *Chametz* form." The one taking medication (a *choleh*, a sick

---

1. Psalms 103:13; Isaiah 66:13.
2. Deuteronomy 6:9, 11:13–21; Exodus 13:1–10; Yore Deah 286.

person) obviously doesn't consider it an "edible" food item. Medicines that are flavored or coated to make them taste better should be avoided.[3]

May Day

Q Can Jews participate in this day?

No. This may seem like an ordinary holiday dedicated to the working man and the socialist, but its origins are primitive paganism, described and decried by the Torah as "an abomination of the heathen." On May Day, concerned about the fecundity of their crops and cattle, the ancients, in bloody rites of magic and sorcery, would "offer up" (i.e., sacrifice) those they treasured most to Moloch, god of vegetation. Phoenicians, in a frenzy of revelry and dancing, even threw their own cherished children into the fiery mouths of makeshift idols!

Mirrors for *tefillin*

Q I've started putting on *tefillin*. Can I use a mirror to make sure they're on right?

Yes, although many Chassidic Rebbes were against it. The Sanzer Rebbe called it "a *minhag* for fools!" Why? Looking in a mirror was considered vain and feminine. But Rav Ovadia Yosef allows mirrors, as did Rav Zalman of Lubavitch, who once emptied a snuffbox gift in order to use the silver as a mirror to check that his *tefillin* were on straight.

Means and ends

Q I believe that the ends justify the means. Am I right?

No. On the verse, "Justice, justice shall you pursue," our rabbis explain the "doubling" as an indication of "justice, by just means!" Why should it

---

3. Biur Halacha 442:9; Chazon Ish, Orach Chayim 116:8; Shulchan Aruch Harav 24; Iggeros Moshe, Orach Chayim 2:92, 3:62; Orach Chayim 442:1, 4; Mishne Berura 20, 43; Da'as 2:60.

matter? If the destination is correct, why worry about the route? Jewish law is clear: *means* matter as much as *ends*! An example? You cannot make a blessing (an admirable act) over a stolen *lulav* (an admirable aim – when it's not stolen). You cannot give *tzedaka* to a worthy charity with stolen cash. "He who steals a measure of wheat and says a prayer over the bread is a blasphemer!" Any loopholes? Sure. You can steal from a thief (*gonev min haganav*), because Jacob stole the birthright from his unworthy brother. In other words, it's OK *in an emergency*, especially if *both* ends and means are upright, and if there is *no* other viable option.[4]

Matza as *mazal*?

Q Is matza considered *mazaldik*?

It isn't. Considering it a "good-luck" amulet, Italian-Jewish women would bite into matza during childbirth. Others hung it up at home, some carried matza crumbs in their wallet or purse for good luck.

Medical records

Q Should patients have access to their medical records?

Yes, unless it's hazardous to their health. The analogy, derived from Job, is Rosh Hashana's famous *Unesanneh Tokef* prayer wherein "every human sets his seal [in God's Book of records]." A Midrash describes how God (and if God, then *why not* a doctor?) shows everyone his or her personal record, and each "signs off on it." Consideration of a patient's mental anguish allows the doctor, friends and family to lie in the face of a serious medical diagnosis. The Hebrew prophets were not consistent. Elisha tells an aid to ben Hadad, King of Aram, to lie to his boss about his terminal condition, whilst Isaiah walks up to a critically ill King Hezekiah and tells him straight out, "You're gonna die!"[5]

---

4. Deuteronomy 16:20; Baba Kamma 94a.
5. Job 37:7; Tanchuma, Bereishis 29; Schach, Siftei Kohen, Yore Deah 338:1; II Kings 8:7–15, 20:1; Isaiah 38:1; Shulchan Aruch, Yore Deah 337:1.

Marital advice

Q I'm looking for a wife. Any ideas?

Here's God's marital advice. When choosing a wife, select substance over form, concentrate your search on inner beauty, examine such (invisible) qualities as the spirit. How does one recognize "inner beauty?" It reveals itself, says Proverbs, if the "woman fears God" and speaks "*Torah Chesed*, a Torah of Love, with wisdom." After you find such a woman, adds King Solomon, only then can "she and her beauty be lauded!" Good luck!

Macho or *nebbish*?

Q The Torah tells us what to look for in a wife, but what about a husband?

"The great question that has never been answered," confessed Sigmund Freud, "despite my thirty years of research into the female soul, is: 'What does a woman want?'" Unlike Tu b'Av there is no day in the Jewish calendar when men go and dance while women pick and choose a mate. However, the Torah gives Jewish girls three pointers: search for *yichus* (a Yiddish word from the Latin *dignitas*, "rank, status"), education (as in *limudei kodesh*, "sacred study"), and potential financial stability (in the context of supporting a wife and family). And looks? The Torah doesn't just associate beauty with women. It describes Jonathan as "lovely" and David as "comely" and admires Samson's flowing curly locks. The traditional ideal of masculinity is far from society's image of a male macho, or the nebbishy Woody Allenish *persona*. Our rabbis considered wisdom, piety, and self-reflection signs of masculine strength (a thoughtful, quiet Jacob is chosen over his hairy hunter brother!). Dr. Freud was probably absent that day in *cheder* when they read the Psalmist's philosophy on the ideal man, an *Ish yarei es Hashem*, a "God-fearing man," one "who has the strength of a male and the compassion of a female!"[6]

---

6. Psalms 112:1.

═ Mezuza ══════════════════════════════

Q I'm putting one up. Anything I should know?

The *mezuza*, written on a single piece of rolled parchment, contains the famous Judaic affirmation ("Hear, O Israel"), and is affixed to the right-hand side (as one enters) of the "doorpost" tilted to face inward at least two-thirds up (the "right" side of interior doors is the side with hinges). When the text uses the word *beitecha* for "your home," Raba links the term to *bi'a'techa*, which refers to how one enters a home (walking in "with his right foot first"). What if everyone in the house is left-handed? No matter. We go by how the majority, not the individual, enters a home. The diagonal direction is the result of a respectful compromise between two Sages, Rashi, who wanted a vertical position, and Rebbenu Tam who preferred the horizontal. Many Jews refer to the case itself as a *mezuza*; this is incorrect. It's *only* a case. The parchment is the *mezuza*! Why is there a single Hebrew letter (*shin*) on the scroll's reverse side, on the back of the case, visible to the public? It stands for *Shaddai* (one of God's many names), an acronym for *shomer daltos Yisrael,* "guardian of the doors of Israel." What's the point of a *mezuza*? Contrary to common popular myth, it is *not* a protective-type amulet but simply a reminder of God's obligatory commandments (and a means of identifying which house is Jewish).[7]

═ Moving on up ══════════════════════════

Q Does the Torah recognize class distinction in real estate?

Sure. If anything, the Torah accepts reality. Shelter first starts in the desert with "tents," then moves on to "houses," and finally, for the man who has it all, "palaces." The earliest palace unearthed in Israel is that of Ai in the mid-second millennium BCE.[8]

---

7.   Yoma 11b; Taz, Yore Deah 289:2.
8.   1 Kings 7:1–12.

Mockery music

Q Is it my imagination – but aren't a lot of Yiddish songs "satirical"?

You're right. Yiddish songs introduced a whole new industry: mockery music. These anti-Chassidic tunes were written and sung by Lithuanian litvaks, whom the Chassidim called *klein kepeldik*, "pedantics." Many are so melodically catching that it's hard to tell they are offensive parodies. If you enjoy music, it's hard not to like the whimsical *Zog-zhe, Rebenyu*, or the jolly *Az der Rebbe tanzt*, or the sing-along *Der Rebbe Elimelekh*, or the biting *Kum aher, du filozof* with such lyrics as, "See here, you philosopher, with your cat-sized brain/Come sit at the Rebbe's table and learn some sense/ You've gone and invented the steamship and think a lot of yourself/But the Rebbe spreads his handkerchief and crosses the ocean in no time"!

Moses with horns?

Q I just came back from Rome and saw a sculpture of Moses with horns. What is this?

In 1505 Pope Julius II commissioned the Florentine artist Michelangelo to design a grand statue of Moses for the papal tomb. The correct translation of Moses' facial skin, after his face-to-face ethereal *mysterium tremendum* with God, is "beams of splendor" or "Divine rays of glory." Michelangelo, wanting to please the Vatican which showed the devil always in horns, chose "horns" instead of "rays."

Mother's "side"

Q My father's Jewish, my mother's not. Why does my Jewishness flow only from my mother?

The answer is obvious: The certainty of maternity overrides the doubt of paternity...even if there is no doubt!

Messiah, singing

Q Is it true that we will be able to identify the Messiah by his ability and willingness to sing?

Yes. Initially, according to the Talmud's Bar Kapara, God was going to appoint King Chizkiyahu, one of the most righteous, devoted and moral of all Jews, as the Messiah, but He did not. Why? Because he was unable to educate his own son (King Menashe) in "the fear of God," watching helplessly as his boy entered into a world of wickedness. When our rabbis tried to comprehend this family tragedy, they concluded that the boy's descent into evil was a result of his father's not singing songs. This deprived his son of Torah warmth and inspiration; the boy was shocked when his father didn't even celebrate after Israel was miraculously saved from the wicked Sancherib, the Assyrian king. Thus, it became inconceivable that the Messiah, the redeemer of mankind, would not be able to carry a tune. Jewish history has the final say: after Chizkiyahu died, all Jewish learning ceased (temporarily), unable to function in the absence of a song and a smile![9]

Mamzer

Q What defines a "bastard" in Judaism?

There are two central categories: a child of parents who committed incest, or a child from a Jewish woman who, though still married to a Jew, had relations with a Jewish man other than her husband. It is a myth that any child born out of wedlock is automatically a *mamzer*; in fact, since Jewish law prohibits self-indictment, even a woman's confession of adultery is not evidence unless supported by certain halachic requirements. And be careful whom you accuse! "Those who are constantly disqualifying others as *mamzerim*," warns the *Shulchan Aruch*, "are themselves under suspicion of being *mamzerim*, because people who are in the habit of disqualifying are only projecting their own defects onto others!"[10]

---

9. Sanhedrin 94a.
10. Even HaEzer 2:2.

Mazal months?

Q Do the Hebrew months have their own "*mazal*"?

Yes. Each was given its own "*mazal*," a character constellation, a zodiac-style "personality" all of its own. This theological dabbling into *tekhuna* ("astrology"), a Psalmist term that describes God's establishment of the universe, inspired Jewish mystics to be, well, mystical! For example: they took the Aramaic meaning of *tammuz* ("heating") and combined it with the Hebrew meaning of Reuben ("to see"). Since Reuben was the first to "see" God purely out of love, this act turned the "heat" of his personality into light. *Voilà!* God's aim for Tammuz was to improve our "sight." And so that month's zodiac sign is a crab, which sees and walks sideways! Since Nisan was synonymous with Pesach, the "kid" (the young goat worshipped in Egypt and symbolically used for the Pesach sacrifice) became its celestial sign. Mar Cheshvan became the "bitter Cheshvan" (thus the scorpion) because it contained no holidays. For obvious reasons, Tishrei's sign was a scale of judgment. Adar is linked to joy, Av to comfort, Shevat to water, Teves to a goat, Adar to a fish (two of them!), Kislev to an arching bow, Elul to a young child, Sivan to twins, Av to a lion and Iyar's sign is an ox.[11]

Moses' birth certificate

Q What is Moses' real birth name?

No one knows. The name Moses, literally "I drew him [*m'sheetihu*] out of the water," was chosen *ad hoc* by a "rebellious" daughter of Pharaoh (Princess Bithyah, who had fifty-eight siblings). The princess finds a baby floating in a papyrus box-basket amongst the willowy reeds of the Nile. Yehuda Leibush ben Yehiel Michal (*Malbim*), the preeminent Volhynia-born Torah commentator of the nineteenth century, combines the two Egyptian words *mo* (water) and *sheh* ("to exit," or "escape") to arrive at *Moshe*, or in English *Moses*. Obviously the royal daughter used Egyptian, rather than Hebrew, to name her find. Moses is more likely to be derived from the Egyptian *mes* (or *mesu*), which means "child, son." It is ironic, in

11. Psalms 8:4–5.

light of a Midrash that credits not changing their Hebrew names as saving the Jews from perpetual servitude, that God continues to call Moses only by his Egyptian name *Moses*. Moses' father, according to Frankfurt Rabbi Shimon Hadarshan, called his son *Chaver*, his mother called him *Yekusiel*, his sister called him *Yered*, his brother called him *Avi Zandach*, and his nurse called him *Avi Socho*. These multiple names perplexed some scholars, who suggest that the diversity results from the non-conformity of *mo*, since water, with no identity of its own, always adjusts to any container into which it is poured.[12]

Malpractice

Q How can doctors be sued if God is the ultimate Healer?

Are you a doctor? When asked if a doctor can be held liable for damages and sued for errors that endanger patients, Rabbi Eliezer Yehudah Waldenberg responded "yes," despite Ben Sira's statement, "Honor the physician for the Lord has created him." Mishnaic Judaism recognizes the fact of medical negligence and that no doctor is infallible. When the text declares that "the best of doctors is destined for *gehinnom* [hell]," it didn't seem to scare off the rabbis. In the Middle Ages, about fifty percent of Torah scholars were physicians![13]

Mikva

Q Is immersion in a *mikva* intended to fulfill a hygienic purpose?

No. In fact, you have to be physically clean *before* entering a mikva! The term means "gathering" or a "collection" of water, and is used to refer to a small pool built according to specific rules (it has to contain forty *se'ahs* – about 120 gallons – of natural rain, or spring water). If you only have enough money and energy to open one out of three – a *mikva*, *shul* or *cheder* – the mikva comes first. It is, since the early days of ancient Israel, an essential act of spiritual dedication. Even the High Priest was not allowed to conduct his Yom Kippur rituals until he immersed himself in the *mikva*.

---

12. Exodus 2:10.
13. Tzitz Eliezer 4:13; Ecclesiastes 38:1; Kiddushin 4:14.

Money vs. mitzvos

Q I'm trying to keep up with all the mitzvos, but, quite frankly, it's very expensive.

Two thousand years ago exploitative merchants extorted women by raising the cost of the Temple offerings that women were required to bring after childbirth. Shimon ben Gamliel, the highest rabbinic authority of the time, warning that he wouldn't sleep "until the price is lowered," waived the obligation and allowed Jewish women to bring one offering for every five births. The result? Prices dropped drastically. Gamliel had no problem altering a Divine command to correct an injustice, arguing that that was the job of the rabbinate, based on the Torah's "Pursue justice, for I am just!" Over the centuries other courageous Torah leaders have done the same. One Chassidic rebbe threatened to replace his *shtreimel* with a cap unless the price of *shtreimlach* came down. In the *shtetlach* of Eastern Europe, Jews made do with one *esrog* and *lulav* for the whole community, rather than each man buying his own. Bar mitzvas and weddings don't have to be so lavish, and *tefillin* don't need silver containers for the performance of the mitzva. In summary: where there's a will, there's a way!

Magic

Q I'm seven years old, and I wanna be a magician when I grow up. Can I?

I'm not a job counselor, but let me quote you those with more wisdom than mine. According to Levi, a third-century Palestinian *amora*, "Who practices magic will be harassed by magic!" *Sefer Chassidim* warns that "a magician will come to no good." What does the Rambam say? You don't wanna know! He was outright hostile to anything not grounded in the rational, calling magic practitioners "authors of nonsense"! The rabbis threatened the Jew "who acquires a single item of knowledge from a magician" with forfeiting his share in "the World to Come" Olam Haba). So, you still wanna be a magician?[14]

---

14. Shabbas 75a; Sanhedrin 90a.

Mouse? Half animal, half dirt?

Q Is there a conflict between religion and science?

How can there not be? The Torah is not a science manual, and Moses did not receive lessons in geometry and physics during his days and nights on Mount Sinai ("Moshe received Torah from Sinai!"). The knowledge (*emunas chachamim*) that Moses transmitted to the elders via Joshua was not arithmetic or calculus but Torah ethics and truths. When Rashi explains the sanctification of the moon (Rosh Chodesh), he has no interest in explaining how it rotates, or orbits, or disappears by day. This is not to say that our rabbis had no interest in the sciences. They did. They consulted scientists and doctors (from Hippocrates they accepted the fact that a heart has two chambers), followed current findings (the Mishna talks about a mouse that was discovered to be half animal and half dirt), and even conducted experiments to better their comprehension of the world – all in the pursuit of making correct decisions in Jewish law. These conclusions were only as good as the level of science at that time. Is it heretical to point out that rabbis are sometimes wrong in connection with science? No. Anybody can make a mistake, even divinely inspired Sages. Infallibility (except for God) is simply not a notion of Sinai but a component of Christianity. Not only can Sages and halachic communal deciders err, allowances are made for them to do so, and an entire tractate of Talmud (*Horiyot*) is dedicated to the fallout from rabbis who rule in error (e.g., in the wake of a mistaken ruling which affects a whole *shul*, the *rav* is to blame and is ordered to bring sin-sacrifices). The Ramban brushed aside, respectfully, any rabbinic astronomy that clashed with reality ("the science of those days was deficient"), whilst Rav Sherira Gaon and his son, Rav Hai Gaon, took the same approach when medical cures suggested in the Talmud proved to be useless ("Our Sages were not doctors. Therefore, there is no commandment to listen to [their medical advice] because they only spoke based on what they saw in their day."). Tosafos disagreed with this approach, arguing that the medical cures in the Talmud were correct, but that nature had changed, making them no longer effective. The final word belongs to the *Sefer Hachinuch* which, after admitting that mistakes are inevitable, warns that it's better to follow one accepted and respected Torah authority ("even if he says that the right is left and the left is right") rather than multiple, contradictory rulers whose existence would "disrupt the religion, cause disunity among the people, and destroy the nation entirely."[15]

═ Minyan ═

Q How do we know a *minyan* requires ten Jews?

When Abraham, acting as a self-appointed advocate for human rights, passionately pestered the Heavens to save the corrupt and immoral cities of Sodom and Gomorra, he did so in the merit of their pious inhabitants (*tzadikim*). His legendary assault ("Will You sweep away the innocent with the guilty?") wins a Divine reprieve, but only on condition that he identify at least ten "righteous" people. Did he? No. Abraham fails, but ten then becomes the minimum standard for a *tzibur*, the basic unit for communal prayer, and *davening mit a minyan* became mandatory. The Chofetz Chaim once quipped that a *minyan* of thirteen was better than ten because, he reasoned, two Jews are always *shmoozing* and a third is always yelling *Sha shtil!*, "Keep quiet!" That leaves ten to make a functioning *minyan*.[16]

═ Miracles ═

Q If man can split the atom and concoct the Internet, what's the big deal about God splitting a sea?

Miracle in Hebrew is *nes*, from the Latin *mirari*, "to wonder, marvel at, be amazed by." But it can also mean a sign (*oe*) or a test (*nissa*). A *nes* is simply seeing the common in an uncommon way, or as the Rambam puts it, "A miracle does not prove what is impossible; rather it is an affirmation of what is possible!" That a "miracle" must contain some virtuoso supernatural component is a common myth. What turns it into a *nes* is its timing and consequence. That a waterway in Egypt split in two is *not* a miracle *in and of itself*; that it parted just at the right time to save Jewish lives made it

---

15. Rashi, Exodus 12:2; Chullin 45b, 57b, 77a; Leviticus 4:13–21, 23:2; Sifra 9:9,10; Chullin 9:10, 45b, 57b, 77a; Guide for the Perplexed 3:14; Teshuvos Hage'onim; Mo'ed Katan 11a; Sefer Hachinuch 496.
16. Makkos 24a; Hilchos Tefillah 8:1; Orach Chayim 90:9; Mishne Berura 90:29; Y.S. Elyashiv, Avnei Yashfei on Tefillah.

one. This is based on the belief that God, through the forces of nature and history, still actively directs the world. Thus, the presence of faith (*emuna*) is a prerequisite to recognizing miracles. Or as Mendel of Rymanov put it, "If a thousand believing Chassidim were to gather around a block of wood, it too would work miracles!"[17]

Matchmaker, Matchmaker

Q Why is a matchmaker called a *shadchan*?

As a distinct profession, *shadchanus* entered Jewish history courtesy of the bloody Crusades, when Franco-German Jewish life was so disrupted that parents worried their children (especially daughters) might forever stay single. This explains why there is a sudden halachic interest in *shadchanus* in thirteenth-century texts. The responsa are full of such questions as "How much of a fee to ask for?" (Answer: two percent of the dowry, but if the couple live more than ten miles apart, it's three percent!). *Shadchan*, derived from a talmudic term, means "to persuade, negotiate." It was originally a rabbi's job and primary source of income, but marriage-brokerage-for-fees soon took on a "laymen's" life of its own.[18]

Matza size

Q My stomach and matza don't get along. What's the minimum I need to eat?

Before you try to wiggle out of eating matza, remember that this is the *only* Biblical mitzva of "eating" still with us in the absence of the Temple. Here's some good news. Legally, other than the *afikoman*, you only have to eat a *k'zayis* of matza once. This is about the size of an olive. But if your stomach holds out, and you want to comply with *matza lishma*, "[eating just] for the sake of the mitzva," you should eat a *k'zayis* from *each* of the three matzos, in order to make *both* blessings (*hamotzi* and *al achilas matza*). This fulfills the "basic" halachic obligation for elderly gastrically-challenged Jews

---

17. Genesis 22:1; Rambam, Guide for the Perplexed, 3:24.
18. Shabbas 150a.

like me who find eating matza difficult. Remember: if you're only going to eat a small amount you must eat it "all in one go." You cannot chew or linger over it for hours. In the olden days, the minimum amount was defined as an egg's worth. Rosh said *half an egg*; Rambam said a *third of an egg*! But those days are gone. Why? Because no one knows what the size of eggs was back then.[19]

Miss America, U.S.A.

Q My daughter is beautiful. Can I enroll her in the local beauty competition?

No. Jewish girls, because of the laws of *tznius* ("modesty") are not paraded in public contests that exploit the physical. That doesn't mean we are shy in ratings. The Torah describes how "beautiful of form and appearance" was Rachel, and that her sister Leah had soft, beautiful eyes. Judaism encourages women to be "attractive" but *only* for their husbands, not for society at large. The Talmud may describe weddings in old Palestine where brides wore "powder, rouge and hair-dye," and used precious spices and oils to "look better," but our rabbis never defined beauty and desirability in such superficial terms as walking, talking mannequins, supermodel features or Barbie Doll proportions. The only model of perfection and beauty was that created by the Creator, which is why "How to Get from a Size 12 to a Size 10"-type manuals are not at the top of any recommended Judaic list.[20]

A postscript: In London, in the late nineteenth century, a disappointed husband told the judge that he didn't realize until the morning after his wedding (when his wife removed her makeup) that she was not the *sizkeit* ("sweetness") he had courted but a *miskeiti* ("ugly girl"), and asked the court for damages from her father based on "her real, and not her assumed, countenance." He won.

---

19. Shulchan Aruch Harav 475:5, 477:3; Seder Ha'aruch 97:8; Mishne Berura 486:1, 475:9; Yom Tov Sheini K'hilchaso 1; Kitzur Shulchan Aruch 119:5; Aruch Hashulchan 4; Chazon Ish, Dinim v'Hanhagos 17:34.
20. Proverbs 31:30; Genesis 29:17; Shir Hashirim 3:6; 5:13.

═ Mother of all Questions! ═══════════

Q I know, I know, you've been asked this a zillion times, but why do the righteous suffer?

This is the Mother of all Questions. And the answer is…no one knows! God introduces Evil right up front, with no delay, with the Hebrew *ra* ("bad, wrong"), in a tantalizing murder mystery with no motive. In the first fratricide confrontation, the Torah begins, "Cain said to his brother Abel…," but leaves the verse incomplete. Why? Again, no one knows. Evil appears right at the beginning of the Torah ("God saw that the wickedness of man was great!"), not as a force of Creation in its own right but as a metaphysical faculty *within* human nature. What inspires and causes evil will never be known because of God's creation of "free will" as a basic privilege. Jewish mystics call evil an "inclination" (*yetzer hora*), an irresistible, seductive, God-created ingredient in human nature. *Sefer Chassidim Zuta* calls it "an inner thief!" The *Zohar* refers to it as the *Sitra achra*, the "other side," implying that evil is a concept alien even to the Heavens. From the moment God refuses Moses' plea, "Please let me know Thy ways," our Sages were worried. They knew that the radical "Why do the righteous suffer?" was merely a subtle "Where was God?" question, one that placed Jewish scholars under a severe spiritual Mission Impossible, the pressure to come up with the "right" answer. Of course, there is none even remotely fathomable to the human mind in the shadow of the ashes of Auschwitz. God doesn't provide any answer to this mother of all questions, other than the generic, "Things are never what they seem to be!" But He does give the antidote: a *yetzer tov*, the inherent good force within man.[21]

═ Money, money, money ═══════════

Q I like money. I want more of it! Anything wrong with that?!

If you send me some unmarked dollar bills in a large white envelope, I'll send you an answer! Meanwhile, here's an overview. When the fictional

---

21. Rambam, Guide for the Perplexed, 3:12; Genesis 1:31; 6:5–6; 4:7, 8; 8:21; Jeremiah 3:17, 12:1–2, 16:12; Job 2:10.

Mendele declares that "money is the best advocate," he echoes Rav Ashi from Babylon, "Cash is the best broker [because] if the hands are empty, the 'spirit' cannot soar aloft!" This was obvious to all. "God performs many miracles," notes a seventeenth-century *mussar rav*, "but he doesn't grow corn in the houses of the pious!" The traditional attitude to cash is that money isn't *the* root of all evil, but that it *can* become so if not handled with care: *Ohev kesef lo yisba kesef,* "He who loves money will never be satisfied with money!" A "kosher business" (*bediente gelt*) requires three prerequisites. Money has to be earned in a kosher way, used for constructive purposes, and pursued with "clean hands and a pure heart." The first question in the next world, says the Talmud, is *Nasata v'netata b'emuna?* "Were your business dealings honorable?" This is even *before* the inquiry "Did you set aside time for Torah study?" The Torah's desire is *kedoshim tihyu,* that the Jew "be holy." If making money the "Torah way" means making less money, then, say our Sages, "So be it!" In its pursuit of a curtain of holiness in all things, the Torah includes in its category of *chillul Hashem* such incidents as a rabbi not paying immediately for his meat or a Jew not paying his fair share of taxes.[22]

— Meet you halfway!

Q Is the Jewish year divided in two?

Not only did the mystic wing of Judaism see significance in beginnings, it also granted religious gravity to the end *and the middle*, especially the Jewish calendar which was "halved" by the *Zohar*. Thus, we have "two" beginnings of Jewish time, Rosh Hashana and Pesach. The former is a symbol of the Creation of the individual, the latter the creation of the Jews as a nation. The "halfway" point was granted great spiritual import. The first half, beginning in the spring, in Nisan, was a reflection of God's holy stimulus (*Is'arusa di'le'eila*). The second half, which began in the autumn month of Tishrei, was considered a self-generated reflection of man (*Is'arusa di'le'satta*). Thus the festivals in the first half (Pesach, Shavuos) are more passive than man's active involvement in the latter festivals (Rosh Hashana, Yom Kippur, Succos, Chanukah, Purim). The first night of the first half, that of Pesach, was

---

22. Ecclesiastes 5:9; Psalms 24; Shabbas 31a.

elevated as a *leil shimurim,* a "night of [Divine] protection," a time truly "different from all other nights." The Torah follows the same pattern. The first half of the Five Books (Creation, the choice of Abraham, the Flood, the giving of the Torah) were, in relation to mankind, passive and more God-intensive. The latter half is much more active in human terms (sending spies into Canaan, the revolt of Korach, the wars of conquest).

══ Marriage, miscellaneous ══

Q **I'm getting married soon. Any tips?**

Yes, plenty. The Torah says a man is incomplete until he's married, and then he's *really finished*! Remember: give your bride an engagement gift, but not a ring. Why not? It can be mistaken for the legal marriage "acquisition" (*kiddushin,* "consecration, betrothal"). When choosing the wedding ring, plain will do just fine, thank you, with no ostentatious diamonds, no precious stones. And, it must belong to *you*, exclusively, even if you have to "buy" it (halachically) from your parents (who probably paid for it). Tell the calligrapher not to use excerpts from the Torah on the wedding invitations because they're only going to be thrown out. On the day itself, you can get married anytime, as long as the "legal" portion (*kesuba, kinyan,* etc.) is done before nightfall. Must you have an "open sky" wedding? Halachically no, but you should try to continue this ancient tradition. You should fast until after the *chuppa*. You cannot use a relative as a witness. A wedding without a contract (*kesuba*) is meaningless. Your bride must get something valuable from you, plus a promise to be provided food, clothing, shelter, furniture, utensils, ornaments, marital relations, medical care, children, and, God forbid, a funeral – and a ransom (if held hostage). Finally, remember this: behind every successful man stands a surprised mother-in-law (and if you ever miss your mother-in-law, it's OK to take another shot!).[23]

---

23. Kisvei Harav Henkin, Prushei Ivra 5:13; Even HaEzer 28:1, 45; Deuteronomy 22:13; Iggeros Moshe, Yore Deah 2:135; Y.S. Elyashiv, Apiryon l'Shlomo; Mishne Berura 562:11, 638:24; Rema, Even HaEzer 61:1; Iggeros Moshe, Even HaEzer 1:93; Rema, Orach Chayim 562:2, 573:1; Aruch Hashulchan, Even HaEzer 61:21; Exodus 21:10; Genesis 1:28.

= Menschlichkeit =

Q What's more important? To be a *mensch*, or to do a mitzva?

I didn't know one had to choose between the two, but there are many instances in the Torah which emphasize the concept of "doing the right thing."
An example? Abraham had no halachic obligation to put himself, or his
380 men, in a high-risk position to attack (far more powerful) kings when
trying to save Lot. But by "doing the right thing," our forefathers – argues
the great nineteenth-century Lithuanian commentator Rabbi Naftali Zvi
Yehuda Berlin (*Netziv*) – are deserving of the title *Yesharim*, which means
conducting their lives in a spontaneous, yet "absolutely straight" manner. *Middos* 'n' manners are at the heart of Sinai, summarized as *mitzvos
bein adam l'chaveiro*, "relationship commands" between Jews. Eleazar ben
Azariah was straightforward: "No manners, no Torah; No Torah, no manners!" A Jew with good traits is called a *baal middos*. But who defines "good
traits"? The rabbis of *Pirkei Avos*. The clue is "generosity, humility, modesty." In response to being asked, "What's the test of good manners," Solomon Ibn Gabirol, eleventh-century Spanish Torah poet, replies, "To bear
patiently with bad ones!" In his fourteenth-century *Sefer Hasidim Zuta*,
Moshe Cohen, the proper German moralist, advised, "Both in writing and
in speaking, always say 'he and I,' not 'I and he.'" Well said, Morrie – but
you're not original. The *siddur* insists that before saying anything about loving God, a Jew should first affirm that he loves his neighbor as himself![24]

24. Genesis 14:12; Avoda Zara 25a; Pirkei Avos 5:22; Deuteronomy 6:5; Leviticus 19:18.

N

No bickering allowed!

Q Why are there no arguments between the Sages of the Gemora and the Mishna?

There is a general concept that certain "learnings" stopped at certain times, and that only through the institution that "closed them" (e.g., a later, greater and wiser Sanhedrin) can reopen them. That is why the *amoraim* (scholars of the Gemora) do not directly contradict or get into disputes with the *tannaim* (scholars of the Mishna). The post-talmudic rabbis took this tradition to heart and also do not allow themselves to quarrel or clash with either groups of *tannaim* or *amoraim*.[1]

Nsua or snua?

Q They sound alike! Do these words mean the same?

No, quite the contrary. Hebrew linguists take *snua*, which means "hated," and, surprisingly, consider it an anagram for *nsua*, "married"! How do they do that? By examining a specific Torah text about patriarchal wives, firstborns, inheritance and a father's whims. Specifically, a father with two wives, "one

---

1. Kessef Mishneh, Hilchos Mamrim 2:2; Kol Sifrei Maharatz Chayes, vol. 1; Elchanan Wasserman, Kovetz Shiurim, Kuntres Divrei Sofrim 2.

beloved, and another hated," is not permitted, in matters of inheritance, to bypass the "firstborn son" of the dethroned, hated mother, and show favoritism to the children of the woman he loves. In fact, he is ordered to shower "the firstborn of the hated with a double portion of all that he hath!" Why? Because "he is the beginning of his strength." The rabbis are puzzled. "Could it be," they ask, "that a woman can be loved or hated by God? No. She is "loved *within* her marriage, and hated *within* her marriage." This was not a hypothetical case. After Leah, Jacob's first wife, cries that "I was hated," the Heavens give her a son (Reuben), but Jacob still prefers his youngest (Joseph and Benjamin), born from his beloved wife (Rachel). This favoritism provokes resentment, envy, jealousy and a family tragedy that spirals into a series of bloody events. As he lies dying, Jacob is aware of his acts, and both blesses and curses his firstborn Reuben.[2]

Not a dry eye in *shul*

Q Should Jews cry on Rosh Hashana?

My mother and her generation would cry on Rosh Hashana, and made sure to bring many Kleenex boxes to *shul*. Even the old Eastern European *machzorim* for *yom tov* had instructions in certain places, *Yetz miz men unhoben zu veynin*, "Now you should start to cry," a directive that never made its way into any ArtScroll *machzor*. And yet this very emotion became a topic of halachic debate. Rabbi Isaac Luria (*Ari*), the esoteric sixteenth-century Safed kabbalist, castigated those who didn't cry, suggesting that their *neshomos* ("souls") were malfunctioning. "It is praiseworthy," said Rav Yishayah Horowitz (*Shela HaKadosh*), "to cry during Rosh Hashana prayers." But the Vilna Gaon frowned on crying. Why? He considered Rosh Hashana a joyful festival.

---

2. Deuteronomy 21:15–17.

Numbers, not desert?

Q **Why is the fourth book of the Torah (*Bamidbar*) called "Numbers" and not by its literal translation, *desert*?**

It's called "Numbers," from the Latin *Numerus*, because this portion of Torah is primarily involved in a numerical exercise. God obviously wants the Jews counted, *yet again*! Earlier counts occurred after the golden calf, and after the Tabernacle was dedicated. As all accountants know, "counting" creates order and balance out of disarray. The title (*Bamidbar*) is thus a generic expression describing being "in the desert," a remote place where time has no rules and where the only consistency is a fiery sun, the lack of trees and water, and loads of sand, sand, sand, sand…

Nature and nurture

Q **Were the Jews naturally attracted to "the land," or were they ordered to love it?**

Both. A midrash, inspired by *Koheles* ("Consider the work of God"), describes how God acts as a tour guide to Adam in Eden, pointing out "how beautiful and praiseworthy are My works," accompanied by a stern warning, "Don't spoil or destroy them!" The Jews of Biblical times showed an intimate care about the richness of the Holy Land, about its "spring flowers, mountains dripping with wine, hills waving with grain." Their sensitive portrayal of the landscape, which reads like an opulent libretto of sights, smells and sounds, found its way into the *hekhalos* hymns and metaphors of visionary prophets, intuitive psalmists, and such great Singers of Zion as Yehudah Halevi and Moses ibn Ezra. Jewish poets "borrowed" these Mother Nature themes to describe God Himself, going so far as to compare Him to a *nesher*, a "griffin vulture," a fiercely protective parent which carries its young (Israel) on its back to help them learn how to fly. Rav Nachman of Bratzlav, great-grandson of the Baal Shem Tov, a Chassidic lover of nature (who was convinced that prayer was strengthened by the presence of a single blade of grass), urged his followers to pray in the open fields in the spirit of *hitbodedus* ("aloneness"). To those Jews who sought the holy grail of knowledge, our rabbis, inspired by *Layt atar panui minayh* ("There is no place empty of Him"), advised them to "ask the beasts, and they will teach you; the birds of the sky, and they will tell you; or the fish of the sea, they will inform you." That is why Rav Abraham Isaac Kook, mystical genius and the first chief rabbi of Palestine in the twentieth century, saw the return to nature in the *yishuv* as a sacred task, necessary to create "strong and holy flesh!"

Names, not numbers?

Q Why is the second Book of Moses called *Shemos*, "Names"?

The title of one of the Torah's most momentous portions and ancient Israel's foundation epic (*Shemos*) comes from its opening, *Veleh shemos*, "And these are the names…," a genealogical introduction to the House of Jacob and its twelve sons, "each with his household." Doesn't the Greek word *Exodus* have a more compelling ring to it than "Names"? And weren't these names already enumerated, in great detail, in the final verses in Genesis? Why repeat them? By beginning with a word of continuity ("*And…*"), the Torah deliberately makes a linguistic link between *Bereishis* (the book of Creation) and *Shemos* (the book of actions and redemptions), because Jewish history can only be grasped and appreciated by getting to know the actual individuals involved.

Numerous as sand and stars?

Q Shouldn't there be more than sixteen million Jews in the world?

Yes. To be blunt, we have lost the demographic battle. In fact, since the beginning of Judaism more Jews have succumbed than survived. What does this prove? That the survival strategies of the Jews (from political to economic to national) have all failed when measured in sheer numbers, despite *the* greatest paradox of them all. When God breathlessly tells Moses, "I will make of thee a great nation," no one could have foreseen that a million and a half European Jewish children would meet their Maker through chimneystacks and ovens. And Moses was not alone. Each Patriarch was promised the same: that his progeny would increase into a great nation, as numerous as the sands of the sea and the stars in the night sky. So instead of a God-ordained expansion of the Jewish people, the House of Jacob, historically older for example than the House of China, has sixteen million Jews (instead of the two hundred million that a statistical table would project) versus China's one billion. Consider: some sixty years after the Holocaust, the Jews are the only participants in that world war who have not, as yet, replenished their losses. Even the Soviet Union, with a loss of twenty million, has recovered numerically. And yet, there has been a demographic revolution in the State of Israel during the latter half of the twentieth century, with a population now of over six million, in comparison to only 4,500 during Ezra's return to Zion.[3]

— Not *in* but *at!* —

Q What's more correct? "*In* the beginning" or "*At* the beginning"?

In the sixteenth century, Isaac Luria (the *Ari z"l*), an amazing kabbalistic innovator, tried desperately to comprehend the times, specifically the cataclysmic fifteenth-century Jewish exile from the Iberian peninsula, and concluded that Torah events were an ongoing cosmic process (that still continues). Luria concluded that God, right from the get-go at Creation, had withdrawn into Himself (*tzimtzum*), creating a window of opportunity for the entrée of evil (*klippos*), one so immoral that the Jewish nation, the army of God, would have no choice but to resist, spiritually, via prayer and mitzvos, "repairing" the world back to its original Godly state. He was convinced that something had gone wrong not "*in* the beginning" but "*at* the beginning," a catastrophic event that had "broken" God's conception. The passage of time through history, if occupied by holy efforts, was *the* only vehicle that allowed the Jew to make things right, once again, within the concept known as *tikkun olam*, the "repair of the world."[4]

---

3. Exodus 32:10.
4. Midrash Tanhuma, Teruma, 8.

Non-compete clause

Q I promised my employer that I wouldn't compete with him. But now I want to start my own (competitive) business. Can I?

It depends. If your former boss hired you as an apprentice and trained you in your skills, then competing would fall under "stealing." However, if you already had the skills before working for him (other than a moral obligation), it's OK. Why? Jewish law recognizes that, once an employee has been paid for his services, the employer has no further "rights" over him, including controlling future earning opportunities.[5]

No one to read

Q Our rabbi quit! We have no one who can read the Torah. What do we do?

Do you still have a *minyan*? If yes, then you can still take out the Torah with the usual ceremonial, have one Jew read aloud from a *chumash* and another repeat the words whilst following them in the *Sefer Torah*. Can you make a blessing over the *chumash*? No. Can you read from the Torah if you know the Hebrew but not the cantillation melody? Yes. Meanwhile, look for a new rabbi.

Noahide

Q Are non-Jews supposed to adhere to Jewish law?

No. The mandatory mitzvos are a moral code designed to train the Jew for his mission, creating Heaven on earth. The "gentile mitzvos," known as *sheva mitzvos b'nei Noach*, "seven laws of the children of Noach," the Noahide laws, are named after Noah because they derive from the post-Flood covenant to all of the survivors (i.e., mankind). Who taught these laws? Noah's sons (Shem and Ever). Was Moses also obligated to teach them? Yes, says the Rambam, based on a Midrash that recalls how the Torah was

---

5. Chasam Sofer, Choshen Mishpat 9; Minchas Tzvi, Sechirus Poalim 10.

transcribed into the seventy languages of the world for the benefit of non-Jews. Can a non-Jew voluntarily take on Jewish law? Yes, with two exceptions (Shabbas and Torah study).[6]

National mourning

Q Does Judaism differentiate between personal and national mourning?

Yes. Individual loss usually occurs suddenly, unexpectedly, causing great heartache and emotional intensity, and then slowly diminishes over time. Thus the *halachos* of personal grief apply when the wound is still raw and fresh, and involve a withdrawal from normal activity. The mourner is then gradually (from seven and thirty days, to a twelve-month anniversary) helped back to the normal rhythms of life. National mourning, in sharp contrast, hardly ever arrives by surprise, and thus Jewish law is constructed in the reverse with a series of ever-increasing intensity, plunging the Jew deeper and deeper into the blues of sadness and grief. Since our rabbis were aware of human nature, they understood that to order a sudden cessation in our normal lives purely for the purpose of grief was risky; so they devised a "mourning ramp-up" that started with the Three Weeks, then moved on to the Nine Days, climaxing finally on Tisha b'Av.

No legs to stand on

Q Is there any link between the shape of Hebrew letters and lessons in life?

Yes. Commenting on the Torah verse, "You [*atem*] are standing this day," the charismatic Kotzker Rebbe notes that the words *atem* (you) and *emes* (truth) contain the same Hebrew letters, suggesting that truth gives human beings the capacity for endurance and stability. The evidence? The shape of the letters. The *aleph* stands on two legs, the *mem* has a firm horizontal

---

6. Sanhedrin 57a, 59a; Yoma 67b; Genesis 28:11; Yalkut Shimoni, Yehoshua 4; Rambam, Hilchos Melachim 10:8–10; Sanhedrin 57b, 105a, 59a; Rambam, Mishne Torah, Hilchos Melachim 8:11.

base, and the *tav* has two legs. The word as a whole, and each of its letters, thus has staying power. In contrast, the opposite, *sheker* [falsehood] *ein lo raglayim,* has "no legs to stand on" – as the *shin* of *sheker* swivels in Torah script on a narrow base, and the *kuf* and *reish* each have only one leg. The usual Hebrew word for "standing" is *omdim,* not *nitzavim,* but this expression connotes an act of will, a physical *Hineni* reaffirmation ("Here I am, ready to do Your will!"), a stance described as "steadfast, with permanence." The Torah often compares the body language of angels as *omdim* (standing) in contrast to humans' *holchim* (progressing), in that angels are stationary and, in contrast to mankind, incapable of self-improvement (in other words, there is no such concept of becoming "better angels").

Nepotism

Q **What's the Jewish view on family favoritism?**

When Moses exits with grace and dignity, he sets *the* example on how to pass the torch. The great lawgiver, with thoughtfulness, prudence and no display of any hurt feelings or resentment, bestows blessings, encouragement and affirmation on Joshua ("in sight of all Israel"), assuring him, *twice,* that he is perfect for the task. And more: in choosing Joshua over his *own* two sons (Gershon and Eliezer), the Torah renders the final opinion on nepotism.

Neighbor's wife or neighbor's house?

Q **Why do Catholics and Lutherans count our Tenth (anti-coveting) Commandment as two separate commandments?**

The Torah has two versions. "You shall not covet your neighbor's house, you shall not covet your neighbor's wife, or his male or female slave, or his ox or his ass, or anything that is your neighbor's" (in Exodus), and then, "You shall not covet your neighbor's wife. You shall not crave your neighbor's house, or his field, or his male or female slave, or his ox, or his ass, or anything that is your neighbor's" (in Deuteronomy). The difference is obvious. In the latter version, the Torah highlights the status of women, with "wife" appearing before "neighbor." The blurring began in the third century

BCE, with the Hebrew-to-Greek *Septuagint*, when the Alexandrian-Jewish translators decided to eliminate any disparity and (basically) stick to the Exodus version, *twice*! Was it an accident? No. They left other linguistic differences, like Shabbas, intact! The Torah's reversal of *wife* and *neighbor* shows that desire in thought and action is easily interchangeable between *someone* (neighbor's wife) and *something* (neighbor's house), in contrast to the Catholics who divorce (pun intended) thought from action (which explains Jimmy Carter's famous "I lusted in my heart" confession).[7]

Netilas yadayim

Q I want to start performing this mitzva, of washing hands in the morning. What do I do?

First you have to have a *netilas yadayim* cup. This can be made of any material (paper, plastic, etc.) that allows the water to pour from it in an uninterrupted flow. If you're on a trip and there's no water available, you can use other liquids (e.g., soda, tea, beer, fruit juice). How about wine or oil? No. What's the minimum amount of water necessary? The unit of measure is a *revi'is* (around 3.3 ounces) of water on each hand. Why not just use a tap? Is a vessel (*k'li*) essential? Yes. The water must come from one's own acts, known as *koach gavra*, "by human force." Can you dip your hands in water? Yes, if it's non-salty water, such as a river, pool, etc. (i.e., no puddles).[8]

No Hallel?

Q I just came back from *megilla leyning* in *shul*. How come there's no *Hallel* on Purim?

Here are three reasons: The *Megilla* itself is regarded as praise for God's deliverance of the Jews from Persia; the whole episode occurred outside

---

7. Exodus 20:14; Deuteronomy 5:18.
8. Y.Y. Henkin, Am HaTorah, 1979, Vol. 10; Mishne Berura 47, 158:37, 162:30, 160:3, 38, 40; Aruch Hashulchan 162:15; Rema, Orach Chayim 160:12; Orach Chayim 158:10, 159:14, 16; Biur Halacha 162:2; Chazon Ish, Orach Chayim 24:20; Minchas Yitzchok 4:21, Magen Avraham 159:4; Tzitz Eliezer 8:7.

of Israel; and, unfortunately, the defeat of Haman does not yet represent the "end" of dangerous times for the Jewish people.

Nicknames

Q Are nicknames "kosher"?

A rose, writes William Shakespeare, by any other name smells just as sweet! Not so in Judaism, which lends great significance to each name as defining one's persona, a concept known as *k'shmo ken hu*. Name-giving was a family empowerment, a Jewish child's first life-cycle event, an act that used to be the Jewish mother's responsibility. Remember: it was the mother, *not* the father (*nor* God), who bestowed names on eleven of Jacob's children; and, unlike today's custom of naming children after ancestors, the early Torah practice was to give the child a name reflective of hope, or linked to the state of the nurturing mother's mind, which swung like a maternal emotional pendulum from love to pride to expectation (e.g., Reuven's name is based on "seeing"; Shimon's on "hearing"; Levi's on "touching"; and when Rachel's second boy is born, the mother dies in childbirth, but not before naming her boy, *Ben-Oni*, "the son of my distress.") Nicknames, especially derogatory ones, were frowned upon, because they deflected from, and thus upset, the delicate mystical "essence" of a person's real name. The rabbis of the Talmud were blunt. "Three [types of Jews] descend to *gehinnom* [hell]: the adulterer, one who publicly shames another, and he who creates or calls his fellow by a derogatory nickname!"

New Year's Eve

Q My firm is having a New Year's Eve party? Can I go?

Here's the general principle. Participation in any non-Jewish day whose origin is "religious" is prohibited. So the question becomes: is January 1 linked to December 25, a day that is definitely paganistic and off-limits? If the New Year is linked to the eight-day gap between December 25 and January 1 (leading up to Jesus' *bris mila*), it would be absolutely prohibited; however we don't know, and thus rely on the *psak* given by Rav Moshe Feinstein: "If a holiday is based on religious belief, such celebrations are prohibited to Jewish people. However, the first day of the non-Jewish year, January 1, and American Thanksgiving are not prohibited according to halacha because today they no longer have any religious significance, but those who are particular should be strict in respect of them."[9]

No blessing?

Q Every mitzva has a blessing, right?

Wrong. An example? There is no blessing for saying the Haggada, a very significant mitzva. Why? This is a mitzva of memory ("Remember the day when you came forth from Egypt") that has no limit nor a quantifiable measure, stretching "all the days of your life." Therefore, it's just like endless prayer, which incidentally, also doesn't require a blessing! The *Sfas Emes* considers all "rational" mitzvos (e.g., *tzedaka*, *bikkur cholim*) exempt from blessings, and considers being freed from slavery as rational as rational can get!

No body

Q Is the mourners' kaddish said if there is no body?

There is no presumption of death in Jewish law; however, there is a tradition of leniency with the evidentiary requirements (especially in releasing a wife from the status of an *aguna*).

No time to pause

Q Does Simchas Torah celebrate the end of the Torah, or the beginning?

A bit of each! Since "breaking up is hard to do," we immediately start reading the Torah all over again, which is why the most prestigious portion is *Acharon*, the last aliya, through which the entire cycle of Torah readings becomes complete. Jewish mystics had a field day in closing the circle. They

---

9. Iggeros Moshe, Even HaEzer 2:13.

took the last letter (*lamed*) of the last Torah word (*Yisrael*) and added it to the first letter (*bet*, or *vet* without the dot [*dagesh*]) of the Torah's first word (*Bereishis*) to arrive at *Lev*, Hebrew for heart, indicating that Torah is the heart of the Jewish people. That is why the Torah portion of Simchas Torah (the only one that does not have a Shabbas unto itself, and the only time of the year when a Torah reading is permitted at nighttime) is compared to a concert that resonates with the inspirational symphony of Torah being discussed, dissected, debated like an endless and infinite lyric-free *niggun* whose exhilarating verbal animation is "the words of the living God." And since the beat of the heart keeps one alive, there is no time to pause. This underscores Ezra's principal canon of Jewish faith: that the study of Torah is, like a circle, a never-ending celebratory "renewal of the Covenant."

O

Other gods?

Q Doesn't the second commandment ("Do not have any other gods…")
imply that other gods actually *exist*?!

The emphasis is not on "gods," *plural* but on *others*, as in other people's
imaginary gods. That is why our commentators use such polytheistic terms
as "the gods of *others*," "what *others* call gods," "gods made by *others*," etc.
Jewish mystics call them "nothing gods," an expression from *elil* ("an idol"),
derived from the Hebrew *al* ("not"). They then link the Hebrew word for
"other" (*aher*) with the root "to be late," suggesting that the mere idea of
"other" gods delays and prevents "goodness from coming into the world."
Rashi, quoting a Midrash, suggests that God is saying, "As long as I exist
you must have no other gods," a belief that ended up in the second paragraph of *Aleinu*, as Jews ask God daily to help "excise the false gods." The
question is obvious, and was asked by the Roman philosophers: "Why does
God allow such sham 'gods' to exist in the first place?" To which our rabbis
replied, "Why should God destroy essential things such as the sun, moon
and stars merely because there are fools who believe in them?" The philosophers then exclaimed, "So let Him destroy the unessential things that people
worship!" The Sages answered, "God will not destroy the world on account
of fools" (this is akin to the illogical argument that perhaps food should be

destroyed because some people are gluttonous; or banning sports because some are obsessed with it).[1]

= Olam Haba

Q What does this mean?

The Hebrew words *olam* ("world") and *he'elem* ("hidden") are formed from the same root, an implication that it was up to mankind to find the key of sanctity that opened his world to *mei'ein Olam Haba*, "the World to Come." In Torah times the "afterworld" was only one spot, known as *Sheol* ("pit"), and was not divided into a Heaven (*Gan Eden*) or Hell (*Gehenna*). Originally, the Torah's system of reward and punishment, justice and mercy, were all this-worldly, in *this* life, and not delayed to any future "after." So what happened? Jewish history intervened. And faith needed more, especially in view of the suffering of the righteous and the triumph of the wicked. The change in philosophy was gradual and finally became "belief" during the Maccabean era, as Jews, trying to stay sane in an insane world, became convinced that judgment and justice would be meted out in another world.[2]

= On one leg

Q So, if you had to teach Torah [while standing] "on one leg," what would it be?

This reductionist quest has been a magnet for many. Rabbi Akiva's favorite was an echo of Hillel's "What is hateful to you do not do to your fellow; the rest is commentary," "Love your neighbor as yourself!" whilst his *chaver* (Ben Azzai) preferred the universalistic "When God created Man, He made them in the likeness of God." David reduced the 613 mitzvos to eleven (in Psalms). Isaiah got it down to six, and then down to two in four words ("Keep justice, do righteousness"). Micah minimalized to three ("Do justice and love goodness and walk humbly with God"), whilst several oth-

---

1. Yalkut Shim'oni 288.
2. Brachos 57b.

ers settled on only one concept. Amos had "Seek Me and live!" a summary supported by Rabbi Simlai, third-century CE Sage from the Galilee. The most frugal was Rabbi Nathan ben Yitzhak. He thought it should be just "The righteous shall live by their faith!"[3]

One small step…

Q Why did the Torah design the entry to the Tabernacle via a ramp instead of steps?

The answers vary. They range from modesty ("You shall not ascend My altar on steps so that your nakedness [exposing the lower body] will not be uncovered upon it") to leveling the playing field for all who wish to approach and serve God equally (ramps are accessible to all, from the healthy to the wheelchaired) to the rabbinic advice that, when turning religious, it's far better to be patient and take "small steps" (ramping up) than "large steps" (to ascend the altar).[4]

Or else?!

Q Did the Jews accept the Ten Commandments freely?

It's a paradox! Some say the Torah was accepted willingly, with a *naaseh v'nishma* promise ("we will obey, we will hearken"), whilst others dispute that interpretation, claiming the common folk were reluctant. A Midrash has God suspending a mountain over their heads with an ominous warning, "If you accept the Torah, all will be well, but if you refuse, *sham t'heh k'vuratchem*, there your graves will be!" Another has God threatening, "If you accept the Torah, you will survive, but if not, I will turn the world back to chaos [*tohu vavohu*]!" So, were the masses eager or reluctant? With human nature being what it is, the correct answer is probably "both," with anxiety over a commitment often oscillating between "yes," "no," and "maybe." Ambivalence is normal. The same contradictory nature is

---

3. Psalms 15; Isaiah 33:15–16, 56:1; Micah 6:9; Amos 5:4; Habakkuk 2:4; Makkos 23b-24a.
4. Exodus 20:23.

displayed later by the liberated Jews at the Red Sea – some boldly advocating moving forward, others wavering and hesitating!

= Out of India

Q Is there a problem with Indian "wigs" being used as *sheitlach*?

Probably, but other than the advice to "proceed with caution," it remains an unresolved rabbinic issue. India, a country where idolatry is rampant, exports human hair, of which it has a ton, *literally*, every hour! Why? Because hair shaving is a religious rite (called *tonsure*) for Indian women (and men) who do so not to glorify baldness but to celebrate good news, or seek good news in a stressful situation. Giving up hair is symbolic of surrendering ("sacrificing") something of personal value to their Hindu god (Vishnu). In numerous Temples across the country, six hundred barbers cut twenty-five thousand women's hair *daily*. The customers then dip themselves in specific pools of water, having "donated" their "vanity" (hair) to the Temple. It is then bundled and sold to married Jewish women (mainly in Israel and the United States) for the production of expensive *sheitlach*. The money from the sales goes towards the upkeep and maintenance of Hindu shrines. What's the issue? The Torah makes it crystal clear: one cannot benefit from idolatry, a prohibition so serious that it is classified as *avizraihu d'avoda zara* – one must sacrifice one's life rather than commit such a sin!

= Omer

Q I've always been confused about the meaning of this word.

It simply means a "measure." Of what? Of a sheaf of barley. So how big was it? Approximately 2.2 liters, 3.3 dry quarts, 43.2 eggs, and ten percent of an *eipha*. In fact, this is the only sacrifice called by its own measure, akin to calling something a "Quart or Liter Offering," all the others having descriptive names (e.g., the Pesach sacrifice was called *toda*, "thanksgiving," or *shtei lechem*, "two loaves"). And there is another curiosity. Why, considering that the *omer* was presented on behalf of the entire nation of Israel, was it the smallest and cheapest offering of them all? Its barley component was of such a low quality that its grain was halachically unacceptable for

Temple offerings and used instead as animal feed! Why was barley chosen? Because of its lowly status, symbolic of the slave existence in Egypt and thus matching the start of the *omer* count (the Pesach offering), in contrast to its upcoming and uplifting climax (a Shavuos offering of wheat). Jewish mystics note the similarity between *omer* and *teruma* (a produce tithe given to the *Cohanim*), both being called *reishis* (the "first") and an *avoda* (a worship-act). They share a unique halachic capability: the presence of just one tiny kernel of *teruma* makes an entire silo permissible, and a diminutive quantity of *omer* legitimizes an entire year's crop. Yet Jewish law requires the *teruma* be chosen from the best part of the crop, in sharp contrast to the *omer*, which came from the lowliest grain. Why? Because our rabbis saw this as a valuable moral lesson in practicing Judaism. In the punctilious *l'chatchila* pursuit of Torah and mitzvos one need not wait for the "best" time, or opportunity. Far better to be pragmatic and realistic, secure in the knowledge that, even though the temporal "first" may not necessarily be the "best," its choice (like barley, which ripens months before the human-preferred wheat) is not seen as an act of indolence but as a sensible practicality. In short: reality beats out fantasy, every time![5]

Old age

Q My mother's getting old. Should I keep her at home or send her to a retirement home?

The Torah orders Jews to stand up for the elderly (*mipnei tzeva takum*). What if you're in the middle of, say, saying *kriyas Sh'ma*? No matter, says Rav Chayim Sonnenfeld, stand up! In the olden days, the elderly were not shunted off to some far away old-age home but were revered and their wisdom eagerly sought. Respect (*kovod*) for old age was such a given in Jewish society ("Rise before the hoary head; honor the face of an old man") that Isaiah was convinced that a community could be judged by how it treated those with "gray hair." The Torah disagrees with Benjamin Disraeli ("Youth was a blunder, manhood a struggle, old age a regret") and considers old

---

5. Leviticus 23:10; Exodus 16:36, 18; Menachos 77a; Y. Frand, Commuter Chavrusah Tape # 996, Kovod Habrios: The Concept of Human Dignity; Brachos 40a; Leviticus 23:10; Pesachim 72b; Mishna Terumos 2:4.

age nothing more than a "natural disease." A word of caution from Ben Sira: "Dishonor not the old!" Why? Because, eventually, "we shall all be numbered among them!"[6]

One dollar, or $100?

Q Is it better to give $1 to charity 100 times, or $100 once?

"If your God loves the poor so much," the wicked Turnus Rufus once taunted Rabbi Akiva, "why doesn't He provide for them?" Akiva's reply embraced the merit of giving *tzedaka*: a mitzva which supports the supporter (i.e., to give is to receive!). An opportunity, says the Midrash, for meritorious self-development, a chance to be "God-like" to another. Thus the Rambam, based on *Pirkei Avos*, "All is judged according to the number of deeds," suggests that it's better to donate one dollar a hundred times, rather than a hundred dollars once. The Chofetz Chaim once politely begged off a donation large enough to cover his yeshiva's entire operating expenses, explaining, "I cannot allow one Jew to monopolize the mitzva of *tzedaka* and thus deprive others of the opportunity!"

Off to war we go!

Q When did the Jews become an organized military force?

The Jews became a basic fighting force the moment they had land to conquer, four decades after wandering in the desert. Who was the enemy? Canaanite tribes and nations that lived in the Promised Land (Philistines, Ammonites, Moabites, Amorites, Jebusites, Hivites, etc.). What were their marching orders? "To utterly destroy," was God's firm directive, especially "their altars, pillars…hew down the graven images of their gods, and destroy the names of them out of that place!" This required a regular standing army, and so the military draft was instituted for every Jewish male over twenty who was capable of bearing arms. It stayed in place from King David (the first to use horses and chariots in warfare), through King Solo-

---

6. Leviticus 19:32; Exodus 20:12; Isaiah 3:4–5; Proverbs 20:29; Job 15:10; Immanuel of Rome, Mahberet, 1491; Ben Sira 8:6.

mon (the first to create a distinct Jewish cavalry), down to the end of the period of the monarchy. When Jews went into battle, they blew a shofar, offered sacrifices, and consulted God either through their prophets or their mystical breastplate, *Urim and Thummim* ("light and perfection"), known as *choshen mishpat*, "breastplate of judgment."[7]

Oedipus, schmoedipus

Q Was Sigmund Freud Jewish?

Yes, but by his own admission, he wasn't a good Jewish boy (refusing to mourn after his own mother's death), nor a good Jewish scholar (in his flighty treatise, *Moses and Monotheism*, he claims that Moses was Egyptian, not Jewish). Freud was a secular, audacious, energetic, shrewd, cigar-addicted, radical son of a Jewish wool salesman from Galicia, Poland. From his Vienna office he managed to convince an entire body of Victorian prudes that they were racked with neurotic angst, miserable dreams, childhood fantasies. Nabokov called it all "mumbo jumbo." But it did give us one of the best therapeutic lines of them all, "Oedipus, schmoedipus, what does it matter, so long as the Jewish boy loves his mother?"

Oil to wine

Q Why is Chanukah associated with oil, and Purim with wine?

Here's the *gematria* answer, courtesy of our clever Jewish numerological-mystic tinkerers. Take out a calculator and follow these instructions! Remember, falling exactly in between Chanukah and Purim are the two days of Rosh Chodesh *Shevat* and *Tu b'Shevat*. If you count, from the last day of Chanukah up to, and including, the first day of Rosh Chodesh *Shevat*, you'll get twenty-nine days. Now, starting from the second of Shevat count up to, and include, *Tu b'Shevat*, to arrive at fourteen days. Got it? Good! Straight after *Tu b'Shevat*, starting from the 16th of the month, count to Purim and you'll get twenty-nine days again. Now multiply twenty-nine by two to get fifty-eight (the value of *chen*, which means "grace" or "symmetry"), and

---

7. Deuteronomy 12:2, 3; Numbers 1:3; I Kings; II Chronicles 13:3, 14:8.

then add fourteen to get seventy-two (the value of *chesed*, "loving-kindness"). And seventy-two happens to be the number from the last day of Chanukah to Purim inclusive! Thus the bridge from the *yom tov* of olive oil to the *yom tov* of wine. Not happy with the answer? Buy a different book!

Organ donation

Q Can I donate an organ?

Yes. Saving a life by organ donation is surely one of the most praiseworthy of all mitzvos (as long as you are not causing yourself harm). Originally, when transplantation was in the experimental stage, organ donation was against Jewish law; however now that the survival rate is significantly higher, rabbinic opinion has shifted.

Olympic Games

Q Why were the rabbis against the early Olympic Games?

Well, let's see. Perhaps the reasons range from immodesty and degeneracy (the original Olympic event was the two-hundred-yard naked footrace; the distance being a *stadion*, hence today's "stadium"); to ostentatious (the chariot races were only for the rich who could afford horses); to its elevation of sports as a religious rite (the first games were held in Olympia, home of the god Zeus); to pure paganism (the glorification of man with the participants' artificially scraped bodies to make them look "beautiful"); to fight-to-the-death ritualized blood-letting (the sport of *pankration* required two men to choke, punch, kick, scratch and batter each other to the bloody finish; the games were called *agones*, from where we get "agony"); to blatant corruption (Prince Pelops from Asia Minor bribed his aides to replace the metal in the king's chariot with wax that killed him, the prince's own father-in-law; meanwhile, Nero, the most spoilt emperor of them all, enrolled and won every race!). So why were the rabbis against? Surely it's obvious!

Open and shut

Q I'm annoyed by people leaving their *siddur* open when they leave *shul*. Am I right?

Yes. It is considered disrespectful to leave a *siddur*, or any other holy book, open or even upside down (akin to the insult of walking away from someone while he or she is still talking to you). In fact, Jewish folklore whispers about an angel called *Shed*, from the initials of *Shomer dappin*, "He who guards the pages," who is delegated to punish Jews who walk away without closing holy books with memory and knowledge loss.[8]

Ostriches

Q Are ostriches kosher?

All birds are kosher except twenty types (including the ostrich); but, since we can no longer identify these species, Jews eat only domesticated birds (e.g., chicken, turkey, etc.) that are traditionally accepted as kosher. The ostrich, the largest member of the bird kingdom, was well known during Torah times as an ornamental bird, inhabiting deserted and lonely places, and known for its lack of intelligence ("God has deprived it of wisdom"), cruelty (it would abandon its own eggs which were then eaten by newly hatched chicks), ability to swallow anything (even a set of *tefillin*), and its melancholy cry. (One of its Hebrew names is *bas haya'ana*, literally "daughter of wailing"!)[9]

Out of the way?

Q How did the Jews of Judea, scattered across the Holy Land, manage the back-and-forth trek to Jerusalem for animal sacrifices, given the primitive means of travel?

They didn't. The rabbis divided the country into twenty-four districts

---

8. Shulchan Aruch, Yore Deah 277; Minhagei Y'shurun; Shach, to Yore Deah 277.
9. Leviticus 11:16; Deuteronomy 14:15; Job 39:17; Eicha 4:3.

(*ma'amados*), and assigned a special week to each district during which local delegations would go up to Jerusalem. Once there, these emissaries timed their morning and evening sacrifices to when their back-home constituents gathered to pray in their synagogues (a model for the future practice of daily *shul* prayers). And to ensure that there were no second-class Israelites, offerings were "equalized" (*each* being "a satisfying aroma to God") by way of sliding-scale dues. For example: the Jew who could not afford the choicest sheep or goat could use a pigeon; and if one was too indigent to even afford a pigeon, then a tenth (*eipha*) of plain ground wheat would do just fine.

— Only on Yom Kippur

Q Why is it OK to say God's Name on Yom Kippur?

The original custom of silently murmuring *Baruch shem kavod malchuso l'olam va'ed,* "Blessed is the Name of His glorious kingship forever and ever," the second line in the *Sh'ma,* arose from sheer unadulterated anti-Semitism. With hostile neighbors peeking over their shoulders in exile, Jews were simply too terrified to openly declare allegiance to Sinai, especially when the ruling elite, usually Catholic, considered this accolade to a God other than their god (or emperor) an act of treason. But on Yom Kippur, one day a year, the silence was swept aside as the excited masses openly and defiantly responded to Aaron's sweeping confession with triple prostration and some spiritual scream-therapy that included the kohen gadol (high priest) shouting the *Shem Hameforash* (the tetragrammaton Name of God) so loud that it was heard as far away as Jericho.

— Old, yet new

Q My wife thinks I'm a pack rat and wants to get rid of all my old "stuff." She claims being tidy is a Torah desideratum.

Are we both married to the same woman? Remember, marital compromise is the key to *shalom bayis* (peace in the home)! Whenever my wife and I argue, I always make sure to get the last word in! And that's usually, "I'm sorry!" The key passage to your question is a Torah blessing, "You shall eat old grain long stored [and] you shall clear out the old to make room for the new." This clearly defends "old stuff," whilst suggesting it be "cleared out" from time to time, which clearly leaves room in the basement and the attic for *both* "old and new."[10]

Our bad-omen day

Q Which is the worst day in the Jewish calendar?

The moment God decreed that "Trouble" was to be Tisha b'Av's middle name, the Ninth of Av entered the Jewish calendar cycle as our Annual Bad Omen Day. As one of three non-Biblical commemorative days (the other two are Purim and Chanukah), Tisha b'Av is traced back to the Torah episode of the twelve spies (*meraglim*) who, despite being prominent "princes of each tribe," delivered a devastating intelligence report describing Canaan as "a land that devours its inhabitants," adding, with a stunning lack of confidence and pride, "we were in our own sight as grasshoppers, and so were we in their sight." The Heavens' response? Quick and brutal. "You cried without cause; I will, therefore, make this an eternal day of mourning for you." Thus the ignominy of Tisha b'Av was born, and God's first national ordained death penalty is recorded as the generation of the desert was condemned to die before entry into the Holy Land.[11]

Original sin

Q Does Judaism believe in "original sin?"

No. Jews are not born bad, but simply go through life wanting to do the right thing. Our rabbis put it politely: Jews occasionally get distracted by a *ruach shtus*, a "spirit of stupidity," but in reality we all, in some manner, fall prey to the *yetzer hora* (evil inclination). The goal of the Torah is not to make gods and angels out of men but to bring Godliness into people.

---

10. Leviticus 26:10.
11. Numbers 13:31–33; 14:2–3; 33:38; Ta'anis 29a; Numbers 13:14, 18–20.

Jews are not flawless, but Judaism is (*Toras Hashem t'mima* – "the law of the Lord is perfect").[12]

On one foot

Q Whatever happened to this expression?

This famous heathen-to-Shammai expression, "while standing on one foot" (*al regel achat*) vanished from the texts for the next thousand years, resurfacing in a fourteenth-century responsum from Shimon Ben Zemach Doran, "And these too are things that cannot be taught while standing on one leg!" Why did it disappear? I don't know. Some see the phrase not in a literal sense but simply as exegetic, a figurative idiom meaning "quickly" or "superficially." Others say that it fell out of favor because its Latin origin (*stans pede in uno*) stems from an anti-Semitic text by Horace.[13]

One year older, please

Q What exactly do Jews wish for on each Yom Kippur?

For God to make them at least one year older so they can return on the following Yom Kippur. But how? Judaism tells us that there *is* something we can do about death, without dwelling on it. The art of dying requires an "art of living," defined as fidelity to the Laws of Moses, especially on Yom Kippur, with the focus on rectifying character blemishes. This powerful process is called *teshuva*, which Judaism considers not a right but a privilege, an act of mercy which defies natural law. "If one were given five minutes' warning before sudden death, five minutes to say what it had all meant to us," theorized Christopher Morley, "every telephone booth would be occupied by people trying to call up other people to stammer that they loved them." On Yom Kippur all empiricism falters before the certainty of

---

12. Psalms 19.
13. Shabbas 31a; S.Z. Doran, Responsa R, 14:5; Satire 1, Lexicon Horatianum, vol. 2, by Dominicus Bo, Hildesheim, 1965–66.

death, as synagogues around the world become the "telephone booths" to God used by Jews who are reminded that when they die they leave behind all they have – and take with them all they are!

P

Pets

Q Do I have to buy kosher food for my cat?

No, but you can't feed your cat any meat-milk mixture (*basar b'chalav*) either. Why not? Because the Torah forbids any benefits to flow from anything forbidden for Jews (*asur min haTorah*), which includes pet foods. Can I give it to a neighbor's pet, or to a stray? No. Can I give my household pet *Chametz* on Pesach? No.[1]

Preemption

Q Does America's new policy of preemption have any validity in Jewish law?

Absolutely. The authority for surprise military preemption to forestall an enemy is based on a famous Torah adage, *Haba l'horgecha, hashkem l'horgo*, "If someone comes to slay you, forestall him by slaying him!"

---

1. Rema Yore Deah 87:1; Mishne Berura, Orach Chayim 248:27–28; Sdei Chemed, vol. 1.

Prophet's prophecy

Q When the Hebrew prophets prophesised, was there any "magic" involved?

Before the institution of prophecy at Mount Sinai, the use of magic was considered legitimate. However, although such major philosophers as Saadiah Gaon and Judah Halevi championed the truth of a prophet's prophecy, the Rambam, rooted in his perception of Mother Nature, was not so accepting of the idea that a prophet does not work miracles as proof of the truth of his prophecy. Concerned that prophecy not be confused with witchcraft ("an abomination"), the Torah condemns those who rely on "an augur, soothsayer, diviner, sorcerer, spell caster, ghost consulter…"; instead, the Jew is advised to be *tamim* ("wholehearted"), a combination of *tam* ("innocent" or "innocuous") and *mu'ad* ("forewarned"). According to Ibn Ezra, twelfth-century Spanish Biblical commentator, the concept of *temimus* is sheer non-intellectual obedience (the simplistic naiveté of "innocence"). In the search for a religious consciousness (*avodas Hashem*), God has no need for such phony intermediaries as the necromancer, or those involved in clairvoyance, alchemy, wizardry, magical and gullible voodoo practices which the Rambam, whose entire Torah approach is rooted in rationalism, describes as an insult to "the intelligence and intellect of scholars and pure thinkers (*temimei hada'as*)."[2]

Public service

Q I work in the public service. Are there any Jewish laws that apply to me?

Yes, many! There is a general principle that those who "service" the community must do so *b'emuna*, which means "reliably" and "honestly." This requires you to work amongst the common folk (as exemplified by Moses who went "down from the Mount *to the people*"), not to use your official position for personal benefit (bribery), to be patient and polite ("his deeds must be pleasant and appropriate"), and, most important of all, to be fully

---

2. Saadiah Gaon, Emunot v'De'ot, Part 3; Judah Halevi, The Book of the Kuzari, 1:8.

accountable (even Moses, honest to a fault, pledges to "give a full account" after building the Tabernacle). Here's some rabbinic advice: if you're handling public funds, never go alone, and watch what you wear (no pockets, nor long sleeves). Why? To avert even the suspicion that you are "pocketing" public funds![3]

Prenuptials

Q I'm getting married soon, and my bride wants a prenup. Is this allowed?

When Rav Moshe Feinstein ruled that prenuptial agreements are permissible, he did so with no enthusiasm, cautioning that it be done only "on a case by case basis" after taking into account "the emotional state of the couple." Rabbi J. David Bleich describes these types of agreements as "divisive"; however, in the face of the tragedy of *agunos* ("chained wives" who are refused a *get* from their husbands), a prenuptial contract is encouraged by several rabbis as long as there are no clauses of coercion which are forbidden in Jewish law (e.g., imposing financial fines on a recalcitrant husband).

Pas palter?

Q What does this expression mean?

It describes kosher bread baked in a non-Jewish bakery. Although non-Jewish wine, oil, and cooked foods were all declared off-limits to the Jew for fear of social intermingling, the attitude towards non-Jewish bread was lenient. Why? Because bread was more of a necessity, a *chayei nefesh*, the "vital element" of the dietary staple.[4]

---

3. Deuteronomy 16:19; Rambam, Hilchos De'ot 5:1; Exodus 19:14; 33:8; Midrash Tanchuma; Shekalim 3:2.
4. Chasam Sofer, Yore Deah 120; Kitzur Shulchan Aruch 72:2; Chazon Ish, Yore Deah 49:7.

═ Peace or unity? ═══════════

Q Which one's more important?

The proponents of a House United include the prestigious *tanna* Simeon bar Yohai, who was convinced that "if one Jew had been absent, God would have withheld the Torah" (which is why it was given "in the sight of *all*"). Philo, first-century Alexandrian Torah philosopher, notes that the Ten Commandments were addressed in the *singular*. But not so fast! The ancient Sifra disagrees. The most important blessing is not unity, but that there be "peace [*shalom*] in the land," based on Ezekiel's universal demand to "seek and pursue" it! The Midrash thus elevates *shalom* above all else, and a whole slew of rabbis agreed. Peace was "the climax of all blessings" (Eleazar HaKappar); the "essence of all prophecies" (Eleazar ben Shammua); the very "Name of God" (*Zohar*); and, added Eleazar bar Kappara, one could even *tell lies* to preserve it![5]

═ Pluralism ═════════════════

Q Why, in Hebrew, is "good afternoon" in plural?

In contrast to the singular expressions of "good morning" (*boker tov*), "good evening" (*erev tov*), and "good night" (*lailah tov*), one wishes another a "good afternoon" (*tzohorayim tovim*) in the Hebrew plural. The Ramban explains why: the singular of the noon's plural (*tzohorayim*) is *tzohar*, which, akin to *zohar*, means "light"; *tzohorayim* ("lights") is in the plural because the morning sun, rising in the east, casts a shadow on the west side of objects. The opposite occurs in the afternoon (the sun, descending in the west, causes a shadow on an object's east side). At noon, however, there is no shadow in any direction because the sun is directly overhead; both sides (in the *plural*) are thus a time of *total* light.[6]

---

5. Psalms 34:15.
6. Ramban, Exodus 12:5.

Prayer

Q What's the point of prayer? Does God actually listen? Does He answer?

"Let others rely on their hands!" roars the Midrash, "Israel's weapon is prayer!" That God helps those who help themselves is a common theme throughout a Torah that sees prayer as a natural inclination of every human being, an instinctive tendency of the human soul. To the tenth-century CE Josippon, prayer was "a conversation with God." To the Baal Shem Tov, it was "a window to Heaven." There are ten different Torah expressions for prayer, including praise (e.g., celebrating the greatness of God), thanksgiving (e.g., expressing gratitude to God for the miracle of life), penitence (wherein Jews seek to correct their failures), simple faith ("I lift up my eyes to the hills"). Are some prayers forbidden? Nothing is forbidden, but some are inappropriate (e.g., selfish, useless, vulgar, or immoral prayers). Does God answer? Yes. But sometimes the answer is, "No!"[7]

Parapsychology

Q Are Judaism and parapsychological phenomena compatible?

The term *paranormal* comes from the Greek *para* ("beside," or "beyond") which, when read in conjunction with *Psi*, short for *psyche* ("mind, soul"), refers to an event (*phenomenon*) which science deems physically possible (e.g., precognition, near-death experiences). But these "supernatural" *phenomena* are simply accepted by the Torah as a facet of Mother Nature, as established at Creation, and are openly discussed in the Talmud by several rabbis (Chisda, Rava, Honi) who are theologically unintimidated by the presence of telepathy, dreams, clairvoyance, or extrasensory perceptions.[8]

---

7.   Psalms 23, 121, etc.
8.   Brachos 55a; Sanhedrin 30a, 101a; Ta'anis 19a; Eruvin 43a.

Poverty

Q Is poverty a disgrace?

Poverty is no disgrace, sang the fiddler Tevye, but it's no great honor either! "Poverty in a house is more bitter than fifty plagues!" This is why the mother of all social mitzvos is to support the poor ("God's people"), alleviate their condition, and encourage opportunities for self-help (a fishing rod being a better gift than a fish!). As a reminder that riches are a blessing to be used wisely, Yehudah HaNasi, famed editor of the Mishna, would publicly honor and respect the wealthy for their potential to help the community. Why do we have poverty in the first place? "To provide," writes Jehiel Anav, thirteenth-century Roman scribe, "the well-to-do with an opportunity for charity!"[9]

Pizza

Q Is it true? The Jews invented not just the sandwich, but also pizza?

By placing a slice of the paschal lamb and bitter herbs onto matza, Hillel invented open sandwiches; later, Roman Jews created the world's first (cold) pizza when they put cheese and olive oil on matza. Did they ever warm it up in a pizza oven? Who knows, who cares!

Pork Ahoy!

Q Why, out of all the forbidden (*treif*) animals, is the pig singled out as the most abominable?

Originally the pig was *not* singled out by the Torah; it simply fit the not-chewing-its-cud definition of a non-kosher animal. But eventually swine became abhorrently unclean in the eyes of Jews for several reasons, ranging from idolatry (pigs were once worshipped, offered as sacrifices to alien gods and idols, their meat eaten in "spiritual" banquets) to health reasons

---

9. Baba Basra 116a; Exodus Rabba 31:12, 14; Exodus 23:11; Leviticus 23:22, 25:35; Deuteronomy 15:11; Eruvin 86a.

(because pigs reveled in filth and ate dirt, they were seen as infected and contaminated, prone to certain diseases such as trichinosis) and ethical contempt (pigs, in fits of infanticide, ate their own young, a disgusting irreverence for life). Even early non-Jews detested pigs. At a time when primitives believed they were what they ate (or as the Germans would put it, *Der Mensch ist was er esst*, "Man is what he eats!"), the pig was scrupulously avoided by Arabs and by the Caribs (who thought they would develop small "piggish" eyes), and Zulu women (who were scared they would give birth to "pig-like" children). Egyptians who raised pigs were so socially ostracized that they could only find wives among other pig-raisers, and if a Greek accidentally touched a pig, he would jump, fully clothed, into the river to wash off any trace!

Polygamy

Q If my forefathers had multiple wives, why can't I?

During a political campaign in Utah, some spinsters complained to Theodore Roosevelt about a candidate for the Utah Senate because the man was a polygamist. "Ladies," Teddy told them, "I prefer a polygamist who does not polyg to a monogamist who does not monog." The Torah refers to Eve as a wife in the singular. Monogamy eventually became synonymous with God's special relationship with Israel, the idea of having multiple wives being compared to worshipping more than one god. Polygamy within the Torah always came with special circumstances. Abraham takes a second wife *only* when he thinks Sarah cannot conceive; Jacob marries Rachel, his second wife, *only* after being deceived into marrying Leah, etc., but it was never presented as the Jewish ideal. In fact, not a single rabbi in the Talmud is recorded as having more than one wife, although there is one view that says one can marry as many wives as one can support!

Parental blessings

Q Where did Isaac get the idea for his deathbed firstborn blessings?

I don't know. Did Isaac receive a similar firstborn blessing from his own father? No. What about the precedent of Noah blessing Shem and Japheth?

This was not a spiritual "Jacob-like" testament but a way to add potency to his curse of Ham, his wayward son. How many parental blessings appear prior to Isaac's? Only one. When Rebecca is about to leave home to marry a man sight unseen, her mother (and brother) see her off with, "O sister! May you grow into thousands of myriads; may your offspring seize the gates of their foes." This blessing is still in use today, the traditional prenuptial blessing for Jewish brides, expressing similar conflicting parental emotions of hope and fear, in seeing their daughters leave the familial nest.

Play it again, Sam

Q How important was music in early Judaism?

Very! Music was important to the early prophets, starting with Samuel, but it reached its high point under King David (and later under Hezekiah and Josiah) who oversaw four thousand musicians (i.e., more than ten percent of the entire tribe of Levi!) whose Temple job was to use music, both vocal and instrumental, to praise God. This chorus was led by two hundred eighty selected and well-trained musicians, each twelve-section of singers having its own leader (conductor, the most famous of whom were Heman, Asaph, and Ethan). What kinds of musical instruments were used? Three types: stringed instruments (like the harp, psaltery), wind instruments (like the flute, pipe, trumpet), and those that were beaten or shaken (like the timbrel, castanets, cymbals) to produce sound.

Pest controllers

Q Does Judaism have a fixation with health and sickness?

Yes. Where does this come from? It can be traced to an unusually lengthy double Torah portion (*Tazria-Metzora*), unique in all of Leviticus. In this How-to-Deal-with-Mysterious-Diseases, the Torah confronts a natural human fear: the dreaded risk of contamination and infection spread from person to person, even house to house. What's the difference between *metzora* and *tzara'as*? The former refers to a contagious leprosy; the latter, from the Aramaic *segiruta* ("isolation"), is a collective term for serious diseases (akin to eczema, vitiligo, psoriasis) that appear on skin, clothing, even on walls, a *tuma*, "spiritual defilement" that requires a purification process (*tahara*) which includes seven days of isolation. After delineating five kinds of "impurity" (*tumos hayotzos migufo*), the Torah reminds the common folk, priests, and prophets what they must do in order to become a "priestly nation (*mamlechet cohanim*)." The priest? He is to act as a combined ritual diagnostician, quarantine officer, and residential "pest" controller. The prophet? His duty is to be a spiritual medic. "Follow his prescription!" advises the *haftora*, referring to Elisha's medical counsel.

Priests 'n' prophets

Q Did the priests and Hebrew prophets, as leaders, get along?

No, there was a simmering dichotomy between the two, erupting into *machlokes* (disputes) every now and then. One priest (Amatziah) once drove a prophet (Amos) out of town (Beth-El) because he didn't like his doom-and-gloom prophecy. One prophet (Malachi) attacked the Jerusalem priesthood for being lax during the Temple sacrifices. The catastrophe of a golden calf involved a priest (Aaron) appeasing the crowds against the wishes of a prophet (Moses). Why the friction? The prophets of Israel (who received their messages from God) were *expected* to be critical of others, *including* priests (who were there to assist the people in their search to serve God). Since the existence of prophecy was an essential precondition for a functioning community, the Hebrew prophet played a central role in both the spiritual and politico-social leadership of the Jewish nation, usually as part of the vocal opposition ("Him you shall heed [*tishme'un*]!").[10]

Prozbul

Q What does this mean?

In response to a direct Torah order, "At the end of every seven years [*shmitta*] you shall cancel all debts," Jews began, near the end of the seven-year cycle, withholding loans because of the fear that creditors would not get their money back. So Hillel introduced the *prozbul*, derived from *pros*

---

10. Amos 7:10–17; Malachi 1:6, 2:9; Exodus 32:1–6; Deuteronomy. 18:14–15.

buli ubuti, "an enactment for rich and poor," whereby lenders transferred their debts to the Court and collected them after the seventh year as agents of the Court.[11]

Pass the turkey!

Q **Can I celebrate Thanksgiving?**

The *responsa* of Rav Moshe Feinstein conclude that Thanksgiving is not a religious holiday, but a secular "day of remembrance for citizens of this country." Therefore Jewish simchas may be held on this gentile day (as well as on January 1), usually prohibited because of *maris ayin* (appearances) if the day is "religious" for gentiles. However, Rav Moshe cautions "pious people" (*baalai nefesh*) to be "strict" (i.e., keep your eye on the ball, the day may develop religious overtones in the future). In 1934 President Roosevelt was motivated by purely commercial motives and not the spirit when he pushed Thanksgiving from the last Thursday in November to the second-to-last Thursday in November. Why? Because November had five weeks to increase shopping spending. What about the Thanksgiving meal of turkey (in Hebrew, *hodu*; in Yiddish, *hendika hen*)? Rav Moshe sees no prohibition as long as it's voluntary and not obligatory. In Europe, the turkey was not considered a kosher bird by some authorities (*Rama*); however, this changed after the bird was found to be within the same halachic category as chickens, geese, and ducks. Most scholars came to the same conclusion as Rav Moshe, including – according to Rabbi Hershel Schachter – Rabbi Joseph B. Soloveitchik and his father, Rabbi Moshe Soloveitchik. Rabbis Yehuda Herzl Henkin, Ephraim Greenblatt, Eliezer Silver, Rabbenu Nissim, Maharik, and Rama accept gentile "holidays" if there is no basis of idolatrous practices (the Gra disagrees). Rabbis Yitzchak Hutner and Menashe Klein thought that any annual non-Jewish holiday based on the Christian calendar was uncomfortably close to idol worship and therefore prohibited Thanksgiving feasts. Rabbi David Cohen (of *Gvul Yavetz*) writes, "to eat turkey for the sake of a holiday is prohibited, since this is an irrational rule of [non-Jews] and following it is improper."[12]

---

11. Deuteronomy 15:1–2.
12. Rema, Yore Deah 148:12; Iggeros Moshe, Even Ha'ezer 2:13; Kiddushin 66a; Moshe

Perceptions

Q Does Jewish law recognize the difference between perception and reality?

No. The law of *maris ayin* prohibits something that *is* otherwise allowed if there is the "possibility" that an onlooker might get the wrong impression. An example? You can't go into a McDonalds to get a drink of water (unless you're about to die of thirst) because someone might see you leave and assume you just ate *treif*! What if there's absolutely no chance of being seen? No matter. "If it's forbidden for appearance's sake, it cannot be done even in strictest privacy." Meanwhile, the rabbis of *Pirkei Avos* also warn the bystander to "judge every person favorably!"[13]

Pharaoh Syndrome

Q What is this?

To undertand the "Pharaoh mentality" you rearrange the Hebrew letters of "Pharaoh" to arrive at *arufa,* which refers to the back of the neck, the Biblical symbol of stubbornness. Hence the expression *kesheh oref,* "stiff-necked," a metaphorically speaking description of obstinacy. It is the "hardening," not of Pharaoh's hands or brains, but of his heart that hints at his evil. And so Jews pray to God not with all their might and body but with all their "heart and soul." The Torah term for heart (*lev*) appears no less than 850 times, a recognition that it is *the* central discerning organ (*lev shomaya*) of emotion, intellect, character, morality. Thus, when God judges an individual, He "probes the heart"; and when He wishes to reform, He promises to "replace the heart of stone with a heart of flesh." Pharaoh's ("hardened heart") syndrome is synonymous with a predisposition to cruelty, a cognitive dissonance of those who are so cold and callous ("a heart of stone") as to be immune from feeling the pain of others. This is not just a Jewish

---

Feinstein, Megilla 7; Ramban, Deuteronomy 4:2: Iggeros Moshe, Yore Deah 4:11; Yore Deah 82:3; Y.H. Henkin, Benai Banim 2:30; Ran, Avoda Zara 11a; Rema Yore Deah, 178:1; Gra, Yore Deah 178:7; Yitzchak Hutner, Pachad Yitzchak, 109; Iggeros Me'at, HaChazon Ish, 97.

13. Beitza 9a; Shulchan Aruch 301:45; Pirkei Avos 1:6.

insight. Egyptian tomb paintings show the weighing of dead hearts against feathers, the supposed hieroglyph for truth, to ensure they are empty of evil before rewarding the dead with eternal life.

Pasteurized

Q What happens to kosher wine if touched by a non-Jew?

It becomes forbidden for a Jew to drink. Why? Because, originally, wine was used by pagans in idol worship; however, the more lasting reason is the same as that for not eating bread or food baked or cooked by non-Jews – to limit social contact and partying, which our rabbis say leads to assimilation, intermarriage, and the ultimate: self-destruction of the Jewish people. Is "boiled" (pasteurized; in Hebrew *m'vushal*, or "cooked") wine OK? Yes, if it's heated to at least 175 degrees F.[14]

Panim chadashos

Q What does this mean?

Literally, a "new [male] face," one of three prerequisites for a non-Shabbas *sheva brachos* ("seven post-wedding blessings") meal. This custom requires that one of the *minyan* for the blessings was neither at the wedding dinner nor at a previous meal. What if there's no "new face"? Then only the final blessing (*asher bara*) can be said. Must this "new face" be exactly that, a total stranger? No. The *mitzva* obligation of a "new face" is to recharge the level of *simcha*. Thus a stranger's presence, even if a happy stranger, means nothing to the newly wedded couple, unless he is a recognized dignitary, or a *talmid chacham*, whose distinguished presence "enhances" the *simcha*![15]

---

14. Shulchan Aruch, Yore Deah 123:3; Iggeros Moshe, Yore Deah 2:52; Yabia Omer 8:15.
15. Sova Semachos 1:11; Even HaEzer 62:7; Kitzur Shulchan Aruch 149:5; Moshe Feinstein, Oholei Yeshurun 4:2.

Pacifism

Q Is Judaism a pacifist religion?

No. The Torah's first armed conflict, Abraham's successful battle to free his nephew Lot from northern terrorist captivity, lays the halachic basis *against* a philosophy of pacifism, and leads to a famous Talmudic adage, *shluchei mitzva eynan nizakin*, that those who are in pursuit of a Godly command will come to no harm. In fact, Abraham's militarism, which brought stability to the south, is praised as a *kiddush Hashem* when King Malchitzedek of Salem blesses "Abram of God Most High." Yes, Judaism abhors war and its glorification, but not in a pacifist way. When other cultures considered wearing a sword a symbol of a gentleman, the rabbis, wishing to stress the disgrace of war, prohibited donning weapons as clothing, or bringing them into a synagogue. The stones of the Temple altar were not hewn with metal implements, because the altar symbolized peace, and metal symbolized war. Instead, the Jewish way was peace, the Jewish greeting became "*shalom*," and Isaiah dreamt not just of the day when swords and spears would be turned into ploughshares and pruning hooks, but when entire nations would be struck by mass amnesia and would forget how to wage war (*milchama*) altogether. And yet, even as the Jews must speak, seek and pursue peace, the Torah demanded reality. Thus, in a brutal, still unredeemed world, *failure* to fight was tantamount to moral abdication. So Jewish law defined some wars as being morally permitted and delineated an ethics of warfare.[16]

Pass through, or passover?

Q Who's responsible for the term *passover*?

The word was, ironically, introduced by William Tyndale, a die-hard sixteenth-century anti-Semitic Bible scholar and compiler of the universally accepted King James 1611 English translation of the Torah. The mistranslation of *Passover* lies in the Hebrew language, which is both visual and spoken, and based on roots and vowels that evoke an idea or nuance behind

---

16. Isaiah 2:4; Micah 4:3; Shabbas 6:4; Isaiah 2:4; Micah 4:3; Psalms 28:3, 34:15.

a word's desired meaning. By presupposing a Hebrew root (*a-v-r*) which means "to pass through," instead of its real verb root (*p-s-ch*), the point is missed. Remember: the Jews of Goshen lived side-by-side with their Egyptian neighbors; therefore the Angel of Death would not have passed "over" but "up-and-down" (and/or) "in-between" the doorposts. So, is "Passover" the correct translation of Pesach? No. The etymology of *pesach* comes from its Hebrew root *p-s-ch* which means "to limp, hobble, jump" – as in the destroying angel "jumping" over the homes of the Jews. Philo, the first-century Alexandrian Torah philosopher, saw Pesach as a "crossing feast" that commemorated something totally different, and, in his opinion, even more miraculous – the "crossing of Israel from Egypt to the Red Sea."

Pilpul

Q What is this?

Derived from the Hebrew verb *pilpel*, "to spice," or "to season," it is used in the context of arguing a rabbinic proposition, or opinion, as part of the penetrating search for closing a debatable issue in Jewish law (as a noun, *pilpel* means "pepper," implying that Torah discussions are as piercing as strong pepper!). It can be exasperating when *pilpul* is used for "hair-splitting," serving as an end in itself, rather than to arrive at a satisfying conclusion.

Pause, review, absorb

Q Why is the Torah portion of *Vayikra* considered the "education" chapter?

This portion opens with God addressing Moses not in such aggressive terms as *daber, amar,* or *tzav* ("speak, say, or command"), but by a soft, gentle and loving "call" (*vayikra*). And so the rabbis of the second century chose this particular *parsha*, despite its stern legislation, as the first introductory chapter of Torah to teach Jewish children the "proper way" (*derech eretz*), declaring that, "Small children are pure, the sacrifices are pure, let those who are pure come and occupy themselves with things that are pure!" As *the* educational *parsha*, the structure is different from other Torah readings:

instead of the standard paragraph breaks, we have numerous specific intervals. Why? These breaks, explains Rashi, are intended to make the study of Torah a positive experience for children, a chance to pause, review, absorb. And more: they simultaneously act as a reminder to parents and teachers that *chinuch* (education) requires patience, forbearance, composure.

P'sil techeles

Q What is this?

As every decorator knows, it's a color! The "fringes" that God wants Jews to put "in the corners of their garments" were to contain a "thread of blue [*p'sil techeles*]." How was this blue dye made? I don't know, nor does anybody else, which is why *tzitzis* and *tallis* today are made only with white fringes. One theory of how the blue dye was extracted in Biblical times appears in a 1911 manuscript (*Hilazon*, "Snail"), written by Rabbi Isaac Halevy Herzog, who would later become Israel's first Ashkenazi chief rabbi. Rav Herzog identified the *hilazon*, a "sea snail," as the original source of the *p'sil techeles*, basing his theory on the fact that the Biblical terms of other textiles in antiquity, dyed from sea snails, are *techeles* (violet) and *argaman* (purple). Later Roman and Greek writers also describe how shellfish (a still-extant species) were used to produce hyacinth and purple dyes (Tyrian purple was named after Tyre, where the Phoenicians, two thousand years ago, had an enormous center for the production of shellfish dyes).[17]

Pssst, wanna live longer?

Q Which mitzvos assure me of a long(er) life?

Only two Torah commandments come with the specific reward to "prolong thy days." The first is easy to comprehend ("Honor your parents"), but the second is not, namely the order of *shilu'ach haken*, which means "banishment from the nest." Specifically, you cannot take unhatched eggs or chicks until the mother bird flies away from the nest. At first glance this seems like an obvious word on compassion but, in a startling admonition,

---

17. Numbers 15:37–41.

the rabbis of the Mishna warn that Jews who associate this "with Divine compassion must be silenced!" Why? "Because," explains Rabbi Yossi Bar Zavida, "in doing so, they are representing all of God's traits as compassion, whereas all His commandments are decrees!" This is the general rabbinic attitude. No attempt should be made to apply logic or reason for mitzva performance, *even* when it has an obvious moral basis.[18]

Property

Q Is it true I can't sell my apartment in Israel to a non-Jew?

In order to maintain Jewish supremacy in *Eretz Yisrael*, the Torah has strict guidelines about non-Jews living in, or passing through, God's promised land. Where exactly is this "land"? No one knows the exact geographical boundaries of the "land of Israel" (a continuous dispute among the rabbis of the Talmud – some even include Cyprus), which ranges from the "maximalist" view (which includes Sinai, Jordan, Syria, Lebanon, and parts of Turkey), to the "minimalist" interpretation (which still places Israel's northern border about halfway through Syria and Lebanon, at the latitude of Homs, because it was part of David's kingdom). Jewish law forbids Jews to sell real estate, property, fields and houses (i.e., anything immovable) to non-Jews. Unless they accept the seven Noahide precepts, non-Jews cannot even temporarily "dwell in the land." There is one exception. The resident alien (*ger toshav*), and even that status was only granted every fiftieth year during *yovel* ("Jubilee Year").

Passing the buck

Q Who was ultimately responsible in the Garden of Eden?

This early inquisitive instinct was to plague human nature: a trend, right from the get-go, to gravitate towards the negative, to hop on board the chariot of curiosity and always gallop towards "the enemy," known as the *yetzer hora* ("evil inclination"). In Eden this came in the form of a crafty (*arom*) walking, talking serpent who tricks Eve to stumble into sin, drag-

---

18. Deuteronomy 5:16, 22:6–7.

ging Adam with her. This is the first recorded proof of a famous rabbinic adage, *mitzva goreres mitzva, aveira goreres aveira*, "Good fosters good, evil fosters evil!" The result? In less than a single day, humanity goes from grace to disgrace, from innocent utopia to banishment, from sheltered existence to the grind of reality. Not one of the principal players expresses remorse. A discomfited Adam recoils in humiliation, hides among the trees, and makes history with the first recorded communication from God to Man, "Where are you?" Rabbi Eliezer declares that all of human history begins with these three words, the discovery of shame. In history's first finger-pointing exercise, now known as "Passing the Buck," Adam blamed Eve, Eve blamed the primordial snake. Whom did the generic serpent blame? I don't know.

Pharaoh

Q Is this a title or a person?

A title. The term *Pharaoh* literally means "great house," and refers to the king of Egypt. In fact, two chapters of Torah go through no less than three Pharaohs! Who's on first? There's the Pharaoh who coincides with Abraham and Sarah passing through Canaan, next comes the Pharaoh of Joseph fame, and finally we have the third Pharaoh (who "did not know Joseph"). He is the villain of the Exodus saga. The peak of Egyptian oppression occurred under the sixty-seven-year reign of Rameses II. The Jews rejoiced at his death, prematurely! He was followed by Mernephtah whose tyranny made them "cry to God." The Torah uses the word *vayagar* ("temporary dwelling"), which seems odd for a period of 210 (or 430) years, but the transitory expression reflects the fact that the Jews never considered themselves Egyptians, maintaining hope for a future permanence of their own homeland. But how did the Jews get to Egypt in the first place? As a result of a famine which drove them there. This Pharaoh was a phony Pharaoh! The Midrash describes how he would study the times of the tides of the Nile, and enter the water precisely the moment that the water began to rise, so that it should appear to be rising to honor him.[19]

---

19. Genesis 12:14–20, 13:18, 41:40, 41:45; Exodus 1:8, 1:16, 2:23.

═ Priorities ═════════════════════

Q What's more important? A *mikva* or a cemetery?

The oldest *mikva* in Europe, called Jacob's Well, was discovered in the 1990s at Bristol, England. One can make out on the walls some Hebrew words such as *zochlin*, which means "flowing." It is even older than the 1956 discovery of a ritual bath in Cologne, Germany, dated to 1170. Thus the establishment of a *mikva*, more properly called *mayanot*, "springs," was traditionally accorded priority in any Jewish community. Even over the opening of a *shul,* the purchase of a *Sefer Torah,* or the establishment of a burial ground? Yes.

═ Pork and milk ═════════════════

Q Are there any circumstances in which a Jew can eat pork and milk?

"It's good to fast," goes an old Yiddish folk saying, "with a chicken leg and something to drink," a witty reference to the fact that, although eating on Yom Kippur is considered a great sin, the order to fast is *not* a halachic absolute (children under the age of nine, sick Jews and women who have just given birth are ordered not to fast, even if they want to!). "A Jew who on Yom Kippur lights a fire to boil himself a portion of pork and washes it down with a glass of milk because his doctor has told him that otherwise he might die," writes Rabbi Moshe Kohn, "does not require God's forgiveness, because he is not transgressing a Divine precept. On the contrary! He would be a sinner in need of forgiveness if he ignored the doctor's instructions!" When a severe cholera epidemic hit Vilna in 1848, the saintly master of *mussar* Lithuanian Rabbi Israel Salanter not only ordered the entire town to eat on Yom Kippur but, in a dramatic show of leadership, ate to set an example. When Rav Chaim Soloveitchik, the Brisker Rav, was asked why he was taking the fast day so lightly by allowing someone to eat, he replied: "I am not treating Yom Kippur lightly. I am treating lifesaving seriously!"

═ Pssst, wanna buy a weapon? ═

Q I have a job in the arms industry. Is that OK?

It depends. "It is forbidden to sell weapons to strangers, or to sharpen their weapons, or to sell them anvils [used for making weapons]," warn our rabbis. Why? The assumption is that any arms trade to individuals will eventually harm others. However, if the intent of a weapons trade is to "protect us" (e.g., legitimate governments, police, etc.), then it's OK. Remember: Judaism is not a pacifist religion. The Torah *always* recognizes the reality and responsibility of self-defense until the day arrives when "nation shall not lift up sword against nation, and they shall not learn war any more!"[20]

═ Present tense ═

Q Why are the blessings in the present tense?

God, the *siddur* tells us, "*daily* renews the work of Creation." This concept is in sharp contrast to the Deists who claim that, having created the world, a retired God took a back seat to history, leaving the world *hefker* (out of control). Jews believe in an active and still involved God, which is why the blessings are in the here-and-now, as in "He *creates* the fruit of the vine," "He *brings forth* bread from the earth," etc.

═ Priestly blessings ═

Q If there's no *Cohen* in *shul,* can the rabbi give the priestly blessing?

No. Only a *Cohen* can give the official priestly blessing (*duchaning*), based on the Torah's "Thus shall *you* [the *Cohanim*] bless the Children of Israel." This was such a direct, unambiguous order that laypeople even hesitated to raise their hands in the set cohanic way.[21]

---

20. Avoda Zara 15b, 16a; Shabbas 6:4; Iggeros Moshe, Yore Deah 2:158; Isaiah 2:4.
21. Numbers 6:23; Kesubos 24b; Shulchan Aruch, Orach Chayim 128:1; Shabbas 118b.

═ Priorities ══════════════════════════════

Q I don't have a lot of time, so what should I learn? Torah, Talmud, halacha?

As the wise rabbi once said: You should learn a few minutes of *mussar* (manners, how-to-behave, etc.) a day, then your entire value system will change, and you will suddenly realize that you have much more time than you think to learn Torah!

═ Privacy ══════════════════════════════

Q I live in a crowded apartment building and wonder if Judaism has a policy of privacy?

Jewish law has long-established principles regulating the behavior of people who live in or around "a joint courtyard," the ancient equivalent to a block of flats. For example: all neighbors are duty-bound to respect and contribute towards the privacy and security of one another, loud noises and parties were ruled an unacceptable intrusion, and doors or windows should not directly face a neighbor – even Bilaam complimented the Jews ("How goodly are your tents, your dwelling-places") for "not aligning the openings of their tents one opposite the other."[22]

═ Probabilities ══════════════════════════════

Q Is there any order to the Jewish festivals, or were their dates arrived at purely by chance?

It's orderly, with many moving parts, and yet there are many dependable "constants" in the Jewish calendar. For example: no Jewish (non-leap) year begins earlier than September 16, nor ends later than October 5. What's the most probable first day of Rosh Hashana? Thursday (a frequency of 31.9 percent). And least probable? Tuesday (11.5 percent), an oddity. Why?

---

22. Baba Basra 7b, 60a; Numbers 24:2–4.

Because even though tradition says that Pesach occurred on a Thursday, it's more likely to fall on a Tuesday!

Professional privileges

Q Does a rabbi have professional privilege?

It's a complicated issue. A rabbi must respect the privacy of those who tell him things in professional confidence ("You shall not go as a tale-bearer amongst your people"), yet he is still subject to the Torah verse "He who is a witness, if he does not tell, he bears his iniquity!"[23]

Prophets

Q How many Hebrew prophets were there?

I don't know, nor does anyone else – but it's somewhere between forty-eight and over a million. According to the Talmud, the number of prophets (*nevi'im*) who existed in the history of Israel was twice as many as the Jews who left Egypt, yet only forty-eight are listed by name. What happened to the rest? They were ignored. Why? Because the Torah only concerned itself with "eternal" [*netzach*] prophecies, as "needed by future generations."[24]

Pursuer pursued

Q What is a *din rodef*?

In simple English, it's the universal right of self-defense; in Hebrew, it literally means "the case of the pursuer!" This rabbinic concept is common sense, as articulated by the Rambam: "Every Jew is obligated to save a pursued person from his pursuer, even if this means killing the pursuer." Thus *din rodef* defines one's options when faced with a threat: Kill It First!

---

23. Leviticus 5:1, 19:16.
24. Megilla 14a.

Parking spaces

Q Is it OK to cut in ahead of another when spotting a parking spot?

The answer seems obvious: of course not! But how do we know? From the Torah's advice to a judge (*dayan*) to accept litigants on a "first-come, first-served basis." The "pushing-ahead-of-others," and not waiting patiently in line, involves two impolite breaches: *Lo sonu ish es amiso*, "don't take advantage of a friend," and "stealing time" (pure theft) from others who are, halachically, entitled to be reimbursed. How do we know? If two vessels approach an opening only big enough for one, the rabbis conclude that the one who goes first gets an advantage, and must therefore compensate the other boat. So, what's the value of lost time? The rabbinic formula is not based on actual damages, but halves the average salary that exists in that particular community in order to determine a symbolic monetary loss.[25]

25. Sanhedrin 8b, 32b; Choshen Mishpat 272:14; Taz, Choshen Mishpat 333:1.

Q

Qumran, unearthed

Q So what's the significance of the Dead Sea Scrolls?

I don't know; neither does anyone else! Don't let all the body of research fool you; so far, it's led to nothing very conclusive. But there's no doubt: the nine hundred ancient Hebrew scrolls, an astounding homogeneous collection consisting of a hundred thousand words, excluding the Biblical books amongst them, but including a Psalms Scroll, an Aramaic targum of Job, and a twenty-nine-foot-long Temple Scroll, accidentally discovered in 1947 (on the eve of Israel's war of independence), in the barren Judean Desert by a young Ta'amireh Bedouin shepherd boy seeking a stray goat, is an unprecedented treasure, the most important archeological find in centuries. The initial find was seven scrolls. Hebrew university Professor E.L. Sukenik clandestinely bought three from a Christian-Arab antiquities dealer in Bethlehem. The other four scrolls ended up in the possession of Mar Athanasius Yeshua Samuel, Metropolitan of the Syrian Jacobite Monastery of St. Mark in Jerusalem, who spent five years trying (unsuccessfully) to find a buyer. He eventually placed an ad (on June 1, 1954) in the *Wall Street Journal* ("Four Dead Sea Scrolls" for sale). Professor Sukenik's son, Yigael Yadin (a onetime chief of staff of the Israel Defense Forces) paid $250,000 (with the assistance of New York philanthropist D.S. Gottesman) and all seven scrolls were reunited; they can now be seen at the Shrine of the Book in Jerusalem's Israel

Museum. Talk about frustration! You would think that the Dead Sea Scrolls should reveal something new, *anything*, about the crucial history of the Second Temple period (520 BCE–70 CE), but it doesn't. But a certain *minhag* has now come up: every few years a new theory arises to shoot down the old theories (there are about a dozen) about the Qumran Scrolls. We still don't know if these folks lived in a fort, hostel, farm or monastery. In an area of only four dunam, about an acre, there are ten mikvas, including the second largest mikva ever discovered. In fact, we're still not sure if they were Sadducees, Pharisees, Essenes, Karaites or Christians!

Quarantine

Q Is this the modern equivalent of the isolation of a leper?

Yes; although the word derives from the Latin, it has a base in Jewish history. It comes from *quarantena*, which is a term of measurement for forty, and refers to such "isolated" incidents as Moses' "missing" forty days and nights on the Mount, the Jews' forty "lost" years in the desert, and Elijah's forty-day fast. This is the basis of the Christian forty-day Lent and the old legal custom whereby a widow was allowed to stay in *quarantine*, which meant "forty days" in the home of her deceased husband.

Queens, or just kings?

Q Were there "Jewish" Queens?

Yes. The most famous queen in the Bible, attracted to King Solomon because "of the name of the Lord," was the Queen of Sheba from southwest Arabia – who was not Jewish! Jewish history is not so kind to many of the early Jewish queens (e.g., Michal and the evil Jezebel, wives of David and Ahab, respectively), but later rained credit on such female rulers as Salome Alexandra, wise wife of Yannai, who brought peace and prosperity to Judea; and Helen, courageous wife of king Monabazus of Adiabene, a convert to Judaism who helped the Jews stand up to Rome.

R

Round or braided?

Q Rosh Hashana is approaching. Do I bake the *challa* round or braided?

Round, according to the Chasam Sofer, in contrast to braided the rest of the year. Why? Because the circle is an "unending" shape, with no end to it, and Jews want a never-ending *bracha* for the year!

Rambam's "premier" mitzva

Q Which law did the Rambam consider the most important?

Other than his declaration on belief in the One God, the Rambam, inspired by Rabbi Assi, declared that the mitzva of *tzedaka* was "greater than all other positive commandments." Abraham was praised because of his concern for the weak and helpless. Since poverty would "never disappear," Jewish law developed pragmatic priorities, based not only on the obvious (the donor's resources, the needs of the recipient), but on the cost of living ("one must not give the wandering poor less than a loaf's worth, a *pondion* [a coin]!"). The Rambam understood human nature. The art of *tzedaka* is one of the few mitzvos that allows the Jew to see *himself* at his best – and at his worst![1]

---

1. Rambam, Laws of Charity 10:1; Baba Basra 6a; Midrash Shoher Tov; Deuteronomy 15:11; Rambam, Yad, Hilchos Matnat Aniyim 7:1, 7:5; Kesubos 67b; Leviticus Rabba 34:6.

Rabbinical mitzvos

Q Where do the rabbis get the authority to "make up" their own mitzvos?

Their authority is derived from a Deuteronomic verse which tells every generation to heed "the judge that shall be in those days." There are seven "rabbinic" mitzvos (including Chanukah, lighting Shabbas candles, saying Hallel and reading the Megilla). For *gematria* lovers, if you add these seven to the 613 traditional ones, you get 620, the numerical value of *keter*, "crown" (of the Torah).[2]

Remove those markers?

Q I heard that it is prohibited to take down a landmark, or marker signpost. Is that true?

There is a concept of *hassagath gevul*, which refers to the removal of landmarks, a practice that Jewish law prohibits ("You shall not remove your neighbor's landmark...cursed be he who does!"). Why? Because in ancient Israel, landmarks, usually fashioned from piles of stones, defined the boundary of one's property in the absence of fences, title companies, aerial maps and land measurements. Removing them was tantamount to the crime (theft) of encroachment, because their absence inevitably "enlarged" someone's estate.[3]

Revenge, revenge!

Q May Jews take revenge in their own hands?

Unlike the other religion, the Torah does not stipulate that we love our enemies, but it does demand restraint, which prohibits seeking revenge. We expect God to mete out the ultimate punishment to our enemies. In the *siddur* we find the daily prayer, "May no person be made to suffer on my

---

2. Deuteronomy 17:8–11.
3. Deuteronomy 19:14; 27:17.

account!" Revenge is sweet when served…not at all? With a few isolated exceptions (e.g., after Haman's defeat), Jews have not gone on the rampage of revenge and physical retribution (although the full story of post-Holocaust settling of scores has yet to be written). Perhaps the ultimate of magnanimity is the image of Rabbi Levi Yitzhak of Berdichev standing before an open Ark, praying that no harm come to the Jews who threw his family out of town. When his supporters asked Rabbi Wolf of Zhitomir to call for God's wrath upon Reb Levi's adversaries, he replied that his prayers were powerless in the face of Levi Yitzchok's call that no harm befall them![4]

Respectful salutations

Q Why do we add *zt"l* after certain names?

It is customary to remember the dead with brief Hebrew letter abbreviations, including *Ayin-Heh* (for *Alav Hashalom*, "Peace be upon him"); *Zayin-Lamed* (for *Zichrono Livracha*, "May his memory be for a blessing," a higher degree of respect); *Zayin-Tzadi-Lamed* (for *Zecher Tzadik Livracha*, "May the memory of the righteous one be for a blessing," a more respectful salutation that indicates the deceased was a distinguished person of piety, moral stature or rabbinic learning).[5]

Reincarnation

Q Isn't this a Christian belief?

Yes, and a Jewish one, too. However the *Tanach* contains no clear statement of a "recycled-souls" dogma, and the rabbis of the Mishna never deemed it essential. Reincarnation as a doctrine was "resurrected" (pun intended) around the eighth century CE, but Saadia Gaon called it "foolish," and such super-rationalists as Chesdai and Yosef Albo thought it opposed the true spirit of Torah. Yet other scholars, such as Isaac Abravanel, Menashe ben

---

4. Leviticus 19:18; Proverbs 17:16; Shabbas 149b.
5. These abbreviations are not used in this book not out of disrespect but only to conserve space.

Israel, and the *Zohar* ("All souls must undergo transmigration!") all supported it.[6]

═ Racism ═

Q **Were Miriam and Aaron racists for calling Moses' wife (Zippora), a "dark-skinned" Midianite woman?**

There is no word for race in the Torah, nor in any of the early rabbinic texts. "Others" are never described by the color of their skin but by their fidelity to God (they are called "idolaters," or "eaters of *treif*"). Was there prejudice against dark-skinned people? Yes, admits the Talmud. Although the Midrash links the "ugly and dark-skinned" nature of Noah's son Ham, progenitor of the Cushites, to a curse, Rashi points out that the *gematria* of Cushite equals *yefas mar'eh*, "of beautiful appearance," an acknowledgment that no human being or group is inherently better or worse, superior or inferior. The great defense of the Cushites is by Amos, who asks in the name of God, "Are you not as the children of the Cushites to Me, O children of Israel?" Nevertheless, God sternly rebukes the siblings for displaying prejudice against Moses' choice of spouse. The punishment? Speedy and severe! The Heavens strike and disfigure Miriam, the instigator, with "snow-white scales" of leprosy (*tzara'as*), causing her removal from the camp for seven days. And Aaron? He is humbled into begging God for a cure for their "sin of folly." The normative Jewish view on racism and bigotry is expressed in an exchange between Rabbi Shimon ben Eleazar and a man who, after being mocked for his appearance, replies, "So go to the Craftsman who made me and tell him, 'How ugly is this vessel which You have made!'" Bias based on appearance is thus an insult to God who made all in His image.[7]

---

6.   Mishpatim 99b.
7.   Mo'ed Katan 16b; Bereishis Rabba 60; Genesis 10:6; Habakkuk 12:7; Amos 9:7; Genesis 1:27; Ta'anis 20a–b.

Raisin wine

Q Can I use raisin wine for the four cups at the Pesach seder?

Yes. Wine from raisins is acceptable for those who cannot tolerate wine (or grape juice), although one could, instead, dilute the wine with water. Some rabbis even allow the four cups to contain "the beverage of the country," which, theoretically, could mean tea (or even coffee), although this would be odd (when asked if he could drink soda water instead of wine, Rabbi Moshe Feinstein said "no," because this drink merely fulfilled thirst, not a mitzva!).[8]

Run, run, run

Q How do we know that we must rush to do a mitzva?

From Abraham. On the third day after his *bris mila*, whilst still in pain, the Patriarch refuses to designate tasks to a servant. Instead he "runs" to greet his guests in the sweltering heat, "runs" to tell his wife to prepare a meal, and "runs" to choose a bull from the herd, showing an alacrity in his old age that would put today's young folks to shame. All this frantic activity caused Joshua ben Levi to conclude, "The merit of a mitzva lies in the running to it!"[9]

Rain

Q Why is there a difference in dates as to when to begin the prayer for rain?

There are two prayers for rain and each has its own basis. *V'sen tal umatar* ("Grant dew and rain") is fixed to a secular, diaspora date (December 4 or 5) that falls sixty days after the autumn equinox, which is determined by the solar calendar. Why? Rashi claims that less rain is needed there, whilst the Mishna views it as simply a date of convenience (to allow Jews who had

8. Mishne Berura 472, 37; Iggeros Moshe, Orach Chayim, vol. 2.
9. Brachos 6b.

been in Jerusalem for Succos time to get home before the rains begin). The other prayer, *Mashiv haruach umorid hagashem* ("He makes the wind blow and the rain fall"), is for Israel only (thus its Hebrew date), and is timed for the rain's appropriate season, at the end of Succos (on Shemini Atzeres). In fact, this is not a "prayer" *per se* but a general praise for the unique "power" (*gevuros*) of the Giver of rain.[10]

Rice

Q I went to a wedding and rice was thrown at the couple. Why?

In the olden days, they threw grain or wheat seeds (today it's rice), which symbolized the hope of fertility and prosperity for the newlyweds. This is the Judaic version of *confetti*, from the Latin *confectionary*, which means "sweet meats," and refers to the Italian custom of throwing nuts and sugared almonds at the bridegroom. Come to think of it, thrown rice seems more civil than throwing old shoes (today, they're tied to the backs of limousines), an ancient (non-Jewish) custom that stemmed from the belief that shoes were extensions of fertility (in fact, Eskimo women never left home without a piece of old shoe for luck).

Rashi doesn't know?

Q What stumped Rashi, the greatest of all commentators?

The Talmud tells a Sage to be honest and humble enough to say, "I don't know," rather than pretend, or tell an untruth. In the Torah portion *Vayetzei*, Rashi, the eleventh-century French-born teacher *par excellence*, answers his own question with, "I don't know." Now that's what I call humility and honesty! What caused this theological headache? When Rebecca urges Jacob to leave his parents' home, the text declares that Rebecca is the mother of *both* Jacob and Esau. This is so obvious that it leads Rashi, the master of *p'shat* (plain-meaning) to ponder, "Why restate it?" Of course, if Rashi doesn't know neither do I, yet Rashi's response is important. It's an admission that it is OK not to know, that to admit lack of knowledge is

---

10. Ta'anis 1:3, 10a.

perfectly acceptable as long as a sincere and unskeptical search for information continues.[11]

Religious animals?

Q Are giraffes, snakes, monkeys, or ants religious? Are they aware of God?

The Midrash describes a scene of arrogance: King David is boasting that no one can sing praises as well as he can, when suddenly God's rebuke comes through loud and clear, "Every creature has its own way of praising its Maker;" and Isaiah is even bolder, claiming that animals *always* know that their water and food come from the Heavens, whereas Man is complacent vis-à-vis these miracles.[12]

Return to sender

Q Last year I received a package during Pesach that contained *Chametz*. What should I have done?

If you know what's inside it, don't open it; in other words, just leave it "ownerless" (*hefker*) until after *yom tov*. If you didn't know until after you opened it, then don't touch the *Chametz*. If the arrival is during *chol hamo'ed*, you have to get rid of the *Chametz* (destroy it, actually) ASAP. And more: it's possible that the packaging insulation itself is *Chametz* (polystyrene is OK, but biodegradable "peanuts," made from edible corn or wheat starch, are not).[13]

---

11. Brachos 4a.
12. Isaiah 43:20.
13. Orach Chayim 446:1, 10; L'ehoros Nossan 5:30; Mishne Berura 15, 41–42; Chazon Ish, Orach Chayim 116:8.

Ribbis

Q If I lend money through my corporation, do I still have to worry about charging interest?

It's in dispute. Rav Moshe Feinstein takes the lenient position, saying it's OK for a corporation to pay *ribbis* for deposits, loans, etc. (even if it's totally owned by Jews), because these are not "personal" Jewish obligations, but promises to pay that are, presumably, backed by assets of the company (in this context, there are no personal guarantees). Others disagree. They still prefer a proper *heter iska* be drawn up. All agree, however, that it is not permitted for an *individual* to borrow money from a Jewish-owned company or bank (incidentally, free gifts from Jewish-owned banks to depositors in exchange for deposits are also a form of *ribbis!*). What about buying shares in a publicly traded bank, which is either majority-owned by Jews, or has a board controlled by Jews, and doesn't use a *heter iska*? Not allowed. Just remember that old Yiddish adage, "Borrow, and you'll sorrow!"[14]

Rose

Q Why is the Jewish nation compared to a rose?

The Shem MiShmuel traces the comparison to a Psalmist expression, *Lamnatzeiach al Shoshanim* ("For the conductor on the roses"), which was composed in honor of Torah scholars (*talmidei chachamim)* whom Rashi likens to soft, beautiful roses.[15]

Ruach

Q What does this mean?

It's not clear. Some translate *ruach* as "spirit," from Creation's "the spirit of God hovered over the surface of the waters." Others, such as Ibn Ezra, ap-

---

14. Exodus 22:24; Leviticus 25:36; Iggeros Moshe, Yore Deah 2:63; Y.E. Henkin, Eidus l'Yisrael; Minchas Yitzchak 1:3, 4, 16–17; Rambam, Hilchos Malveh V'loveh 4:2; Bris Yehudah 38, 40; M. Feinstein, Y. Roth, Mishnas Ribbis 2.
15. Psalms 45:1.

proach *ruach* literally, as wind, claiming that the Heavens, by means of the wind, made the waters dry up and the land appear. Does Rashi agree with either? No. He interprets *ruach* to mean, metaphorically, "breath," in that the Glory of God was suspended above the waters by the breath of God.[16]

Royte bendel

Q What is the red ribbon I see people wearing around their wrists? Should I get one?

No. In Yiddish it's called a *royte bendel* (*bendlach*, in plural); but today it's just a pseudo-kabbalistic cheap trinket, a design statement of mystic chic. It has its roots in Yiddish Eastern Europe where red ribbon amulets were tied to the posts of a baby crib (or on a child's collar or underclothes, but never on the wrist!) to protect against the *ayin hora* ("evil eye"), or the demonic Lilith. Why red? This bright color was thought to be anathema to the evil powers. During the catastrophic 1887 cholera epidemic in Russia, desperate Jews resorted to superstition to protect their children, tying red ribbons around their necks. Originally, the rabbis opposed this practice, but eventually went along with it grudgingly because the masses sought it. This was not just a Jewish custom. Russian peasants wrapped knotted wool around their children's arms and legs; German women used red ribbons as headbands; and the Scots used red to keep witches away.

Rationality

Q Is Reason the enemy?

It shouldn't be, but has been. The spectrum of Torah mitzvos is divided into three categories. Traditional (*eidos*), logical (*mishpotim*), and obscure (*chukim*). The first refers to those that are undiscoverable through self-deduction (*tefillin, tzitzis, bris mila*); the next are those that logically form the basis of civilized law, even in the absence of Torah (murder, robbery); and then we have *chukos*, which means "statutes," or "edicts," a reference to mitzvos that defy reason or logic. Examples? The prohibition of meat and

---

16. Genesis 1:2.

milk (*basar b'chalav*), marrying a brother's widow (the *levir*), not mixing wool and linen (*sha'atnez*), the Yom Kippur scapegoat (*sa'ir la'azazel*) – and, the Mother of all Mystery Mitzvos, the ritual slaughter of a red heifer (*para aduma*), a seemingly illogical concept that ashes can both purify the impure yet make the pure impure (even the wisest of them all, King Solomon, admits non-comprehension: "Its purpose is far from me!"). That God's Law is inviolate rests on the philosophy that human thinking is all relative; if one is allowed to succumb to one's subjective notions, then what might be unethical to one may be ethical to another.

Rolling Stone

Q Is the custom of laying coronation or foundation stones a Jewish one?

No, it's not a Jewish custom, but it is Jewishly inspired. When Jacob was fleeing Esau's wrath, he used a stone as a pillow for the night, and had his famous ladder dream. In the morning, convinced that both the stone and site were sanctified, the third Patriarch set up a pillar, anointed it with oil, and declared the place a *Beth El*, "House of God." This "foundation stone," having linked heaven and earth, somehow found its way into British mythology: King Edward I claimed he possessed *the* stone of Jacob and ordered it built into Westminster Abbey's coronation chair (which is still in use!) How did it get there? Here's what the King of England said: after Nebuchadnezzar destroyed the Temple (586 BCE) the Jewish refugees took the stone from the Sanctuary and went to Ireland, where, now known as the "Stone of Destiny," it was used during coronations. A thousand years later, according to the king, the most valued stone in all of Jewish history somehow made its way to Scotland (specifically, a place called Scone, two miles north of Perth), where it was embedded in a special wooden chair and used in the coronation of Scottish kings. And it had a new name! Jacob's stone was the Stone of Scone (a tongue-twister) and caught the fancy of King Edward who, in 1296, made it part of the throne of England (over the years, the Scots and Brits actually fought over who was the rightful heir to this holy stone!)

Rebels

Q My son is in a rebellious mood. What should I do?

To rebel was once serious business, especially for the Sage who didn't agree with his Sanhedrin contemporaries. The punishment for this "rebellious elder," for "the man who acts willfully not to listen"? Death! The same penalty in ancient Israel for the son who rebels against the top commandment, "Honor and fear your father and your mother." But not today. When it comes to your own child, the best response is that of the Baal Shem Tov, "Love him all the more!"[17]

Rejoice, not

Q Why does the Torah instruct us to "rejoice" on only two of the three pilgrimage festivals?

Because Pesach, the third pilgrimage *yom tov*, symbolized a *chutz la'aretz* event in exile, whilst Succos and Shavuos are intrinsically tied to the Holy Land itself.

Rosary

Q Is there any "Jewish" link to the rosary?

The Jewish equivalent would be the counting of *sefira*, or the guide posted in some *shuls* as to the order of prayers. The rosary (from the French *ro-saire*, a "bead"), originally an Indian "invention," was simply a mechanical aid that many religions used for memory, a string of prayer beads intended to keep track of prayers that used to be recited by heart. In fact, today's necklace, a secular item of jewelry, is simply an extension of the religious bead (which means "prayer").

---

17. Deuteronomy 17:10–12; 1:1–2, 5; 2:1; 3:4; 2:4–5, 9; 17:9; 5:1, 5; 6:1; 7:1; 21:18, 5:16; Leviticus 19:3, 20:9; Exodus 13:1, 21:15,17; 20:12.

Relationships

Q Am I imagining things? Isaiah's metaphors of affection seem far from the "love is a many-splendored thing" sung by pop artists!

Isaiah's vivid *Shivas Zion* poetry, of God-Israel as husband-wife metaphors, sets the stage for unusual relationships. With Jerusalem a "barren woman" and Israel the "abandoned and brokenhearted" wife, whose husband had once left her but now returns, the Torah is acknowledging that not all unions are ideal. With remarkable bluntness, the Torah discusses all sorts of unusual spousal relationships such as the "permissibly desired" women captured in conquest (*taavah shel heter*), dysfunctional two-wife families (one loved, one scorned) and levirate marriages (*yibbum*). Concerned with a balance between law and mercy, Judaism thus focuses not on the spiritual challenges within normal, "healthy" marriage relationships as a microcosm of society (i.e., love and marriage go together like a horse and carriage), but on the abnormal, "out-of-the-ordinary," disharmonious union.

Round or square?

Q Why was the matza round when I was a child, whilst these days it is square?

Because machine-made matza is easier to bake and pack if it is square, though hand-baked matza follows the traditional round shape. The Torah's *uggos matzos*, "cakes of unleavened bread," refers to circular cakes, because its Hebrew root (*ug*) means "round," or "drawn in a circle." Jewish mystics see a round shape as denoting eternity, with God and Israel existing without limit.

Republic or monarchy?

Q Does the Torah prefer rule by a republic or a monarchy?

Monarchy. "When you come to the land you shall set over yourself a king whom God shall choose from among your brethren." However, Samuel castigates the Jews when they demand, "Give us a king to judge us," and even

God warns that the appointment of a king is fraught with danger: "This is what the king will do: He will take your sons, and make them serve with his chariots and horses! He will take your daughters to be perfumers and cooks and bakers! He will take the best of your fields and vineyards and give them to his attendants. He will take a tenth of your flocks, and you yourselves will become his slaves! When the day comes, you will cry out for relief from the king you have chosen!" The Heavens obviously prefer rule by piety rather than royalty, an educated judge shorn of pretensions and pomposity. Others look at the verse "You shall surely set over yourself a king" and conclude that a king is not really needed unless the people insist. The more normative view is that a nation must have a king, but he must be approved by God; he is not above the law, and must conduct himself with restraint and dignity – and not have too many wives or horses! *Sefer Hachinuch* explains that a nation needs one head, even a bad one, so that society will not disintegrate into chronic disputes. In reality, it was not an issue for a powerless people and thus not often debated until the Middle Ages, when Don Isaac Abravanel, an accomplished Spanish Torah states-man and adviser to kings, decided, choosing experience over the Torah's preference, that the monarchies were "abominations and corruptions," and that a republican form of government was better.[18]

Rabbis

Q Rabbis! Who needs them?!

Technically, you're right. The Jewish rabbi, despite his traditional impressive title, *Mara d'asra* ("master of the place"), has not a single essential function that (in theory) cannot be performed by someone else. In fact, any ordinary learned and respected Jew can accommodate the needs of an entire Jewish community. Since Torah "is neither in the Heavens nor beyond the sea," it enters Jewish history as the heritage and destiny of *all* Israel. Thus no priest, prophet, rabbi, or educator can claim exclusivity. In reality, though, with the pressures of earning a living, it simply doesn't work this way. This is why all the scholars in the Talmud also worked as carpenters, shoemakers, blacksmiths, woodchoppers, water-carriers, cobblers (and even gladiators!).

---

18. Deuteronomy 17:14–20; I Samuel 8:11, 13–14, 17–18.

"I love work, but hate the rabbinate," whispered the first-century Rabbi Shemaia. His was not an isolated voice. In Eastern Europe anti-rabbinic scorn was indiscriminate, pouring forth from Chassidic masters (Nachman of Bratzlav: "It was hard for Satan alone to mislead the whole world, so he appointed prominent rabbis in different localities!"), to *misnagdishe* giants (Israel Salanter: "A rabbi whom they don't want to drive out of town isn't a rabbi; and a rabbi whom they actually drive out of town isn't a man!").

Reverence

Q Why are the words "Know before Whom you stand" placed above the synagogue Ark?

As a reminder about how to behave in *shul*, a constant cue to maintain an atmosphere of holiness and reverence. The synagogue is not a park or beach, so one's attire must be respectful; it's not a restaurant, so eating and drinking is inappropriate; it's not a mini-United Nations, so politics should be kept out; it's not an insider's tip haven, so stock and real estate prices should be kept outdoors; and, finally, it's not a marketplace, so buying and selling should be avoided.

Right is left and left is right

Q Huh?

The Jewish attitude is: *Yiftach b'doro kiShmuel b'doro,* "We must unite behind the less-than-great leader just as we would behind the great leader!" This is a rabbinic *leitmotif*; the idea is explained by Rashi, quoting the Sifrei, that Jews must listen to the rabbis in *all* circumstances, *even* if they claim that "right is left and left is right." Doesn't this imply infallibility? No. No one's flawless nor perfect; however this is a recognition that rabbinic rulings merit *siyata d'Shemaya,* "Divine guidance." Both the Rambam and Ramban agree: one is obligated to obey, even if rabbis err. Why? Because spiritual leaders deserve the benefit of the doubt. Even if right *is not* left? Yes, on the theory that Judaic unity overrules factionalism and religious anarchy. "Far better," said Rav Isser from Bobroisk, "to accept a crooked answer from a straight person whose relationship with Torah is of a singular nature than a straight answer from a crooked person!"

Real estate

Q Location, location, location!

In the Torah's first real estate transaction, Abraham buys not a commercial building or an apartment complex, but one field and a double cave in Hevron ("an estate for a burial site"). And, wonder of wonders, the first Jew pays "four hundred silver shekels" (*kintirin*), the full retail price, after turning down an offer from Efron the Hittite (the seller) for a free site! From this incident, Jewish law introduces the most disregarded law amongst Jews, *lo sachmode*, wherein you cannot pay less than fair market value for an object, branding the buyer "a *gazlon!*" The seller's greed does not escape the Torah terminology. When his name first appears, it is spelled with the letter *vav*, but not this time. The *gematria* of Efron minus a *vav* is four hundred (the price), which equals the *gematria* of *ra ayin* ("evil eye"), an observation of his low moral stature. And more: the *gematria* of his full name (Efron ben Tzochar, with a *vav*) is identical to a famous Koheles saying, *Hakessef ya'aneh es hakol*, "Money ain't everything!"

Ring around a rosy

Q **My daughter wants to put rings in her nose, tongue, and navel. I'm a pretty tolerant father, but isn't this going a bit too far?**

Yes, and not just for the obvious reasons (hygiene and modesty); Judaism still remembers that ear piercing was a mark of servitude in Biblical times. Incidentally, if your son also wants to wear rings, it's prohibited under the Jewish law against cross-dressing![19]

---

19. Exodus 21:6; Deuteronomy 22:5.

S

Semitic Schmaltz syndrome

Q **What is philo-Semitism?**

It is the unusual focus on all things Jewish in a non-Jewish atmosphere. In America, for example, the word "Jew" has become a metaphor. But don't confuse philo-Semitism with the acceptance of "Jewishness" just because a wave of perverse fondness for such fictional Broadway Jews as Tevye the Milkman or Max Bialystock sweeps through American culture. This is the symbiotic Semitic Schmaltz syndrome, a benevolent, warm and fuzzy identification that permits non-Jews (e.g., Madonna and her kabbala infatuation) to cuddle up to the Judaic pop culture of *Seinfeld kvelling*, or to seek some obscure Jewish "hooks" in early Superman comics, or to worship the gastronomic sacrament of Borscht Beltish bagels and lox.

Seichel

Q **How important is "common sense" (*seichel*) in understanding the Torah?**

In Moses' third, and final, farewell address, he concludes with a blueprint for Judaic prosperity that involves a proviso ("if you safeguard this covenant") and a promise ("you will be successful [*taskilu*]"). The Hebrew root of *taskilu* is connected to *seichel*, "common sense." In other words: if you have the *seichel* to occupy yourself with Torah, you'll find prosperity. Does that mean *seichel* guarantees success? Yes, says Rav David Kimchi (*Radak*), thirteenth-century Provence scholar, but not necessarily in material possessions, for if the road to "success" is paved with the Torah's business ethics, those who walk it do so in a successful atmosphere of well-being, merited with *Shuttaf l'HaKadosh Baruch Hu b'ma'aseh bereishis*, being "partners with God in building the world."

Sela

Q What's a *sela*?

This word is prevalent in both the *siddur* and Psalms (where it appears more than seventy times), usually at the end of a sentence, or paragraph. Its Hebrew root is *sal*, from *sullam*, "a ladder," and denotes "to raise up," or, "continually." Rashi and Onkelos, the authoritative second-century CE Aramaic translator of the Torah, read *sela* as *l'almin*, "eternally," or "forever." The word performs an important service by acting as a musical pause, a practice that began in the Temple when the leading singers "raised" their voices with a *sela*, a solemn "elevation" of tones, as they neared the end of a sentence. Why? In order to alert the musicians that they were about to pause, allowing the silence from both vocals and music to act as a liturgical guide to the overflow festival crowds in the outer Temple Court.[1]

Sa'ir la'azazel

Q What does this mean?

I don't know; nor does anyone else. See "Scapegoat!"

---

1. Jeremiah 1:26; Isaiah 57:14; 62:10.

Scapegoat!

Q I thought you'd never ask! Does this word have Jewish connotations?

Yes. After the Temple was destroyed, the Jewish mind adopted the declaration of the prophet Hosea, "We shall offer, instead of bulls, the words of our mouth," a spiritual battle cry that resulted in the liturgical heights of Yom Kippur majesty. Meshulam ben Kalonymus, a tenth-century Italian rabbi, richly describes the day's mysterious ritual, an act known as *kappora*, which means "to wipe out," as in to "wipe out" Israel's sins via sacrifice. This ceremony required a special offering of an unblemished bull and two he-goats (of equal size, cost, appearance), chosen via the drama of lottery (*goral echad la'Shem*), a subtle nod to the "random" element of human existence. One goat was inscribed with the words "for God" and then sacrificed. The other was chosen as a "confession vehicle" and sent (*sa'ir la'azazel*) "into the inaccessible wilderness" as a symbolic courier of the iniquities of the people. This "escaped" goat became the "scapegoat," a term still in use by westernized society to censure or castigate one for the sins of others. "When the goat reached the wilderness," Rabbi Yishmael records, "a thread of crimson wool tied to the door of the Temple turned white ("Though your sins be as scarlet they shall be as white as snow"). This served as a veritable spiritual barometer of God's forgiveness, a sign that caused the entire community to erupt in ecstatic joy, spontaneous dancing, mass celebration (emotions that we no longer see on our Yom Kippurs!). So what does *sa'ir la'azazel* mean? We know that *la* means "to," and *sa'ir* means "goat." But *azazel*? It's a mystery. Why? The word appears nowhere else in the Torah and thus has no clear etymology. Remember: the ancient proto-Sinaitic letters of the Hebrew alphabet are named after objects resembling them (e.g., the *beis* is derived from the word *bayit*, a "house;" the *dalet* from *delet*, a "door," and so on). There is no match for *azazel,* but there's lots of speculation. Menachem Azarya DeFano, guided by a Midrash, suggests the word is an acronym for *Zeh le'umat zeh asa Elokim*, "God has made one [good] and the other [evil]." Rabbi Ishmael links it to two sinful angels (Aza, Aza'el), who mislead the "sons of God" prior to the Flood, which is the source of the Hebrew slang, *lech la'azazel*, "Go to hell!" a reference to the goat sent to *azazel*. Perhaps this is why so many ancient drawings show the devil as a goat?![2]

Sholem Aleichem

Q Is this a greeting, a Shabbas song, or the name of an author?

All three! When Sholem Rabinovich, a young government-employed Ukrainian rabbi was searching for a pseudonym for his writings, in order not to lose his job, he flirted with *Der Yiddisher Gazlen* ("the Robber Jew") and *Solomon Bikherfresser* ("Solomon the Book Eater"), before settling on *Sholem Aleichem*. Today the expression is not only the name of the popular Friday night *erev* Shabbas meal song, but also modern Yiddish for "Hello," "How are you," or "Great to see you!" (or in Aussie slang, "How ya goin', mate!"). The Anglo-Saxon greeting *hello* (with its variants *hallo, hullo,* etc.) comes from *hale* (as in "hale and hearty") and originally meant "I wish you well." But in classical Hebrew, *sholem aleichem* means "peace be with you." The reply is reversed: *aleichem sholem*, "With you should [also] be peace!" The Jewish custom to greet another Jew with a *sholem aleichem* was originally intended to extend the concept of God between brethren, since *Shalom* is one of God's Names ("God is Shalom, His name is Shalom, and all is bound together in Shalom!"). Thus, its correct meaning is not "peace be upon you" but "God be with you," a prayer that all Jews be met and blessed with Divine Presence.[3]

Sh'ma

Q Is this the primary prayer of Israel?

Yes. The *K'rias Sh'ma* is Israel's ultimate, unambiguous declaration of allegiance and manifestation of faith, because of its opening verse, "Hear, O Israel, the Lord our God, the Lord is One," which is why it can be said in any language. It is the first prayer taught to a Jewish child (upon arising in

---

2. Yoma 4:1; Leviticus 16:1–32; Ecclesiastes 7:14; Pesikta D'Rav Kahana 28; Leviticus 17:7; Yoma 69b.
3. Zohar, Leviticus 10.

the morning and going to sleep at night), and the last words recited prior to death. Thus, the Torah enlarges the *ayin* and *daled* of the first verse in order to spell out *aid*, the Hebrew word for "witness," in that by declaring the *Sh'ma*, comprised of three sections of the Torah ("Hear, O Israel…," "If you listen to my Commandments…," and "…they shall make fringes…"), Jews are testifying to the Oneness of God.[4]

Short of cash

Q I am buying a house and am short of cash. Can I delay buying the *mezuzos*?

No. Putting up a *mezuza*, which means "doorpost," is a direct "positive" Torah obligation, on both men and women. Jews simply cannot live in homes without kosher *mezuzos* (although you can go into another Jew's home even if there's no *mezuza* there). When does the obligation to start hammering begin? It's immediate, the moment you move in with furniture. No, a thirty-day delay is not, despite the myth, allowed unless you're renting (just in case you change your mind). The sole purpose of this is to remind the Jew to act and behave as a Jew when he comes in or out of his home. Are there security "rewards" or "good luck strings" attached to having a *mezuza*? No, these supernatural ideas are prevalent today, but are secondary to the ritual.[5]

Sooner the better!

Q How effective is a deathbed repentance?

The succinct answer can be found in the Yom Kippur service, *Ad yom moto t'chakkeh lo liteshuva*, "To the day of one's death God waits for a person to repent." Deathbed repentance might be acceptable ("Even if one is a complete evildoer all his days and repents at the end, no wickedness shall be recorded against him"); however, the sooner (i.e., the younger) the bet-

---

4. Brachos 10b; Deuteronomy 6:4–9, 11:13–21; Numbers 15:37.
5. Yore Deah 291:3, 286:22; Sefer Hachinuch 423; Aruch Hashulchan 286:49; Iggeros Moshe, Yore Deah 1:179, 2:141; Menachos 44a; Rambam, Hilchos Mezuza 5:4; Shabbas 32b.

ter. Why? "The choicest repentance," writes Yonah, "is that of one's youth, when one subdues his evil inclination while he is yet in possession of his energies!"

Smoking

Q To smoke, or not to smoke? What's the verdict?

Smoking falls within the halachic category of not taking risks with life or health, a warning the Torah repeats twice ("You shall carefully guard your life"). The Chazon Ish determined that smoking is bad for both the body and the soul, and frowned upon Jews who took risks on the basis that "God protects the simple." Yehezkel Ashayak, a driver working for Rav Schach, recalls how the *rosh yeshiva* of Ponevezh would ask him to refrain from smoking. Even before the dangers were well known, one of the Lubavitcher Rebbes (Joseph Isaac Schneersohn), more than half a century ago, banned smoking in his yeshiva for young students (under twenty), and urged others to smoke only in moderation. Rav Moshe Feinstein, America's foremost halachist, urged parents not to let their children pick up smoking as a habit. Was it always so? No. When tobacco first came out, its pleasure was so apparent that Chassidim compared it to offering incense in the Temple, and asked their *rabbonim* whether smoking required a blessing (as in smelling sweet spices, for which a *bracha* is required).[6]

Seeing, hearing, smelling

Q Why are there no blessings related to sight and hearing, only to smelling?

According to legend, Adam lost some degree of his senses (sight and hearing) after he ate the forbidden fruit in Eden, thus we have no blessings relating to these senses. However, smell, an ephemeral sense, remained, and has a blessing attached to it. Jewish mystics then linked "fragrance" to the relationship between God and man, based on its first Torah appearance as

---

6. Deuteronomy 4:15; Psalms 116:6; Orach Chayim 210:2.

a verb ("And He smelled the pleasant smell") when God accepted a sacrifice from Noah as he left the Ark.[7]

Selling crabs and lobsters

Q Is *kashrus* only food-related?

No. It is a myth that non-kosher simply means it cannot be eaten (*asur b'achila*). In fact, one cannot derive any "benefit" whatsoever from anything not kosher (*asur b'schora*). That's why fishing for crabs and lobsters, or raising pork, is not at the top of every Jewish boy's fantasy of how to get rich.

Same-sex marriage

Q What would the Torah say about this new trend?

It would simply see it as an oxymoron of morals, and a contradiction in terms.

Solicitation

Q A rabbi from Israel asked me for the names of my rich friends so he could solicit them for charity funds. Is this OK?

Yes. If he is legitimate and his intentions are honorable, and if your friends are known as being generous and already give to charity, Rav Moshe Feinstein defines helping collectors as a mitzva. However, like all things in life, it should be done in moderation (Rashi was concerned that a local rich man's house would be "flooded" by people who will "eat all his food!").

---

7. Genesis 8:21.

Shiduchim

Q I know a boy and a girl who might be suitable for each other. Should I introduce them?

Anything anybody does to accelerate matrimony is considered a great mitzva. God himself arranges matches! Even a professional *shadchan*, who gets paid for his work, can arrange "a match" (*shiduch*, Aramaic for "peaceful" or "tranquil") on a Shabbas, and even discuss his fees on Shabbas. Who's liable for the fee? The parents, *not* the young couple, on both sides, should pay the *shadchan*, equally. How much? That's negotiable. When is the payment due? Immediately after the *shiduch* has been arranged, and, if the engagement is broken later, there is no such thing as a refund, unless it can be shown that the *shadchan* lied in such matters as physical or mental illness, financial status, level of religious observance, etc.[8]

Sins, on a scale

Q On the Richter scale of sins, what's more damaging? Fiscal or ritual crimes?

A quick look at the sins listed in the daily *Vidui* prayer of repentance shows a larger number of monetary-type than ritual offenses, such as Shabbas desecration, *kashrus* violations, etc. Five of the eleven curses recited at Mount Eival are for economic evils (robbery, corruption, bribery, extortion, etc.), leading French Rabbi Moshe Mekotzi to blame the length of the exile on fraud and lies practiced by Jews against gentiles.

---

8. Midrash Rabba, Tzav 8:1; Ran, Shabbas 12a; Orach Chayim 306:6; Ketzos Hashulchan 107:8; Avnei Netzer, Choshen Mishpat 36; Rema, Choshen Mishpat 87:39, 185:10; Akiva Eiger, Choshen Mishpat 185.

Slichos

Q When should I say them? Do I have to take my wife and daughters? Do I need a *minyan*?

Preferably *Slichos*, an abbreviation of *pesukei Slichos*, "verses of forgiveness," should be said at the end of the night that follows the last Shabbas before Rosh Hashana [or the Shabbas before that, if Rosh Hashana falls early in the week]), when it's *eis ratzon*, the traditional "time of appeasement"; however, they're still valid if you read them any time after midnight (or once "a third of the night" has passed). Want to take your wife? That's OK, but it's not obligatory. No, you don't need a *minyan*; however, in its absence you can't say certain sections (e.g., the Thirteen Attributes).[9]

Slander

Q I have a friend who can't stop spreading slander. What should I do?

The Chofetz Chaim, in his epochal work on gossip (*loshen hora*), puts as much blame on the listener as on the speaker; he would urge you to politely, yet firmly, say you're not interested in hearing slander. "A man of understanding," says Solomon, "will make himself deaf to such words," a warning that the one who listens to prattle is no better than the one who spreads it. Or, as that cynical Yiddishist said: "I don't like to repeat *loshen hora*, so listen carefully the first time I tell you!"[10]

Slavery

Q What's the Torah's view of slavery?

Rav Avraham Pam, twentieth-century *rosh yeshiva* of Yeshivah Torah Va'daas, noted that the only quality that differentiated a slave from a free human being was the ability to control one's free time. Italian Rabbi

---

9. Orach Chayim 581:1; Mishne Berura 565:12; Iggeros Moshe, Orach Chayim 2:105; Yechave Da'as 1:46; Birkei Yosef, Sha'arei Teshuva 581:1; Orach Chayim 565:5.
10. Proverbs 11:12.

Ovadiah Sforno, a major commentator of the Middle Ages, went one step further: the significance of the "day," as a unit of Jewish time, was meaningless until after the Exodus. Why? Because a day meant nothing to a slave who was deprived of any power to shape it. When Ludwig Boerne cried out, "Because I was born a slave, I love liberty more than you," he was confirming that only the liberated, emancipated from tyranny, could appreciate time as a precious gift. The noble eighteenth-century words on the Liberty Bell in Philadelphia, "Proclaim liberty in the land to all its inhabitants" (a universal theme expressed by the French national slogan, *Liberty, equality, fraternity*), is first found in Leviticus.

Sssh! Don't tell the insurance companies

Q Are Jews, who take their health seriously, a better insurance risk?

In 1873 Dr. John Stockton Hough published "Longevity and Other Biostatic Peculiarities of the Jewish Race," a treatise that concluded Jews in America were a good bet, medically speaking. First, they were no longer threatened with extinction by natural causes (the murderous plagues and diseases of Europe) nor by non-natural causes (the murderous Cossacks, blood libels, Inquisitions, Adolf's gas chambers). Their physical resilience and safety precautions against sickness led Dr. Hough to write that "the average Jewish life span is eleven years longer than that of the average gentile." However, with the rise of modern technology, it is now certain (but don't tell the insurance companies!) that Jews suffer a disproportionate number of genetic diseases and other such "modern-day" infirmities as Tay Sachs, breast cancer, diabetes, migraine headaches, manic depression, and the devastating Niemann-Pick disease, which disproportionately affects Ashkenazi Jews in its most damaging form, subtype A.

Silence is golden!

Q Is this a "Jewish" saying?

Sure is! Silence, reveals Rabbi Akiva, "is a protection for wisdom," an echo of King Solomon's observation in Proverbs, "Even fools, if they keep silent, are deemed wise!" Our Sages preferred *miyus sicha*, "a minimum of small talk or chatter!" To Rav Hiyya it wasn't "necessary to tell a wise man to hold his tongue," whilst his colleague, Joshua ben Levi, measured the "worth" of each word: "A word is worth a *sela* [a small coin], but silence is worth two [*sela'im*]!" Koheles, as usual, was direct: "There is a time to keep silent and a time to speak!"[11]

Satmar and Zionism

Q Why are the Neturei Karta against the State of Israel?

Neturei Karta, Aramaic for "Guardians of the City," a phrase from the Talmud, was a "breakaway *minyan*" in 1938 of *Yerushalmi Litvaks* from the Polish-Lithuanian-Russian-German rabbis of Agudas Israel, "Society of Israel," an organization founded in 1912. Its founder, Rav Amram Blau, was inspirational, courageous, dedicated, and so in love with the land of Israel that he never travelled abroad. He married a convert who had fought in the French Resistance, and who had rescued him during the Holocaust. Why did he "break away"? He thought Aguda, despite the presence of such Ivy League *gedolim* as the Rashab, Chazon Ish, and the Brisker Rav, were not tough enough on Zionism. His ideology was based on that of Rabbi Yoel Teitelbaum, the Satmar Rebbe (although the Satmar Rebbe criticized Neturei Karta for meeting with Arab "murderers"). Rav Teitelbaum was an outstanding Talmud scholar, charismatic, brilliant, prolific, and a man of uncompromising principles who opposed the establishment of Israel. His position is based on a single sentence in the Talmud, known as the "three solemn oaths," that only God, in a cosmic display of the supernatural and miraculous, would redeem Israel, thus making His power manifest to the nations of the world. Until then, the Jews were to remain passive, submit to the degradation of exile, retain fidelity to the Laws of Moses, and not interfere with "God's finger" (*Yad Hashem*) in history. The Satmar Rebbe viewed Zionism as a satanic creation of Samael, God's demon-in-charge of history, despite the fact that Israel is the largest ever financial contributor to Torah causes, and that, by absorbing 700,000 Jewish refugees from concentration camps, giving them food and housing, Israel performed the

11. Pirkei Avos 3:17; Ben Sira 4, 23; Proverbs 10:19; Derech Eretz Zuta 7:4; Ecclesiastes 3:7.

largest act of *pikuach nefesh* in history. The majority of scholars disagree with Satmar. Specifically, the oath that "the nations swear not to subjugate Israel overmuch," was negated by the Holocaust, and the United Nations vote to establish Israel negated the other "oath" (not to "rise up against the nations"). Rabbi Shraga Feivel Mendlowitz made a blessing at the good news from the United Nations, and Rav Aharon Kotler later assured him his *hatov v'hameitiv* blessing was in order. The Boyaner Rebbe and Rabbi Yosef Eliyahu Henkin fiercely opposed the Neturei Karta philosophy. The Brisker Rav, a fierce opponent of Zionism, called the United Nations vote "a smile from Heaven" (although he never supported the individual leaders in the Knesset). Rabbi Moshe Feinstein, America's pre-eminent halachist, approved the words in the prayer for Israel. Rabbi Yehiel Yaakov Weinberg, although opposing Yom Ha'atzmaut (Independence Day; because it was declared unilaterally by the Israeli Rabbinate), expressed great joy at the establishment of Israel. Rabbi Joseph B. Soloveitchik, although he refused to call the establishment of Israel a messianic event, was an ardent lifelong Zionist, and Rabbi Ya'akov Kamenetsky, foremost Torah educator in the United States, wrote, "After the great destruction and despair that overtook the remnant [of the Holocaust], God caused the establishment of the state of Israel in order to strengthen the connection to Judaism and to sustain the link between the Jews in exile and the Jewish nation." Israel's most revered halachist, Rabbi Ovadia Yosef, encourages the saying of *Hallel* and *Sheheheyanu* on Israel's Independence Day ("I wish to emphasize first that the State of Israel and independent Jewish reign in our Holy Land is of the highest historical and religious significance!"). The majority of Torah Sages did what the Lubavitcher Rebbe did. A fierce critic of Zionism before the Holocaust, the leader of Chabad changed his tone after the establishment of Israel. He told his followers that the "new reality" of six million Jews slaughtered and the Jewish people still in existential danger demanded that Jews unite and nothing be done or said to harm Jewish interests, religious or secular![12]

12. Kesubos 111a; Ovadia Yosef, Yabi'a Omer, vol. 6, Orach Chayim 41–42.

Simanim

Q What is this?

These are "cuisine signs;" namely, the different foods (apples, dates, leek, etc.) we eat with a *Yehi ratzon* blessing on the nights of Rosh Hashana as a symbolic part of our plea for, say, a "sweeter year," a "positive year," etc. (Pomegranates are a favorite because they are said to contain 613 seeds, symbolic of the 613 commandments in the Torah.) This *minhag* is derived from several Talmudic analogies. An example? The coronation-inauguration ceremony of a new king would occur near a wellspring. Why? In the hope that his wisdom would flow like a wellspring!

Squaring the circle

Q If God is omnipotent, can He square a circle?

God can do whatever He wants to, although Jeremiah places limits *even* on God, and poses the real question, *Why* would He want to? According to the prophet, God is restricted to acts that give Him "pleasure." These are guided by principles of loving-kindness, justice and righteousness; in other words, even God cannot turn Himself into a forbidden idol, or into an evil force![13]

Shortest prayer?

Q What's the shortest prayer in the Torah?

Aaron begs God, *El na rifah na la*, "O God, pray heal her," a five-word plea for his sister, Miriam, who has been disfigured by the Heavens with the "snow-white scales" of leprosy (*tzara'as*), punishment for calling Moses' wife (Zippora) a "dark-skinned" Midianite woman. Our early Sages tried to make *davening* "stress free"! They followed a principle of *Torah tzibur*, not to bother the congregation, which saw no particular merit in stretching out

---

13. Psalms 135:6; Genesis 18:14; Jeremiah 32:26; 9:23–24; Numbers 11:23; Exodus 34:6–7; Leviticus 20:23; Deuteronomy 12:32; 24:16.

prayers. When *davening* with others, Rabbi Akiva kept his prayers short, but when alone he was so animated in his prayers that he started in one corner and ended in another![14]

Shtetl sleuth

Q How do you say "private eye" in Hebrew?

The Hebrew slang is *shamus*, derived from the Yiddish *shammes* (in Hebrew, *shamash*), a "synagogue beadle" who runs the *shul* (no, it has no link to the common Irish name Shaymus!). What's the link between a beadle and a private detective? There's an old Yiddish proverb on how to get information (the "dirt") on anyone in the *shtetl: Ich ken dem shammes un der shammes kent di gantze shtot!* "I know the *shammes* and the *shammes* knows the whole town!" It was the job of the *shammes* sleuth to know everything about everybody! He had to know each one's correct full name, and his father's name (to call them up to the Torah); where they lived (to knock on their door to wake them up for midnight *slichos*); and such basic "gossip" as who was engaged, had a baby, escaped from harm, was sick, died, etc., in order to make announcements in *shul*.

Sex-changes

Q Any problem with sex-change operations?

All sex-related questions can be summarized in two words: procreation (anything that interferes, harms, or negates human reproduction is forbidden) and modesty (anything that dilutes the "*kedusha* [holiness] in the daughters of Israel"). This includes those who voluntarily change their sex by surgery (also a transgression of self-mutilation and cross-dressing). Would a wife of an "ex-male" need a *get* (divorce)? No, the moment her husband's sexual status changes, her marriage is automatically terminated. What if the surgery is a "done deal"? In Jewish law, is he still a *he*, or a *she*? Surgery does not change one's birth identity; however, a man lacking male

---

14. Tosefos Brachos 3:5; Brachos 12b, 31a, 34a.

genitalia cannot, according to Rabbenu Asher, marry (neither as a woman nor as a man; the former, says Ibn Ezra, being an act of homosexuality).[15]

Secretarial gossip

Q I'm uncomfortable about my doctor's secretary being familiar with my medical records. Is this OK?

The prohibition against *rechilus* (slander) and *loshen hora* does not apply to the inter-office communication between a professional and his/her (necessary) staff, such as a doctor's secretary, documenting your diagnosis and forwarding it to another physician or to a laboratory. This also applies to any information passed from a lawyer to his staff, who must, in order to provide proper service to you, the client, be privy to your confidential, even if negative, information. In Hebrew, this is called *michila*, "implied consent," because it's of benefit to the patient or client.

Separation of Church and State

Q Does Jewish rule favor decentralized government?

In the Torah portion on justice and judges (*Shoftim*), which introduces the ideal workings of urban civilization, the Jews learn that "separation" is a key component. The branches of judicial and legislative power in government are divided, the administrative duties are broken into two categories of magistrate (*shofet*) and official (*shoter*), and the justice system is clearly decentralized: "Establish courts in *all* communities, *throughout* your tribes" (*b'chol sh'o'recho*), which is the forerunner for today's *beis din* structure.

---

15. Deuteronomy 22:5, 23, 23:1; Tzitz Eliezer 10, 25–26; She'elot Yavetz 1:171; Besamim Rosh 340; Rabbenu Chananel, Leviticus 18:22; Sefer Hachinuch, # 209; Tosafos, Nedarim 51a; Sanhedrin 7a.

Seventy, or sixty-nine?

Q How many Jews originally went to Egypt?

Jewish history has "seventy" (souls) from Jacob's family who go "down to Egypt" as guests under Joseph's protection. The oldest? Serach, daughter of Asher, whose great longevity makes her *the* only known eyewitness to the entire Egyptian-Judeo experience. The question is obvious. That a "great and populous nation" emerges from only "seventy" is an extraordinary demographic harvest; but was it *exactly* seventy? Perhaps this is simply a symbol of a "large" number? The Torah itself lists only sixty-nine, a number that excludes daughters-in-law but includes one wife, Rachel ("proof" of her unique status in the family). Since seventy *is* recognized as a precise count, who is missing? I don't know, but rabbinic speculation focuses on three possibilities: Jacob, Yocheved, daughter of Levi (born "between the Egyptian entrance walls"), or God Himself ("I will go down *with you* to Egypt")!

Symbol

Q What's the single most important symbol of Judaism?

The Ark of the Covenant, God's only earthly physical manifestation. The Ark was in existence from the wanderings in the desert through to the destruction of the First Temple. What was inside? The first (broken) and second (complete) tablets of the Ten Commandments, although one opinion in the Talmud has two Arks, each containing one set of tablets.[16]

Sew-what!

Q I went to buy a suit and the tailor asked if I wanted it "kosher"! Is there "kosher clothing"?

Yes, there is. A "kosher" garment (the "sew-what?!" mitzva) prohibits "mixing" such as wool and linen in a single piece of clothing. This is called

---

16. Baba Basra 14b; Brachos 8b.

sha'atnez (or *kilayim*), an abbreviation for *shua* (combing, brushing), *tavuy* (drawn into fiber), and *nuz* (braided). Does *sha'atnez* only apply to clothes? No. It also includes any item which wraps around, or rests, on part of the body (e.g., towels, pillows, blankets). Can you wear a woolen suit and a linen shirt? Yes, they're two separate garments. What about polyester suits with synthetic fibers? They're OK, even though they contain linen in the padding, collar supports, and seam bindings. What's the rationale behind this prohibition? I don't know, but there are several hypotheses. Some trace it to God's desire at Creation that every species (or category) preserve a distinct identity; others link it to the clothes of idol-worshiping clerics (even during the Rambam's time, it was still "fashionable" for twelfth-century Egyptian priests to wear wool-flax wardrobes); whilst Jewish mystics see it as a permanent reminder of the disaster in Eden following the "merging" of linen (symbolic of Cain's offering) and wool (a reminder of Abel's offering).[17]

---

17. Leviticus 19:19; Deuteronomy 22:11; Yevamos 5b; Kilayim 9:8; Yuma 60b, 69a.

T

Tree tax deadline

Q Tax-paying trees? Is there such a thing?

Yes! When Jews applied tithing to fruit, they had to create a fruit "tax year," a "cutoff" day, akin to a Jewish-IRS tax deadline. And so, trees had their own "New Year's," when they were "judged." This took place on Tu b'Shevat, the night with a full moon chosen by Hillel as the halachic vehicle which enabled the agricultural community of Israel to count the age of each tree, determine in which specific year the tree's tithes belonged, and thus calculate exactly what percentage of their harvest went to the Temple. No fruit was allowed to be eaten during the first three years after planting, when it was called *orla*, a recognition that only Heaven creates Life (human or plant). This is the basis of the *ofsherenish* custom, a boy's first haircut at age three. Did this apply to all food products? Not at first. In the Bible, it only applied to grain, wine, and oil. The rabbis later extended this to all agricultural-horticultural produce; and, in order to help the farmer decide which fruits were suitable to be eaten, and thus subject to a tithing tax, the Mishna handed out "generic" rulings: figs (the moment their tips turn white); grapes (when berries first appear); mulberries (when turning red); pomegranates (when the core becomes "pulpy"); dates (at swelling, like dough); peaches (when they acquire red veins); walnuts-almonds (after their kernel skins have formed); pears (when the skin is smooth) and so on.[1]

Third Temple

Q Are we obligated to rebuild the Temple in Jerusalem?

Yes. "It is a positive commandment to build a house to the Lord," based on the Torah's demand, "They shall make for Me a sanctuary, and I shall dwell in their midst." So why don't we? Because there are seven preconditions (which have nothing to do with today's political problems, such as access to the Temple Mount) that do not currently exist. They are: the majority of the Jewish people must be living in Israel; there must be conditions of peace; the wish for a Temple must arise from a Jewish spiritual reawakening; there must be a supernatural act of God's approval; a true prophet must give the command to rebuild; the site must be resanctified (although the Rambam argues that the original sanctity still persists); and the Torah's ordained measurements, proportions and specifications of the Temple must be scrupulously followed. Rabbi Shlomo HaCohen Aviner (*Tal Hermon*) adds another caveat: the halachic requirement that mitzvos be performed according to a certain procedure. In the case of the rebuilding of the Temple one prerequisite, as per the Rambam, is the eradication of Amalekism from the planet – a near impossibility in the foreseeable future![2]

Trumpets

Q Is the shofar a "Jewish" instrument?

There are many Torah instruments, but *only* the shofar is uniquely Jewish. Why? It is not a contrived musical instrument but a reminder of the faith that surrounds the binding of Isaac (*akeda*). This is why, says Rabbi Abbahu, a ram's horn was chosen, because its curved shape, preferably unadorned (i.e., no silver coating or colors added) resembles humble submission. Its religious undertones, its eerie sounds, are not meant to serenade us but to

---

1. Rosh Hashana 10a; Ma'aseros 1,2,3.
2. Meoros Hadaf Hayomi, 2; Rambam, Hilchos Beis Habechira 1:1; Exodus 25:8.

wake us from our slumber; that is why this Jewish "trumpet" can only be made from a kosher animal – but not a cow! Why not? Because of its association with the golden calf. "A prosecutor," notes the Talmud, "cannot be a defender at the same time!"

Trickle-down economics

Q Were the Jews subject to agricultural taxes?

Jews, since Biblical times, have been required to contribute towards supporting the poor, widows, orphans, strangers, and those who, around *yom tov* time, find themselves unfortunately reliant on communal generosity (e.g., donations of wheat and wine before Pesach). The Laws of Sinai thus imposed taxes that were later, during the time of the Talmud, extended to pay for community maintenance, which included synagogues, security, town walls, upkeep of roads, etc. Were rabbinic scholars exempt? Yes, from some taxes, but not from those which benefited every citizen. How were the taxes determined? Sometimes unfairly. King Solomon's over-taxation led to disastrous national consequences. But generally the amount depended upon one's income and the degree of benefit one derived from the services provided. The income from Jewish farmers' income was subject to agricultural taxes under the laws of *ma'aseros* ("tithings") or *terumos* ("uplifted," or "separated" offerings). A second tithe (*ma'aser sheni*) was put aside for one of two purposes – either to be eaten later in Jerusalem, or sold and the proceeds used later to buy food to be eaten in Jerusalem. A third category (*teruma gedola*, a "major heave offering") was an optimistic voluntary tithe with no set amount, based purely on each individual's generosity. Were there guidelines? Yes! Giving a sixtieth of one's produce was considered cheap ("mean"). Giving a fiftieth was "average." Giving a fortieth was "generous." The Levites received ten percent (*ma'aser rishon*), the "first tithe" of whatever was left, and were required to give the poor and needy a tenth of this (*ma'aser min hama'aser*, "offering from the offering") every third to sixth years of the Sabbatical cycle (*ma'aser oni*, the "tithe for the poor"). Why the special treatment for priests and Levites? Because they had no ancestral land holdings of their own, and were too busy attending to the Temple's religious, educational and administrative duties to earn a livelihood. Enforcement was strict! The Midrash frowns on "grudging givers"!

Rabban Gamliel warned his followers not to "give by guesswork." Yochanan ben Zakkai made the stunning claim that the destruction of the Second Temple was the fault of delinquent taxpayers, and Jewish law considers tax cheating a "public robbery," a serious profanation of the Divine Name.[3]

Turban

Q **What is the meaning of the early morning blessing that praises God "who crowns Israel with glory"?**

The early morning *brachos* are wake-up liturgical calls, derived from a passage in the Talmud that goes into one's early-morning sequence of actions. Thus, when the rooster crows its wake-up call, Jews praise God who gave the bird the intelligence to tell the difference between day and night. When a person wakes up and realizes he's a man, he praises God for not creating him "a woman" (giving him the honor and opportunity of performing more mitzvos). Opening a morning eye? You bless God "who opens the eyes of the blind." Putting on shoes? You praise God "who has supplied all my wants." Strapping on a belt? He is praised "who girds Israel with might." And when donning a cap (literally, his turban), Jews praise Him "who crowns Israel with glory." Remember: the Jews of ancient Babylon regarded the turban, wound around the head, as a mark of morality, piety, humility. Why did Jews stop wearing turbans? Because the rise of Islam hijacked the turban headgear as a "crown of Arabs, the badge of Islam." Drawings of the Rambam, created long after he lived, show the Spanish Sage wearing a turban, but this is pure fiction; no one knows what he wore![4]

Two or three Temples?

Q How many Temples have there been?

Everybody talks about the destruction of the "first" and "second" Temples and building a "third," when in fact there have already been three Temples,

---

3. Magen Avraham, Tosefta Baba Kamma, 10a; Gittin 10b; Deuteronomy 1:3; 27:8; Pirkei Avos 1:16; Baba Basra 8a, 35b; S'machos 44b; Seder Zeraim; Baba Metzia 106b; Jeremiah 14:1; Megilla 5b.
4. Brachos 60b.

all built on the same site. The first, which took over seven years to erect, was Solomon's. It stood for 410 years, until the master arsonist Nebuchadnezzer burnt it to the ground. Fifty years later construction was started on the next Temple by Jews returning to Judea. It took them twenty years. Groundwork for the third, white-marbeled Temple, much larger than Solomon's, began twenty years before the Common Era and was destroyed ninety years later by the Romans (586 BCE).

Tractate Purim

Q Is there a Tractate Purim?

Yes, but only if your mind recognizes that on Purim nothing is as it seems. What you see is not what you get, and vice versa. In the olden days, yeshiva boys would "study" Tractate Purim, except that there is no such tractate, an act that led to today's Purim custom of the "spoof" newspaper, a refreshing tonic by Jews who believed that religion is healthy when it can laugh at itself. Such rabbinic writers as twelfth-century Judah Ibn Shabbetai and Solomon Ibn Saqbel were master satirists, and the fourteenth-century Kalonymos ben Kalonymos penned a parody of the Mishna on Exodus called *Massechet Purim l'layl shikkurim*, a play on the words *leil shimurim*, "A Night of Watching"! Since it was a Purim treatise, Jacob Israelstam felt safe enough to translate the title into "The Tractate of Lots for the Night of Sots"! Yep, it's playtime! Purim, as per usual, is the only occasion Jews can "make *hoyzek*" (Yiddish for "joke," or "make fun of"), as in *mach nisht kayn hoyzek*, derived from *hosche*, German for a "jest (or) prank." A *New York Jewish Week* Purim parody ("*The Jewish Weak*") ran such stories as "Husband Gets Get after Wife Dates 100 Rabbis," "Reform to officiate at same-sheep ceremonies," and an exposé that the *yom tov*'s villain's name was Hey-man! because when he entered the palace he said, "Hey, man! I have to see His Maj!"

Tribes

Q There are twelve Hebrew Tribes, right?

Wrong. There are thirteen tribes (*shevatim*), but "twelve" is the number that tradition uses. How do we get to thirteen if Jacob only had twelve sons? Because Joseph eventually splits into two tribes (Ephraim and Menashe), making thirteen, but then, later, the tribe of Levi is excluded from the census which brings it back to twelve, although this "twelve" no longer has a *Joseph* or *Levi*.

Tombstones

Q Do graves need tombstones?

Yes, and no. Although the "words of the righteous are their memorials" (Simeon ben Gamliel), the erection of a tombstone has been the norm in Judaism from ancient days, derived from Jacob's action in placing a stone over the grave of his wife Rachel near Bethlehem.[5]

Testimony

Q I saw a crime but don't want to testify. Do I have to?

It depends. If you're a relative, ignoramus, child, blind, woman, unstable, proselyte, old, *mamzer*, eunuch, a friend of the defendant's enemy, can benefit from the verdict, or just plain "evil," then, no, you don't have to testify. If you ticked "none of the above," then, yes, Jewish law orders witnesses to give testimony (*eidus*) ("If he saw or knew and does not tell, he bears his sin"), and to be truthful ("You shall not answer as a false witness").[6]

Take two aspirins and call me in the morning

Q Were our rabbis knowledgeable about medicine?

Yes, in fact, parts of the Talmud read like a Judaic version of the amazing fifth-century BCE Hippocratic medicinal corpus; but remember, their interest in medicine or astronomy, science or physics was incidental. There was no motivation to become physical healers (especially after God de-

---

5. Genesis 35:20.
6. Deuteronomy 5:17, 24:16; Exodus 20:16, 23:1; Leviticus 5:1.

clared, "I wound and I heal; there is no rescue from My grasp!"), but *only* a desire to arrive at correct halachic conclusions. The Talmud may not be a medical treatise but, for example, its rabbis became pioneers of the science of pathology, obsessed with understanding the slaughter of animals in order to perfect *kashrus* (e.g., by inserting a tube into the trachea of an animal, and inflating its lungs, they were able to list eighteen defects that made the animal unfit for Jews).[7]

That's a stretch!

Q Why are Jews called a *yud*?

Reb Simha Bunim, great Chassidishe master, tells us: "Just as the letter *yud* is the only one in our alphabet that cannot be magnified (if written longer vertically it becomes a *vav*, and horizontally a *daled*), so the Jew who magnifies himself ceases to be a Jew!" When Yisro became a Jew, according to Rashi, a *vav* was added to his name. The *Pardes Yosef*, after asking why not add a *heh*, a more traditional custom (given to both Abraham and Sarah), replies in *gematria* terms: Yisro is broken down into *yud* (for *Yehudi*, "Jew") with the rest (*taf, reish, vav*) adding up to 606. So? What's the relevance of this number?! If you add the extra seven Noahide laws that Yisro came with, we get 613, the number of obligatory mitzvos of a Jew.

Temple treasures

Q What happened to the Temple treasures?

How would I know? Some claim they never left Jerusalem and were buried there for safekeeping, or that Heraclius, Byzantine emperor, had the vessels buried in the Monastery of the Cross. Others, based on depictions on the Arch of Titus and a report from the historian Josephus, believe they were taken to Rome. And then what? According to Procopius, a fifth-century author, Geiseric, king of the Vandals, stole them from Rome and hid them in his Carthage palace, only to have them reclaimed two years later by Belisarius, a Roman general who stored the gold candelabrum in

---

7. Deuteronomy 32:29; Brachos 60a.

Constantinople (where it was lit on Christian festivals), and the rest of the golden Jewish vessels in "a holy Christian place in Jerusalem." Heinrich Graetz, nineteenth-century Jewish historian, was convinced that none remain, all victims of plunder and destruction.

Trees 'R' Us

Q Why are Jewish mystics so foliage-fixated on trees, grass, greenery?

The Torah pays homage to the tree and salutes its ubiquitous symbolic contribution to the cosmic oasis of Life itself. In the chronology of Creation, God occupies Himself with the tree *before* humans by "planting a garden in Eden," and then extending it to the future: "When you enter the land, occupy yourselves first with naught else but planting!" Yochanan ben Zakkai took this seriously. "If you have a sapling in your hand, ready for planting, and you are told: the Messiah is here – go and plant the sapling first and then welcome the Messiah!" The presence and perpetuation of trees in Israel was vital; they represented not just an investment in the future, but the in-bred optimistic expectation that there will be a future. Food emanated from their branches and their leaves provided shelter to earthly nutrient seedlings which, in turn, produced more food. This explains why Moses, in sending his twelve spies (*meraglim*) on their ill-fated reconnaissance mission, assigned to them such a strange intelligence request: "Does the [holy] land have a tree or not?" Fixation on trees is not restricted to Jews or Judaism. The Bohemians would fashion a tree into a puppet called Death and then "drown" it in the local pond. Russians would dress up birch trees as girls. The English and Irish would celebrate around maypoles and whitethorn altars whose little red fruit was symbolic of Diogenes's lantern. The ancient Celtic Druids not only blanketed the countryside with forests, but named all eighteen letters of their Gaelic alphabet after trees and then, in an act that borders on foliage-idolatry, allocated native spirits to each tree. This is why the rabbis of the Talmud forbade Jews from using the wood of the "tree of idolatry," a directive that goes back to the time of Jezebel (a hundred years after the First Temple), when Asa, king of Judah, tried to wean the Jews away from "tree spirits" linked to Baal and Ashera, the main Canaanite god and goddess whose rituals centered on tree worship.

Theocracy, or Torahcracy?

Q Should Israel be a theocracy?

If you mean run by rabbis, the answer is no. If you mean a legislation run according to *mishpat ivri*, Jewish civil law, then the answer is yes: in other words, not a theocracy but a Torahcracy! The original plan for Israel was unique. A theocracy that required no central government. God was "the Head" of the nation, intending to sustain a unifying force of faith by personally interacting with His covenantal people, leaving all the local issues to the priests and judges. Did this theocratic structure work? Only in the desert and during part of the era of the Judges. Eventually, the Jews themselves clamored for "a king to judge us like all the nations." God got the message ("They have rejected Me, that I should not reign over them"), and relented, giving Samuel the go-ahead ("Hearken unto their voice, and make them a king"). This was the ominous beginning of the end. The kingdom, divided, created two rival kings, two capitals, two armies, and conflicting laws, until the social fabric of a people had so unraveled that the Jewish king (Rehoboam) simply ignored the counsel of the Jewish elders.[8]

Terrorists

Q How did the word *mehabel* for "terrorist" enter the Hebrew language?

The ancient Hebrew expression (*mal'achei habalah*) was used to describe the "punishing angel-demons" who tortured sinners after their death. Meanwhile, the Hebrew root for *mehabel*, derived from the *Shir Hashirim* (Song of Songs), which describes a mother's "travail" (*hiblatcha imcha*) and a "spoiling" (*mehablim*) of vineyards. Modern Hebrew adopted the word to describe one (e.g., a terrorist) who "deliberately hurts or causes pain."

---

8. 1 Kings 11:1–8, 11; 1 Samuel 8:5, 7, 22.

Teaching with teeth?

Q I was told that the Sh'ma's *"v'shinantam"* is linked to teeth! How is that possible?

Rashi sees *v'shinantam,* derived from the verb *shana,* "to repeat" (i.e., learn by repetition), as an expression for *chiddud,* "being sharply impressed." However, some Torah linguists also connect it to *shen,* "a tooth," in that, in order to "teach them diligently" you need to bite like teeth, deeply! The Talmud describes a certain Sage known for his incisive mind as a *shin'na,* one "with prominent teeth." Of course, these are all metaphorical, inspired by a rabbinic fixation that teeth equaled peace and friendship. Once upon a time, showing one's teeth to a stranger was even better than offering him "milk to drink." And the opposite is true. To provoke another would "set his teeth on edge"![9]

The Taliban's yeshiva?

Q When did the concept of a "yeshiva" begin?

Originally, we had the *beis sefer,* a "House of the Book" (for beginners), the *beis Talmud,* "House of Learning" (for older children), or the *beis medrash* (for advanced students), a term derived from the verb *darasa* or *darash,* "to study," or "to seek." In Arabic, *madraseh* also denotes a Muslim religious seminar; and *Taliban* comes from *talaba,* "to seek." Today it is known simply as the *yeshiva,* literally, "a sitting," suggestive of intense study. In later years, the *beis medrash* also referred to a "House of Gathering," which was usually a *shul,* because that's where the *seforim* usually were available. When did yeshiva study begin? Under the ancient auspices of Shem and Ever. However it was not until the beginning of the nineteenth century that the modern *yeshivos* with international reputations (e.g., Reb Chayyim Volozhiner's yeshiva in Volozhin near Vilna, Lithuania, established in 1802) emerged, attracting students from out of town.

---

9. Deuteronomy 6:7; Hagiga 15b; Kesubos 111b, on Genesis 49:12; Jeremiah 31:29.

Teetotaler

Q Who was the first teetotaler in the Torah?

Not only does Noah get credit for being the first person in the Torah to make wine, he's also the first to discover the mystic powers of the grapevine – and get drunk! The moment he drinks from its fermented juice, Noah begins to act so strangely as to plunge into indecent exposure. Why was Noah drunk? The Torah is mute on the subject, but it's easy to imagine how many problems Noah must have had looking after such a large, diverse animal population for a whole year! Welcome to the arrival of drunkenness; no wonder Isaiah and Hosea would later bitterly attack Jews for letting wine "take away the heart"! The Rechabites, inspired and encouraged by Jeremiah (precursor to the later prohibitionist Elliot Ness!), swore off wine, forming a temperance faction. Their descendants were known as *teetotalers*, a word that entered the English lexicon when a Lancashire working man (Richard Turner) once ended a speech advocating "total abstention" but, burdened by a stutter, he said *t-t-total*. Opponents ridiculed Turner, and referred to those who abstain as being members of *t-totalism* who prefer drinking cups of (sissy) *tea* to the real McCoy.

Toys (and Torah) 'R' Us

Q What do toys have to do with Torah?

While singing his praises in *tehillim*, King David called Torah a toy ("Were not Your Torah my plaything, I would have perished in my affliction"), and others picked up the unusual comparison. For if playing with toys is "imaginative and joyful," then so should creating new insights into Torah (*chidushim*) be "imaginative and joyful"![10]

---

10. Psalms 119:92.

═Taking care of business ═══════════

Q Is business a worthy pursuit?

"To be a successful businessman you need extraordinary talents," notes Rabbi Israel Salanter, *mussar* master, "and if you have such talents, why waste them on business?" Nachman of Kasovier, eighteenth-century rabbi from Galicia, adds, "Some people think of business when they are at the synagogue. Is it too much to ask them to think of God when they are at business?"

═Twinkle, twinkle little star ═══════════

Q We just bought a new house and want to have a housewarming party. What's the best day to have it on?

Rosh Chodesh. The moment the Torah inserted this as a "day of your gladness" in the same sentence with "the beginnings of your months," our Sages wrapped the day in a mantle of optimism, and Jewish mystics covered Rosh Chodesh Nisan with ten crowns, symbolizing ten wonderful things that happened on that day. After celestial sightings inspired King David to sing about "the work of Your Fingers," and Ben Sira waxed poetic at how the "stars are the beauty and glory of Heaven," Rosh Chodesh became infused with Jewish mysticism. To catch a falling star became a kabbalistic obsession, and "Twinkle, twinkle, little star" more than just a children's ditty (stars do not actually twinkle; they only seem to when the air that surrounds the earth bends the light that the star produces). The nation of Israel became convinced that Rosh Chodesh guided its rise and fall. Jews quickly infused the cheerful day with pomp, ceremony, festive meals and positive greetings (*Chodesh tov*) for a good month, one of health, peace, fulfillment. Embraced as *the* "Day of Good Beginnings," Rosh Chodesh then became the chosen date on which Jews held housewarming parties, known as a *chanukas habayis*, "dedication of a new home," a symbolic and optimistic harbinger of a new start in life. So go for it![11]

---

11. Psalms 8:4–5, 119:19; Ecclesiastes 43:9; Numbers 10:10.

=The mystery revealed! =

Q Who is responsible for kabbala?

Jewish history notes three important milestones in the development of kabbala: the first is in the third century, with the release of the *Zohar*, a book of parables in Aramaic from Rabbi Shimon Bar Yochai (*Rashbi*, pupil of Rabbi Akiva), as dictated to his student, Rabbi Aba. This book disappeared almost as soon as it was written, only to resurface several hundred years later in Safed (legend has it that it was found by a Jew buying fish from an Arab that was wrapped in *Zohar* pages). This led to the second dynamic period, that of Rabbi Yitzhak Luria (*Ari*), who "opened" its wisdom to all (legend has it that he spent seven isolated years in mystic study on the island of Roda on the Nile), as recorded by his follower, Rabbi Chaim Vital. We then have the great Chassidus era, from 1750 to the end of the nineteenth century, when any grand rebbe, *tzadik* or *chacham* – from Poland and Russia to Morocco and Iraq – worth his *smicha* ("rabbinical ordination") was a kabbalist!

=*Tevilas keilim* =

Q I just got married and received utensils as wedding gifts. What do I do?

If the utensils were manufactured by or bought from a non-Jew, you must immerse them in a kosher *mikva* (based on the verse "Everything that will not come in fire you shall pass through water"). Which utensils need "dipping"? Only those used for a meal (*klei seuda*). The Torah mentions six types of metal utensils that require immersion, but the rabbis of the Talmud redefine them as any utensil made out of material which "when broken can be melted down and reformulated" (e.g., gold, silver, copper, iron, tin, lead). What about glass? No. It can be "reformulated" when broken. Utensils made out of wood, stoneware, plastic, paper, styrofoam, non-glazed earthenware? No. Do you have to say a blessing (*…al tevilas keilim*)? It depends. Yes, on a utensil made out of any type of metal; no, on disposable pans. What about china dishes? There is no consensus on this (yet).[12]

---

12. Avoda Zara 75b; Aruch Hashulchan, Yore Deah 120:25; Shabbas 15b; Yore Deah 120:6;

Ten plagues?

Q Were there exactly "ten" plagues?

It depends. On what? On who's counting, and who's interpreting. As J.M. Keynes put it so well, "I'd rather be vaguely right than precisely wrong!" The Hebrew word for plagues (*makkos*) doesn't even appear during the ten plagues; it shows up, only *once*, in the Book of Samuel, and is spoken not by a Jew but by a gentile Philistine: "He is the same God who struck the Egyptians with every kind of plague [*makkos*]." But which *makkos* is he referring to? Rashi limits it only to God's blow against the Egyptians at the Red Sea. Why? Because the Torah does the same, using the word only in this context, identifying the splitting of the Sea as the greatest of all the Exodus miracles. Since *makkos* was a *goyish* word, our early rabbinic tradition used the expression *otot mofetim* ("signs and marvels") for the first nine plagues, and characterized only the last one (firstborn slayings) as "a true plague (*nega*)." Wait! It gets even more confusing. Several scholars insist on including Moses' rod-into-a-serpent (*tanin*) act, ordered by God, to get a total of eleven, not ten! And if you then add "the greatest of them all (the Red Sea)," you get twelve. So how does Rabbi Judah fit "ten" plagues into his mnemonic *detzach-adash-b'ahab* device? By combining "boils" and "pestilence" into one plague!

Tree lessons

Q Am I imagining this? Everywhere I turn in the texts I stumble over a tree! What's the significance?

You're right. Rabbi Shimon bar Yochai reacted to the "pleasant shade" of a particular tree by immediately crying out, "We must crown this place with words of Torah!" Halachists then allocated a special blessing for fruits that grow on a tree (*borei pri ha'etz*) to differentiate them from foods that do not (*borei pri ha'adama*). The tree was created, says a Midrash, "for man's com-

Chelkas Ya'akov 2:163, 3:115; Kisvei Harav Henkin 2:60; Tzitz Eliezer 7:37, 8:26; Be'er Moshe 2:52; Minchas Yitzchak 3:76–78, 5:32; Iggeros Moshe, Yore Deah 3:23, 120:1; Moshe Feinstein, l'Torah v'Horaha; Kitzur Shulchan Aruch 37:3.

panionship." Nachman of Bratzlav, nature lover *extraordinaire*, warned, "If you kill a tree before its time, it is the same as murder!" Another Chassidic giant, Rabbi Avraham Yehoshua Heschel (the Apter Rebbe), reminded his followers that the Hebrew word for tree (*ilan*) was numerically the same as two of God's Names (*Havaya* and *Adnut*). This foliage mesmerization was not limited to Chassidim! Rabbi Eliyahu (the Vilna Gaon), misnagdic leader *par excellence*, tinkered with Genesis numerology and discovered a delightful symmetry: an arithmetical relationship that thematically twinned the tree of the third day of Creation to man and woman formed on the sixth. In order to reinforce the notion that "a man is like a tree of the field," Talmud linguists note that whenever the Torah refers to trees (*etz*) or man (*adam*, formed from *adama*, the earth itself), it does so in the singular. And by describing the original menorah of antiquity, which resembles a tree with its trunk and its branches, in botanical terms (branches, calyxes, petals, cups, etc.), God ensured that the tree (which appears a hundred nine times in the Bible) entered Jewish tradition as a calligraphic metaphor of Torah itself. This is why Torah was called an *etz chayim*, "Tree of Life," and why ancient *shuls* were always surrounded by trees.[13]

Too many chefs?

Q Why was there a need for so many levels of leadership in ancient Israel?

For checks and balances! Decentralization, already during the Jewish people's wanderings in the desert, was seen as a complex but necessary component, in order to ensure a stable leadership to oversee a proper legal and ethical society. By the time the Jews enter Canaan, there is a gallery of Torah-defined leaders that includes judges, officers, kings, priests, Levites and prophets (both true and false!). What came first? The pursuit of justice. The first to be appointed were the "judges and officers," individuals chosen not for their wealth or *yichus* but from the common folk, as long as they were able to "judge the people with just judgment." And if they couldn't? The Torah then expanded the leadership apparatus to include "the priests

---

13. Brachos 43b; Genesis 2:7; Deuteronomy 20:19; Exodus Rabba 44; Zohar, 2:127a; Brachos 40a; Genesis Rabba 13.2; Psalms 93:13.

and the Levites" who not only serviced the needs of the Temple but also lent a hand to the judiciary. Some powers of leadership were then given to the monarchy ("I will set a king over me"), preferably one who was not overly obsessed with "wives and horses, silver, gold." The main difference between the three levels of power was this: judges were appointed, kings were elected, priests inherited their positions.[14]

Torah scroll

Q Can a Torah be written on paper?

No. It must be written on ruled lines on parchment, with either the entire skin on its outer side, or the outer layer on its inner side. The parchment sheets are then sewn together with sinews. What about the first and last sheets? They are sewn onto wooden rollers.

Time

Q What's the Jewish concept of time?

The concept of now (i.e., "the present") does not exist in classical Hebrew where *z'man*, the word for Time, is related to *hazmona*, "preparation." The value of counting days, weeks, or months lies only in time being used towards the attainment of an identifiable end, a Godly destination called *Makom* in Hebrew, which, not uncoincidentally, is God's name for space. This suggests that between past and future there is nothing, time having no reality of its own. It was like the circus, always packing up and moving on, which is why the Jews were expected to be *l'ma'alah min haz'man*, a people uniquely transcending its shackles, secure in the knowledge that God had split time into holy segments. This belief inspired Joseph B. Soloveitchik (the *Rav*) to declare that absolutely nothing in life is sacred unless, and *until*, man made it so. In other words, there is time and there is Jewish time, and since the latter waits for no man, it must not be squandered but preciously collected as a significant family and community experience.

---

14. Deuteronomy 17:8–9, 17:14, 16–17.

=Tay-Sachs

Q Am I allowed to be screened for this potential disease?

Yes. In the spirit of *sakanas nefashos*, "potential dangers," the prohibition of looking "into the future" (i.e., "soothsayers, fortunetellers"), does *not*, according to Rav Moshe Feinstein, apply to genetic-medical screening.[15]

=Timely payments

Q I run a small business and always struggle with meeting my payroll. Can I ask my staff to wait?

No. There is an employer obligation known as *lo salin*, "timely payment," based on sensitivity for a worker's needs and expectations, whereby a direct worker (not a third party, or subcontractor's worker) must be paid "timely" (i.e., either before the day, or night, of his employment is over, or on the day, or night, that his wages are due). Thus delaying payment is a form of "cheating and robbing." Does this apply to corporations, *yeshivos*, day schools? Only if "the buck stops" somewhere (i.e., with one definitive "boss"); in other words, *lo salin* does not apply (other than morally) to boards, directors, fund-raisers, etc.[16]

=Tehillim

Q How do I know which daily chapter of *Tehillim* to recite?

There is a custom to pick the chapter associated with the year or your age, plus one. My mother doesn't have this problem: she says *all* of *Tehillim* *every* morning, getting up before sunrise in order to finish together with the miracle of the morning light.

---

15. Rashi, Deuteronomy 18:13; Iggeros Moshe, Even Haezer, vol. 4, #10.
16. Makkos 24a; Choshen Mishpat 339:7; Tosafos Rid, Ritva, Baba Metzia 110b; Deuteronomy 24:14; Baba Metzia 61a, 111a; Y.S. Elyashiv, Shulchan Aruch Harav, Sechirus 18.

=Tzu Gott's Nomen

Q What does this mean?

It is Yiddish, literally "In God's Name," to describe the day after Yom Kippur, a nod to reverting to the usual phrase (*ha'El haKadosh*, "Holy God") from the Yom Kippur's *haMelech haKadosh*, "Holy King," which, in order to be characteristic of this time of the year, specifically referenced God as *the* King and Creator Who brought the world into being.

=Tuesdays

Q Why is it considered good to get married on a Tuesday?

This idea is traced to the Creation story itself, wherein a constant refrain is God commenting on His latest work by saying, "it is good." On the third day (Tuesday), however, this refrain is repeated twice, making the day "doubly good" (as in, twice-blessed). What's that got to do with marriage? In the next chapter, having concluded that man should not be alone, God provides Eve, the missing "good" factor. Some Jews choose Thursdays as an auspicious day for weddings. Why? Because all the out-of-town guests and relatives will leave immediately to go home for Shabbas? No, because this day in Creation is blessed with fertility ("Be fruitful and multiply").

=Tefillin, on God?

Q Can you explain the rabbinic idea that God has *tallis* and *tefillin*?

Certain metaphors cannot be taken literally. Since God has no physical form, He obviously cannot perform such corporeal mitzvos. Therefore these expressions are read within their poetic context. The notion of God wearing *tefillin* was intended to rebuke those Jews who, during the time of the Talmud, were lax in this mitzva – as in, "Hey! If God Himself wears *tefillin*, why can't you!"[17]

---

17. Brachos 6a.

Trinity

Q Are the Trinitarian ideas of Christianity idolatrous?

Yes, says the Rambam. No, says Rabbenu Jacob Tam.[18]

Theodicy

Q How could God take our ancestors out of Egypt "on the wings of eagles," and yet allow their holy descendants to be agonizingly reduced to crematoria ashes?

Our rabbis clearly understand the theologic enigma of theodicy, the potentially devastating overdose of "too much suffering," and the generations of martyred Jews who had perfect faith in the coming of a Messiah who had, indeed, tarried! The paradox has been around since an innocent Job was punitively tested by God to counter a Satanic challenge. His friends, limited by man's ignorance of the Divine plan, search for but can find no solace. When Job pleads (unsuccessfully) for an explanation, the reply is, "Don't ask, I won't tell!" Job then does what all victims do; he plunges into a self-examination that changes the question from "Why, God?" to an inward "Why me?" – as in, "What possible sin have I committed to deserve this grim destiny?" And it is Job who provides Jewish history's traditional "Jewish" answer: "Though He may slay me, yet will I believe in Him, but I will argue my ways before Him," in the spirit of Abraham's J'Accuse: *HaShofet kol ha'aretz lo ya'aseh mishpat*? "Shall the Judge of all the earth not act justly?"[19]

To me

Q What's the most crucial word under the *chuppa*?

Li, "to me"! The groom can say, "You are betrothed," a million-zillion-trillion times to his bride, but if he doesn't add the *li*-word, it means nothing.

---

18. Sanhedrin 56–60.
19. Pirkei Avos 1:7; Job 13:15; Genesis 18:25.

They stay unwed until he completes the sentence "You are betrothed *to me*." The moral? All is partial and incomplete, without a total and personal commitment; in other words, the sum *is* greater than the parts.

U

Use paper, not parchment

Q Why is *Megillas Eicha* read from ordinary paper and not from parchment?

As one of the Five Scrolls, *Eicha* is read from inexpensive paper with simple binding, because parchment was considered a permanent means of recording something. Since the Jew had to have faith in a speedy redemption (when Tisha b'Av would be a time of happiness instead of sorrow), printing *kinos* was seen as a waste of money.

Unlucky?

Q Is "thirteen" an unlucky number in Judaism?

No. Thirteen, in fact, has a special Judaic status (i.e., it's the age when a Jewish boy becomes obliged to keep *Torah un mitzvos*). Thirteen as bad luck is a widespread non-Jewish superstition. Consider: Australian skyscrapers have no thirteenth floor; American airlines have no thirteenth row; in France, street numbers go from twelve to fourteen; in Italy, lotteries avoid the number; British sailors refuse to leave port on the thirteenth of the month; and Friday the thirteenth is, well, Friday the thirteenth! Its origin is pure pagan, derived from a tale in ancient Norse mythology describing a dinner in Valhalla to which twelve gods were invited and which was "gate-crashed" by Loki, a "thirteenth" god of evil who kills the favorite god Balder. The number thirteen was then adopted as an omen of misfortune and death by all, except the Jews!

Upside down prayer?

Q Why do we pray for rain on Shemini Atzeres?

The prayers for rain make perfect sense in Israel, but in the Antipodes it might seem strange to speak of rain when summer is around the corner. Because the antipodean seasons are (from the northern hemisphere point of view) upside down, certain down-under (i.e., Australian) *shuls* used to reverse the prayers for rain and dew, reciting the former on Pesach and the latter on Shemini Atzeres (this custom has since been abandoned). Rain is one of the supreme Divine blessings. The *Sh'ma* promises it as a reward for obedience to God's commands, Elijah warns King Ahab that drought will come as a punishment, whilst the Mishna declares that "the world is judged through water." No wonder our ancestors prayed and fasted in times of drought. The Shemini Atzeres prayers for rain are intended to remind God of the righteousness of the Patriarchs, Moses, Aaron, and the tribes of Israel ("For their sake, withhold not water!")…and end with a plea that, when the rain finally comes, it be "for blessing, and not for a curse; for life, and not for death; for abundance, and not for famine." Jews were realists. They knew: boon or bane, precious or not, the gift of rain could either revive Mother Nature – or engulf it in flood![1]

Utensils and kids

Q I'm too busy; can I send my young children to dip my *keilim* (utensils) in the *mikva*?

Sure, if they're under adult supervision; they can even say the *bracha* (…*asher kiddeshanu b'mitzvosav v'tzivanu al tevilas keilim*). What if they go

---

1. Rosh Hashana 1:2; Deuteronomy 11:11–17; 1 Kings 17:1.

alone? Is their "dipping" kosher? It depends: "no" if the utensil is of metal (a Torah dictate), "yes" if it's of glass (a rabbinical order).

Underestimated

Q **What's the most undervalued day, Jewishly, of the year?**

The day before Rosh Hashana. This day, according to the Midrash, has the ability to grant atonement for a full third of one's sins – which is why some fast on this day, starting at dawn (*alos hashachar*). Another third is forgiven on Rosh Hashana itself and the ten days (*aseres yemei teshuva*) to Yom Kippur; and the final third on Yom Kippur.

Unadorned and uncomplicated

Q **Sorry to be so morbid, but I need to buy a coffin. Any rules?**

Here are your choices: plain, bare, straightforward, unadorned and uncomplicated. In short, keep it simple! When asked by the angels why Moses had to die, God's response was blunt, "That he may be equal to all men." The grave was *the* ultimate equalizer. Thus a coffin should be the same for rich or poor, famous or unknown, the learned or the ignoramus. Rabban Gamliel's will demanded that he be buried in plain linen garments (*tachrichim*) to discourage the display of *yichus* (pedigree) and wealth. Judaism frowns upon expensive coffins, magnificent tombs, garish floral displays, ornate stone markers. Even visitors to a house of mourning are warned to tone it down. "They used to carry food, the rich in silver and gold caskets, the poor in wicker baskets. Then, in deference to the poor, all had to carry wicker baskets." Why wooden coffins? Because of a Torah text ("Dust you are, and to dust you shall return"), which excludes, say, metal coffins which interfere with the body's "return" to the earth.[2]

---

2. Sifre 339, to Deuteronomy 32:50; Job 3:19; Mo'ed Katan 27a; Genesis 3:19.

═ Ur Kasdim ═══════════════════════════════

Q Is this city important to Jewish history?

Very. This Sumerian city in southern Babylon is where Abraham began his journey into monotheism. Ancient Babylonia (now Iraq) has, with the exception of the Holy Land, had more influence on Jewish history, culture and religion than any other country. It appears in the Bible more than two hundred times! Jews daily recognize the incalculable scholarship contribution of the "scholars and teachers of Babylon" in the (*Yekum Purkan*) morning prayers.

═ Use it or lose it ═══════════════════════

Q Can I save my *ma'aser* money for the future? Or is it use-it-or-lose-it?

Generally speaking, the allocation of *ma'aser kesafim*, one's obligatory portion of income dedicated to charity, is up to the discretion of the giver, as long as it qualifies as a mitzva. However, it's not so simple. Since it's not obligatory to give a tenth, some Jews announce, when they are giving for the first time, that it is done *b'li neder,* which means in the absence of a vow. This means they are not obligated to continue the practice each year, and are exempt from any halachic complications such as *hataras nedarim,* the "annulment of vows." But in order for *ma'aser kesafim* to qualify, it must be donated to a cause to which the giver had no previous obligation. A child paying for a parent's burial, for example, would not qualify as it is *already* a mandatory duty. Some scholars extend this "obligatory" cause to the cost of education; however, if a parent pays more tuition than is customary, this counts as *ma'aser.* Are there priorities? Yes. The preferred charities should be support of the poor or enabling others to learn Torah. Poor relatives, and one's own grown children, take precedence over supporting unrelated Torah scholars. Can you save *ma'aser* moneys for a future mitzva use? Yes. For example: to support a child in learning Torah after marriage, even though this learning is not a halachic obligation. When did the practice of *ma'aser* begin? From our forefathers. "All that You will give me," says Jacob, "I will surely give a tenth to You!"[3]

---

3. Yore Deah 249:1; Kisvei Harav Henkin 2:81; Iggeros Moshe, Yore Deah 1:114, 1:153, 2:113;

Until death do us part!

Q Is this a Jewish expression?

If your marriage contract includes the phrase "to love, cherish and honor until death do us part," you're in the wrong religion! These words were added by the Church. In contrast, Judaism made allowances for divorce.

Ufaratzta

Q My Chabad friends use this term all the time. What does it mean?

Jacob, on his deathbed, reserves his most extensive blessing for Joseph, using the singular when referring to himself as "thy father." This choice of words raises scholarly eyebrows. Is Jacob hinting that his blessings are more valuable than those bestowed by Abraham and Isaac? No, explains Rashi, to whom "the blessings of thy father" simply meant "the blessings thy father has received." Jacob seeks to merge *all* the blessings, from Abraham (who was promised the land of Israel), to Isaac (who was promised a broader territory, "all these lands"), to his own: "You shall spread abroad to the west, east, north, and south" (i.e., all four corners of the earth). The Hebrew for "spread abroad" is *ufaratzta*, which was originally understood not just in geographic or demographic terms, but in spiritual and cultural modes.

Unknown anniversaries

Q What if someone's date of death is unknown? When should the *yahrzeit* be observed?

A day is designated for annual observance. Polish Jews, for example, commemorate the Holocaust victims with unknown death dates on the Warsaw

---

Mishna Berura 605:6, 694:3; Aruch Hashulchan 249:10; Chasam Sofer, Yore Deah 231; Tzitz Eliezer 9:3; Chofetz Chayim, Ahavas Chesed 19:1; Akiva Eiger, Pe'ah 1:1; Chasam Sofer, Yore Deah 331; Iggeros Moshe, Even HaEzer 3:43; Genesis 14:20, 28:22; Rashi, Genesis 26:12.

Ghetto anniversary; Hungarian Jews remember their victims on Sivan 20, a date already in the Jewish calendar for previous massacres.

═ Up, or down? ═

Q Do I have to stand during *leyning* (the reading of the Torah)?

There is no consensus on this. In my *shul*, everyone stands, on the grounds that everyone stood at Mount Sinai when the Torah was given. Others say it's a personal preference, and some (*Arizal*) even claim that it's better to sit. So what to do? Follow the custom of the *shul* in which you are *davening*.[4]

---

4. Rema, Orach Chayim 146:4; Orach Chayim 146:6; Shulchan Hatahor 146:4; Iggeros Moshe, Orach Chayim 4:22; Yechaveh Da'as 6:8.

V

Verses, sing along

Q Why is a part of the morning *davening* called "verses of songs"?

It is a rabbinic adage that praise always precedes prayer; thus, with *baruch she'amar* and *yishtabach* acting as foreword and epilogue, the *pesukei d'zimra*, literally "verses of songs," a mosaic of passages and quotes from Psalms, Chronicles, Nehemiah and the *shir* of Moses, is said first. Whose idea was it originally? Rabbi Meir of Rothenburg (*Maharam*), thirteenth-century scholar revered as the *Meor Hagolah*, "Light of the Exile."[1]

Vidui

Q Who compiled the Yom Kippur confessions?

Nobody. The art of Jewish confessions (*vidui*) simply evolved; from the unscripted Cain ("My punishment is heavier than I can bear"), to Jacob ("I am not worthy of all the true and steadfast love which Thou hast shown"), to David ("I have done a very wicked thing…I have been very foolish!"). These *ad hoc* guilty pleas then became standardized into such (unimaginative) phrases as "We have sinned and acted perversely and wickedly," or "We have sinned, erred and done wrong." The High Priest was the first to use an

---

1. Brachos 32a; Exodus 14:30–15:18; Psalms 100, 145–150.

orderly confession, starting with himself, his household, priests, and then, finally, the people.[2]

=Verboten vessels =

Q I'm buying a candelabrum as a wedding gift. Should I buy one with seven or with eight branches?

The latter. Why? Because Jews are forbidden to make, let alone own, replicas of any of the vessels (keilim) used in the Mishkan, which includes a seven-branched imitation candelabra. What if it's not an exact copy (e.g., it is made out of wood or porcelain instead of gold; or has no decorative cups, knobs, or flowers; or is shorter than eighteen tefachim [about four feet])? Then it's OK, although not all scholars agree. What if it's electric and seven-branched? Some say "yes," others "no." Well, what if I've already bought it, do I have to throw it out? No; you can keep it. What if my menora started with eight branches, and one fell off? I don't know, which doesn't mean the question hasn't been asked![3]

=Voodoo, you do?! =

Q If everything is biy'dei Shamayim, "in the hands of Heaven," are there explicit references in the Torah to astrology?

No. However, some terms (e.g., diviner, soothsayer) are definitely related. The Torah strongly warned the Jews to avoid these acts of "abomination" when they entered the land of Canaan, for fear that believing in stars, demons and witches was tantamount to accepting planetary deities. This was a blasphemous repudiation of the rabbinic adage hakkol biy'dei Shamayim, that everything is in the hands of Heaven. Astrological consistency was not exactly your ordinary pagan's asset. Some embraced, for example, Friday as the luckiest day of the week because it was considered ruled by Venus,

---

2. Genesis 4:13, 32:9; II Samuel 24:10; I Kings 8:47; Psalms 106:6.
3. Rosh Hashana 24a; Tosefos, Avoda Zara 43b; Exodus 20:20; Schach, Yore Deah 141; Rosh Hashana 24a; Darkei Teshuva 141:56, Iggeros Moshe, Yore Deah 3:31; Pischei Teshuva, Yore Deah 141:8, 14–15; Yesodei Yeshurun 1; Yabia Omer 1:12; Yechaveh Da'as 3:61; Darkei Teshuva 141:52–53.

in honor of Freya, goddess of Love; in contrast, the Christians associated Friday with gloom and doom because the sin of Adam occurred on a Friday, as did the crucifiction of Jesus. Christian countries once considered Friday a day of such bad luck that England refused to send ships to sea on this day, and the French steered away from riding on buses on Fridays. At the University of Wisconsin, the Hebrew Studies department is on the thirteenth floor, an "unlucky" number for non-Jews but a neutral one for Jews. Other than being the age at which Jewish boys reach maturity (bar mitzva), the number thirteen holds no important role within Judaism. But the rabbis sent mixed messages, giving both credence to, and lecturing against, the belief that astrology has power over the destiny of Israel. "If you want to discover demons," admits the Talmud, "take sifted ashes and sprinkle them around your bed, and in the morning you will see something resembling the footprints of a cock. If you want to see them, take the afterbirth of a black she-cat, the firstborn of a firstborn, and roast it in fire and grind it to powder, and then put some in your eye, and you will see them!" We read about King Saul and the witch of Endor, and how Rabbis Joshua ben Hanania and Jannai invoke magic invocations to defeat evil witches. Another Talmudic Sage, sensing the contradictions, elaborated, "If one actually performs magic, he is stoned; if he merely creates an illusion, he is exempt!" By the time we get to the *shtetlach* of Eastern Europe, Jewish folklore, seeking relief from misery and fears, was possessed with dybbuks; stillbirths were blamed on a vengeful she-demon (Lilith); and tales of ghosts, speaking corpses, vampires and werewolves were being spread as a cathartic release from the daily terror. Over the centuries, rabbinic skeptics of astrology (Rambam, Judah Halevi, Hasdai Crescas) were up against an array of other rabbinic heavyweights (Ramban, the Vilna Gaon, Abraham Ibn Ezra). The great Talmudic Sage Rava was blunt: "Life, merit and sustenance depend not on merit but on the stars"; and the captivating *Zohar* breathlessly declares that "there is not a single blade of grass in the world over which a star or planet doesn't preside!"[4]

---

4. Deuteronomy 18:9–14; Shabbas 75a, 156a; Sanhedrin 90a; Yore Deah 179:1; Jeremiah 10:2–3; Genesis 33b; Melammed L'ho'il, 2:63; Mo'ed Katan 28a; Zohar 2:171d; Brachos 6a; Sanhedrin 67b.

Vav columns

Q Why is the *vav* the most frequent letter in the Torah?

Other than the first column in the Torah, which begins with the word *Bereishis*, scribes would go to great lengths to ensure that columns start with a *vav* at the top ("the *vav* columns," *vavei chomdim*), a literary "jockeying" that required stretching or "squishing" letters closer, discarding the Torah's customary form and spacing. The result makes the text look uneven (although not invalid), which is why several scholars (e.g., the thirteenth-century *Semak*, and Rabbi Meir of Rothenburg, the *Maharam*), tried (unsuccessfully) to abolish this practice (today, with the help of computers, the layout can be evenly designed with a *vav* on top of every column). Why a *vav*? In the courtyard that surrounded the desert Tabernacle (*Mishkan*) the Jews hung tapestries between the columns which were held up by "little hooks," (the Hebrew word for hook is "*vav*"). Jewish mystics have another reason! *Vav*, as a prefix, means *and*, which makes it *the* Hebrew letter of "connection," implying that the *vav* in this location acts as a reminder of the Torah's "connection" to the life of a Jew.[5]

Vot? Anuder drink?!

Q Isn't this an odd Purim custom? To drink, drink, drink?

Yes. It's the strangest Purim practice of them all; a *minhag* of intemperance, a custom of inebriation, so incongruous for Jews that the cynic Yiddishists would sing, *Ganstz yor shikkur, Purim nikhter*, "all year drunk, on Purim sober" (which applies to folks always doing things out of season). The formidable Sage Rava laid down the lighthearted dictum that, on Purim, the Jews, the most abstinent of all people (despite the fact that a baby boy's first taste after his *bris* is wine), must drink so much alcohol that *ad d'lo yada*, their intoxicated senses become so blurred that they "cannot tell the difference" between two expressions whose *gematria* (502) is identical: *arur Haman* ("curse Haman"), and *baruch Mordechai* ("bless Mordechai") – a

---

5. Maharam Responsa, ii, 150; Rema, Yore Deah 273:6; Tikunei Zohar, Parshas Terumah.

category of a mitzva known as *haba'a b'aveira*, a "good deed brought about through wicked means!"

Vulgate

Q Is this a bird?

No, it's the Latin version of the Torah, written by Jerome (340–420 CE) who relied on an earlier monumental polyglot Greek translation of the Bible compiled by Origen of Alexandria (185–254 CE). Origen, using the original Hebrew in square style, created the *Hexapla* ("six," because its six texts are laid out in six columns), which quotes contemporary second-century Torah Sages whilst incorporating several other Greek Torah works. It was commissioned for the benefit of the ignorant Jews of the Roman Empire, which included Aquila and Theodotion, converts to Judaism. Aquila produced the first substitute to the Greek Torah (*Septuagint*) and the Aramaic Onkelos version. What motivated Aquila? He was bothered by the many mistakes and blunders, as well as the editing, in the *Septuagint* which bordered on blasphemy (in one Psalm, the phrase "from the cross" was added to "the Lord reigns"). Is there an extant complete *Hexapla*? No. Only fragments of it were discovered in the Cairo Genizah. If any reader has a complete one, please mail it to me. I'll pay for postage![6]

Valentine's card

Q I'm engaged. Can I send my bride a Valentine's card on February 14?

No. Buy her flowers *erev* Shabbas or a nice piece of jewelry *erev yom tov* instead. On the surface, these cards seem to be just lighthearted playful missives of love ("the honey's sweet and so are you") – but to Jews, Valentine's Day reeks of paganism. The day is based on the Lupercian festival when boys celebrated *Februata Juno* (the "ox-eyed" Roman sex goddess, queen of heaven, guardian of women and marriage) by choosing girls for pleasure. Even one of the popes (Gelasius) declared it an "indecent" festival

---

6. Psalms 96:10.

and replaced it with St. Valentine's Day, a "Friend of Lovers" day in honor of Valentine, the martyred third-century Bishop of Interamma who was decapitated for presiding over the marriage of young lovers in secret (an act of "treason" according to the mad emperor, Claudius II).

Vaccinate

Q If vaccination is not a hundred percent safe, are we still obligated to immunize our children?

Jewish law admits to not being expert, nor having the final say, in such (medical) matters. Ask a doctor who has expertise in this field and follow his advice.

Village of Idiots

Q Was there really a place called Chelm?

Yes, and no. Although there was a town in Poland called Chelm, the Chelm of the humorous stories (a charming city full of gentle, simpleton Jews infused with an abundance of egregious "wisdom"), is a fiction of Jewish folklore built upon the statement of Socrates, that he is the wisest of them all because he knows how stupid he really is! And yet the silliness of Chelm tales and frolicking Gimpel fables, using the tools of *bashert* (fate), lunacy, whimsy and irony, is Jewish *reductio ad absurdum* in moral disguise: "We're not fools! It's just that foolish things are always happening to us!!"

Verbal agreements

Q I agreed verbally to do a job but have changed my mind. Am I obligated?

It depends on many factors (financial loss, embarrassment, etc.); however the general rule is that one should stand by one's word in a business transaction. "Your 'yes' should be righteous!" If you act irresponsibly, don't be surprised if your reputation is sullied, or, as the rabbinical phrase puts it, you find yourself, "out of favor."[7]

Vowels

Q I don't understand the Hebrew vowels. Are they letters or not?

Hebrew vowels (such as "o," "u" and "i"), from around the eighth century CE, were never considered nor written as letters, but as punctuation (i.e., as "accent" marks placed above, below, or after a consonant). Still don't get it? Here's an example: the word *shalem* ("whole") has three consonants, SH, L, M. To help vocalize this word, two vowels are used (a *kamatz*, which looks like a small "T," appears under the SH, and a *tseirei*, two horizontal dots, is placed under the L). What are the other Hebrew vowels? There are the *segol, cholem, shuruk,* and *chirik* (the first composed of three dots forming a triangle). What does *k'tiv malei* mean? Literally, "full spelling." This refers to a "non-accent" system whereby, in modern Hebrew, the vowels are expressed as consonants (e.g., a *vav* represents either "o" and "u," and a *yud* means "i"; in Yiddish, the "a" and "e" are represented by an *alef* and *ayin*). Why are there no vowels in the Torah? Pragmatically, it would be hard to have vowels if there are none in the Hebrew alphabet. Mystically, the words of Torah are meant to be understood on many different levels, and vowels would simply "get in the way." However, there is (technically) one Torah with vowels. At the end of his life, Moses wrote and gave a Torah scroll to each of the twelve tribes, and then wrote a "thirteenth" *Sefer Torah* with vowels and accent marks which he placed in the Holy Ark (which explains the reference to the "vowels in the Torah of Moses").[8]

---

7. Baba Metzia 49a; Shulchan Aruch, Choshen Mishpat 204:7.
8. Tzefanat Pa'aneach, Deuteronomy 31:9; Rabbeinu Bachya, Deuteronomy 7:2, Genesis 18:3.

═Villains ═

Q Why are there so many villains in the Torah?

Every good saga needs a crook! Every moral needs a rogue! My favorite Torah rascal is the despicable, detestable Lavan, Jacob's uncle and future father-in-law, a boorish and vulgar man who lives up to his name. Our rabbis trace the term *lavan* to the color "white" (as in "glowing with wickedness"), and link his nickname ("the Aramean") not just to the place of his birth (Aram) but to *ramma'i*, which means "impostor, deceiver." And that he was! A fraudulent thief who cheats Jacob both emotionally (by marrying him off to Leah instead of the promised Rachel) and financially (forcing him to labor for years before marrying his first love). By forcing Jacob to work for nothing, Lavan sets the stage for businesspeople to be thought of as being less than honest. And yet, Jacob and Lavan, surely the oddest couple in the Torah (the former a paragon of ennobled spirituality, the latter a master con artist and abuser), are family, for better or for worse!

═Veils ═

Q Is the bridal veil a Jewish custom?

It has become so and is associated with the concept of bridal modesty and humility (*tznius*). This can be traced back to Rebecca, who, upon meeting her future spouse (Isaac), bashfully "took a veil and covered herself with it." It also indicates submission to the husband (who unveils the bride to check if she is the "right one," a custom referring back to the dishonest Lavan who tricked Jacob into marrying his older, rather than his younger, daughter). Yiddish folklore saw the veil as a curtain to "hide" the beauty of the bride from the "evil eye" (*ayin hora*), hoping the disguise would distract this potent wicked force (Moroccan girls cover their eyes during the entire *chuppa* ceremony).

═Vulgarity ═

Q Can I watch porn films?

No. Just a quick glance through the Torah and Talmud shows that Judaism is far from being prudish; in fact, it is quiet frank about intimacy – but *always* in a dignified context.

═Visitors, hospital ═

Q I don't have time to go to the hospital and visit my friend. Can I call on the phone?

Sure you can, but it doesn't fulfill the requirement of visiting the sick, as laid down by the example of God visiting a recovering Abraham on the third day after a painful circumcision, the world's first *bris mila*. Rav Moshe Feinstein encouraged phone calls to the sick, but cautioned that they show a lesser level of respect and are not the ideal. Rav Ovadia Yosef agrees and claims that prayers said for the sick are not as effective in the absence of a personal visit. Why not? Because one needs to see the effects of the illness in order to reach an appropriate level of *kavana* (intention). Rabbi Akiva once entered his *beis medrash* and announced that he who does not visit the sick acts as though he killed them. What caused this outburst? Rabbi Akiva had just returned from visiting one of his sick *talmidim* and, whilst there, swept the student's room. The boy sat up and told his teacher: "Rabbi, you brought me back to life. When the room was dirty I was like a dead man."[9]

═Visitors, cemetery ═

Q I'm just about to make my first visit to a cemetery. What should I do?

The proper behavior is a mixture of Jewish law and customs, both Yiddish and mystic. First, take a *siddur* and *tehillim*, and remember to wash your

---

9. Nedarim 40a.

hands before leaving home. When you arrive, you say the blessing *asher yatzar eschem badin*, place your left hand on the marker (no leaning, or stepping on the grave) and say some *tehillim* or *kaddish*. It's disrespectful to eat, drink, greet a friend, discuss business, learn Torah, or even *daven* within four *amos* (about six to eight feet) of the grave. When you leave, you place a small stone, pebble or some grass on the marker, throw some soil and grass over your shoulder (but not on Shabbas), and wash your hands again, three times, preferably from a vessel, and dry them naturally (i.e., without a towel).[10]

Vort

Q What's a *vort*?

It's a Yiddish word for "word" and refers to a pre-marriage ceremony called "The Breaking of the Plate." This involves smashing a plate against a hard surface, after it was wrapped up so no one gets hurt from flying broken pieces. But why break a plate? Because this act is serious and irreversible, symbolic of the seriousness of the marriage commitment – and by tempering the joy of the moment, it is akin to breaking the glass under the *chuppa*, a reminder of the destruction of the Temples. Who breaks the plate? The mothers, together. Why? I don't know. Can one break something else? You mean, the caterer's jaw after you get the bill? No. How about a vase, or a window? I don't think so. Originally, the *vort* occurred at the engagement when the couple legally commit (i.e., give their "word") to a formal marriage, but this proved complicated. Why? If either side changed their mind, several serious halachic issues suddenly arose (e.g., breaking a vow, etc.). So the custom today is to time the *vort* as close as possible to the *chuppa* so as not to allow enough time to cancel the engagement.

---

10. Orach Chayim 224:8, 12; 547:12; Mishne Berura 4:39, 43, 23:3, 559:41, 4:42, 224:17; Kitzur Shulchan Aruch 128:13; Schach, Yore Deah 363:3; Birkei Yosef, Yore Deah 344:17; Rema, Yore Deah 343:2; Yore Deah 376:4.

=Vows and obligations

Q What's the difference between them?

It's simple. A vow is a promise *to do* something, an obligation is a promise *not to do* something. Are a vow (*neder*) and an oath (*shevuah*) the same? No. The former changes the status of an object. For instance, if you "vow" not to watch TV, you have made TV a forbidden object. The latter places an obligation on the person. An example? If you make an "oath" to lose weight, this obliges *you*, not the status of any food. The Chofetz Chaim, the saintly twentieth-century leader of world Jewry, noted that four Torah personalities (Eliezer, Caleb, Saul, and Jephthah) began their careers with an oath, in order to show the importance of proper speech; and Rav Samson Raphael Hirsch explains that the reason God specifically directed the mitzva of vows to the tribal heads (*rashei hamatos*) was to warn them that only by guarding their language could they join Him as a "partner."

Will I go mad?

Q Will I go mad if I study kabbala?

No. According to Isaac Luria, the popular sixteenth-century kabbalistic innovator, from his generation onwards kabbala was intended for everybody, including children. Yehuda Ashlag (*Baal Hasulam*), the great nineteenth-century Lodz-born Polish kabbalist, created a new study method especially "for this generation." Kabbala comes from the Hebrew *l'kabbel*, "to receive," and describes the motives of kabbalistic actions as "the desire to receive" wisdom in order to understand the metaphysical aspect of Judaism. The general rules concerning its study (i.e., not until you're forty, or only if you are married and have children, etc.) are basically a guide that, in the pursuit of Torah knowledge, it's best to walk before running. Jews and non-Jews who turn to kabbala for "quick fixes" for success in life and business are searching in all the wrong places. Thanks to one pop star (Madonna), kabbala has been transformed from the ancient, revered, holy text that blended Torah and mysticism into just another adjunct to the New Age movement. Yes, the publicity is great. More non-Jews are aware of the term than ever before in history but have absolutely no clue as to what it truly reflects (to cult fans, kabbala could just as easily be devoted to Feng Shui or Indian gurus). Madonna has commercialized kabbala and turned it into an artsy entertainment fashion trend. The movement was started in Los Angeles in the eighties and has a stunningly successful marketing program, which cheapens Jewish tradition. The only people going "mad" from kabbala are those paying ridiculous prices for red wrist strings, candles to scare away the *ayin hora* ("evil eye"), boxes of white powder to "cleanse the *ruach* (atmosphere)" of the house, bottles of water that bubble with "the wisdom of generations," and how-to books of Judaic spiritual knowledge that have our ancient Jewish mystics rolling over in their *Zohar*s!

═ Why Ruth? ═══════════════════════

Q If Ruth was just one of many proselytes, why is *she* selected for such prominence?

You're right: a list of other contestants would be highly impressive. There's Yisro, Moses' Midianite father-in-law priest; Joseph's wife Asenath (daughter of the Egyptian priest of On), David and Judah's wives (Philistine and Caananite); Rahab (one of the world's four outstanding beauties, along with Sarah, Avigail, Esther), who not only married Joshua, but became ancestor to no fewer than eight priests and nine prophets (including Jeremiah and Hulda); Onkelos, the Ger, was a Jew-by-choice, and a whole line of distinguished talmudists (e.g., Rabbis Akiva, Shmaiah, Avtalyon) were all descendants of proselytes. So why the emphasis on Ruth? As the great *bubba* (grandmother) of David, "the Sweet Singer of Israel" and author of the indispensable Book of Psalms, Ruth's role in Jewish history is prominent (this is why David, aware of the public unease of his "non-kosher" genealogy, reminds his nation in his farewell speech, that *all* are "strangers" in front of God). Remember: Ruth, as a Moabite, had come from one of the nations that the Torah explicitly excludes from converting to Judaism (*Lo yavo Amoni u'Moavi b'kahal Hashem*, "An Ammonite or a Moabite shall not enter into the assembly of God"). This is why the prophet Shmuel, author of *Megillas Ruth* (and the one who anointed David as King), felt obligated to set the record straight: by ordering that the story of Ruth ("Your God is my God…") be publicly read on Shavuos, the prophet cleared any doubts as to the proud lineage of David.[1]

---

1. Ruth Rabba 2; Yalkut Ruth 601; Brachos 2:8; Megilla 14b, 15a; Psalms 39:13.

═What, no more? ═

Q Did the beginning of the third millennium CE create some Jewish calendar oddities?

Yes. The year 2000 saw the start of a rare five-year cycle in which Rosh Hashana and Succos fall on a Shabbas and Sunday, four years out of five (1999, 2000, 2002, 2003). The last such cycle began in 1928 (1928, 1929, 1931, 1932). This phenomenon will not occur again in this, the twenty-first century.

═Where is he? ═

Q Why hasn't the Messiah come yet?

Isaiah provides the answer: everything happens in God's good time, adding, *Hama'amin lo yachish*, "The believer must not be in a hurry!"[2]

═Whose money is it? ═

Q A salesgirl gave me more change than I was entitled to. Whose money is it?

It ain't yours! This falls under the obligation of *hashavas aveida*, "returning lost articles." What if returning it is not an option? The excess money must then be forwarded to the city, or county, where the store is located so they can use it for public service. That way, the seller will receive some degree, even indirectly, of compensation.[3]

═Well, well, well ═

Q Was the Biblical "well" also the local social hangout place?

Yes. Remember, there was no indoor plumbing, and water aqueducts weren't invented until Roman times (and even then existed only in major

---

2. Isaiah 28:16, 60:22.
3. Choshen Mishpat 366:2.

urban areas). Thus water had to be "drawn" daily, making the well (*be'er*), an artificial man-made shaft that tapped into underground springs, not just a means of survival but a social magnet as *well* (pun intended!). Once out of the desert, the Jews collected water in pools (which were built in Hebron, Gibeon, Samaria, and Jerusalem), and by the mother of all elaborate engineering feats: the hidden underground water tunnel (e.g., Hezekiah's tunnel in Jerusalem) which ensured water supply during enemy sieges.[4]

Widows and orphans

Q Why are these two always mentioned in the same sentence?

In Hebrew, both *almana* (widow) and *yasom* (orphan) are derived from the verb "to mutilate" or "cut off," both closely linked categories of the disadvantaged. In the widow's case it is the loss of an emotional and financial companion, whilst the orphan's loss of parents is a deprivation of both, someone to hold hands with, to lean on, depend on. The characteristic factor in many of God's statutes is empathy, which is why the order not to make a stranger suffer is one of the few mitzvos that come with an explicit reason: "because you were strangers in the land of Egypt." Unlike today's definition of an orphan (a child who lost both parents), an orphan in those days was also a minor whose father had died. This left *both* widow and child (or children) deprived of any source of financial support, since it was practically impossible for a single woman with a family to earn a living. Since inheritance laws gave all the property to the oldest son, this left the care of the widow and daughters to the benevolence and mercy of a son-brother. That is how Ruth and Naomi, left destitute after their husbands died, found themselves searching in the fields for scraps to eat. Any community that tolerated the abuse of an *almana* or *yasom* was considered a "failed society."[5]

---

4. Genesis 21:17–18; II Samuels 2:13, 4:12; I Kings 22:38; II Kings 20:20.
5. Exodus 22:7, 21–23; Job 24:3, 9; Psalms 94:6, 146:9; Isaiah 10:2; Sanhedrin 19b; Yad, De'oth 6:10.

Whose *Tanach* is it?

Q can a printing of the *Tanach* be protected by copyright?

Two people share in a copyright – the author and the publisher – under a Torah law known as *hassagat g'vul*, "encroaching upon another's territory." Obviously, if a new translation comes out, then the printer-publisher is protected. What if it's a Hebrew edition? The Chasam Sofer was asked this question and understood that publishing classical Torah works must, for continuity purposes, remain economically feasible, and renders even a Hebrew edition subject to copyright laws (especially its design, and typeface). He uses a Talmud analogy, "One must keep fishing nets away from a fish which another fisherman is trying to catch"; in other words, although fish belong to no fisherman, others must respect the initiative and efforts of the first fisherman who staked out the fish. Similarly, although the Hebrew text of Torah belongs to us all, any publisher who has made a special effort to produce an attractive edition must be respected and protected.

Whistle-blowers

Q Does Judaism agree with "whistle-blowing?"

I don't know. On the surface "whistle-blowing," the spreading of stories and gossip, seems to fall under the category of *loshen hora* which the Torah finds abhorrent; and yet an employee is obligated to tell the truth, with no motivation of spite or self-interest, if staying mute leads to financial loss. This is Jewish law: if you know of a misdeed, even if there is *no* explicit duty to disclose it, staying silent makes you an accessory, culpable for the damages; and if those being harmed are fellow Jews, then you are treading on the genetic duty of *areivus*, "all Jews being responsible for one another."

Where there's a will...

Q Who gets what, when?

When the Torah introduces us to the laws of inheritance (in Hebrew *yerusha*, akin to *morasha*, "heritage," God's term that describes both the Torah and the land of Israel), we realize that this is much more than a method of asset redistribution. The intriguing thirteenth-century *Sefer Hachinuch*, a classic medieval Spanish work by an unknown teacher, found that it is human nature to seek to value one's property as a forced appreciation of the "Will" of God; a trickle-down act of spiritual and not just physical gains. In a clever play on words, the Mishna's Gamliel III advised his colleagues, "Make His will yours, so that He may make your will His," a metaphysical power that even the fictional *Mendele* respects: "When God wills it; even a broom can shoot!" And the Yiddish cynics add, "Where there's a will, there's a relative!" Is there a pecking order in Torah inheritance? Yes, first place goes to the son, and after that the daughter. A husband has prior claim to his wife's estate, but his priority is not "inheritable" if he predeceases her. What if there are several equally entitled heirs? They share equally, unless they are all sons. Then the father's first child gets a windfall double share of the estate. And a levirate marriage? The Jew who marries his brother's wife "maintains the name of his dead brother" in all respects, including inheriting his estate. Can I show preference? No, the Torah frowns on heir selectiveness. However, you can give away parts of an estate in accordance with your preference whilst alive, making it "effective" upon death.[6]

White lies

Q Can I lie for a worthy cause?

That's a tough one! Who's to decide what's "worthy"? The Torah considers lying a despicable behavioral trait ("Keep far from falsehood"), equivalent to idol worship. Even Abraham, the "straight-as-an-arrow" forefather, is accused by the Ramban of "a great sin" when he twists the truth to save his life (claiming his wife is his sister), instead of "trusting God to save him." Commenting on Jacob, known as the *amud ha'emes*, "pillar of truth," lying to his father about his true identity, the twelfth-century Radak respectfully says he was "economical with the truth." The general consensus is this: White lies are OK "in the interests of peace," based on Rashi's observation that Jacob's sons "altered matters for the sake of peace [family unity]." Rashi even catches God himself in a little "deviation from the truth for the sake

---

6. Numbers 27:8–11; Deuteronomy 21:17, 25:6.

of peace." When repeating to Abraham Sarah's response on being told of the pending birth of a son, God changes her uncomplimentary references to her husband "for the sake of peace between husband and wife." Thus is a principle established. Harmony is more important than truth; one *can* lie ("I don't know") when keeping a secret; avoid telling bad news; and about one's wealth (to avoid jealousy, and the *ayin hora*, "evil eye"). And Hillel adds another category. You can lie about a bride's beauty. As usual, Shammai disagrees, saying, "Each bride – as she is!" Does a *shadchan* have to tell the truth? Yes, but only if it's a "major deficiency" (in fact, *not* telling is a halachic crime, *lifnei iveir lo sitein michshol*). What about age? Can you say a girl is nineteen when she's in fact twenty? I don't know.[7]

Who heard what?

Q At Sinai, were the Ten Commandments issued directly from God to Israel?

No one is sure. Ibn Ezra says "yes," the Rambam says "no." He argues that only Moses understood, whereas the Jewish people "heard," but without comprehending. And the Ramban? He compromises, with a "yes, but," in that the Jews only comprehended the first two commandments (regarding the existence of an infinite, invisible, incomprehensible God), requiring Moses to repeat the next eight. Why the confusion? The tradition of "613" (*taryag*) is derived from the *gematria* (611) of the verse *Torah tziva lanu Moshe*, "The Torah was commanded to us via Moses," plus, in order to get up to 613, an additional two commands issued directly by God (the first two, *Anochi Hashem*, "I am God," and *Lo yihyeh*, "You shall have no other gods"). This conclusion is not based just on *gematria* but also on grammar. There is a switch from first-person in the first two Commandments to third-person in the remaining eight.

---

7. Exodus 23:7; Sanhedrin 92a; Makkos 24a; Yevamos 65b; Genesis 12:10, 18:12; 50:16; Yore Deah 402:12; Kesubos 16b–17a; Tzitz Eliezer 16:4; Chelkas Yaakov 3:136.

═White ═

Q *Why wear white on Rosh Hashana and Yom Kippur?*

In pre-war Frankfurt-am-Main, on the High Holydays, *even* the carpet was changed to white! So were the Ark and Torah covers, as well as the chazan's cap. Why white? "When Jews fast on this day they become like the angels," read the poetic lyrics of Israel's master poet Yehudah Halevi, "humbling themselves, lowering their heads, standing, bending their knees and singing hymns of praise!" White also symbolizes purity and acts as a reminder to God of His promise that our sins shall be as white as snow; it is also symbolic of the color of the High Priest's robes worn in the Temple on these holy days; and according to Isaiah, it's a "clean color." "Though your sins be as scarlet, they shall be white as snow," and Isaiah thus challenges one to focus on "getting better." And so Jews wear a plain white *yarmulke* and robe in *shul* (a *kittel*), angelic reminders of the white burial shrouds of death itself. Judaism has many paradoxes: so too the *kittel*, which is worn at the peak of *simcha*, under the *chuppa* at a wedding, and is also placed on the body of a deceased at his burial.[8]

═Worker's compensation ═

Q *Does Judaism have a method of worker's comp?*

The final chapter in *Bechukosai* contains the Torah's most explicit method of how to properly assess a person's worth in money (*shekalim*). How? By recounting an oath, which Judaism takes very seriously, to donate the value of one's own life to the Temple. But how is this "worth" determined? The Torah, way ahead of modern personal-injury claims, uses a formula that analyzes age, gender, and the capacity for future labor (i.e., contribution to society).

═Why remember Temples? ═

Q Why, with so much contemporary tragedy crowding the highways

---

8. Kuzari 3:5; Isaiah 1:18.

of Jewish history, do our rabbis keep reverting to the destruction of the ancient Temple as *the* most catastrophic event?

Because the Temple's absence constitutes the defining moment of the troubles of the children of Israel. If you take a quick glance at the Rambam's list of the 613 mitzvos, you'll see that more than half are no longer applicable since the Temple's abrupt disappearance, which led to the sudden removal of the *Shechina*, the "Divine Presence," from the nation's midst. Remember: without the Temple we only have Three Books of Moses, not Five. It is as though a broom of history abruptly, without warning, swept aside a vast part of the national-spiritual foundation of Judaism, its core creed so to speak. All subsequent tragedies have therefore been experienced by an orphaned nation, a crippled folk, a people deprived of their life's original and central axis.

Witnesses

Q How many witnesses are required in a Jewish trial?

It depends. If capital punishment is involved, it's a minimum of two (who must be unrelated); but the twenty-three judges, sitting in a semi-circle, did not consider all witnesses as "equal" witnesses. The Torah forbade minors, slaves, women, gamblers, deaf-mutes, ignoramuses and *apikorsim* (those who knew the law but ignored it). Second-hand testimony was disallowed, as were self-confessions by the accused ("no man can by his own testimony incriminate himself in a capital charge"). So strict are the rules of evidence that if, say, only one out of a hundred witnesses contradicted the others regarding date, time and place, then all the testimony was thrown out![9]

Wisdom

Q I want wisdom! Where can I find it?

Stand in line! Job asks the same question! The one to ask would have been King Solomon, who is granted both "wisdom and knowledge." Why?

---

9. Numbers 35:30; Deuteronomy 17:6; Sanhedrin 9b.

Because he asked for them, instead of "silver or gold." Learned Jews are known as *chachamim*, the "wise ones" – but, "who is wise and what is wisdom?" According to Shakespeare, "There are sermons even in stones," yet we turn to the fourth chapter of *Pirkei Avos* for a definition: "A wise person is one who learns from all human beings." (In short: if you think you know everything, you know nothing!) Wisdom is thus not measured in terms of how many books one has read – in the rabbinic phrase, even a donkey can carry books – but in a continual interaction and openness to the knowledge of others.[10]

Women at war

Q Can Jewish women go into the military?

No. "It is not the way of a woman," say our rabbis, "but the way of a man to make war" (which is why Jewish law exempts women from fighting Amalek). Are there exceptions? Yes. Devorah, Yael and Judith fought and destroyed the enemy. If the nation of Israel finds itself in an "obligatory" (i.e., self-defensive) war, then *every* Jew, *even* a bride standing under her *chuppa*, must go; however, Eliezer ben Ya'akov, not wanting to give up on a women's modesty and dignity, adds that she should not wear a military uniform, nor carry weapons.[11]

Why Abraham?

Q What did Abraham do to deserve being chosen as the first of the Chosen People?

We don't know for sure. Why? Because the Torah never explicitly explains Heaven's selection process that chooses only one person over ten generations (since Noah) to become the progenitor of the Jewish people – but it sure leaves plenty of clues. After establishing Abraham's prime role, the first outreach program in Jewish history, known as *koreh b'Shem Hashem*, to

---

10. Job 28:2; 2 Chronicles 1:12; 1 Kings 5.
11. Kiddushin 2b. Sefer Hachinuch, Mitzva 603; Avnei Nezer, Orach Chayim 509; Judges 4:4–16, 17–24; 5:24–27; Sotah 8:7; Nazir 59a; Onkelos, Deuteronomy 22:5.

"call out" in God's Name, the *haftora* has God calling Abraham "my friend." This is an unusual title reserved only for this Patriarch, but takes into account that its Hebrew root also forms the word "love." Aguila, the English novelist, describes love as "the voice of God, the rule of Heaven" ("To live," shouted Ludwig Boerne, "is to love!"), whilst Immanuel, thirteenth-century poet of Rome, writing in his treatise *Mahberet*, sees love as "the pivot of the Torah." The credo and protocol of Abrahamic teachings was pure *emuna* ("faith," or, more literally, "trust") – that all will end well, that he is only a small cog in Tevye's vast eternal master plan, that life's travels and travails come with both fortune and misfortune, that all obstacles and adversaries are to be met with faith, and occasional quick thinking (as in passing his wife off as his sister when in danger of her being abducted into Pharaoh's harem). God's new best "friend" earns his humble title by leading an unassuming life, treading a paragon path of humility (regarding himself as *afar v'eifer*, only "dirt and ashes"), punctuated by an ever-ready alertness (*z'rizus*), a term for liveliness that is derived by combining the Hebrew *zehirus* ("meticulous care") with *nekius* ("cleanliness"), to imply a life totally detached from sin, animated only with concern for others to whom he rushes to offer help. But the main reason for Abraham's selection must surely be his ingenuity in "discovering" the One God in an immoral evil climate of rampant idol worship, abominable practices and polytheistic cults.

Why no women?

Q Why are women rarely depicted in most Haggadas?

During the mishnaic years, the *seder tisch* (seder table) was attended only by men, and the Haggada was crafted for fathers and teachers to teach their sons and (male) students. It was not until the thirteenth century that medieval Haggadas began to illustrate women, daughters, and servant girls as seder participants. By the fifteenth century, German-Jewish women (now literate, and able to read) were shown (e.g., the Darmstadt Haggadah) holding their own Haggadas.

P.S. Why no children? After the Inquisition, the Haggadas of the sixteenth century show the seder table with no Jewish children. This seems odd? In those days, artists drew what they saw rather than from the imagination. The absence of children at the Pesach *tisch* was because of a Guide to Hidden Jews (*Marranos*) that the Catholic Church distributed. This listed certain Jewish customs around the time of Jewish holidays which, if practiced, were signs of a "secret" Jew. An example? Spies were on the lookout for homes where no smoke came out of chimneys on Shabbas. One of the "giveaways" was young Jewish children staying up late on Pesach night.

Whoops!

Q What happens when old beliefs about *treifos* are suddenly contradicted by science?

This happens all the time. Our rabbis were once convinced that an injured animal could only live for a year and thus declared it unkosher. But veterinary science experimentation has disproved this "fact," and notes that injured (*treife*) animals live much longer than twelve months. The Talmud also defines as *treif* any animal pierced by a predator's nails (*drusa*), on the basis that venom is secreted during the withdrawal of the claw. But science has proved this theory wrong; there is no venom in the predators mentioned in the Talmud. Another Gemora, supported by the *Shulchan Aruch* and the Rivash, claims that an animal whose liver is removed (yet remains with two olive-sized pieces of liver) can live, and is thus not *treif*. However, modern medicine tells us exactly the opposite, that this animal cannot survive. Do we alter Jewish law or ignore science? Neither. "One must not add or subtract to laws," warns the Rambam, "that were given to Moses on Sinai." Some scholars (Rashba, Rivash, Shlomo Heiman) advise a continuing skepticism regarding all science findings. Others (Maharshal, Schach) are less incredulous, and suggest that God's laws of *treifos* only apply to the majority of animals (*ruba deruba*), which always allowed for exceptions. Other scholars (Bechor Shor) say both can be correct at different times. This was also the Chazon Ish's position, that the *halachos* of *treifos* depended on nature as it was during the time of Torah, with about two thousand years between Abraham and the close of the Mishna.[12]

---

12. Chullin 3:80, 42a, 46a, 53a, 54a, 58a; Shulchan Aruch, Yore Deah 30:2, 41:1; Rivash, Responsa 447; Hilchos Shechitah 10:12–13; Rashba, Responsa, 1:98; Schach, Yore Deah 57:48; Chazon Ish, Yevamos 57:3; Avoda Zara 9a.

Who lost Jerusalem?

Q Who's to blame for the loss of our holy city?

There is a startling Talmudic statement that "Jerusalem was destroyed because the rabbis insisted on fulfilling the letter of the law" instead of the spirit of the law. Earlier devastations were related to such economic sins as social injustice, corruption and robbery. The sixteenth-century Maharal of Prague saw God's presence as an essential component of the First Temple's existence because it came about only through His Will and was destroyed via the same Divine Will after the Jews violated certain of God's injunctions. In contrast, God's presence in the Second Temple was a result of the unity and will *not* of God, but of the people, and the Temple could have stood forever had it not been for their own ill-advised behavior. The Talmud blames the First Temple's fall on idolatry, murder and sexual immorality and stresses that the Second Temple's downfall was for one reason only: *sinas chinam,* "baseless hatred" amongst Jews. Our rabbis interpreted this to mean that because unfounded hatred attacks the cohesiveness of the Jewish people, it is worse than the other three combined. How's this for irony? Because of its position in the *alef beis, sinas chinam,* despite its profound halachic seriousness, ended up at the bottom of the *al cheit* Yom Kippur list of sins! That explains why the loss of Jerusalem is placed above *all* other tragedies, to maintain an immutable, continuous reminder to all Jews in *all times* of the core of Judaism: "Love your fellow as yourself. This is the whole Torah. The rest is commentary!" And so it is customary to read Isaiah's *haftora* just before Tisha b'Av. Why? Because the prophet not only reminds Jews of why the Temple was destroyed but what it will take to get it back. His conclusion is startling. A call for ethics and justice *over* ritual and mitzvos! The link is crystal clear. The presence (or absence) of *ahavta l'reiacha,* "love of our fellow Jews," dictates whether the tangibility of God's Presence stays around in a protective role.[13]

---

13. Baba Metzia 30b; Sanhedrin 108a; Isaiah 1:10–17.

═Wicked, or just plain stupid? ═══════════════

Q Who was more wicked? Ahasuerus or Haman?

Our rabbis are careful not to overtly paint King Ahasuerus with the anti-Semitic brush. Why not? I don't know. They seem divided as to whether, as wicked as he was, he was inherently evil like Haman. The consensus? Ahasuerus was an intellectual midget, manipulative, "fickle-minded," unpredictable, stupid and obtuse, a serial bumbler who swayed between good and bad, wisdom and foolishness – but not as immoral as Haman.[14]

═Where did Esther go? ═══════════════

Q What ever happened to Queen Esther?

No one knows! The last we hear of her is when she asks future generations of Jews to remember Purim. What of her children? No one knows. One scholar claims her son became the next king, others claim that her descendants lost their Jewish identity only to return in the future as Righteous Gentiles. Ironically, we know more about Haman's descendants. They converted to Judaism and "learn Torah in B'nai Brak"![15]

═Who's on first? ═══════════════

Q How can Yom Kippur, the "tenth" of the month, be the official "beginning" of the New Year?

When God announced that "the tenth day of the seventh month [Tishrei] shall be a sacred occasion for you," Yom Kippur entered Jewish history as *Yom HaKodesh, the* Holy Day of the year, and *the* Shabbas of Absolute Rest (the "Sabbath's Sabbath"). But Heaven's date immediately caused a paradox: how could the "tenth" be the "beginning"? Reasons abound. Jewish mystics equate the tenth of Tishrei with the day God gave Moses the second set of Tablets, thus creating a "new beginning," the first national day of forgive-

---

14. Megilla 15b.
15. Gittin 57b, Sanhedrin 96b.

ness for the Jewish people after the Golden Calf fiasco. But there is a more pragmatic explanation that has to do with the Jewish calendar itself. Prior to the incorporation of the leap year and its extra month, there was a ten-day "discrepancy" between the solar (365 days) and lunar year (354 days), which our rabbis reconciled by adding ten days to the end of the previous year. The result? The beginning of Tishrei remained the month's "first" day; however Yom Kippur, ten days later, became Tishrei's "official first" day.[16]

Where's Sinai?

Q So, where is it?

I have no idea, nor does anyone else. Why? Because the route of the flee-ing Jews and the locations of their stopping places are shrouded in mys-tery. Since the fourth century CE, Sinai was believed to be one of the clus-ter of peaks (Jebel Musa) near the southern tip of the Sinai peninsula (but which peak?). This "guesstimate" is based on conjecture that the Jews left Egypt, crossing the marshy swamp areas, and simply walked the Road of Shur, a major trade route of the ancient world. Yet the Jebel Helal mounts can also be accessed from Egypt by the coastal route, along the Way of the Philistines, over the land strip of Lake Sirbonis (known as the Sea of Reeds; another "road block," because this "sea" is either at the tip of the Red Sea in the Gulf of Heroonpolis, or simply one of the many papyrus swamps in the Gulf of Suez). Others, convinced by the Torah's "volcanic" descriptions of Sinai, place it in the volcanic Midianite mountains, east of the Gulf of Akaba (choosing El Khrob, because it resembles the name Horeb). Both sites ignore the Torah verses that position Sinai in Edomite territory![17]

What's the point?

Q Should we observe Tisha b'Av now that we have a State of Israel?

The emergence of the State of Israel, according to Rav Moshe Feinstein,

---

16. Leviticus 16:29, 23:27, 32; Numbers 29:7; Ta'anis 30b; Pirkei d'Rabbi Eliezer 46; Rashi, Deuteronomy 9:18; Rambam, Guide for the Perplexed 3, 43.
17. Numbers 33:1–37; Judges 5:4; Deuteronomy 33:2; Exodus 19:16.

America's greatest halachist, radically altered the status of Jerusalem, in that Jewish sovereignty eliminated the halachic status of *churban* (destruction and ruin) on Jerusalem. And yet, that didn't nullify the continuing need for Tisha b'Av, for several reasons: the establishment of Israel has not, as yet, been the fulfillment of Judaic messianic yearnings. Jerusalem still "sits solitary" and in danger, the Temple has yet to be rebuilt, and worse – Jews are still quarrelling amongst themselves! Remember: Tisha b'Av not only symbolizes physical suffering and regeneration, but the need for a spiritual redemption that requires international justice and local peace amongst Jews, both of which are still lacking.[18]

Who started it?

Q Who established the idea of blessings?

The basic concept of blessings is derived from the Torah: "You shall eat and be satisfied, and bless the Lord your God."[19] Later, Moses, Joshua, David, Solomon, the rabbis of the Mishna, and Ezra's rabbinical court, inspired by the belief that blessings are a blessing, laid out which *brachos* to say and when, taking the words from a mosaic of traditional thanksgiving sources. Their logic? "If, when a person is full, he blesses God, how much *more so* should he say a blessing when he is hungry, has food in front of him and is about to eat!" And so the occasions to *give thanks* to the One "who has bestowed all goodness on me" was extended to before eating, drinking, smelling fragrant odors, doing certain mitzvos, when receiving good, or bad, news, recovering from an illness, being released from prison, a safe journey, seeing unusual creatures, natural phenomena, the New Moon, etc. Or as King David would sing, "Every day I shall bless you!"

Wealth

Q Is it OK to be rich?

Sure. Judaism views wealth as a privilege (given by God) and an opportu-

---

18. Iggeros Moshe, vol. 8; Orach Chayim 27:1; 561:1, 2; Mo'ed Katan 26a.
19. Deuteronomy 8:10.

nity (to do something for the community). When *Pirkei Avos* asks, "Who is rich?" the answer ("He who is content with his lot") comes *not* in financial, but psychological, terms. This is not a tirade against ambition or drive, but a nod and a wink that fortune is at times measured in such simple things as peace and tranquility, and satisfaction with one's lot in life.

With or without a blessing?

Q Do I say Hallel with or without a blessing on Yom Ha'atzmaut?

Rav Moshe Feinstein, concerned that the issue is divisive, advises Jews to follow whatever the custom of their *shul* is, in order to maintain harmony.

White rooster for men, for women a hen

Q Why a chicken when doing *kappora*?

The custom of *kappores shlogen* began when Babylonian Jews, desperate for a symbolic non-sacrificial act of sin cleansing, sought to "wipe out" the past via its transfer to another living creature. The men used a white rooster, the women a hen – swinging it over one's head, whilst saying a little prayer that asked (naturally) that the fowl be killed instead of the Jew. Many great rabbis abhorred this custom, concerned that it would undermine the seriousness of the whole idea of vows. The thirteenth-century Shlomo ben Avraham Adret (Rashba) prohibited it in his Barcelona community; the Ramban called *kappores shloggers* "idol-worshippers"; Rabbi Yosef Caro called it a stupid custom. All to no avail. It was wildly popular, especially in Eastern Europe. In my home, at dawn on the day before Yom Kippur, my father and mother would each *shlog kappores* by swinging a chicken three times over their heads, each time saying *Zeh califasi, zeh temurosi, zeh kapporosi*, "This is my substitute, this is my exchange, this is my atonement." Why a chicken? Why not a fish or a house pet? Because of an old Polish superstition. When roosters crow in the early morning to announce the first lights of day, they scare away the evil spirits which shun daylight. Why "three" times? In Judaism this number is representative of something permanent, as the Yiddishists would say: a triple braid is not easily undone! That is why the obligation to ask another for forgiveness must be carried out three times, after which one has fulfilled the requirement (even if there is no response). I was too chicken to swing a live chicken around the kitchen. So my father would let my sister Hannah and me swing money tied in a white cloth handkerchief instead, whilst saying the same invocation. How much money? Any amount as long as it was in multiples of *chai* ("eighteen"), which means Life. We then donated the money (but not the handkerchief) to charity, because this was one of the three mitzvos (*tefillah, tzedaka u'teshuva*, "prayer, charity and repentance") that mitigated God's decree.

Weapons of mass destruction

Q Are Jews allowed to go to war to find and destroy such weapons?

A word of advice from Rabbi Yania, Talmud Sage, was eventually codified into Jewish law: "A man should never put himself in a place of danger and say that a miracle will save him, lest there be no miracles…" In short, when faced with danger, imminent or not, one must not hesitate to respond in accordance with the mother of all mitzvos, *pikuach nefesh*.[20]

Was he Jewish?

Q Was Jesus a Jew?

No doubt about it. He was born of a Jewish mother, lived in a Jewish milieu, prayed Jewish prayers, observed Jewish practices, died because he was a Jew, and *never* considered himself to be a Messiah. If he in fact "returned" today, he would feel more at home in a Young Israel *shul* than in a Catholic church. Remember: Christianity, as a religion, only developed *after* he died. Was he a rabbi? No, despite the Gospels that address him as such. How do we know? Because the term did not become common until later. All Jewish Sages at that time were known by their personal names (Hillel, Shammai) without a rabbinic title. Was he a prophet? No. Biblical prophecy was over by then (and a preacher is not a prophet!). Was he an

---

20. Sotah 32a.

Essene, Pharisee, Sadducee? He was a borderline Pharisee Jew from the Galil, the world's first "reform Jew," with negative views about Torah. What about those who join "Jews for Jesus"? They are practitioners of Spiritual Schizophrenia.

Y

Yoreh, yoreh, yadin, yadin

Q What is this?

These are the essential words found on the *smicha* or *heter hora'ah* (ordination) certificate of a rabbi. They literally mean "here is one [well-versed in civil and religious law] who can surely make a decision, and surely render judgment!"

Yom kalla

Q What is this day?

There were famous Torah academies in the days of the Talmud, not necessarily for full-time students but for anyone who wanted to discover the inner meaning of Judaism. Twice a year, during Adar and Elul, when agricultural work had slowed down, the academies were crowded for adult education courses, not to train rabbis (professional rabbis did not emerge until the late Middle Ages) but to produce learned laymen. These were known as *kalla* months. *Kalla* is derived from the initial letters of *k'nesset lom'dei haTorah*, "assembly of students of Torah." Today, some communities put aside one day a year, a *yom kalla*, for the same purpose.

═Yizkor ═══════════════════════════════

Q Is it compulsory for children whose parents are alive to leave *shul* during *Yizkor*?

No, but it's now the practice. Originally, *Yizkor* was for every Jew because it began as a communal act of respect and remembrance by the survivors from the Rhineland Jewish community massacres during the First Crusade. It was then expanded to embrace the memory of the thousands who had been martyred *al kiddush Hashem*, which soon gave rise to an erroneous custom that has now become the norm, that the *Yizkor* plea is restricted only to those who have lost a parent (later, the Eastern European Yiddishists introduced a superstition that the presence of children with parents still alive would tempt the Angel of Death).

═Yichud ═══════════════════════════════

Q What is this?

This term describes the complex status of a male over the age of nine being alone with one or more females over the age of three to whom he is not related by marriage or immediate family relationship (he is her/their grandfather, father, brother, son or grandson). Its status is complicated. There is a question as to what "alone" means. Does "alone" apply if the woman's husband is in town, acting as an absent "deterrent"? Driving in a closed car on an open highway? If a door is slightly open? In an elevator? How much time must pass before *yichud* becomes an issue? Two minutes, twenty minutes? In other words, consult a *rav*![1]

═You've got to know *tashnat*! ═══════════

Q How do I determine which English year matches the Hebrew year?

With difficulty – extreme difficulty, if you're not good at math. Jews rely

---

1. Iggeros Moshe, Even HaEzer 4:60, 4:64–3, 65–1, 3, 4, 7, 9, 16, 19, 21, 22:8, Yore Deah 2:35, 2:82.

on a letter-math formula (*tashnat*), which requires one to vocalize the letters of a Hebrew year into numbers. For example: the letters of the Hebrew
year 5759 are vocalized as *taf-shin-nun-tet*, which numerically stands for
400, 300, 50 and 9. You then add them up (759), affix a 5 at the beginning
(which represents the millennium), and arrive at 5759. To "play" this dating game you need the patience of Job, the wisdom of Solomon, a pen and
lots of paper. The year 5759 is *hameshet-alafim-shva-me'ot-hamishim-v'tesha*,
but there are not enough letters in the twenty-two-character Hebrew alphabet, so you take the first ten letters (from *alef* to *yud*) which represent
the numbers one to ten; the next eight letters (from *kaf* to *tzadi*) represent
multiples of ten, from twenty to ninety (i.e., *kaf* = 20, *lamed* = 30, *mem* =
40, etc.). But there are only four Hebrew letters left. Thus *kuf* suddenly becomes an unwieldy 100, *resh* 200, *shin* 300, and *taf* 400. What if you need
higher multiples of 100? That's where you have to sharpen your skills and
start combining: 500 is *taf-kuf*, 600 *taf-resh*, 700 *taf-shin*, 800 *taf-taf*, and
900 is *taf-taf-kuf*. What happens during the millennium year? In the year
1000 our math-Sages agreed to use the letter for the number of the millennium; i.e.; *dalet* for 4; *heh* for 5 (with a diacritical slash over it). You think
this is complicated? Chassidus is even harder. Why? Chassidim don't use
numbers or words, but complete sentences. For example: when dating the
book *Likutei Moharan*, "The Collected Sayings of Moharan" (Moharan
being the acronym for *Moreinu Harav Nachman*, "Our teacher Rabbi Nachman [of Bratzlav])," his followers utilized the Psalmist's verse, *Bishnat lev
tahor bara li Elokim lamed-peh-double-slash-kuf*. This is a date? Yes: the
charismatic Rav Nachman expected his adherents (without even the use
of a hand calculator!) to add up the numerical values of each word (i.e., *lev*
is 32; *tahor* is 220; *bara* is 203; *li* is 40; *Elokim* is 92), and arrive at 587; plus
5 for the millennium and you get 5587 (the year of the book). But what if
we want the English year? Ah, that requires some subtractive arithmetic:
to get to the English Common-Era year equivalent, you always deduct a
"constant" of 3761. Therefore, 5587 minus 3761 gets an English year of 1826.
What if you want to figure the Hebrew year from the English year? Simple,
do the reverse: add 3761 (e.g., the year 2005 + 3761 = 5766, the Hebrew
year). But wait! There's still another problem. Since the Jewish year begins
at Rosh Hashana (September–October), and the secular year on January 1,
this formula sometimes lands you smack in the middle of the three- to
four-month gap, *in between* one of two consecutive years (in other words,

unless you know the month in which a book is published, you can never be certain of its exact year). And so, when Bratzlaver Chassidim use the above formula to claim 1826 as the secular year of their Rebbe's publication, they are wrong. It's 1827!

Yarmulke – part of the uniform?

Q When did Jews start wearing head-coverings?

Originally, the *yarmulke* had no religious significance. Today it is so predominant that both daughter religions have adopted it. The pope wears one, and all Muslims cover their heads at prayer. Before the establishment of the synagogue, Jews prayed in the open at altars exposed to the sun. In those days covering the head was purely pragmatic, and preventive, but, worn while standing before God, it soon became such a symbol of humility and submissiveness that to go bareheaded was considered disrespectful. This custom now borders on law, despite its absence from the Torah, Talmud, and a wealth of halachic *responsa*. In fact, there is no Jewish law that a Jew walking around without a head-covering (*b'gilui rosh*) is committing a sin. The origin of the *yarmulke* also led to the popularity of the handkerchief (sometimes used as an emergency substitute when no *yarmulke* is around). Early man would use a simple cloth to cover his head from the searing heat of the sun; when British sailors landed in France, the fashion-conscious French called it a *couvre-chef*, "a covering for the head," but the Brits shortened it to *kerchief*. As a covering in cold London, the kerchief was useless and ended up being carried openly by hand (thus the new hybrid name, *hand-head-kerchief*, eventually shortened to *handkerchief*). Two new uses were then found. Wiping perspiration from the face, and blowing noses, both of which, for obvious reasons, turned what started as a head-covering into an item best hidden in the pocket. The only Jew ordered by God to wear special clothing and cover his head with a *mitznefes*, a headdress made of fine linen coiled around the head like a turban, was the priest, and only then during his services in the Temple. *Yarmulke* is not even a known Hebrew word (traditionally, it's a *kippa*) but a merger of two words, *yiras* and *Malke*, which literally mean, "fear of the King." This originated as an outward sign of a Jew's belief in God, akin to a uniform shouting its fidelity to a certain government, and an act of respect for being "under" God's Watch.

Yovel

Q When's the next *Yovel* year?

No one knows exactly. The best guesstimate is 2027/8, based on the *Yovel* years of antiquity occurring in years 24 and 74 BCE, and 27 and 77 CE.

Year in Israel

Q My son wants to study in Israel for a year. Should I send him?

No question! And you want to know why? I can tell you in four words: *Avira d'eretz Yisrael machkim*, because "the very air of the land of Israel makes one wise!"[2]

Yosef the Golem

Q What does the expression mean, "the golem that turns on its creator"?

Its English slang equivalent would be "biting the hand that feeds you," or in rabbinic lore, "the petard that hoists its own maker." In Yiddish (*ven der goylem buntevet zikh kegn zayn beshefer*), the phrase refers to the artificial man-out-of-clay (a *golem*) "created" by the sixteenth-century Prague Rabbi Yehuda Loew ben Betsalel (*Maharal*, acronym for *Morenu Harav Lev*, "our teacher, Rabbi Loew"), the greatest defender of traditional Judaism of his time, which turned on its "master," forcing the rabbi to "destroy" it. This dumb-but-strong "creature," called Yosef, was fully clothed, wore a cap, and had two chores: to help the rebbetzin around the house *erev* Shabbas, and patrol the Jewish quarter of Prague between Purim and Pesach, protecting the Jews from the seasonal Christian blood libels. Yosef was "operational" as long as a piece of parchment on which was written the Tetragrammeton [the four holy letters of God's name], placed under its tongue, stayed in place (when the parchment was removed, it reverted to "a lifeless clod of earth"). The rabbi would remove the parchment every *erev* Shabbas so the

---

2. Baba Basra 158b.

golem could rest on the holy day; until he forgot one week – and the *golem*, confused, ran amok, strangling the cats 'n' chickens of Prague. After the rabbi snatched the parchment, he was afraid to revive his "dead creation," so he *shlepped* the lifeless body to the attic of Prague's *Altneuschul* ("Old New Synagogue") where Jewish tourists still go to catch a glimpse of it.

Yayin nesech

Q What type of wine is this?

Originally there was a problem with "wine consecrated for heathen worship" (*yayin nesech*), a forbidden beverage extended to include *stam yeynam*, "wine made (or handled) by non-Jews." This prohibition sought to minimize the social group practice of wine drinking out of fear of potential mixed marriages. The result? Wine had to be manufactured, *and* served, by Jews to and for other Jews. The exception was *yayin m'vushal*, "boiled or pasteurized" wine? Why? Because it is not associated with early idolatrous worship.

Yahrzeit

Q What does this mean?

"*Jahrzeit*" is literally German for "year time," and was originally observed only by orphans for their parents (and by others for Torah scholars) in the belief that the departed soul received added merit when associated with the sanctification of God's Name. The first year cycle of mourning is memorialized annually (by repeating the *kaddish*) with a twenty-four-hour *yahrzeit* candle being lit privately in the home. This is not to be confused with the communal *yizkor*, "remembrances" in *shul* during Yom Kippur, the last day of Pesach, Shavuos, and on Shemini Atzeres. These times were set as days of commemoration, reiteration of the tragedy, and withdrawal into a sentiment of sadness. Why light a candle? Rabbi Aaron Berechia of Modena traces this to the verse "Man's soul is the candle of God," whilst the *Sfas Emes* paired the numerical value (*gematria*) of *ner daluk*, "a burning candle" to *Shechina*, "God's Spirit." Although now associated to one's parents, the *yahrzeit* ritual was not universally accepted, especially amongst the Sephardi rabbinate. A disapproving seventeenth-century Menashe ben Israel called it "a strange custom," in contrast to the sixteenth-century Isaac Luria who sang its praises: "Kaddish elevates the soul every year to a higher sphere in paradise!"[3]

Yichus

Q What does this mean?

It's a hard word to translate accurately, but *yichus* is akin to prestige, or status, and is similar to *dignitas*, Latin for rank or esteem. Is it inherited? Yes, sometimes. Can it be acquired? Yes, through Torah knowledge. Does it have to do with family, occupation? Yes.

Year One?

Q From which year do Jews start their calendar?

The Judaic measure of calendar time is straightforward. Year One begins at the Creation of the world, a time of "waste and void." But how do we know the year of Creation? By adding up the ages of those mentioned in the Torah going back to the "beginning." God's cosmic clock started to tick on a Sunday (the twenty-fourth of Elul) with a command, "Let there be light!" and completed its first weekly cycle the following Saturday (Shabbas). This starting point (August 22, 3760 BCE if calculated by the future Gregorian calendar) was 3,760 years and three months before the commencement of the Christian Era, designated as AM 1 (*Anno Mundi*, "year of the world"). This allocation of a "date" to a year is a practice nowhere found in the Torah. Why not? The Jews preferred to place the succession of years in relation to some outstanding historic event, as in "so many years *after*" the deliverance from Egypt, the formative event of its existence as a people; or the Flood, the formative event of universalism; or by the accession of rulers to the monarchy (as "in the year X of the reign of King Y"); or from the Seleucid era, beginning 312 BCE, used by the Jews after the Babylonian exile up to the twelfth century. The destruction of the Temple

---

3. Proverbs 20:27; Shabbas 30b; Maabar Yabbok, 15:94b; Nishmas Chayim 2:27.

in 70 CE was such a cataclysmic event that it replaced (temporarily) the use of the Exodus as the inaugural date.

Young Jewish Singles Dance-a-Thon

Q Jews actually had "dating" parties?

Yes. The holiest singles party of the year entered the Jewish calendar on Tu b'Av as a Judaic Valentine's Day (a "Tu b'Av Young Jewish Singles Dance-a-Thon"), a desire-driven entrepreneurial moment that bravely stapled Jewish feminism to matchmaking (*shadchanus*), "a yearly festival of God at Shiloh [today about forty minutes by car north of Jerusalem, the then-capital of Israel] when the maidens come out to [the vineyard's] dance." Why? Because there were no "Personal Columns" in ancient Israel, so Jewish girls hoped to catch the eye of their "destined one" (*bashert*). The timing was perfect! Spring was in the air as eligible males were attracted to the Tu b'Av bonfires in the fields. Their mission? Select a wife. Or was it a reverse psychology of mating? Rav Zvi Elimelekh Shapira of Dinov, master Chassidic Sage, claims it was the women, and not the men, who chose their husbands on that day!

Yemach shemo v'zichro

Q Is this Judaism's ultimate curse?

Yes. It is a custom to add these words ("May his name and memory be obliterated!") when mentioning an exceedingly wicked person, based on the verse *V'shem reshaim yirkav*, "May the name of the wicked rot!" Our rabbis considered the "ultimate" punishment to be the obliteration of one's "name and memory." Why? Because the loss of a good name, "more valuable than the crowns of priesthood and royalty!" meant denial of an afterlife. The term *Yemach shemo v'zichro* (which I heard regularly in my home in the context of Adolf and his Hitlerian hordes) was originally associated with the ultimate enemy, Amalek, where the word *yibum* appears in the context of a levirate marriage wherein "his name not be blotted out of Israel." Thus *yimcheh shemo* deals with the wiping out of one's future genealogic line, an order from God directed at exterminating the entire nation of Amalek, thus eliminating their future.

Z

Zechus avos

Q What does this mean?

It is a famous rabbinic concept that Jews throughout the generations are blessed, and *continue* to be blessed, because of the *zechus avos* ("merit of the father"), the righteous deeds of Patriarchs and Matriarchs (and our ancestors). It is this irrevocable blessing from God, according to our rabbis, that prevented a gentile prophet (Balam), hired by a gentile king (Balak) from cursing the nation of Israel ("Do not curse the people," the Heavens warn him, "for it is blessed") to which Balam humbly replies, "Blessed are those You bless, and cursed are those You curse." Jewish mystics note that the word for "blessed" is a passive one, *baruch*, but can also be used as an adjective, as in *chanun* or *rachum*, "gracious" and "compassionate," the twin qualities that lie behind God's blessings.

Zealotry, or plain homicide?

Q Is zealotry a good or a bad trait?

Zealots is a Greek term (*zelotes*), itself a translation of the Hebrew *kana'im* from the verb *kanei*, "to be jealous." In God's vocabulary, being "zealous for My sake" (*b'kano es kinati*) was a badge of honor. Or was it? When discussing zealotry and zeal, Rashi, the preeminent medieval Torah commentator, compares Elijah to Pinchas, and notes that the Torah uses near-identical words (*b'kano, kinati, b'kinati*) when describing their special circumstances. These terms suggest an "impassioned jealousy," fueled by an obsessive anger at those who trample over a God who ascribes the same intense emotions (jealousy, envy, passion, rage) to Himself. Yet this is one of the few characteristics of God that Jews are *not* encouraged to emulate. The mysterious Elijah acts in a similar Pinchas-style burst of genuine ardor, fervently killing hundreds of idolatrous prophets, bloodshed that forces him to run for his life from an angry Queen Jezebel. The contrast is startling: Pinchas, despite the fact that zealotry was *not* a positive trait, is exonerated and even *rewarded* for homicide with a Covenant of Peace and everlasting priesthood. In contrast, the enigmatic Prophet is forced to hide in wilderness caves for his multiple manslaughters. Yosef Ben Matisyahu, better known as Josephus Flavius, the Jewish historian, when describing the Maccabean fighters, preferred the Moabite term for Pinchas, *lista'a*, "the bandit." The rabbis agreed, and called the zealous rebels *baryonim*, "outlaws," or *sikarikon*, from *sicarii*, "knife wielders" (*sica* was a short dagger, an assassination tool; one of the Jewish leaders was even nicknamed *Abba Sikra*, "Daddy Knife!").

Zion, or Arabia?

Q So, whose land is it?

Our link with *ha'aretz*, "the land [of Israel]," accompanied by an uninterrupted love and significant yearning for Zion, dates back nearly four thousand years to the moment God told Abraham to leave his homeland (Ur Kasdim), and go "to a land that I will show you." By using a past tense Hebrew verb (*natati*), God reveals He has "*already* given," indicating that the "good, blessed and beautiful" land was allocated to the House of Israel prior to this promise (part of the fabric of Creation itself). And more: this promise didn't *end* with Abraham but *began* with him, being extended not just to include our forefathers and their wives, but to Abraham's descendants as an eternal inheritance ("for an everlasting possession"). Thus *Eretz Yisrael* is the Holy Land, *par excellence*, the very core of Jewish identity, the lifeblood of the Jewish people; any attempt to repudiate the link between Jews and Israel is to rebut the Torah, denigrate Judaism, and distort God's

Word. Jewish mystical tradition claims its very oxygen makes one wiser. Tradition has it that the land will, stubbornly, "refuse" to bear fruit unless the Jews cultivate it. And, incredibly, Jewish history has proven this belief: until the mid-nineteenth century, the land was desert and swamp, awaiting the waves of pioneering Zionists to till its soil and fulfill Isaiah's promise, "God will comfort Zion, her waste places, and make her wilderness like Eden!"[1]

Zugot

Q What's a *zugot*?

In mystic terms, a *zugot* is a thing which forms a "pair," and is used by demons and evil spirits to cause damages. This belief is based on an ancient Judaic superstition, that even numbers are derived from "less-than-holy" spheres and thus cause spiritual damage. Why? Because odd numbers are based on the number One, and the number One represents the omnipotence of One God. Therefore, even numbers, based on the number two, represent the heretical opposite, a disbelief in God, which "attracts" impure forces. An example? After the rabbis of the Talmud classified a second cup of wine as being dangerous, Rashi defined this cup as constituting a *zugot*. The question then is obvious: if "pairs" are suspect, and considered a bad omen, what about the *two* loaves of Shabbas *challa*? Negative ("demon") dangers are powerless against those involved in doing a mitzva.[2]

Zebra

Q What's my responsibility towards the zebra, and other animals?

When Proverbs searches for the definition of a "righteous man," it concludes that he is one who "cares about the soul [life] of his beast." Johanan ben Nappaha makes a startling declaration: "Had the Torah not been given to us, we would learn modesty, honest toil and chastity from cats, ants and doves!" The general principle is this. "Make no other living creature suffer,"

---

1. Isaiah 51:3.
2. Brachos 51b; Pesachim 110a.

which means cruelty against animals is forbidden (ritual slaughter, *shechting*, for food must be done as painlessly as possible). Thus the Torah directives include unloading over-loaded donkeys (even if the owner is your enemy!), not working animals on Shabbas, helping them find their way back to their owners, not muzzling beasts while they work (they should be able to eat during work just as freely as their owners), showing compassion by not emptying a nest of its fledglings in front of the mother bird and so on. Therefore, killing animals for sport (hunting), fashion (fur), or vanity (showing off stuffed heads over the cozy fireplace), is strongly *verboten* – some scholars even consider socializing with hunters ("sinners") as abhorrent, influenced by the fact that whenever the Torah mentions "hunting" it is related to such wild characters as Nimrod and Esau. What about medical experiments on animals? If the end result produces new, and nearly immediate, methods to treat diseases and mitigate human pain and suffering, they are allowed – but again, they must be conducted in the most respectful, least painful manner. Do animals speak? "Who can say for certain that they do not?!" replies the Mabit, sixteenth-century kabbalist from Safed.[3]

=Zohar=

Q Is the *Zohar* Sephardi or Ashkenazi?

The *Zohar* is a pluralist tapestry of Jewish culture with a rich, halachic component; described as *the* magnum opus of Sephardi mysticism, despite the fact that its original form also has an abundance of Ashkenazi halacha and customs (courtesy of Rabbi Jonah Gerondi, a relative of the Ramban who first studied in the Ashkenazi *yeshivos* of Evreux, France, before becoming the head of Spain's Ashkenazi community, where he introduced French-Ashkenazi customs to the "*Zohar* circle"). The writings of Yosef Caro, of *Shulchan Aruch* fame, whose broad wall-to-wall authority also crossed Ashkenazi-Sephardi lines, was influenced by a "maggid" of *Zohar*, an enigmatic heavenly mentor he credits in his remarkable diary (*Maggid Mesharim*) for helping him become the world authority on Jewish law.

---

3. Proverbs 12:10; Eruvin 100b; Exodus 20:8–10; 23:4, 5; Deuteronomy 22:6, 7; 25: 4; Leviticus 22:26, 27; Psalms 1: 1.

=Zachor=

Q How can I "wipe out" Amalek if I don't even know who he is?

In three short verses, the Torah, in one of the most important readings of the year, makes it a positive command to forever remember "that which Amalek did to thee (*Zachor es asher asah lecha Amalek*)." Our Sages position the obligatory public hearing of *Parshas Zachor*, which discusses this concept, on the Shabbas before Purim and identify Amalek as *the* persona of all evil, in fact, the only one whose nefarious memory all Jews through all generations must "wipe out." Who was Amalek? I don't know. In fact, no one knows. The question is obvious: how can it be an "eternal" battle if we don't know who the descendants of Amalek are? Rabbi Yitzchak Hutner, head of the Chaim Berlin Yeshiva, had an answer: to focus on destroying the amalekite qualities within, thus improving one's character traits.

=Zaken=

Q What is this?

Not *What*, but *Who*! *Zaken* is Hebrew for "elder" (*presbuteros* in Greek, *senatus* in Latin), which literally means an elder member of the Jewish community, since authority was once measured in age (the Torah applies the term to non-Jewish leaders as well, such as the Egyptians and Midianites). Originally the title didn't mean scholar but described the powerful Jew, local and national, who dispensed justice and advised kings (Samuel, David) on the formation of government. Wisdom and knowledge were added much later, during the tannaitic period, as labels for those graduating from the yeshiva of Shammai. Soon there was no distinction between *chachamim* and *zekeinim*, the latter being considered the bearers of the tradition of Joshua and thus the forerunners to the Sanhedrin. Even a dangerous, contrary Sage (partially) kept this title (*zaken mamreh*), despite facing the death penalty if he dared rule against his Sanhedrin contemporaries as they sat in the *lishkath hagazith* ("chamber of hewn stone"), an unacceptable act that the Torah saw as forcing schisms among His people.[4]

---

4. Genesis 50:7; Numbers 22:7; I Samuel 8:4; II Samuel 3:17; Brachos 11a; Pirkei Avos 1:1;

═*Ze'ah*═

Q What is this?

Can you use a gas or electric oven, for both milk and meat preparation? Yes, but it's preferable not to. The problem with a single oven is what Jewish law calls *ze'ah*, which literally means "a sweat." This refers to the "vapor" which emits from cooked food that "sticks" onto oven walls (especially liquid-type foods, such as roasted gravy, rather than dry items, such as cake). The rabbinic concern? That this "vapor" would later drop onto dairy food, thus making it forbidden to eat. Rabbi Ovadia Yosef advises that "liquid" meat food be covered with tin foil, for instance, or to allow for a twenty-four-hour lapse between *fleischigs* (meat) and *milchigs* (dairy), and a fifteen-minute "burning" of the oven. Rav Moshe Feinstein is more lenient, and, with dry items, doesn't require any waiting period at all (especially if the fire is from the top of the oven, which obviates the risk of any lingering *ze'ah*).

═*Zara*, as in *avoda*═

Q Is this an absolute prohibition for *both* Jews and non-Jews?

Yes. Judaism considers *avoda zara*, "idol worship," as its main enemy, considering evil as being rooted in its practice. In fact, the law against idolatry "outweighs all other commandments." What's the punishment? Death? Not necessarily! Although the verse *tov sheba'akum harog* is usually translated as "kill the best of the idolaters," some interpret "idolaters" as *Mitzrim* (Egyptians), *K'na'anim* (Canaanites) or even just *goyim* (gentiles). Why so many versions? Because rabbinic references to gentiles have been subjected to so much censorship that it's unclear what the original meaning was; in fact, the Hebrew *harog* may not be an imperative ("kill!") but a verbal noun meaning "a killer." This changes the whole tone of the sentence, and, ironically, reflects the bitter historic experience that Jews have had: "The best of the idolaters is a killer!"[5]

Sanhedrin 88a,b, 14b, 52a, 87a; Sota 7b
5.   Exodus 20:3; Deuteronomy 5:7; Mechilta, Exodus 12:6

Index

From Fasting to Feasting

A Sophisticated Guide to the Jewish Festivals

From *Fasting to Feasting* takes us on a dramatic journey through all the Jewish holidays. Joe Bobker's light and refreshing approach to asking questions and seeking answers brings two-thousand-year-old Jewish practices into easy focus.

HB · ~240 pp · Publication date: June 2007 · ISBN 978-965-229-378-7 · $14.95 · 70 NIS

And You Thought There Were Only Four

400 Questions to Make Your Seder Enlightening, Educational and Enjoyable

One of the main themes of Pesach is the Four Questions that are asked… but do not be mistaken, there are still many other questions to be asked and lessons to be learned!

Joe Bobker addresses amusing and fascinating questions you never thought about or perhaps always wanted to ask, but never did! Have fun this Pesach, entertain and enlighten your guests around the Seder table.

Paperback · 228 pp · ISBN 965-229-366-0 · $14.95 · 70 NIS